W9-CRS-526

Frommer's
3rd Edition

Puerto Vallarta, Manzanillo & Guadalajara

by Marita Adair

Macmillan • USA

ABOUT THE AUTHOR

Marita Adair's lifelong passion for Mexico's culture, people, and history began at age 11 on her first trip across the border to Nogales. An award-winning travel writer, she logs about 10,000 miles a year traveling in Mexico—by all means of conveyance— and is the author of six Frommer guides to that country. Her freelance photographs and articles about Mexico have appeared in numerous newspapers and magazines.

MACMILLAN TRAVEL

A Simon & Schuster Macmillan Company
1633 Broadway
New York, NY 10019

Find us online at **http://www.mcp.com/mgr/travel** or on America Online at Keyword: **SuperLibrary.**

ISBN: 0-02-860870-4
ISSN: 1060-3727

Editors: Ian Wilker, Blythe Grossberg
Digital Cartography by Stephen Martin
Design by Michele Laseau

Maps copyright © by Simon & Schuster, Inc.

SPECIAL SALES

Bulk purchases (10+ copies) of Frommer's travel guides are available to corporations at special discounts. The Special Sales Department can produce custom editions to be used as premiums and/or for sales promotion to suit individual needs. Existing editions can be produced with custom cover imprints such as corporate logos. For more information write to Special Sales, Simon & Schuster, 1633 Broadway, New York, NY 10019.

Manufactured in the United States of America

Contents

List of Maps

AN INVITATION TO THE READER

In researching this book, I discovered many wonderful places. I'm sure you'll find others. Please tell us about them, so we can share the information with your fellow travelers in upcoming editions. If you were disappointed with a recommendation, I'd love to know that, too. Please write to:

Marita Adair
Frommer's Puerto Vallarta, Manzanillo & Guadalajara, 3rd Edition
Macmillan Travel
1633 Broadway
New York, NY 10019

AN ADDITIONAL NOTE

Please be advised that travel information is subject to change at any time—and this is especially true of prices. We therefore suggest that you write or call ahead for confirmation when making your travel plans. The authors, editors, and publisher cannot be held responsible for the experiences of readers while traveling. Your safety is important to us, however, so we encourage you to stay alert and be aware of your surroundings. Keep a close eye on cameras, purses, and wallets, all favorite targets of thieves and pickpockets.

A FEW WORDS ABOUT PRICES

In December 1994, the Mexican government devalued its currency, the peso. Over the ensuing months, the peso's value against the dollar plummeted from 3.35 pesos against U.S. $1 to nearly 7 pesos against U.S. $1; the peso's value continues to fluctuate—at press time it was slightly more than 6 to the dollar. Inflation in Mexico for 1995 and 1996 is predicted to be between 40% and 60%. Therefore to allow for inflation, prices in this book (which are always given in U.S. dollars) have been converted to U.S. dollars at a rate of 4.5 pesos to the dollar. Many moderate-priced and expensive hotels, which often have U.S. toll-free reservation numbers and have many expenses in U.S. dollars, did not lower rates in keeping with the sinking peso.

Mexico has a Value-Added Tax of 15% (*Impuesto de Valor Agregado,* or IVA, pronounced "*ee*-bah") on almost everything, including hotel rooms, restaurant meals, bus tickets, and souvenirs. (Exceptions are Cancún, Cozumel, and Los Cabos, where the IVA is 10%.) This tax will not necessarily be included in the prices quoted by hotels and restaurants. In addition, prices charged by hotels and restaurants have been deregulated. Mexico's new pricing freedom may cause some price variations from those quoted in this book; always ask to see a printed price sheet and ask if the tax is included.

WHAT THE SYMBOLS MEAN

✪ Frommer's Favorites

Hotels, restaurants, attractions, and entertainment you should not miss.

⑤ Super-Special Values

Hotels and restaurants that offer great value for your money.

The Best of Mid-Pacific Mexico

In September, in the mountain village of Mazamitla, south of Lake Chapala, I snuggled neck to ankle in long johns; donned heavy socks, gloves, and a jacket; and covered my lower body under layers of heavy blankets. I longed for a wool muffler and ear muffs. This elaborate effort to brace myself against Mazamitla's nightly chill had one purpose—to enable me to beat out a few paragraphs for this book on my portable computer.

Only days before, I concluded that the region around Lake Chapala (only two hours north of Mazamitla) is God's earthly experiment in perfect, heavenly weather. Awakening to the chirping of tropical birds fluttering amid lush vegetation in a climate of perpetual spring makes one ask, "Why live anywhere else?" That's why an eclectic mix of artists, writers, and retirees have settled there permanently or stay for months on end.

A couple of weeks after my teeth chattered in Mazamitla, I thawed out on the sunny Pacific coast and gladly settled in for afternoon siestas—the only sensible way to beat the heat. I prefer to be droned to midday sleep by the white noise of a speeding ceiling fan that billows the curtains and sheets, but I noticed other tourists taking their daily naps on the beach by the aquamarine water beneath the shade of a wide thatched palapa. I watched limp hands slip away from paperback novels as the rhythm of scalloped waves lulled them into timeless relaxation as gently as a rocking cradle.

The surprising variety of climates covered in this regional guide is matched only by its rich cultural diversity and its wide range of accommodations and restaurants. The Pacific coast claims some of Mexico's best eateries and hotels.

For this edition, I luxuriated in the remarkably renovated Hotel Bel-Air Costa Careyes; found both comfort and prime location at the remodeled Hotel Calinda Roma in Guadalajara; marveled at the primordial forest setting of the new Hotel Bel-Air El Tamarindo; and felt sumptuously ensconced in the village setting of the Hotel Krystal Vallarta. Someday, I'll rent the oceanfront Casa del Sol at Las Alamandas and prop myself up like a princess on the grand patio sofa cradled by giant colorful pillows.

Hotels that were easy on my wallet afforded me some true Mexican moments. I enjoyed memorable days at the charming Los Cuatro Vientos in Puerto Vallarta, where a casual but graciously presented breakfast is included in the price of the room. In addition, the best sunset perch in "PV" costs nothing from the rooftop of the hotel. At the Hotel Yasmin in Puerto Vallarta, strains of music from wandering troubadours drifted from the street up to my room as they serenaded diners at the Café de Olla in the street-side restaurant below.

As my mind drifts back over the year's travels, I remember truly special meals at Mark's in Bucerías; Los Pibes and Adobe in Puerto Vallarta; Colina de los Ruiseñores in Mazamitla; Manix and Los Telares, both in Ajijic; and the terrific salad bar at La Trattoría Pomodoro Ristorante in Guadalajara. Fond memories linger of breakfasts at Memo's La Casa de Hotcakes and the Hotel Bel-Air, both in Puerto Vallarta, and at the restaurant of the Hotel Delfin in Barra de Navidad.

You can have similar memorable experiences no matter what your budget. This book covers the full range of hotels and restaurants, from the best in the budget category through those in the top luxury resorts.

While pausing to reflect on the year, and on the progress I've seen in Mexico during the last 20 years—the growth of luxury travel, the construction of new freeways, and the expansion of air access—it would be glib not to mention that the country has had its share of grief this year and last. Mexico's problems— political assassinations, the peso devaluation, curtailed international business, Popocatepetl spewing volcanic ash, violence in Chiapas, and a cloud hovering over a once-revered president—have been such prominent news in the United States that they have perhaps skewed our perception about what it really means to travel south of the border.

You won't see the grim face of depression. The country bustles with commerce as much as ever, and ready smiles greet visitors as they always have.

If you are so brazen as to ask, as I have, "How difficult has the devaluation been for you?" you may catch a glimpse of resignation, but it's quickly followed by a look of set-jawed determination and a vow to work harder and get through it, most often with a sense of humor. Mexicans have a deep reservoir of personal strength. Bringing up the subject of devaluation, however, touches the Mexicans' deep sense of personal and national pride, both of which are best left alone.

Mexico is also blessedly free of depressing news from home. Yes, you can buy U.S. newspapers or catch CNN, but you can avoid them if you wish and forget your own thorny set of local and national problems, while focusing instead on Mexico's sun, sand, surf, mountain villages, or shopping bazaars. This is a country that asks "O. J. who? Newt who?" Absorbed as we are in our own world, we forget that our dramas aren't news in Mexico.

And then there are the bargains. It's been 10 years since prices were this good. As I write this, inflation has yet to spiral prices out of sight, and Mexico is a true travel bargain. It's so value packed and food is so inexpensive, for example, that I found myself tipping more than necessary, aware that wages have not kept pace with the cost of feeding families. All over the country, I resisted the urge to crow out loud about the fabulous windfalls I was finding. And the savings I enjoyed? I'll use them to return to Mexico as soon as this year's round of books are off to the publisher.

This promises to be a great year for Mexico travel.

1 The Most Luxurious Hotels

Within the region covered by this book, there are a number of special hotels where the service is as polished as the quality of the establishment. Below are a few that should be on any list:

- **Las Alamandas, Costa Alegre:** A superexclusive, mega-expensive, beachfront hideaway, the 70-acre resort sits on a sparsely inhabited stretch of coast between Puerto Vallarta and Manzanillo. With only five sumptuous villas, Las Alamandas can accommodate only 20 people at a time.
- **Hotel Bel-Air El Tamarindo, Costa Alegre:** As remote and exclusive as Las Alamandas (see above), this resort accommodates guests in luxurious individual villas spread out on grassy lawns facing the ocean, against a backdrop of dense forest and mountains.
- **Hotel Bel-Air Costa Careyes, Costa Alegre:** Wonderfully stylish and relaxing, this stand-alone, posh resort has an equestrian center, a complete spa, tennis courts, and a full lineup of water sports. It shares golf and other facilities with the Hotel Bel-Air El Tamarindo.
- **Hotel Bel-Air, Puerto Vallarta:** A stay here is like falling deep into the lap of luxury—there are spacious, beautifully furnished rooms, gleaming marble floors, and excellent service. And it's all right on the golf course.
- **Hotel Krystal, Puerto Vallarta:** Built like a self-contained village, the Hotel Krystal is a low-rise oasis in a line of high-rise hotels. Rooms, all of which are large, often have balconies overlooking the palm-filled lawns. With seven restaurants in the resort, you never have to be hungry and never are compelled to head off to town for a meal.

2 The Best Budget and Moderately Priced Hotels

Some inns stand out for their combination of hospitality and simple, but colorful, surroundings to which guests want to return again and again.

- **Los Cuatro Vientos, Puerto Vallarta:** A quiet, cozy inn set on a hillside overlooking Banderas Bay, Los Cuatro Vientos features colorfully decorated rooms built around a small pool and central patio. Amenities include a complimentary daily continental breakfast, and the best place to watch the sun sink in Puerto Vallarta.
- **Las Artistas, Bed and Breakfast, Ajijic:** This lovely home, secluded behind walls, lies on a shady, cobblestoned street. The six rooms are on beautiful grounds with a swimming pool. The attentive hosts greet each morning with a delicious breakfast.
- **Hotel Sierra del Tigre, Mazamitla:** Cozy and centrally located, this hotel is a great choice for those cold Mazamitla nights. Cuddle up in the warm plaid bedspreads.
- **Posada Alpina, Mazamitla:** This hotel is in a rustically charming late 19th-century home on the town's main square. A small restaurant on the patio serves coffee and pastries in the late afternoon and evening.
- **Hotel San Francisco Plaza, Guadalajara:** Not far from the Plaza Tapatía, this hotel is comfortable in every way. Guests can enjoy a taste of class while remaining on a budget. Readers who have stayed here give this place high marks.

- **Hotel La Posada, Manzanillo:** Located on the beach of Las Brisas Peninsula, this popular small hotel offers a winning combination of casual comforts, camaraderie among staff and guests, and great beach location.

3 The Best Beach Destinations

A trip to one of the towns below combines good beaches, accommodations, and dining.

- **Manzanillo:** Beaches spread out all along **Bahía Manzanillo** and **Bahía Santiago,** the two big bays on which Manzanillo is built. One of the best beaches and certainly the most accessible is **Playa Las Brisas,** fronted by small hotels and condominiums.
- **Barra de Navidad:** The golden sands of Barra de Navidad Bay spread from this village to its neighbor **Melaque:** There are inexpensive hotels and good restaurants right on the beach or very nearby.
- **Puerto Vallarta:** The spectacularly wide **Banderas Bay** is lined with fine beaches. Boat excursions take you to other nearby beaches to spend the day and dine on fresh fish beneath a woven palm umbrella.

4 The Best Outdoor Activities

There are endless opportunities to be active on the Pacific coast if you can remove yourself from the sands. Refer to individual chapters for specific information about outfitters who cater to outdoor activities.

- **Mountain Biking:** Several outlets in Puerto Vallarta now feature mountain-bike trips into the mountains surrounding this picturesque village.
- **Diving:** There's a fascinating sea world on the Pacific coast, offshore from both Puerto Vallarta and Manzanillo.
- **Fishing:** Billfishing for graceful marlin and sailfish is among the popular sports in Manzanillo and Puerto Vallarta.
- **Surfing:** Surfers congregate on **Las Islitas Beach,** near San Blas, where there's a magnificent swath of sand fronting a section of ocean with mile-long waves.
- **Birding:** The area around **San Blas** has one of the highest bird counts in Mexico. Nearby, **Tovara Springs** is well known for its abundance of colorful tropical birds.

5 The Best All-Around Restaurants

In Mexico, dining out in a charming atmosphere where good food is served doesn't have to be expensive. This list incorporates some of the region's best places to eat in a variety of price categories. All my selections feature a special blend of atmosphere, service, and good food.

- **Willy's, Manzanillo:** Willy's is open only five hours nightly, so make a reservation and expect to pamper your palate with such grilled specialties as red snapper tarragon, dorado basil, robalo with mango and ginger, and other memorable combinations.
- **Restaurant Argentino Los Pibes, Puerto Vallarta:** At this Argentinean restaurant, you can expect perfect quality and taste. Select your beef cut from a tray

of fresh meat (portions are huge) or choose the scrumptious homemade sausage or baby pig or the lamb or chicken fixed several Italian ways. Douse the meat with the most savory chimchuri sauce, then waddle home to nap and dream of returning.

- **Café Adobe, Puerto Vallarta:** Owner Rudolfo Choperena serves excellent food with a southwestern flair at his cool, casually chic, central village restaurant.
- **Chef Roger, Puerto Vallarta:** European-trained chef Roger Drier offers eager diners an original lineup of fine food that combines elements of the cuisines of Europe, the American Southwest, and Mexico.
- **Mark's, Bucerías:** It's worth a trip from Puerto Vallarta to dine on pasta, steak, and seafood at this evening-only, casually charming restaurant.
- **La Trattoría Pomodoro Ristorante, Guadalajara:** Main courses at this Italian restaurant include garlic bread and a trip to one of the best salad bars in the country, which is worth mentioning since salad is usually only served à la carte in Mexico.
- **Recco, Guadalajara:** Housed in an old mansion, this popular restaurant serves the city's upper crust fresh pastas and other Continental favorites at reasonable prices.
- **Mariscos Progreso, Tlaquepaque:** One of the most pleasant places to dine in this village near Guadalajara, this shaded patio restaurant specializes in charcoal-grilled seafood.
- **Manix Restaurant, Ajijic:** Here, you can always count on a delicious meal that's politely served in a serene setting. The servings of Continental favorites are always generous.
- **Los Telares, Ajijic:** Diners in this new, open-patio restaurant are surrounded by art and music while savoring a sophisticated selection of Continental specialties.
- **La Rusa, Ajijic:** For casually chic dining, La Rusa offers an array of international food at moderate prices beside Lake Chapala. This popular village dining/drinking establishment is *the* place to meet local foreigners residing in the area.
- **Colina de los Ruiseñores: Mazamitla:** Family recipes handed down through the generations are the backbone of this delightful little restaurant. The meat marinades transform ordinary food into something special.

6 The Best Java and Juice Joints

Mexico produces some of the world's finest coffee, and a few places on the Pacific coast excel in serving coffee with a flair. Another of Mexico's delicacies is fruit, which is sold everywhere from street vendors to great juice bars, where it's artistically displayed before it's devoured. Savor the juice from such fresh fruits as mango, papaya, oranges, and banana, all together or separate and mixed with water or milk.

- **Tutifruti, Puerto Vallarta:** What this place lacks in seating it makes up for in great fresh juice drinks. Take your selection to go, or grab one of the few stools facing the senoritas and rows of fresh fruit.
- **Café San Cristóbal, Puerto Vallarta:** This is a delightful small place to meet friends and settle in for a cup of fresh brew prepared most any way imaginable—over ice, hot, with milk, latte, as cappuccino or espresso—you name it. Mexican chocolate is mixed in drinks as well.
- **Café Madrid, Guadalajara:** This place is neither trendy nor chic, with its decor of chrome and Formica. It is the best place in the downtown area to

linger over tall glasses of café con leche, espresso, or cappuccino behind the wide windows facing the street.

7 The Best Breakfast Places

When I'm at home, hungering for a breakfast that I could only have in Mexico, these places come immediately to mind:

- **Hotel Bel-Air, Puerto Vallarta:** The prices are moderate, the harpist and food are exquisite, and the shaded outdoor setting by the golf course is perfect. It's a special place to start or end the day, with a round of golf in between.
- **Memo's La Casa de Hotcakes, Puerto Vallarta:** Owner Memo Barroso serves up mouth-watering pancakes and waffles imaginatively mixed with apples, caramel, raisins, granola, chocolate, nuts, and even peanut butter. It's hard to top the eggs Benedict, eggs Florentine, breakfast burritos, huge omelets, and positively wonderful hash browns. The coffee keeps coming, but you pay for it only once.
- **Hotel Delfin, Barra de Navidad:** Owner/manager Herlinda Madrigal concocts the best and most relaxing breakfast you'll find for a long, long while. On a small second-floor patio decked out in umbrella-covered tables, guests select from among fresh fruit, juices, granola, yogurt, milk, pastries, eggs served your way, and delicious banana pancakes—all for a low price that includes a large pot of coffee delivered to your table. What a terrific way to start the day.

8 The Best Places for Sunsets and Margaritas

Many visitors to the coast plan their days around the perfect place to gaze upon the magnificent sunsets (*puestas del sol*), which are extraordinarily good on the Pacific coast. The combination of gazing upon the sun until it disappears below the horizon and sipping the perfect chilled and tangy margarita is a fitting end to any day.

- **Barra de Navidad:** Beachfront restaurants in this laid-back village host sunset happy hours that bring in resident Americans and locals alike.
- **Manzanillo:** When the sun starts to set, *the* place to be is the outdoor patio of the cozy **Hotel La Posada** on the Las Brisas Peninsula. Here, you join guests in the daily sunset ritual honoring the last rays with a toast of margaritas.
- **Puerto Vallarta:** Anywhere along the beach facing the magnificent Banderas Bay you'll see people pausing until the sun casts its last orange-gold rays of light. Though the beach is a great place to be for sunset, from the rooftop of the **Hotel Los Cuatro Vientos,** the whole town is silhouetted against the entire bay as visitors reverently watch the sun disappear while imbibing some of the best margaritas in town.

9 The Hottest Nightlife

In Mexico, nightlife runs the gamut from a few quiet supper clubs with a dance floor to beachside dance floors with live bands to rousing extended "happy hours" in seaside bars to some of the flashiest discos known to humankind. Yes, discos. They may be passé in the rest of the world, but in Mexico, *dees kohs* are more than alive and well. The party in most nightspots starts up at around 9:30 or 10pm and ends between 2am and sunrise. Refer to individual chapters for specific establishments and hours.

- **Puerto Vallarta:** Here, you can find hot spots to listen to mariachis and rhythm and blues until the wee hours, or work yourself into a dancing frenzy at one of several discos open almost all night. For something completely different, join a crowd at one of the special Mexican fiestas that include dinner and a splendid show of Mexican folk dancing.
- **Manzanillo:** This slow-paced coastal resort may not have Puerto Vallarta's variety of nightly entertainment, but discos thrive here nevertheless. There's always the local standby **Carlos 'n' Charlies,** where a night out can be wild, loud, and silly.
- **Guadalajara:** Here, visitors can enjoy a cultural evening at the famous **Ballet Folklórico Nacional** at the Instituto Cultural Cabañas, or join a group for literary readings. You can also be entertained by rousing mariachis, take in a cozy jazz club, or disco the night away.

10 The Best Shopping

Among the sure bets for superior shopping are Tonala and Tlaquepaque, two craft villages near Guadalajara, and the streets of Puerto Vallarta.

- **Tonala and Tlaquepaque:** These two villages near Guadalajara are renowned for pottery, papier-mâché, and hand-blown glass. Most crafts are mass produced in workshops in the two villages, but they include items, especially pottery and blown glass, that are hard to find or are more expensive in other parts of Mexico. More than 400 artisans have workshops in Tonala. Market days are Sunday and Thursday in Tonala, when the streets are awash with crafts shaded under colorful suncloths stretching across village streets.
- **Puerto Vallarta:** In the last several years, the cobblestoned downtown village section of Puerto Vallarta has become a haven for fine shops selling imported goods and the best of Mexican crafts, including original fine art; *equipal* furniture; brass, gold, and silver jewelry; regional dance masks and costumes; and Huichol Indian yarn "paintings."

11 The Best Museums

Mexico excels in creating truly fine museums that draw both tourists and locals alike.

- **Museo de Occidente de Gobierno de Estado, Colima:** Also known as the Museo de Antropología, this small museum has an exquisite selection of pre-Hispanic pieces primarily from western Mexico and including hundreds of the famous clay dancing dogs of Colima.
- **Museo de las Artes de la Universidad de Guadalajara, Guadalajara:** Opened in 1994, this museum promises to be one of the most exciting contemporary art museums in Mexico.
- **Museo de la Ciudad, Guadalajara:** Housed in a wonderful old stone convent, this fine museum opened in 1992 and chronicles Guadalajara's fascinating past.

12 The Best Cultural Experiences

The following experiences are indelibly imprinted in my memory and recall the best of Mexico whenever they come to mind.

- **Mariachis:** On the Plaza Garibaldi in Mexico City and under the portals of **El Parian** in **Tlaquepaque,** near Guadalajara, numerous groups of elegantly clad musicians play their lustrous horn and string instruments and belt out their songs. In Puerto Vallarta, **Santa Cecilia,** the patron saint of mariachis, is honored for a solid 24 hours on **November 22,** when different mariachi groups take turns playing in the cathedral. Anywhere you hear mariachis in Mexico, you settle back and say, "Now *this* is Mexico."

- **Fireworks:** Pyrotechnic displays are seen so frequently in Mexico that it's easy to take them for granted. Their makers are often so creative that displays of fireworks surpass even the most fantastic laser show, with spinning wheels casting off into the blackened sky; whirring noisemakers blasting forth in brilliant fiery colors; and figures of trees, dancers, food, drinks all ablaze in synchronized order. Fireworks appear at almost every festival countrywide.

- **Regional Dancing:** Whether you see the **Ballet Folklórico** in Guadalajara or take part in hotel fiesta nights countrywide, performances of regional dances never become tiresome no matter how many you've seen. Swirling, foot-stomping dancers wear brilliant satin costumes and step to the rhythms of dances from all over Mexico. The Jarabe Tapatío, known as the Mexican Hat Dance, was created in this region and is a part of every show, as are the *alegre* tunes of rousing mariachi bands, yet another regionally born form of entertainment.

2

Unmistakably Mexico: The Mid-Pacific Region

Mexico's Pacific coast has become known for its flashy resorts filled with upscale accommodations and pulsating nightlife. Beneath all the lush vegetation, however, you'll also find tranquil seaside villages and authentic Mexican culture.

This book focuses on the resorts and villages along Mexico's stunning Pacific coast—**Puerto Vallarta** and **Manzanillo,** two world-famous coastal resorts, and between them the villages of **Barra de Navidad** and **Melaque.** Inland through the mountains lie sophisticated **Guadalajara** and nearby villages, including **Chapala, Ajijic,** and **Mazamitla.** These cities are located in two neighboring states—Jalisco (*hah-LEEZ-coh*), Mexico's sixth-largest state, and Colima (*coh-LEE-mah*), the second-smallest state, both on Mexico's Pacific coast. **San Blas,** which can be visited as an excursion from Puerto Vallarta, is in the state of Nayarit.

Puerto Vallarta, Jalisco, a resort city, has a picturesque, cobblestoned town center flanked by high- and low-rise resort hotels leading in and out of town. Manzanillo, Colima, 175 miles south of Puerto Vallarta, is built around a major port and a string of beaches and bays. A long-time haven for condo owners from north of the border, Manzanillo is a more tranquil alternative to beachside vacationing, as are the rustic coastal villages of San Blas, north of Puerto Vallarta, and Barra de Navidad, north of Manzanillo. Between Puerto Vallarta and Manzanillo lie some of the Pacific coast's most beautiful mountains and undeveloped coastal landscape, with enticing beaches all along the coast. Thick mountain vegetation and plantations of banana, mango, lime, and coconut hide remote vacation spots.

Inland, 260 miles east of Puerto Vallarta and 167 miles northeast of Manzanillo, is Guadalajara, Jalisco, capital of the state and Mexico's second-largest city. A delightful deviation from the resorts, the city features a colonial-era center, museums, and the nearby artisan villages of **Tlaquepaque** and **Tonalá.** And 34 miles south of Guadalajara is **Lake Chapala,** blessed by a perennially spring-like climate. The nearby mountain resort village of Mazamitla shows another completely different, more mellow side of Jalisco. Surrounding Jalisco and Colima are other culturally interesting states—Nayarit, Zacatecas, Aguascalientes, Guanajauto, and Michoacán—all of which have influence on Jalisco and Colima where their borders touch.

Mexico

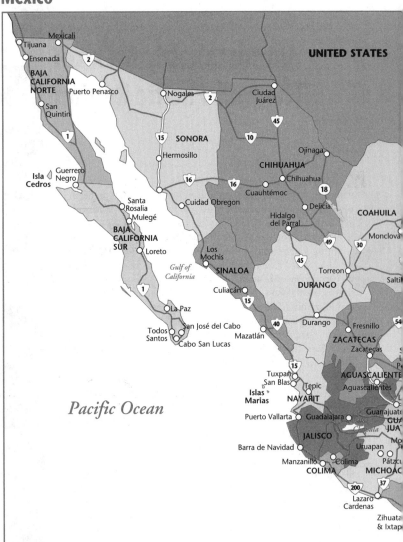

What's Special About Mexico's Mid-Pacific Region

Bird Watching
- San Blas's famous trips into the mangrove, with its 300 bird species.
- The rich bird life in Colima—especially around Laguna Cuyutlán, Manzanillo's lagoon, and near the volcanoes east of Colima City.

Beaches
- Some of the country's best beaches, stretching from San Blas to Manzanillo— many are completely unspoiled.

Fishing
- The mid-Pacific coast has an abundance of marlin and sailfish.

Food & Drink
- A host of regional delicacies—*ceviche, birria,* red *pozole,* and *menudo* of Jalisco; Colima's white *pozole* and *frijoles bodas* (married beans); and *tortas ahogadas* from the Lake Chapala region.
- The town of Tequila—the heart of the tequila-producing region near Guadalajara.

Museums
- Colima's Museum of Western Cultures—its pre-Hispanic artifacts include the famous clay dancing dogs.
- Colima's Museum of Popular Culture Pomar—displaying regional clothing from throughout Mexico.

Nightlife
- Puerto Vallarta—with pulsating nightlife on the beach and in discos and bars.

Shopping
- Guadalajara—for huaraches and silver.
- Tonalá and Tlaquepaque—which feature fine decorative objects, *equipale* furniture, blown glass, and pottery.
- Colima—where you can purchase pre-Hispanic reproductions.
- Puerto Vallarta—for pottery, Huichol Indian art, and contemporary art.

Weird Phenomenon
- The magnetic field near Comala that causes vehicles to move without being powered by their motors.

SEEING THE REGION

Thirty years ago, reaching Puerto Vallarta meant a two-day bus trip from Guadalajara, a journey over an unpaved mountain road from Manzanillo, or a flight to Puerto Vallarta's new airport from Tepic or Guadalajara—all cities more developed and well known than Puerto Vallarta. What a difference three decades has made! Within the last several years, Puerto Vallarta has doubled the number of its luxury hotel rooms; it now rivals Acapulco in the number of accommodations.

Mexico's Mid-Pacific Coast

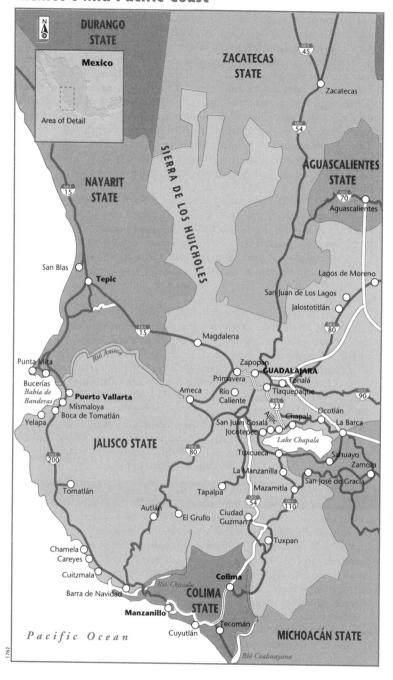

DURANGO STATE

ZACATECAS STATE

Mexico

Area of Detail

Zacatecas

AGUASCALIENTES STATE

NAYARIT STATE

Aguascalientes

San Blas

Tepic

SIERRA DE LOS HUICHOLES

Lagos de Moreno

San Juan de Los Lagos

Jalostotitlán

Magdalena

Río Ameca

Zapopan

GUADALAJARA

Punta Mita

Bucerías

Bahía de Banderas

Puerto Vallarta

Mismaloya

Boca de Tomatlán

Yelapa

Primavera

Ameca

Río Caliente

Tonalá

Tlaquepaque

Ocotlán

Chapala

La Barca

San Juan Cosalá

Jocotepec

Lake Chapala

JALISCO STATE

Tuxcueca

Sahuayo

Zamora

La Manzanilla

San José de Gracia

Tomatlán

Tapalpa

Mazamitla

Autlán

El Grullo

Ciudad Guzmán

Chamela

Careyes

Cuitzmala

Tuxpan

Barra de Navidad

Río Chacala

Colima

COLIMA STATE

Manzanillo

Cuyutlán

Tecomán

MICHOACÁN STATE

Pacific Ocean

Río Coahuayana

1762

There are plans for even further expansion. Developers who have long eyed the coastline between Puerto Vallarta and Manzanillo (an area dubbed the Costa Alegre, or "Happy Coast") broke ground in a big way in early 1993. In addition to the established resorts of El Tecuan and Las Alamandas, the first phase of work on the grand Isla Navidad resort development adjacent to the village of Barra de Navidad is nearing completion; a 27-hole golf course and hotel should be finished by the time you travel. Also new is the secluded and sophisticated Hotel Bel-Air El Tamarindo. Under new ownership, the former Hotel Costa Careyes has been transformed into the secluded Hotel Bel-Air Costa Careyes with a state-of-the-art health spa, and the new Grand Bay Hotel in the Isla Navidad project has plans for a spa as well. International airports in Manzanillo, Guadalajara, and Puerto Vallarta make getting there easier; the latter two have the most frequent connections.

Distances are easily manageable by car; most drives between major points take from 45 minutes to 6 hours. Roads throughout both states are generally good. A new toll road between Guadalajara and Puerto Vallarta, which should be finished by the time you travel, will shorten travel between the two cities to around 4 hours.

If you decide to visit this region, you have several choices about how to allot your time. Most people pick one coastal resort and stay there for the duration of their vacations, but you can easily enjoy more than one resort during your time in Mexico.

Barra de Navidad, for example, is so close to Manzanillo that it's easy to combine several days there with a stay in Manzanillo. From Puerto Vallarta, Bucerías and San Blas are options if you want a change of pace and scenery. With the exception of Las Alamandas (which is closer to Puerto Vallarta), the luxury coastal resorts between Manzanillo and Puerto Vallarta are nearer to Manzanillo. There are more frequent flights, however, to and from Puerto Vallarta than Manzanillo, and many people find Puerto Vallarta has the best access to the coastal area. The resorts located between the cities are self-contained and far from anything else, so they are intended as vacation destinations in their own right. Although these resorts can arrange transportation from either Manzanillo or Puerto Vallarta, renting a car may be more econo-mical and will allow unrestricted explorations of the little-known beaches and other secluded resorts in the area.

1 The Lay of the Land

Colima and Jalisco claim 265 miles of some of the country's most beautiful mountain coastline, fringed by beautiful beaches and rocky outcroppings. The area is studded with volcanoes. At 14,302 feet, the snowcapped Volcano de Nevada lies completely in Jalisco, although it is better seen from Colima City. The still-active Fire Volcano, at 12,870 feet, looms only 35 miles from Colima's city limits. After years of producing nothing but willowy plumes of smoke, it sent out a stream of lava as recently as 1991.

In Jalisco, the mountains reach to the sea, but the mountainous part of Colima lies inland for the most part. Mexico's largest lake, measuring 666 square miles, is Chapala, near Guadalajara.

Jaguars, alligators, and ocelots roam the untouched coastline of both Colima and Jalisco. The area is populated by 70 species of mammals, 30 of which are species of bats, including the vampire bat. Hundreds of bird species have been counted between Cuixmala and Teopa, near Careyes.

2 The Mexican People

The population of Mexico is 85 million; 15% are ethnically European (most of Spanish descent), 60% are *mestizo* (mixed Spanish and Indian), and 25% are pure Indian (descendants of the Maya, Aztecs, Huastecs, Otomies, Totonacs, and other peoples). Added to this ethnic mix are Africans brought as slaves (this group has been so thoroughly assimilated that it is barely discernible); a French presence that lingers on from the time of Maximilian's abortive empire; and other Europeans.

Although Spanish is the official language, about 50 Indian languages are still spoken, mostly in the Yucatán peninsula, Oaxaca, Chiapas, Chihuahua, Nayarit, Puebla, Sonora and Veracruz, Michoacán, and Guerrero. Nahuatl, the language of the Aztecs, is still spoken in some parts of Jalisco and Colima.

Modern Mexico clings to its identity while embracing outside cultures; Mexicans enjoy the Bolshoi Ballet as easily as a family picnic or village festival. Mexicans have a knack for knowing how to enjoy life, and families, weekends, holidays, and festivities are given priority. They also enjoy stretching a weekend holiday into 4 days called a *puente* (bridge) and, with the whole family in tow, fleeing the cities en masse to visit relatives in the country, picnic, or relax at resorts.

The Mexican work day is a long one: Laborers begin around 7am and get off at dusk; office workers go in around 9am and, not counting the 2- to 3-hour lunch, get off at 7 or 8pm. Once a working career is started, there is little time for additional study. School is supposedly mandatory and free through the sixth grade, but many youngsters quit long before that or never go at all.

Sociologists and others have written volumes trying to explain the Mexicans' special relationship with death. Death and the dead are at once mocked and mourned. The Day of the Dead, November 1–2, a cross between Halloween and All Saints' Day, is an opportunity to observe Mexico's relationship with the concept of death.

Mexico's social complexity is such that that it's difficult to characterize the Mexican people as a whole, but some broad generalizations can be drawn.

CLASS DIVISIONS

There are vast differences in the culture and values of Mexico's various economic classes, and these differences have grown even more over the last 10 years. On the one hand there are the fabulously rich; according to *Forbes* magazine, Mexico has the fourth-largest number of billionaires in the world, with at least 24. Upper-class Mexicans are extremely well educated and well mannered; they are very culturally sophisticated and often speak several languages. Many of Mexico's recent presidents have been educated in the United States.

The Mexican middle class—merchants, small restaurant and souvenir-shop owners, taxi drivers, and tour guides, and the like—swelled from the 1950s through the 1980s but is struggling to stay afloat after a decade of massive inflation. And yet these middle-class Mexicans are educating their children to higher standards—many young people now complete technical school or university. The middle-class standard of living includes trappings of life many take for granted in the States—maybe a phone in the home (a luxury that costs the equivalent of U.S. $1,000 to install), fancy tennis shoes for the children, occasional vacations, an economy car, and a tiny home or even smaller apartment in a modest neighborhood or high-rise.

Mexico's poorer classes have expanded. Their hopes for a decent future are dim and the daily goal for many is simple survival.

ETIQUETTE & BEHAVIOR

Residents of the big cities—like Mexico City and Guadalajara—are more formal than residents of smaller Mexican cities, in dress as well as conversation. Many may form friendships slowly because they hold to traditional politeness and formality in business and personal dealings. To a foreigner, the formality may seem stiff and somewhat standoffish. With time and familiarity, the stiffness eases gradually.

MACHISMO & MACHISMA

The subject of *machismo* and *machisma* in Mexico is fraught with subtleties better suited to sociological studies. Suffice it to say that in Mexico, and especially in Mexico City, the roles of men and women are changing both slowly and rapidly. Both sexes cling to old gender roles—women in the home and men in the workplace—but they are relinquishing traditional ideas, too. More women are being educated and working than ever before, and men are learning to work side by side with women of equal education and power.

Though women function in many professional positions, they encounter what they call the "adobe ceiling" (as opposed to the see-through "glass ceiling" in the United States): The male grip on upper-level positions in Mexico is so firm that women aren't able to even glimpse the top. Some women opt to set up their own businesses as a result. Anyone used to a more liberated world may be frustrated by the extent to which Mexico is still a man's world—not uncommon are women who pander to old-fashioned negative stereotypes and flirtatious Mexican men who have difficulty sticking to business when dealing with a woman, even a serious businessperson who is dressed accordingly. Typically the Mexican man is charmingly polite and affronted or embarrassed by the woman who won't permit him to open doors, seat her, and in every way put her on a respectful pedestal.

THE FAMILY

As a rule, Mexicans are very family oriented. Family takes priority over work. Extended families routinely spend weekends and holidays together, filling parks and recreational spots until the last minute of the holiday. During those times men are often seen playing with, tending to, and enjoying the children as readily as women. In the home, girls are supervised closely until they are married. The untethering of boys begins around age 15, when they are given more freedoms than

Considering the variety of nations, tongues, cultures, and artistic styles, the unity of these peoples comes as a surprise. They all share certain ideas and beliefs. Thus it is not inaccurate to call this group of nations and cultures a Mexoamerican civilization. Unity in space and continuity in time; from the first millennium before Christ to the sixteenth century, these distinct Mexoamerican peoples evolve, reelaborate, and re-create a nucleus of basic concepts as well as social and political techniques and institutions. There were changes and variation . . . but never was the continuity broken.

—Octavio Paz, 1990

> **❓ Did You Know?**
>
> - During the 300 years that Mexico belonged to Spain, no Spanish king ever visited the country.
> - Nearly 300 Union veterans of the U.S. Civil War joined the side of Benito Juárez and fought against French intervention in Mexico in 1866.
> - The Mexican territory ceded to the United States by the Treaty of Guadalupe Hidalgo in 1848 after the Mexican-American War makes up almost one-third of U.S. territory, encompassing Texas, New Mexico, Arizona, Nevada, California, Utah, and part of Colorado.
> - In 1519, Mexico's Indian population was approximately 30 million; by 1550, it was reduced to three million due to smallpox, measles, and other diseases to which the Indians had no immunity, brought to the New World by the Spaniards.

their sisters. It's customary, however, for all children to remain in the home until they marry, although there are more young people breaking the mold nowadays.

Family roles among indigenous people are clear cut. Women tend the babies, the home, the hearth, and often the fields. Men do the heavy work, tilling the soil, but women often join them for planting and harvesting. Theirs is a joint life focused on survival. Though not so much an unbendable custom now among these cultures, it's common to see a woman walking behind her spouse, carrying a child on her back and heavy bundles on her shoulders. When these people reach Mexico City, these roles shift somewhat; for example, a husband and wife will take turns tending their street stall with a child sleeping in a box or playing nearby, but she will always prepare the food.

Generally speaking, children are coddled and loved and are very obedient. Misbehaving children are seldom rebuked in public, since Mexican parenting style seems to favor gentle prodding, comforting, or nurturing instead.

THE MEXICAN CHARACTER

Describing the Mexican character is at least as complex as trying to describe the difference between New Englanders and southerners in the United States. At the risk of offending some, I'll try to describe the values of the average Mexican. He or she is generous, honest, loyal, and accepts acquaintances at face value. Visitors are far more likely to have something returned than to discover it stolen. But just as Mexicans are accepting, they can become unreasonably suspicious, and nothing will divert them from suspecting ill will.

The fierce Mexican dignity doesn't allow for insult. An insulting shopper, for example, may discover that suddenly nothing in the store is for sale, or that the prices have suddenly become ridiculously high for the duration of the shopper's visit.

Longtime friendships can fall apart instantly over a real or imagined wrong. Once wronged, Mexicans seldom forgive and never forget. The expression of indifference and distrust a Mexican wears when taking exception can appear to have been set in concrete. The more you try to right a wrong, or to correct a wrong impression, the more entrenched it can become. This goes for personal friendships as well as dealings with the government.

Mexicans' long-term memories harbor the bad and the good. A Mexican will remember a kind deed or a fond, but brief, acquaintance, until death. They will never forget the number of times the United States has invaded Mexico, or the government massacre of peaceful demonstrators at Tlatelolco Square in the capital in 1968.

Mexicans seem to thrive on gossip, which runs the gamut from what the government is doing behind the public's back to neighborhood squabbles. It figures prominently in the breakdown of personal and business relationships as well as the lack of confidence the public has in the government. During Mexico's recent investigation of the assassinations of two prominent government leaders, newspapers published the intrigue and conspiracy the public believed caused both events, alongside different official government reports. Mexicans often express the belief that their president takes his orders from the U.S. president.

No matter how poor or opulent their lives may be, all Mexicans love festivities, whether simple family affairs or the citywide parades on Revolution and Independence days. Often this celebratory spirit is just as evident when dining in a festive place.

When it comes to foreigners, Mexicans want visitors to know, love, and enjoy their country and will extend many thoughtful courtesies just to see pleasure spread across the face of a visitor. They'll invite them to share a table in a crowded restaurant, go out of their way to give directions, help with luggage, and see stranded travelers safely on their way. An entire trip can be joyously colored by the many serendipitous encounters with the people of this nation, whose efficiency and concern will be as memorable as their warmth and good humor.

3 A Look at the Past

Timeline

- 1500–300 B.C. Preclassic period: Olmec culture spreads over Gulf coast, southern Mexico, Central America, and lower Mexican Pacific coast. La Venta Olmec cultural zenith in 600.
- 500 B.C. Zapotecs lay out great mountaintop plaza of Monte Alban.
- 100 B.C. Olmec culture disintegrates.
- A.D. 100 Building begins on Sun and Moon pyramids at Teotihuacán, which eventually becomes largest city in the world. Palenque dynasty emerges in Yucatán.
- 300–900 Classic period: Xochicalco established in

continues

PREHISPANIC CIVILIZATIONS   The earliest "Mexicans" were Stone Age men and women, descendants of a people who had crossed the Bering Strait and reached North America before 10,000 A.D. These were *Homo sapiens* who hunted mastodons and bison and gathered other food as they could. Later, during the archaic period (5200–1500 B.C.), signs of agriculture and domestication appeared: baskets were woven; corn, beans, squash, and tomatoes were grown; turkeys and dogs were kept for food. By 2400 B.C., the art of pot making had been discovered (the use of pottery was a significant advance). Though life in these times was still very primitive, there were "artists" who made clay figurines for use as votive offerings or household "gods." Many symbolized Mother Earth or fertility. (Use of these figurines predates any belief in well-defined gods.)

It was in the **preclassic period** (1500 B.C.–A.D. 300) that the area known by archaeologists as Mesoamerica (running from the northern Mexico Valley to Costa Rica) began to show signs of a farming culture. The inhabitants farmed either by the "slash-and-burn" method of cutting grass and trees and then setting fire to the area to clear it for planting, or by constructing terraces and irrigation ducts. The latter method was used principally in the highlands around Mexico City, where the first large towns developed. At some time during this period, religion became an institution as certain men took on the role of shaman, or guardian of magical and religious secrets. These were the predecessors of the folk healers and nature priests still found in modern Mexico.

The most highly developed culture of this preclassic period was that of the Olmecs, which flourished from 1500 to 100 B.C. They lived in what are today the states of Veracruz and Tabasco, where they used river rafts to transport the colossal multiton blocks of basalt out of which they carved roundish heads that are the best-known legacy of their culture. Archaeologists are still unsure what these sculptures signify. The heads seem infantile in their roundness, but all have the peculiar "jaguar mouth" with a high-arched upper lip that is one identifying mark of Olmec art (this feature was borrowed and adapted by many later cultures). The artists seemed obsessed with deformity, and many smaller carved or clay figures represent monstrosities or mis-shapen forms. Those with open eyes are slightly cross-eyed. In addition to their achievements in sculpture, the Olmecs were the first in Mexico to use a calendar and to develop a written language, both of which were later perfected by the Maya.

The link between the Olmecs and the Maya has not been clearly established, but Izapa (400 B.C.– A.D. 400), a ceremonial site in the Chiapan cacao-growing region near the Pacific coast, appears to have been one of several places where transition between the two cultures took place. When discovered, its monuments and stelae were intact, having escaped the destruction wrought on so many sites.

Most of pre-Hispanic Mexico's artistic and cultural achievement came during the **classic period** (A.D. 300–900), when life centered in cities. Class distinctions arose as a military and religious aristocracy took control; a class of merchants and artisans grew, with the independent farmer falling under a landlord's control. The cultural centers of the classic period were Yucatán and Guatemala (also home of the Maya), the Mexican Highlands at Teotihuacán, the Zapotec cities of Monte Albán

300. Maya civilization develops in Yucatán and Chiapas.

- **650** Teotihuacán burns and is deserted by A.D. 700. Cacaxtla begins to flourish.
- **650–800** El Tajín reaches cultural zenith on coast of Veracruz.
- **750** Zapotecs conquer Valley of Oaxaca. Casas Grandes culture begins on northern desert.
- **800** Bonampak battle/ victory mural painted.
- **900–1154** Chichimecas descend on the territories of today's Jalisco and Colima. Cacaxtla begins decline.
- **900–1500** Postclassic period: Toltec culture emerges at Tula and spreads to Chichén Itzá by 978.
- **1156 or 1168** After a fire, the Toltecs abandon Tula.
- **1230** El Tajín abandoned by this year.
- **1290** Zapotecs decline and Mixtecs emerge at Monte Alban and Mitla becomes refuge of Zapotecs by this year.
- **1325–45** Aztec capital Tenochtitlán founded. Aztecs dominate Mexico until 1521 when they are conquered by Spaniards.
- **1519–21** Conquest of Mexico: Cortés and troops arrive near present-day Veracruz and conquest of Mexico is complete when Cortés defeats Aztecs at Tlaltelolco near Tenochtitlán in 1521.
- **1521–24** Hernán Cortés organizes Spanish empire in Mexico and begins building Mexico City on top of ruins of Tenochtitlán.

continues

- 1523 City of Colima founded.
- 1524–35 First Franciscan friars arrive from Spain. Cortés removed from leadership. Spanish king sends officials, judges, and finally an audiencia to govern.
- 1531 Tepic founded. Nuño de Guzmán begins the conquest of western Mexico, terrorizing and killing inhabitants of Jalisco, Colima, Michoacán, and Nayarit.
- 1535 Cortés visits Manzanillo for the first time.
- 1535–1821 Viceregal period: Mexico governed by viceroys appointed by king of Spain; landed aristocracy emerges.
- 1537 Mexico's first printing press is installed in Mexico City.
- 1538 Nuño de Guzmán imprisoned for his reign of destruction across western Mexico.
- 1542 Guadalajara founded for the final time.
- 1571 The Inquisition is established in Mexico.
- 1703 Population of Guadalajara is 6,000.
- 1742–48 Construction on the Seminario Conciliar de San José is finished; today it's the Regional Museum of Guadalajara.
- 1767 Jesuits expelled from New Spain.
- 1792 Guadalajara's first printing press starts operation.
- 1803 Guadalajara's population is almost 40,000.
- 1804 In Guadalajara, construction begins on

continues

and Mitla (near Oaxaca), and the cities of El Tajín and Zempoala on the Gulf Coast.

The area covered by this book flourished during the classic period; however, little of the architecture of these ancient cultures still exists. Remains of pottery and intricate underground burial chambers show a mixture of influences, including some from as far away as South America.

In the **postclassic period** (A.D. 900–1500), warlike cultures developed impressive societies of their own, although they never surpassed the classic peoples. All paintings and hieroglyphs of this period show war, migration, and disruption. Somehow the glue of society disintegrated; people wandered from their homes, and the religious hierarchy lost influence. During these years Colima and Jalisco were inhabited by Otomis, Toltecs, and Tarascans and later by nomadic Chichimecas, who left abundant pottery and underground tombs but few buildings. Finally, in the 1300s, the warlike Aztecs settled in the Mexico Valley on Lake Texcoco (site of Mexico City), with the island city of Tenochtitlán as their capital. Legend has it that as the wandering Aztecs were passing the lake, they saw a sign predicted by their prophets: an eagle perched on a cactus plant with a snake in its mouth. They built their city there, and it became a huge (pop. 300,000) and impressive capital. The Aztec empire was a more or less loosely united territory of great size. The high lords of the capital became fabulously rich in gold, stores of food, cotton, and perfumes; skilled artisans were prosperous; state events were elaborately ceremonial. Victorious Aztecs returning from battle sacrificed thousands of captives on the altars atop the pyramids, cutting their chests open with stone knives and ripping out their still-beating hearts to offer to the gods.

The legend of **Quetzalcoatl,** a holy man who appeared during the time of troubles at the end of the classic period, is one of the most important tales in Mexican history and folklore and contributed to the overthrow of the Aztec empire by the Spaniards. Quetzalcoatl means "feathered serpent." Learned beyond his years, he became the high priest and leader of the Toltecs at Tula and put an end to human sacrifice. His influence completely changed the Toltecs from a group of warriors to peaceful and productive farmers, artisans, and craftsmen. His successes upset the old priests, and they called on their ancient god of darkness,

Texcatlipoca, to degrade Quetzalcoatl in the eyes of the people. One night the priests conspired to dress Quetzalcoatl in ridiculous garb, get him drunk, and tempt him to break his vow of chastity. The next morning, the shame of this night of debauchery drove him out of his own land and into the wilderness, where he lived for 20 years. He emerged in Coatzacoalcos, in the Isthmus of Tehuantepec, bade his few followers farewell, and sailed away, having promised to return in a future age. Toltec artistic influences noted at Chichén-Itzá in the Yucatán seem to suggest that he in fact landed there and, among the Maya, began his "ministry" again, this time called Kukulkán. He supposedly died there, but the legend of his return in a future age remained.

THE CONQUEST OF MEXICO   When Hernán Cortés and his fellow conquistadors landed in 1519, in what would become Veracruz, the enormous Aztec empire was ruled by Moctezuma (a name often misspelled Montezuma) in great splendor. It was thought that these strange visitors might be Quetzalcoatl and his followers, returning at last. Moctezuma was not certain what course to pursue; if this was in fact the god returning, no resistance must be offered; on the other hand, if the leader was not Quetzalcoatl, Cortés and his men might pose a threat to his empire. Moctezuma tried to bribe them with gold to go away, but this only whetted the Spaniards' appetites. Along the way from Veracruz to Tenochtitlán, Cortés made allies of Moctezuma's enemies, most notably the Tlaxcaltecans.

Though the Spaniards were outnumbered by the hundreds of thousands of Aztecs, they skillfully kept things under their control (with the help of their Tlaxcalan allies) until a revolt threatened Cortés's entire enterprise. He retreated to the countryside, made alliances with non-Aztec tribes, and finally marched on the empire when it was governed by the last Aztec emperor, Cuauhtémoc. Cuauhtémoc defended himself and his people valiantly for almost three months but was finally captured, tortured, and ultimately executed.

What began as an adventure by Cortés and his men, unauthorized by the Spanish Crown or its governor in Cuba, turned out to be the undoing of a continent's worth of people and cultures. Soon Christianity was being spread through "New Spain." Guatemala and Honduras were explored and conquered, and by 1540 the territory of New

Hospicio Cabañas designed by Manuel Tolsá.

- **1810** Independence War begins. Father Miguel Hidalgo starts movement for Mexico's independence from Spain and leads a large group of insurgents to Guadalajara.
- **1818** Earthquake destroys the towers of Guadalajara's cathedral.
- **1821** Independence from Spain achieved.
- **1822** First Empire: Agustín de Iturbide, independence leader, orchestrates his ascendancy to throne as emperor of Mexico. Guadalajara's population is 70,000.
- **1823** Jalisco becomes a free state.
- **1824** Iturbide is expelled, returns, and is executed by firing squad; Priciliano Sanchez is elected first governor of Jalisco. Federal Republic period begins: Guadalupe Victoria is elected first president of Mexico.
- **1828** Slavery abolished.
- **1833** Cholera epidemic kills thousands in Guadalajara.
- **1835** Texas declares independence from Mexico.
- **1836** Santa Anna defeats Texans at Battle of the Alamo, at San Antonio, Texas, but is later defeated and captured at the Battle of San Jacinto outside Houston, Texas.
- **1838** France invades Mexico at Veracruz; after 34 years of construction the Hospicio Cabañas is finally finished in Guadalajara.
- **1845** U.S. annexes Texas.

continues

- **1846–48** War with U.S.; for a payment of $15 million Mexico relinquishes half of its national territory to the U.S. in treaty of Guadalupe Hidalgo.

- **1855** Santos Degollado is named governor of Guadalajara. Reform years begin. Country wages three-year war on itself, pitting cities against villages and rich against poor. Benito Juárez becomes president, in fact and in exile.

- **1862** England, Spain, and France send troops to demand debt payment and all except France withdraw.

- **1864–67** Second Empire: French Emperor Napoléon III sends the Hapsburg Ferdinand Maximilian Joseph, 32, and his wife, Marie Charlotte Amélie Léopoldine, 24, to be emperor and empress of Mexico.

- **1866** Guadalajara is seized by troops loyal to Juárez.

- **1867** Juárez orders execution of Maximilian at Querétaro and resumes presidency in Mexico City until his death in 1872.

- **1872–84** Post-Reform period: Only four presidents hold office but country is nearly bankrupt.

- **1876–1911** Porfiriato: With one four-year exception, Porfirio Díaz is president/dictator of Mexico for 35 years, leading country in tremendous modernization at the expense of human rights.

- **1880** Mule-drawn trolleys serve as public transportation in Guadalajara.

continues

Spain included Spanish possessions from Vancouver to Panama. During that time the cruel Spaniard, Nuño de Guzmán was president of the governing audiencia. Before he could be deposed, he led an army of conquest to western Mexico, killing, terrorizing, and exploiting native inhabitants of the present states of Michoacán, Jalisco, Colima, and Nayarit. In the two centuries that followed, Franciscan, Augustinian, and Dominican friars converted great numbers of Indians to Christianity, and the Spanish lords built up huge feudal estates on which the Indian farmers were little more than serfs. The silver and gold that Cortés had sought and found made Spain the richest country in Europe.

THE VICEREGAL ERA   Hernán Cortés set about building a new city and the seat of government of New Spain upon the ruins of the old Aztec capital. Spain's influence was immediate. For indigenous peoples (besides the Tlaxcaltecans, Cortés's Indian allies), heavy tributes once paid to the Aztecs were now rendered in forced labor to the Spanish. In many cases they were made to provide the materials for the building of New Spain as well. Diseases carried by the Spaniards, against which the Indian populations had no natural immunity, killed millions.

Over the three centuries of the viceregal period (1535–1821), Mexico was governed by 61 viceroys appointed by the king of Spain. From the beginning, more Spaniards arrived as overseers, merchants, craftsmen, architects, silversmiths, and the like, and eventually African slaves were brought in as well. Spain became rich from New World gold and silver, chiseled out by backbreaking Indian labor. The colonial elite built lavish homes both in Mexico City and in the countryside. They filled their homes with ornate furniture, had many servants, and adorned themselves in velvets, satins, and jewels imported from abroad.

A new class system developed: The *gauchupines* (Spaniards born in Spain) considered themselves superior to the *criollos* (Spaniards born in Mexico). Those of other races, the *castas* or castes, the pure Indians and Africans, and mixtures of Spanish and Indian, Spanish and African, Indian and African, all occupied the bottom rung in society.

It took great cunning to stay a step ahead of the money-hungry Spanish crown, which demanded increasingly higher taxes and contributions from its well-endowed faraway colony. Still, the wealthy prospered grandly enough to develop an extravagant society.

Discontent with the mother country simmered for years over such issues as the Spanish-born citizen's advantages over a Mexican-born subject; taxes; the Spanish bureaucracy; and restrictions on commerce with Spain and other countries. Dissatisfaction with Spain boiled to the surface in 1808 when, under the weak leadership of King Charles IV, Spain was invaded by Napoleón Bonaparte of France, who placed his brother Joseph in the Spanish throne. To many in Mexico, allegiance to France was out of the question. Mexico seemed left without leadership. After nearly 300 years of restrictive Spanish rule, Mexican discontent with the mother country reached the level of revolution.

INDEPENDENCE   The independence movement began in 1810 when a priest from Colima, Father Miguel Hidalgo, gave the cry (known as the *grito*) for independence from his pulpit in the town of Dolores, Guanajuato. The revolt soon became a revolution, and Hidalgo, Ignacio Allende, and another priest, José María Morelos, gathered an "army" of citizens and threatened Mexico City. Battle lines were drawn between those who sided with the Spanish crown and those who wanted Mexico to be a free and sovereign nation. Ultimately Hidalgo was executed, but he is honored as "the Father of Mexican Independence." Morelos kept the revolt alive until 1815, when he too was executed.

The nation endured a decade of upheaval (1810 until 1821), and then the warring factions finally agreed on a compromise, Augustín Iturbide's *Plan de Iguala*. It made three guarantees: Mexico would be a constitutional monarchy headed by a European prince; the Catholic church would have a monopoly on religion; and Mexican-born citizens would have the same rights as those born in Spain. He thoughtfully tagged on another proviso allowing for a Mexican emperor, should no European prince step forward to take the role of king. When the agreement was signed, Iturbide was positioned to take over. No suitable European monarch was located, and the new Mexican congress named him emperor. His empire proved short-lived: his administration fell the very next year. The new nation

- **1884** Electric lights go on in Guadalajara for the first time.
- **1887** Gen. Ramón Corona is elected governor of Jalisco in 1887.
- **1888** The Mexico City-to-Guadalajara railroad is inaugurated.
- **1907** Electric trolleys are installed in Guadalajara.
- **1909** Francisco Madero's political tour of Mexico includes Manzanillo and Guadalajara as he becomes a more visible anti-Díaz leader. The Guadalajara-to-Manzanillo railroad is inaugurated.
- **1911–17** Mexican Revolution: Díaz resigns and many factions jockey for power. Period of great violence, national upheaval, and tremendous loss of life. Starvation reaches epidemic proportions, dramatically affecting Guadalajara.
- **1913** President Madero assassinated.
- **1914–1916** Two U.S. invasions of Mexico.
- **1917–40** Reconstruction: Mexican constitution signed. Reforms initiated, labor unions strengthened, and Mexico expels U.S. oil companies and nationalizes all natural resources and railroads. Presidents Obregón and Carranza assassinated as are Pancho Villa and Emiliano Zapata.
- **1926–29** The Cristero Rebellion in response to President Calles's action limiting the Catholic church; violence between church and government is particularly strong in Jalisco, Colima, and Michoacán.

continues

- **1940–present** Mexico enters period of political stability and economic progress though with continued problems of corruption, inflation, national health, and unresolved land and agricultural issues.
- **1955** Women given full voting rights.
- **1982** Nationalization of banks.
- **1988** Mexico enters the General Agreement on Trade and Tariffs (GATT).
- **1991** Mexico, Canada, and the United States begin free-trade agreement negotiations.
- **1992** Sale of *ejido* land (peasant communal property) to private citizens is allowed; Mexico and the Vatican establish diplomatic relations after an interruption of 100 years.
- **1993** Mexico deregulates hotel and restaurant prices; New Peso currency begins circulation.
- **1994** An Indian uprising in Chiapas sparks protests countrywide over government policies concerning land distribution, bank loans, health, education, and voting and human rights. In an unrelated incident PRI candidate Luis Donaldo Colossio is assassinated five months before the election; replacement candidate Ernesto Zedillo Ponce de Leon is elected and inaugurated as president in December. Within weeks, the peso is devalued, throwing the nation into turmoil.

continues

became a republic but endured a succession of presidents and military dictators, as well as invasions, a war, and devastating losses of territory to its neighbor to the north, the United States.

Capping the half-century of political turbulence that followed independence was the French Intervention, in which three old colonial powers—England, France, and Spain—and the United States demonstrated continued interest in meddling with Mexico's internal affairs, and found, in the fractured world of mid-19th-century Mexican politics, plenty of help in carrying out their intrigues. Before it was over, Mexico had seen troops from the three European powers occupy Veracruz (the English and Spanish withdrew before long, but the French remained and declared war on Mexico); had enjoyed a glorious, if hollow, victory over the French at Puebla (the event that birthed the nation's Cinco de Mayo celebrations); had watched the Mexican president, Benito Juárez, retreat to the countryside to bide his time while the French marched on Mexico City and with the help of anti-Juárez factions, installed a naive young Austrian, Archduke Maximilian of Hapsburg, as emperor of Mexico; and finally had rolled its collective eyes at the three-year-long spectacle of Maximilian trying to "rule" a country effectively in the midst of civil war, only to be left in the lurch when the French troops that supported him withdrew at the behest of the United States, and then summarily executed by Juárez upon his triumphant return.

Benito Juárez, a Zapotec lawyer, who would be remembered as one of the nation's great heroes, did his best to unify and strengthen his country before dying of a heart attack in 1872.

THE PORFIRIATO & THE REVOLUTION

From 1877 to 1911, a period now called the "Porfiriato," center stage in Mexico was occupied by Porfirio Díaz, a Juárez general who was president for 30 years and lived in the Castillo de (Castle of) Chapultepec in Mexico City. He was a terror to his enemies—that is, any-one who dared challenge his absolute power. Nevertheless, he is credited with bringing Mexico into the industrial age and for his patronage of architecture and the arts, the fruits of which are still enjoyed today. Public opinion forced him from office in 1911; he was succeeded by Francisco Madero.

After the fall of the Porfirist dictatorship, several factions split the country, including those led by

"Pancho Villa" (whose real name was Doroteo Arango), Alvaro Obregón, Venustiano Carranza, and Emiliano Zapata. A famous photograph shows Zapata and Villa taking turns trying out Díaz's presidential chair in Mexico City.

The decade that followed is referred to as the Mexican Revolution. Around two million Mexicans died for the cause. Drastic reforms occurred in this period, and the surge of vitality and progress from this exciting, if turbulent, time has inspired Mexicans until the present day. Succeeding presidents have invoked the spirit of the Revolution, which lives in the hearts and minds of Mexicans as though it had happened yesterday.

BEYOND THE REVOLUTION   The decades from the beginning of the revolution in 1911 until stabilization in the 1940s and 1950s were tumultuous. Great strides were made during these years in distributing land to the peasant populations, irrigation, development of mineral resources, and the establishment of education, health, and sanitation programs. However, the tremendous economic pressure Mexico faced from its own internal problems and the world depression of the 1930s did little for political stability. From 1911 to 1940, sixteen men were president of Mexico. Some stayed in power for a year or less.

■ **1995** The peso loses half its value within the first three months. The government raises prices on oil and utilities. Interest on debt soars to 140%; businesses begin to fail, people are laid off. The Chiapan rebels threaten another rebellion, which is quickly quashed by the government. Former President Carlos Salinas de Gortari leaves Mexico for the United States under suspicion over his economic leadership that led to the devaluation. A government investigation leads to the arrest of Salinas's brother, who is accused in the assassination of their brother-in-law, the head of the PRI. International confidence in Mexico's once-thriving economy slows down.

The longest-lasting (1934–40), and one of the most significant leaders of the period, was Lázaro Cárdenas. He helped diminish the role of Mexico's military in national politics by dismantling the machine of Gen. Plutarco Calles and exiling him from the country. He is remembered fondly as a president who listened to and cared about commoners. He made good on a number of the revolution's promises,

Impressions

When we [Cortés and Moctezuma] met I dismounted and stepped forward to embrace him, but the two lords who were with him stopped me with their hands so that I should not touch him. . . . When at last I came to speak to Mutezuma himself I took off a necklace of pearls and cut glass that I was wearing and placed it around his neck; after we had walked a little way up the street a servant of his came with two necklaces, wrapped in a cloth, made from red snails' shells, which they hold in great esteem; and from each necklace hung eight shrimps of refined gold almost a span in length.
—Hernán Cortés, *Letters from Mexico* (1519)

When they arrived at the treasure house called Teucalco, the riches of gold and feathers were brought out to them: ornaments made of quetzal feathers, richly worked shields, disks of gold, the necklaces of the idols, gold nose plugs, gold greaves and bracelets and crowns. . . . The Spaniards . . . gathered all the gold into a great mound and set fire to everything else. . . . Then they melted down the gold into ingots.
—*The Broken Spears: The Aztec Account of the Conquest of Mexico* (1528)

Blood, Passion & Skill: Mexican Spectator Sports

The precise rules of the ball game played by pre-Hispanic Mexicans are not known, but it is fairly well established that some of the players were put to death when the game was over—whether it was the victors or the losers is unknown. Stone carvings of the game left on the walls of ball courts throughout Meso-america depict heavily padded players elaborately decked out. Ever since that interesting beginning, team sports have been popular in Mexico. Probably the most popular team sport today is soccer; you can turn on the TV almost anytime to catch a game.

Bullfighting, introduced by the Spaniards, is performed countrywide today; the best venues are in Aguascalientes, Guadalajara, and Mexico City. Jai alai, another Spanish game, is played in arenas in Mexico City and Tijuana. By the 18th century, the Mexican gentleman-cowboy, the *charro*, displayed skillful horsemanship during the *charreada*, a Mexican-style rodeo; today charro associations countrywide compete all year, usually on Sunday mornings. Cockfights, although supposedly illegal, are held in specially built arenas in many places.

distributing nearly 50 million acres of land, primarily to *ejidos*, or communal farming groups; putting money into education; and encouraging organized labor. In one of his most memorable and controversial decisions, he nationalized Mexico's oil industry in 1938, sending foreign oil companies packing. Although Mexicans still view this act with great pride—the government stood up for Mexican labor—it did considerable damage to Mexico's standing with the international business community.

Despite many steps forward during the Cárdenas era, jobs could not keep pace with population growth. With foreign investors shy of Mexico, and the world mired in the Great Depression, the Cárdenas era ended in 1940 with the nation in dark economic circumstances.

From the 1930s through the 1970s, socialism had a strong voice in Mexico; its impact was most marked in the state's attempts to run the country's businesses—not just oil, but railroads, mining, utilities, hotels, motion pictures, the telephone company, supermarkets, and other industries. Miguel Aleman, president from 1946 to 1958, continued progress by building dams, improving highways and railways, encouraging trade, and building the Ciudad Universitario (University City) in Mexico City, home of Mexico's national university. North Americans began to invest in Mexico again. Yet problems remained, many of which still plague the country today. The country's booming population created unemployment, the wages of the common people were appallingly low, and Aleman's administration was plagued by corruption and graft.

In 1970, Luis Echeverria came to power, followed in 1976 by José López Portillo. During their presidencies there emerged a studied coolness in relations with the United States and an activist role in international affairs. This period also

Impressions

Without more chin than Maximilian ever had, one can be neither handsome nor a successful emperor.

—Charles Flandrau, *Viva Mexico* (1908)

Impressions

[Porfirio Díaz] looks what he is—a Man of Iron, the most forceful character in Mexico. Whatever was done in the sixteenth century was the work of Cortez . . . who was responsible for everything but the climate. Whatever is effected in Mexico today is the work of Porfirio Díaz.

—Stanton Davis Kirkham, *Mexican Trails* (1909)

saw an increase in charges of large-scale corruption in the upper echelons of Mexican society. The corruption, though endemic to the system, was encouraged by the river of money from the rise in oil prices. When oil income skyrocketed, Mexican borrowing and spending did likewise. The reduction of oil prices in the 1980s left Mexico with an enormous foreign bank debt and serious infrastructure deficiencies.

The country inherited by Miguel de la Madríd Hurtado in 1982 was one without "king oil" and with new challenges to build agriculture, cut expenditures, tame corruption, and keep creditors at bay. He began the process of privatizing government-held businesses (airlines, hotels, banks, and the like) and led the country into membership in GATT (the General Agreement on Tariffs and Trade), an important preparation for entering NAFTA (the North American Free Trade Agreement), which was accomplished during his successor's presidency.

Nevertheless, a soaring rate of inflation of 200% faced Carlos Salinas de Gortari as he took office in 1989. Salinas's accomplishments included decreasing inflation to 15% annually by adeptly gaining the necessary agreement of industry and labor leaders to hold wages and prices; continuing the privatization of government-held businesses; and leading the country into NAFTA, which over a 15-year period would reduce trade barriers and allow business to flourish more freely between Mexico, the United States, and Canada.

During Salinas's six-year term, Mexico's position in the global economy as a country poised for great prosperity strengthened, and Mexican public opinion held his administration in high esteem. A cloud arose over the country toward the end of the Salinas era, however, when disgruntled Maya Indians staged an armed uprising after the NAFTA agreement was signed, and assassins' bullets felled both the PRI presidential candidate and the head of the PRI party. The presidential elections, while automated for the first time and more honest than they had been in the past, were still marred by allegations of corruption. Still, these incidents failed to dampen Mexico's hope for continued progress when Ernesto Zedillo assumed office in December 1994.

TOWARD THE FUTURE   From the time of the revolution to the present, political parties and their roles have changed tremendously in Mexico. Although one political party, the **Partido Revolucionario Institucional** (PRI, called *el pree* in Spanish) has been in control under that name since 1946, opposition to it has become increasingly vocal and effective in recent years. In the beginning, the forerunner of the PRI, the Partido Revolucionario Mexicano, established by Lázaro Cárdenas, had four equal constituent groups—popular, agrarian, labor, and the military. At the risk of greatly oversimplifying its complex history, the widespread perception that the party is out of touch with the common Mexican and its current problems retaining leadership are the result of a change in focus away from those original four groups. The PRI today is heavily backed by, and in turn run by, business and industry leaders.

Heroes & Villains: Some Giants of Mexican History

Hernán Cortés Brash, bold, greedy, and a brilliant military leader, 34-year-old Hernán Cortés conquered Mexico in the name of Spain without the knowledge of that country's king. He sank his ships to prevent desertion and with only 550 men and 16 horses, he conquered a nation of 30,000 and a territory larger than his native country. He became governor and captain general of New Spain immediately after the conquest and later he was given the title of Marqués of the Valley of Oaxaca and substantial landholdings. He began silver mining in Taxco and introduced sugarcane cultivation around Cuernavaca. But by 1528 he was removed from governorship and the king sent other Spaniards to take charge. Cortés (1485–1547) died in Spain while seeking proper recognition and a more significant title from the Spanish court, which shunned him. Mexicans regard him as the destroyer of a nation and no monuments honor him. He is buried in a vault in the Church of the Hospital of Jésus Nazareño, Mexico City.

Porfirio Díaz Born in Oaxaca and schooled in law, at age 32 Díaz distinguished himself at the famous "Cinco de Mayo" Puebla battle and within 14 years became president of Mexico. Díaz (1830–1915) remained as dictator for the next 34 years, with one 4-year interruption. His contributions were enormous: He moved the country from turmoil and bankruptcy into peace and stability through improvements in communication, railroads, agriculture, manufacturing, mining, port enlargement, oil exploration, and foreign investment. He built lavish public buildings, and sent promising art students to Europe on full scholarship. His love for all things French was legendary. He achieved these successes by disregarding the law and at the expense of the poor, Indians, and intellectuals who opposed his methods, all of which brought about his downfall in 1911 and the Mexican Revolution which lasted until 1917. He died in exile in Paris and is buried in the Père Lachaise Cemetery there. A movement is underway to bring his remains to Mexico for reburial in Oaxaca.

Miguel Hidalgo y Costilla In 1792, the man later to be known as the Father of Mexican Independence was the parish priest in Colima. By 1810, however, he was a small-town priest in the town of Dolores, Guanajuato. At the time Hidalgo (1753–1811) was better known for his anticelibacy beliefs and disbelief in papal supremacy. As priest he taught parishioners to grow mulberry trees for silkworms (for making silk) and grapes (for winemaking, prohibited by the crown), and to make ceramics; the latter two still thrive in the region. He was among several in his area who secretly conspired to free Mexico from Spanish domination. On the morning of September 16, 1810, a messenger from Josefa Ortiz de Dominguez brought Hidalgo word that the conspiracy was uncovered. He quickly decided to publicly call for independence (known today as the *grito*

The crisis in Chiapas has become a focal point for many of the nation's problems. Opposition parties such as the **Partido Acción Nacional** (PAN) had taken up the cause of the seemingly disenfranchised masses, but no one had spoken for or paid much attention to Mexico's millions of poor indigenous people for some time. On New Year's Day in 1994, militant Maya Indians attacked Chiapan towns, killing many. They drew attention to the plight of neglected indigenous groups and others in rural society, which the PRI-led government seemed to or "cry") from his parish church, after which he galloped from village to village spreading the news, and gathering troops. His small home, today a museum, is on Morelos Street, corner of Hidalgo in Dolores Hidalgo, Guanajuato, and he is buried in the Independence Monument, Mexico City.

Agustín de Iturbide   In an elaborate ceremony that took months to plan, Iturbide (1783–1824) was crowned emperor of Mexico and created an elaborate imperial monarchy with titles and right of succession by his children. But his brief reign (1822–24) ended when General Santa Anna led a successful rebellion to dethrone him. He returned surreptitiously from exile but was captured and shot by a firing squad in Padilla, Tamaulipas. For years regarded as a usurper and self-interested politician, in a rare move public sentiment recognized his role in gaining Mexico's independence from Spain and his remains were interred more fittingly in the Mexico City Cathedral.

Benito Juárez   A full-blooded Zapotec, Juárez (1806–72) was orphaned at the age of three. He became governor of Oaxaca in 1847 after which he was exiled to New Orleans by grudge-holding President Santa Anna because Juárez refused to grant him asylum in Oaxaca years before. On becoming president of Mexico first in 1858, his terms were interrupted once during the Reform Wars and again during the French Intervention. Juárez cast the deciding vote favoring the execution of Maximilian. He died from a heart attack before completing his fourth term. Devoid of personal excesses, Juárez had a clear vision for Mexico, that included honest leadership, separation of church and state, imposition of civilian rule, reduction of the military, and education reform. He is buried in the San Fernando Cemetery, Mexico City.

Antonio López de Santa Anna (1794–1876)   One of the most scorned characters in Mexican history, he was president of Mexico 11 times between 1833 and 1855. Audacious, pompous, and self-absorbed, his outrageous exploits disgust and infuriate Mexicans even today, but none more than his role in losing half the territory of Mexico to the United States. Defeated and captured at the Battle of San Jacinto outside Houston, Texas, in 1836, among other things he agreed to allow Texas to be a separate republic and to mark the boundary at the Río Grande. When the United States voted to annex Texas, it sparked the Mexican-American War which the United States won in 1848. In the Treaty of Guadalupe Hidalgo which followed between the two nations, the United States paid Mexico $15 million for Texas, New Mexico, California, Arizona, Nevada, Utah, and part of Colorado. Eventually Santa Anna was exiled, but returned two years before he died, poor, alone, and forgotten. He is buried in the Guadalupe Cemetery behind the Basilica de Guadalupe, Mexico City.

relegate to the bottom of the agenda. These groups are still clamoring for land they never received after the Revolution. That population growth has outstripped the availability of distributable land and that Mexico needs large-scale, modern agribusiness to keep up with the country's food needs are realities not understood by the millions of rural Mexicans who depend on their small fields to feed their families. President Carlos Salinas de Gortari's bold, controversial decision in the early 1990s to allow sale of *ejido* land may reflect Mexico's 21st-century needs, but it is at odds with firmly entrenched farm- and land-use traditions born before the 16th-century conquest.

The issues of agrarian reform and the lack of other basics of life (roads, electricity, running water, education, health care, and the like) are being raised in areas besides Chiapas, most notably Oaxaca, Chihuahua, Guerrero, and Michoacán. This is a grave and festering problem, which has become all the more serious now that Mexico is reeling from the devaluation of the peso.

The surprise decision to devalue the currency threw domestic and international confidence in Mexico into turmoil. The peso had already been in a fairly rapid, but controlled, daily devaluation process just prior to the government intervention, and it had been obvious for at least three years that a devaluation was overdue. The Zedillo government erred, however, in not involving industry and labor in the decision, in shocking the population with an overnight devaluation, and in not anticipating national and international repercussions. Within three months of the devaluation, the peso lost half its value and Mexico's buying power was reduced by half. After the government issued its harsh economic recovery program, interest rates on credit cards and loans (which have variable, not fixed, rates in Mexico), soared 80% to 140%. Overnight the cost of gasoline increased 35% and gas and electricity 20%. As a partial solution, a $40 million loan package offered by the United States to ease the peso crisis uses Mexico's sacred petroleum revenue as collateral—a staggering blow to Mexico's national pride. The effect so far has been a loudly expressed lack of confidence in Zedillo and in the PRI, a dramatically slowed and cautious international investment climate, and a feeling among the citizenry of betrayal by the government. Responsibility for paying for governmental mismanagement of the economy has been shifted to ordinary Mexican citizens who were blindsided by this unexpected financial burden. Ordinary costs of daily living exceed the ability of average people to pay; businesses are closing and jobs are being eliminated.

Meanwhile, as the effects of the peso crisis worsened, the Chiapan rebels threatened another uprising, the volcano Popocatepetl began spitting smoke and flames, and inflation predictions of 45% to 60% were heard. Former president Carlos Salinas de Gortari's brother was jailed and accused of involvement in the assassination of their brother-in-law, the head of the PRI party. Carlos Salinas de Gortari and his family left Mexico quickly for the United States after Salinas threatened a hunger strike unless his name was cleared regarding the assassination of his brother-in-law and after he spoke publicly (an unheard-of breech of conduct by a past president) against the present government's handling of the peso crisis.

It seems incredulous that a country so poised for prosperity should career backwards so rapidly and that such an admired president should so quickly fall from grace. However, as grim as all this seems, using Mexico's history just this century as a rule, the country bounces back from adversity to become even stronger. A strong popular will to progress undergirds the Mexican spirit, and despite recent sobering events, the country still bustles with commercial activity. Meanwhile, as long as inflation doesn't outpace the effect of the devaluation, the country is quite a bargain; prices are better than they've been since 1985.

Economically, Mexico, though still a Third World country, is by no means a poor country. Only about a sixth of the economy is in agriculture. Mining is still fairly important. Gold, silver, and many other important minerals are still mined, but the big industry today is oil. Mexico is also well industrialized, manufacturing textiles, food products, and everything from cassette tapes to automobiles.

4 The Visual Arts in Mexico

Mexico's artistic and architectural legacy began more than 3,000 years ago. Until the fall of the Aztec Empire in 1521, art, architecture, politics, and religion were inextricably intertwined in Mexico and remained so in different ways through the colonial period.

The more than 15,000 world-famous archaeological sites in Mexico are individually unique, even those that were built by the same groups of people. Each year scholars decipher more information about the ancient cultural groups who built these cities by studying the bas-relief carvings, sculptures, murals, and hieroglyphics found in them.

Mexico's pyramids are truncated platforms, not true pyramids, and come in many different shapes. Many sites have circular buildings, usually called observatories and dedicated to Ehécatl, god of the wind. Few pre-Hispanic buildings remain in either Colima or Jalisco, although exquisite pottery examples are preserved in museums in both states.

Pottery played an important role in the cultures of Mexico's indigenous peoples; the work of different groups can be distinguished by their use of color and style in pottery. The Cholulans had distinctive red-clay pottery decorated in cream, red, and black; Teotihuacán was noted for its three-legged painted orange ware; Tenochtitlán for its use of brilliant blue and red; Casas Grandes for anthropomorphic and zoomorphic images on clay vessels; and the Maya for pottery painted with scenes from daily and historic life.

In Tonalá near Guadalajara, pottery traditions begun in pre-Hispanic times continue today, and the National Museum of Ceramics in that village contains many good samples of Jalisco pottery as well as pieces from around Mexico. Ancient Jalisco pottery was both off-white and dark red and often decorated with black or red. Many of the figures show the workaday world of unknown peoples, carrying children or water jugs and at play. Good examples are on display at the small museum of anthropology in Guadalajara, across from Agua Azul Park. Both Jalisco and Colima are riddled with underground burial chambers and much of the dark red pottery was found in these multiroomed vaults. Colima is also famous for clay pieces formed into the shapes of potbellied hairless dogs, many of them dancing. The pottery also took the shape of vegetables, especially squash. Excellent museums in Colima display the unusual work of pre-Hispanic peoples of that area. In addition to the museums mentioned above, prime samples from this area are in the Museum of Anthropology in Mexico City.

With the arrival of the Spaniards, a new form of architecture came to Mexico. (The 300 years from the early 16th through the early 19th centuries are known as the viceregal period, when Spain's appointed viceroys ruled Mexico.) Many sites that were occupied by indigenous groups at the time of the Conquest were razed, and in their place appeared Catholic churches, public buildings, and palaces for conquerors and the king's bureaucrats.

Indian artisans, who formerly worked on pyramidal structures, were recruited to give life to these structures, often guided by drawings of European buildings the

Spanish architects tried to emulate. Frequently left on their own, the indigenous artisans sometimes implanted traditional symbolism in the new buildings: a plaster angel swaddled in feathers, reminiscent of the god Quetzalcoatl, or the face of an ancient god surrounded by corn leaves. They used pre-Hispanic calendar counts, the 13 steps to heaven, or the nine levels of the underworld to determine how many flowerets to carve around the church doorway.

To convert the native populations, New World Spanish priests and architects altered their normal ways of building and teaching. Often before the church was built, an open-air atrium was first constructed so large numbers of parishioners could be accommodated for the service. *Posas* (shelters) at the four corners of churchyards were another architectural technique unique to Mexico, again for the purpose of accommodating crowds during holy sacraments. Because of the language barrier between the Spanish and the natives, church adornment became more graphic. Biblical tales came to life in frescoes splashed across church walls; Christian symbolism in stone supplanted that of pre-Hispanic times. Out went the eagle (sun symbol), feathered serpent (symbol of fertility, rain, earth, and sky), and jaguar (power symbol), and in came Christ on a cross, saintly statues, and Franciscan, Dominican, and Augustinian symbolism.

It must have been a confusing time for the indigenous peoples, which accounts for the continued intermingling of Christian and pre-Hispanic ideas as they tried to make sense of it all. The convenient apparition of the Virgin Mary on former pre-Hispanic religious turf made it "legal" to return there to worship and build a "Christian" shrine. Baroque became even more baroque in Mexico and was dubbed *churrigueresque*. Excellent Mexico baroque examples are in Guadalajara in the Chapel of Our Lady of Aranzaú and Guadalajara's Regional Museum. The term *plateresque* was given to facade designs resembling silver design, but these were more planted on a structure than a part of it.

Concurrently with the building of religious structures, public buildings took shape, modeled after those in European capitals. Especially around Puebla, the use of colorful locally made tile, a fusion of local art, and Spain's Talavera style decorated public walls and church domes. Haciendas—massive, thick-walled, fortresslike structures built around a central patio—began to rise in the countryside. Remains of haciendas, some still operating, can be seen in almost all parts of Mexico.

Orozco: Jalisco's Moody Muralist

Born in what today is known as Ciudad Guzmán, Jalisco, José Clemente Orozco (1883–1949) is considered one of Mexico's "Big Three" muralists, along with Diego Rivera and David Alfero Siquieros. His gloomy, angry, but powerful works project his bitter view of politics. His years of struggle included a stint painting street signs and doll faces in the United States. On one trip north across the border, U.S. Customs destroyed his brothel series of paintings. Alma Reed, who owned Delphic Studios in New York, took him under her wing, promoting his career. His best-known murals appear in Guadalajara, and many of his easel works are in the Alvaro Carrillo Gil Museum in Mexico City. He is buried in the Rotonda de los Ilustres of the Dolores Cemetery in Mexico City.

Impressions

The revolution gave us self-confidence and a conscience for our existence and our destiny.

—José Clemente Orozco

Mexico is a country as richly set with architecture as an Elizabethan gown with pearls. Obviously they are not all jewels, but all have their places in the great network from which such buildings as the parish church of Taxco, San Agustín Acolman, the cathedral of Puebla, the Palacio del Gobierno in Guadalajara, or the Casa de los Azulejos in Mexico City stand out.

—Elizabeth Wilder Weismann, *Art and Time in Mexico,* 1985

The San Carlos Academy of Art was founded in Mexico City in 1785, taking after the renowned academies of Europe. Though the emphasis was on a Europeanized Mexico, by the end of the 19th century the subject matter of easel artists was becoming Mexican: Still lifes with Mexican fruit and pottery, and Mexican landscapes with cactus and volcanoes, appeared, as did portraits whose subjects wore Mexican regional clothing. José María Velasco (1840–1912), the father of Mexican landscape painting, emerged during this time. His work and that of others of this period are at the National Museum of Art in Mexico City. The José María Velasco museum in Toluca also showcases this master artist's works.

With the late 19th-century entry of Porfirio Díaz into the presidency came another infusion of European sensibilities. Díaz idolized Europe, and he lavished on the country a number of striking European-style public buildings, among them opera houses still used today. He provided European scholarships to promising young artists who later returned to Mexico to produce clearly Mexican subject paintings using techniques learned abroad. While the Mexican Revolution, following the resignation and exile of Díaz, ripped the country apart between 1911 and 1917, the result was the birth of Mexico and the claiming and appreciation by Mexicans of their homeland—which carried into the arts.

In 1923, Minister of Education José Vasconcelos was charged with educating the illiterate masses. As a means of reaching many people, he started the muralist movement when he invited Diego Rivera and several other budding artists to paint Mexican history on the walls of the Ministry of Education building and the National Preparatory School in Mexico City. From then on, the "big three" muralists—David Siquieros, José Clemente Orozco, and Rivera—were joined by others in bringing Mexico's history in art to the walls of public buildings throughout the country for all to see and interpret.

The years that followed eventually brought about a return to easel art, an exploration of Mexico's culture, and a new generation of artists and architects who were free to invent and draw on subjects and styles from around the world. Among the 20th-century greats, in addition to the "big three" mural-ists, are Frida Kahlo, Rufino Tamayo, Gerardo Murillo, José Guadalupe Posada, Saturnino Herrán, Francisco Goitia, José María Velasco, Pedro and Rafael Coronel, Miguel Covarrubias, Olga Costa, and José Chávez Morado. Among important architects during this period, one standout is Luis Barragán, of Guadalajara, who incorporated design elements from haciendas, Mexican textiles, pottery, and furniture into sleek, marble-floored structures splashed with the vivid colors of Mexico. His ideas are used by Mexican architects all over the country today.

5 By Word of Mouth or Stroke of Pen: Mexico's Storytelling Tradition

LITERATURE

By the time Cortés arrived in Mexico, the indigenous people were already masters of literature, recording their poems and histories by painting in fanfold books (codices) made of deerskin and bark paper or by carving on stone. To record history, gifted students were taught the art of bookmaking, drawing, painting, reading, and writing—skills the general public didn't have.

Unfortunately, very little has survived, for after the Conquest, the Spaniards deliberately destroyed native books. However, several Catholic priests, among them Bernardo de Sahugun and Diego de Landa (who was, ironically, one of the book destroyers), encouraged the Indians to record their customs and history. No authenticated pre-Hispanic Aztec painted books remain. However, Aztec artist survivors of the Conquest painted some that were used to verify Aztec territories, tributes, property, etc., but that also contained Aztec history, ritual, and culture before the conquest. These records are among the best we have to document life before the Conquest.

During the Conquest, Cortés wrote his now-famous five letters to Charles V, which give us the first printed Conquest literature, but the most important record is that of Bernal Díaz de Castillo. Forty years after the Conquest, Díaz de Castillo (a conquistador who was enraged by an inaccurate account of the Conquest written by a flattering friend of Cortés) wrote his lively and very readable version of the event, *True History of the Conquest of Mexico*; it's regarded as the most accurate.

The first printing press appeared in Mexico in 1537 and was followed by a proliferation of printing, mostly on subjects about science, nature, and getting along in Mexico. The most important literary figure during the 16th century was Sor Juana Inès de la Cruz, a child prodigy and later a nun and poet whose works are still treasured. The first daily newspaper appeared in 1805. The first Spanish novel written in Mexico was *The Itching Parrot* by José Joaquin Fernández de Lizardi, about 19th-century Mexican life. It's a classic, satirical 19th-century tale about the wanton life a young man leads after his mother convinces him he is too aristocratic to work, though he has no means of support.

Nineteenth-century writers produced a plethora of political fiction and nonfiction. Among the more explosive was *The Presidential Succession of 1910* by Francisco Madero (who later became president), which contributed to the downfall of Porfirio Díaz, and *Regeneración*, a weekly anti-Díaz magazine published by the Flores Mignon brothers.

Among the 20th-century writers of note are Octavio Paz, author of *The Labyrinth of Solitude* and winner of the 1991 Nobel Prize for literature, and Carlos Fuentes, author of *Where the Air Is Clear* and *The Old Gringo*.

Books in Mexico are becoming very expensive and editions are not produced in great quantity. Newspapers and magazines abound, but the most visible form of literature is the comic-book novel.

RELIGION

Mexico is predominantly Roman Catholic, a religion introduced by the Spaniards during the Conquest. Despite its preponderance, the Catholic faith, in many places (Chiapas and Oaxaca, for example), has pre-Hispanic overtones. One need only visit the *curandero* section of a Mexican market or attend a village festivity featuring pre-Hispanic dancers to understand that supernatural beliefs often run parallel to Christian ones.

MYTH & FOLKLORE

Mexico's complicated mythological heritage from pre-Hispanic culture is jammed with images derived from nature—the wind, jaguars, eagles, snakes, flowers, and more—all intertwined with elaborate mythological stories to explain the universe, climate, seasons, and geography. So strong were the ancient beliefs that Mexico's indigenous peoples built their cities according to the four cardinal points of the compass, with each compass point assigned a particular color (the colors might vary from group to group). The sun, moon, and stars took on godlike meaning, and the religious, ceremonial, and secular calendars were arranged to show tribute to these omnipotent gods.

Most pre-Hispanic cultures believed in an underworld (not a hell), usually of nine levels, and a heaven of 13 levels, so the numbers nine and 13 became mythologically significant. The solar calendar count of 365 days and the ceremonial calendar of 260 days were numerically significant. How one died determined where one wound up after death: in the underworld, in heaven, or at one of the four cardinal points. Everyone first had to make the journey through the underworld.

One of the richest sources of mythological tales is the *Book of Popol Vuh,* a Maya bible of sorts that was recorded after the Conquest. The *Chilam Balam*, another such book, existed in hieroglyphic form at the time of the Conquest and was recorded using the Spanish alphabet to transliterate Mayan words that could be understood by the Spaniards. The *Chilam Balam* differs from the *Popol Vuh* in that it is the collected histories of many Maya communities.

Each of the ancient cultures had its set of gods and goddesses, and while the names might not cross cultures, their characteristics or purpose often did. Chaac, the hook-nosed rain god of the Maya, was Tláloc, the mighty-figured rain god of the Aztecs; Quetzalcoatl, the plumed-serpent god/man of the Toltecs, became Kukulkán of the Maya. The tales of the powers and creation of these deities make up Mexico's rich mythology. Sorting out the pre-Hispanic pantheon and mythological beliefs in ancient Mexico can become an all-consuming study (the Maya alone had 166 deities); below is a list of some of the most important gods of the Aztecs:

> *Coatlíque:* Huitzilopochtli's mother, whose name means "she of serpent skirt," goddess of death and earth.
> *Ehécatl:* Wind god, whose temple is usually round; another aspect of Quetzalcoatl.
> *Huitzilopochtli:* War god and primary Aztec god, son of Coatlique.
> *Mayahuel:* Goddess of pulque.
> *Ometeotl:* God/goddess and all-powerful creator of the universe, ruler of heaven, earth, and the underworld.
> *Quetzalcoatl:* A mortal who took on legendary characteristics as a god (or vice versa) in Tula; he also is symbolized as Venus, the morning star, and

Ehécatl, the wind god. Quetzalcoatl is also credited with giving the Maya cacao (chocolate), teaching them how to grow it, harvest it, roast it, and turn it into a drink with ceremonial and magical properties.

Tezcaltipoca: Aztec sun god known as "Smoking Mirror."

Tláloc: Aztec rain god.

Tonantzin: Aztec motherhood goddess.

Xochipilli: Aztec god of dance, flowers, and music.

Xochiquetzal: Flower and love goddess.

6 Mariachi Serenades & More: Mexico's Music & Dance

One has only to walk down almost any street or attend any festival to understand that Mexico's vast musical tradition is inborn; it predates the Conquest. Musical instruments were constructed from almost anything that could be made to rattle or produce a rhythm or a sound—conch-shell trumpets, high-pitched antler horns, rattlers from seashells and rattlesnakes, drums of turtle shell as well as upright, leather-covered wood (*tlalpanhuéhuetl*) and horizontal hollowed logs (*teponaztli*), bells of gold and copper, wind instruments of hollow reeds or fired clay, and soundmakers from leather-topped armadillo shells and gourds. Many were elaborately carved or decorated, befitting the important ceremonies they accompanied. So important was music that one of Moctezuma's palaces, the Mixcoacalli, was devoted to the care and housing of musical instruments, which were guarded around the clock. In Aztec times, music, dance, and religion were tied together with literature. Music was usually intended to accompany the poems that were written for religious ceremonies. Children with talent were separated and trained to adulthood, especially as musicians and poets, two exacting professions in which mistakes carried extreme consequences. The dead were buried with musical instruments for their journey into the afterlife.

Music and dance in Mexico today are divided into three kinds: pre-Hispanic, post-Hispanic, and secular. In addition to authentic, but often remote, rural village fiestas, one of the best places to see pre-Hispanic dancing is the Ballet Folklórico in Guadalajara. Among pre-Hispanic dances still performed there or elsewhere in Mexico are "The Flying Pole Dance," "Dance of the Quetzales" (the sacred quetzal bird), "Deer Dance," and dances of the Huicholoes and Coras of Jalisco and Nayarit. Post-Hispanic music and dance evolved first in order to teach the native inhabitants about Christianity with such dances as "Los Santiagos," with St. James battling heathens, and "Los Moros," with Moors battling Christians. Others, like "Los Jardineros," were spoofs on pretentious Spanish life. Secular dances are variations of Spanish dances performed by both men and women and characterized by lots of foot-tapping, skirt-swishing, and innocent flirtation. No "Mexican fiesta night" would be complete without the "Jarabe Tapatío," the national folk dance of Mexico, created in Guadalajara.

Besides the native music and dances, there are regional, state, and national orchestras. On weekends, state bands often perform free in central plazas. Performing-arts groups from all over the world frequently tour Mexico. Mexicans have a sophisticated understanding and enjoyment of visual and performing arts, so any special show will draw a sell-out crowd.

7 Margaritas, Tortillas & Pozole: Food & Drink in Mexico

Mexican food served in the United States or almost anywhere else in the world is almost never truly Mexican. The farther you get from the source, the more the authenticity is lost in translation. True Mexican food usually isn't fiery hot, for example; hot spices are added from sauces and garnishes at the table.

While there are certain staples like tortillas and beans that appear almost universally around the country, Mexican food and drink varies considerably from region to region; even the beans and tortillas will sidestep the usual in different locales.

MEALS & RESTAURANTS À *LA MEXICANA*

BREAKFAST   Traditionally, businesspeople in Mexico start their day with a cup of coffee or *atole* and a piece of sweet bread just before heading for work around 8am; they won't sit down for a real breakfast until around 10 or 11am, when restaurants fill with men (usually) eating hearty breakfasts that may look more like lunch with steak, eggs, beans, and tortillas. Things are slowly changing, as some executives are beginning to favor an earlier breakfast hour, beginning between 7 and 8am, during which business and the morning meal are combined.

Foreigners searching for an early breakfast will often find that nothing gets going in restaurants until around 9am; however, markets are bustling by 7am (they are a great place to get an early breakfast), and the capital's hotel restaurants often open as early as 7am to accommodate business travelers and those leaving on early flights. You might also bring your own portable coffee pot and coffee and buy bakery goodies the night before and make breakfast yourself.

LUNCH   The main meal of the day, lunch has traditionally been a 2- to 3-hour break, occurring between 1 and 5pm. However, at least in the capital, an abbreviated midday break is beginning to take hold. Short or long, the typical Mexican lunch begins with soup, then rice, then a main course with beans and tortillas and a bit of vegetable, and lastly dessert and coffee. But here too you'll see one-plate meals and fast food beginning to encroach on the multicourse meal. Workers return to their jobs until 7 or 8pm.

DINNER   The evening meal is taken late, usually around 9 or 10pm. Although you may see many Mexicans eating in restaurants at night, big evening meals aren't traditional; a typical meal at home would be a light one with leftovers from breakfast or lunch, perhaps soup or tortillas and jam, or a little meat and rice.

RESTAURANT TIPS & ETIQUETTE   Some of the foreigner's greatest frustrations in Mexico occur in restaurants, when they need to hail and retain the waiter or get their check. To summon the waiter, waive or raise your hand, but don't motion with your index finger, a demeaning gesture that may even cause the waiter to ignore you. To gesture someone to them, Mexicans will stand up, extend an arm straight out at shoulder level, and make a straight-armed, downward, diving motion with their hand cupped. A more discreet version, good to use when seated, has the elbow bent and perpendicular to the shoulder; with hand cupped, make a quick, diving motion out a bit from the armpit. (Both of these motions may make you feel silly until you practice. The latter one looks rather like the motion Americans make to signify "be still" or "shut up.")

If the waiter arrives to take your order before you are ready, you may have trouble getting him again. Once an order is in, however, the food usually arrives in steady sequence. Frequently, just before you've finished, when your plate is nearly empty, the waiter appears out of nowhere to whisk it away—unwary diners have seen their plates disappear midbite.

Finding your waiter when you're ready for the check can also be difficult. While waiters may hover too much while you're dining, they tend to disappear entirely by meal's end. It's considered rude for the waiter to bring the check before it's requested, so you have to ask for it, sometimes more than once. (To find a missing waiter, get up as if to leave and scrape the chairs loudly; if that fails, you'll probably find him chatting in the kitchen.) If you want the check and the waiter is simply across the room, a smile and a scribbling motion into the palm of your hand will send the message. In many budget restaurants, waiters don't clear the table of finished plates or soft drink bottles because they use them to figure the tab. Always double-check the addition.

FOOD AROUND THE COUNTRY

You won't have to confine yourself to Mexican food during a visit to Mexico— you'll find restaurants that prepare world-class French, Italian, Swiss, German, and other international cuisines. But you can also delve into the variety of Mexico's traditional foods, which derive from pre-Hispanic, Spanish, and French cuisines. At its best Mexican food is among the most delicious in the world. Visitors can fairly easily find hearty, filling meals on a budget, but finding truly delicious food is not so easy. Nevertheless, some of the country's best food is found in small, inexpensive restaurants where regional specialties are made to please discerning locals. Explanations of specific dishes are found in the appendix. Although the foods mentioned below originated in a particular part of the country, they frequently cross state lines and appear on menus countrywide, so you might see *tamales estilo Oaxaca* (Oaxaca-style tamales), or *sopa Tarasca* (Tarascan soup) in Guadalajara or Puerto Vallarta.

Recipes such as mole poblano—a flavorful sauce usually used for turkey or chicken that was developed by nuns in Puebla during colonial times to please priests and visiting dignitaries—have become part of the national patrimony, but the basics of Mexico's cuisine have endured since pre-Hispanic times. Corn, considered holy, was the foundation staple food of pre-Hispanic peoples. These people used corn leaves to bake and wrap food and ground corn to make the *atole* drink in many flavors (bitter, picante, or sweet) as well as tortillas and tamales (stuffed with meat).

When the Spanish arrived they found a bounty of edibles never seen in the Old World, including turkey, chocolate, tomatoes, squash, beans, avocados, peanuts, and vanilla (in addition to corn). All of these ingredients were integral parts of pre-Hispanic foods and remain at the heart of modern Mexican cooking. Also central to the Indian peoples' cuisines were chiles, nopal cactus, amaranth, eggs of ants, turtles and iguanas, corn and maguey worms, bee and fly larvae, flowers of the maguey and squash, grasshoppers, jumiles (similar to stinkbugs), armadillos, rattlesnake, hairless dogs, deer, squirrels, monkeys, rats, frogs, ducks, parrots, quail, shrimp, fish, crabs, and crawfish. Exotic fruits such as sapodilla, guava, mamey, chirimoya, and pitahuayas rounded out the diet. Some of these are mainstream foods today, and others are considered delicacies and may be seen on specialty menus.

Much of what we consider Mexican food wouldn't exist without the contributions of the Spanish. They introduced sugar cane, cattle, sheep, wheat, grapes, barley, and rice. The French influence is best seen in the extensive variety of baked goods available in the capital.

MEXICO'S REGIONAL CUISINES   Tamales are a traditional food all around Mexico, but there are many regional differences. In Mexico City, you can often find the traditional Oaxaca tamales, which are steamed in a banana leaf. The zacahuil of coastal Veracruz is the size of a pig's leg (and that's what's in the center) and is pit-baked in a banana leaf; it can be sampled from street vendors on Sunday at the Lagunilla market.

Tortillas, another Mexican basic, are also not made or used equally. In northern Mexico flour tortillas are served more often than corn tortillas. Blue corn tortillas, once a market food, have found their way to gourmet tables throughout the country. Tortillas are fried and used as a garnish in tortilla and Tarascan soup. Filled with meat, they become, of course, tacos. A tortilla stuffed, rolled, or covered in a sauce and garnished results in an enchilada. A tortilla filled with cheese and lightly fried is a quesadilla. Rolled into a narrow tube stuffed with chicken, then deep fried, they become a flauta. Leftover tortillas cut in wedges and crispy fried are called totopos and used to scoop beans and guacamole salad. Yesterday's tortillas mixed with eggs, chicken, peppers, and other spices are called chilaquiles. Small fried corn tortillas are delicious with ceviche, or when topped with fresh lettuce, tomatoes, sauce, onions, and chicken they become tostadas. Each region has a variation of these tortilla-based dishes and most can be found in Mexico City.

Since a variety of Mexico's cuisines appear on menus, it's useful to know some of the best to try.

Puebla is known for the many dishes created by colonial-era nuns, among them traditional mole poblano (a rich sauce with more than 20 ingredients usually served over turkey), the eggnoglike rompope, and bunuelos (a kind of puff pastry dipped in sugar). Puebla is also known for its Mexican-style barbecue, lamb mixiotes (cooked in spicy sauce and wrapped in maguey paper), and tinga (a delicious beef stew). Chiles enogadas, the national dish of Mexico, was created in Puebla in honor of Emperor Agustín Iturbide. The national colors of red, white, and green appear in this dish, in which large green poblano peppers are stuffed with spicy beef, topped with white almond sauce, and sprinkled with red pomegranate seeds. It's served around Independence Day in September.

Tamales wrapped in banana leaves and a number of different mole sauces are hallmarks of **Oaxacan** cuisine.

The **Yucatán** is noted for its rich (but not *picante*) sauces and pit-baked meat. Mild but flavorful achiote-based paste is one of the main flavorings for Yucatecan sauces.

The states of **Guerrero, Nayarit,** and **Jalisco** produce *pozole,* a soup of hominy and chicken or pork made in a clear broth, or one from tomatoes or green chiles (depending on the state), and topped with a variety of garnishes. Birria (lamb or goat meat cooked in a spicy tomato broth), both red and white, is the specialty of **Colima** and Jalisco. Rompope is a local specialty sold widely in the mountains of Jalisco.

Michoacán has produced a triangular-shaped tamal called corunda as well as uchepo, a rectangular tamal that is either sweet or has meat inside. The state is also known for its soups, among them the delicious *Tarascan* soup, made with a bean-broth base.

Tequila!!!

Perhaps looking to distract themselves from the cares of conquest, the first waves of Spanish colonists in Mexico fiddled around with *pulque* (POOL-kay), a mildly intoxicating drink popular among indigenous peoples. They hit upon a stronger drink in the late 16th century when Cenobio Sauza distilled his first bottle of a special hooch in Tequila, Jalisco—thus was born an 80-proof potation now consumed the world over, which can truly be called the "spirit" of Mexico.

True tequila is made only from the sweet sap at the heart of the blue *agave* (ah-GAH-veh) plant, grown in the states of Jalisco, Nayarit, and Michoacán. The laborious process by which tequila is produced involves roasting the enormous agave heart (it can weigh 100 pounds or more) in a pit; the cooked heart is then pulped and the juice distilled. It is double distilled before it is bottled.

The basic tequila is *blanco,* or white. Many "gold" tequilas are just *blanco* with a little artificial coloring; the true golds are always *reposado,* or "rested" at least six months. The aging process does lend tequila a light-gold tint. Also available, at the super-premium end of the market, are *añejo* tequilas, which must be aged at least two years.

A similar but less-refined drink is *mescal;* it is made from one of the other 400 varieties of agave. It's mescal, not tequila, that comes with a worm in the bottom of the bottle. Pulque, which comes from yet another agave, is still produced.

The hoary old ritual for drinking tequila, dating back long before margaritas began hogging the spotlight, is to put a dash of salt in your left hand, a shot glass of tequila before you in the middle, and a nice fresh slice of lime on your right—consume them from left to right, in bang-bang-bang fashion. This is a bracing combination—I dare you to do it without falling into unconscious mimicry of Jack Nicholson having a snort in *Easy Rider.* (It should be noted that reckless repetition of this procedure has felled many a tourist onto bar-room floors.)

In the 1940s, when Margarita Sames concocted the original tequila-based "margarita" drink, she entertained friends with it in her Acapulco home. She never imagined that sunsets from Anchorage to Argentina would one day be celebrated with the tasty lime-laden cocktail, and sipped from big, long-stemmed glasses named especially for her drink. The concoction became so popular that bartenders far and wide laid claim to its creation, but Sames's story is the most believable. Sames made her drink with tequila, fresh-squeezed lime juice, and Cointreau, a French liqueur made with the skins of both bitter and sweet oranges. The particulars can change, but these three categories of ingredient—real tequila, lime juice, and orange-flavored liqueur—are the holy trinity of margarita making.

Here's a few variations you can work into your bartending. There are a lot of tequilas available beyond the usual Cuervo and Sauza varieties. Herradura is another big-name brand, perhaps the best of these. If your liquor store is enlightened they may be able to procure lesser-known brands; you can also, of course, add a special bottle of tequila to your shopping list for each trip you make south of the border. As far as liqueur goes, these days most people use triple sec instead of Cointreau—both are orange-based liqueurs, but Cointreau is considerably more expensive. If you're using an expensive premium tequila, try the Cointreau—it's delicious. If you're using triple sec, don't buy one of the bargain-basement varieties—it's just not the real stuff. Marie Brizard, Bols, and DeKuyper all make good triple secs. Another substitute for triple sec is Grand Marnier, a top-shelf orange- and cognac-flavored liqueur—it may sound odd, but the cognac flavor lends an interesting character to a margarita. And finally, while traditionalists will tell you there's no substitute for fresh-squeezed lime juice, it can be nearly impossible to procur a decent supply of juicy, ripe limes—the fruit is notorious for inconsistent quality. One solution is to use fresh-squeezed lemon juice; the flavors are nearly indistinguishable in the context of the cocktail, and lemons are much more consistent. Another is to use a bottled lime juice, but if you do, get Rose's Lime Juice—it's just better than any of the other brands.

The proportions of the cocktail are 2 parts tequila, 1 part liqueur, and $1\frac{1}{2}$ part lime juice. Purists will tell you that there's only one way to mix a margarita (in a shaker with fairly coarse chunks of ice) and only two ways to serve it (either "on the rocks" into a kosher salt–rimmed hurricane glass or "straight up" strained from the shaker into a salt-rimmed martini- or champagne-style glass). But why let an ideologue impinge on your fun? If you want to use a blender for frozen margaritas, knock yourself out—just use less expensive brands of tequila and triple sec, as the Slurpee effect will dilute the flavors of the spirits. Or add some fresh fruit—strawberries, raspberries, ripe peaches, and kiwis all are delicious additions to a frozen margarita.

All the squabbles over minor additives, salt or no salt, or who actually created the drink aside, three cheers to the margarita itself: so refreshingly smooth it goes down as agreeably as lemonade on a summer day . . . just watch out for that sneaky wallop—Mike Tyson's got nothing on it for knockout power.

In Chapala, Jalisco, a widow (in Spanish, *viuda*) invented a spicey orange juice–based drink as a tequila chaser and bottled it under the La Viuda label, which is made in Chapala and sold countrywide. Along came bloody mary–style tequila drinks and many more including the tequila sunrise, which blends tequila, orange juice, and a splash of grenadine into a cocktail that looks as promising as a tropical sunrise.

Tequila is making inroads into new territory these days—as a flavoring in food in everything from banana nut bread, cookies, and jalapeño jelly, to salsa, pot roast, baked chicken, and stuffed peppers. If this revolution takes hold the way margaritas did, we could soon see tequila beside wine on the cook's list of pantry staples. Tequila-flavored dishes are already beginning to appear on menus of fine restaurants in Mexico.

At least four books are available that expound at length the versatility of Mexico's most famous liquor: *Tequila: The Spirit of Mexico* by Lucinda Hutson (Ten Speed Press, 1994); *The Tequila Cook Book* by Lynn Nusom (Golden West Publishers, 1994); *Tomás' Tequila Book* by Don and Alice Hutson and Dianne Goss (Pasquale Publishing, 1992); and *The Tequila Book* by Ann Walker (Chronicle Books, 1994).

Veracruz, of course, is famous for seafood dishes. Especially well known is red snapper Veracruz-style, smothered in tomatoes, onions, garlic, and olives.

DRINK

Though Mexico grows flavorful **coffee** in Chiapas, Veracruz, and Oaxaca, a jar of instant coffee is often all that's offered, especially in budget restaurants. Decaffeinated coffee appears on some menus, but often it's the instant variety, even in the best restaurants.

Specialty drinks are almost as varied as the food in Mexico—not everything begins and ends with **tequila.** Hot **ponche** (punch) is found often at festivals and is usually made with fresh fruit and spiked with tequila or rum.

Domestic wine and beer are excellent choices in Mexico, and in the past they have been cheaper than any imported variety. However, NAFTA has lowered trade barriers against U.S.-made alcoholic drinks, and prices for them are becoming lower as well.

Baja California and the region around Querétaro is prime grape-growing land for Mexico's **wine** production. Excellent **beer** is produced in Monterrey, the Yucatán, and Veracruz. The best **pulque,** a pre-Hispanic drink derived from the juice of the maguey plant, supposedly comes from Hidalgo state. Mexicans prefer freshly fermented pulque and generally avoid the canned variety, claiming it's just not the real thing. Visitors to the capital can sample it at restaurants around Garibaldi square. Delicious **fruit-flavored waters** appear on tables countrywide; they are made from hibiscus flowers, ground rice and melon seeds, watermelon, and other fresh fruits. Be sure to ask if they are made with purified water. **Sangría** is a spicy tomato, orange juice, and pepper-based chaser for tequila shots.

Though the rich, eggnoglike **rompope** was invented in Puebla, now other regions such as San Juan de los Lagos, Jalisco, produce it. It's sold in liquor and grocery stores countrywide.

8 Recommended Books, Films & Recordings

BOOKS

There are an endless number of books written on the history, culture, and archae-ology of Mexico and Central America. I have listed those I especially enjoyed.

HISTORY

A Thumbnail History of Guadalajara (Editorial Colomos, 1983) by José María Muriá Rouret, can be purchased in Guadalajara in English. It provides excellent background on the city's early trials and architecture. Dennis Tedlock produced an elegant translation of the *Popul Vuh*, a collection of ancient Maya mythologi-cal tales (Simon & Schuster, 1985). *A Short History of Mexico* (Doubleday, 1962) by J. Patrick McHenry is a concise historical account. A remarkably readable and thorough college textbook is *The Course of Mexican History* (Oxford University Press, 1987) by Michael C. Meyer and William L. Sherman. Bernal Díaz's *The Conquest of New Spain* (Shoe String, 1988) is the famous story of the Mexican Conquest written by Cortés's lieutenant. *The Crown of Mexico* (Holt, Rinehart & Winston, 1971) by Joan Haslip, a biography of Maximilian and Carlotta, reads like a novel. Eric Wolf's *Sons of the Shaking Earth* (University of Chicago Press) is the best single-volume introduction to Mexican history and culture of which I know. *Ancient Mexico: An Overview* (University of New Mexico Press, 1985) by Jaime Litvak, is a short, very readable history of pre-Hispanic Mexico.

The Wind That Swept Mexico (University of Texas Press, 1971) by Anita Brenner, is a classic illustrated account of the Mexican Revolution. Early this century, Charles Flandrau wrote the classic *Viva Mexico: A Traveller's Account of Life in Mexico* (Eland Books, 1985); it's a blunt and humorous description of Mexico. Most people can't put down Gary Jenning's *Aztec* (Avon, 1981), a superbly researched and colorfully written fictionalized account of Aztec life before and after the Conquest.

CULTURE

Five Families (Basic Books, 1979) and *Children of Sanchez* (Random House, 1979), both by Oscar Lewis, are sociological studies written in the late 1950s about typical Mexican families. Irene Nicholson's *Mexican and Central American Mythology* (Peter Bedrick Books, 1983) is a concise illustrated book that simplifies the subject.

A good but controversial all-around introduction to contemporary Mexico and its people is *Distant Neighbors: A Portrait of the Mexicans* (Random House, 1984) by Alan Riding. In a more personal vein is Patrick Oster's *The Mexicans: A Personal Portrait of the Mexican People* (HarperCollins, 1989), a reporter's insightful account of ordinary Mexican people. A book with valuable insights into the Mexican character is *The Labyrinth of Solitude* (Grove Press, 1985) by Octavio Paz.

For some fascinating background on northern Mexico and the Copper Canyon, read *Unknown Mexico* (Dover Press, 1987) by Carl Lumholtz, an intrepid writer and photographer around the turn of the century.

The best single source of information on Mexican music, dance, and mythology is Frances Toor's *A Treasury of Mexican Folkways* (Crown, 1967). *Life in Mexico: Letters of Fanny Calderón de la Barca* (Doubleday, 1966), edited and annotated by Howard T. Fisher and Marion Hall Fisher, is as lively and entertaining today as when it first appeared in 1843, but the editor's illustrated and annotated update makes it even more contemporary. Scottish-born Fanny was married to the Spanish ambassador to Mexico, and the letters are the accounts of her experiences. *My Heart Lies South* by Elizabeth Borton de Treviño (1953) is a humorous, tender, and insightful autobiographical account of the life of an American woman married to a Mexican in Monterrey; it begins in the 1930s.

ART, ARCHAEOLOGY & ARCHITECTURE

A book that tells the story of the Indians' "painted books" is *The Mexican Codices and Their Extraordinary History* (Ediciones Lara, 1985) by María Sten. *Mexico Splendors of Thirty Centuries* (Metropolitan Museum of Art, 1990), the catalog of the 1991 traveling exhibition, is a wonderful resource on Mexico's art from 1500 B.C. through the 1950s. Another superb catalog, *Images of Mexico: The Contribution of Mexico to 20th Century Art* (Dallas Museum of Art, 1987) is a fabulously illustrated and detailed account of Mexican art gathered from collections around the world. Elizabeth Wilder Weismann's *Art and Time in Mexico: From the Conquest to the Revolution* (HarperCollins, 1985), illustrated with 351 photographs, covers Mexican religious, public, and private architecture with excellent photos and text. *Casa Mexicana* (Steward, Tabori & Chang, 1989) by Tim Street-Porter, takes readers through the interiors of some of Mexico's finest homes-turned-museums or public buildings and private homes, using color

Impressions

Jalisco is not only a state but also a magic name. The scenes for many of Mexico's modern movies and popular novels are set in Jalisco and often have the name in the title; practically all of the ranchero songs are about Jalisco or about Guadalajara, its capital. This popularity is probably traceable to a nostalgia for the good old days of Mexico which Jalisco once represented.
—Herbert Cerwin, *These are the Mexicans*, 1947

Jalisco is rich in ancient remains. Burial places are constantly discovered, though the material unearthed falls, at least to a great extent, into the hands of shrewd dealers, who sell it to tourists and thus scatter it over the earth.
—Carl Lumholtz, *Unknown Mexico*, 1902

photographs. *Mexican Interiors* (Architectural Book Publishing Co., 1962) by Verna Cook Shipway and Warren Shipway, uses black-and-white photographs to highlight architectural details from homes all over Mexico.

FOLK ART   Chloè Sayer's *Costumes of Mexico* (University of Texas Press, 1985) is a beautifully illustrated and written work. *Mexican Masks* (University of Texas Press, 1980) by Donald Cordry, based on the author's collection and travels, remains the definitive work on Mexican masks. Cordry's *Mexican Indian Costumes* (University of Texas Press, 1968) is another classic on the subject. Carlos Espejel wrote both *Mexican Folk Ceramics* and *Mexican Folk Crafts* (Editorial Blume, 1975 and 1978), two comprehensive books that explore crafts state by state. The two-volume *Lo Efémero y Eterno del Arte Popular Mexicano* (Fondo Editorial de la Plastica Mexicana, 1974), produced during the Echeverría presidency, is out of print, but it's one of the most complete works ever produced on Mexican folk art and customs. A similarly exhaustive work with excellent photographs in two volumes (Editorial Hermes 1976) is *Arte Mexicano: Danzas y Bailes Populares and Indumentaria Tradicional Indigena. Folk Treasures of Mexico* (Harry N. Abrams, 1990) by Marion Oettinger, curator of folk and Latin American art at the San Antonio Museum of Art, is the fascinating illustrated story behind the 3,000-piece Mexican folk-art collection amassed by Nelson Rockefeller over a 50-year period and includes a great deal of information about individual folk artists.

NATURE   *Peterson Field Guides: Mexican Birds* (Houghton Mifflin) by Roger Tory Peterson and Edward L. Chalif, is an excellent guide to the country's birds. *A Guide to Mexican Mammals and Reptiles* (Minutiae Mexicana) by Norman Pelham Wright and Dr. Bernardo Villa Ramírez is a small but useful guide to some of the country's wildlife.

FILMS

Mexico's first movie theater opened in 1897 in Mexico City. Almost immediately, people with movie cameras began capturing everyday life in Mexico as well as both sides of the Mexican Revolution. All these early films are safe in Mexican archives. As a commercial industry, film had its Mexican start with the 1918 *La Banda del Automóvil Gris* (The Gray Automobile Gang) by Enrique Rosas Priego, based on an actual cops-and-robbers event in Mexico; however, the industry's heyday really began in the 1930s and lasted only until the 1950s. Themes revolved around the Mexican Revolution, handsome but luckless singing cowboys, and helpless, poor but beautiful maidens, all against a classic Mexican backdrop, at first in rural villages (*ranchos*) and later in city neighborhoods.

Classic films and directors from that era are *Allá en el Rancho Grande* and *Vamonos Con Pancho Villa*, both by Fernándo de Fuentes; *Campeón sin Corona* (Champion without a Crown), a true-life boxing drama by Alejandro Galindo; *La Perla* (The Pearl) by Emilio Fernández, based on John Steinbeck's novel; *Yanco* by Servando González, about a poor young boy of Xochimilco who learned to play a violin; and the sad tale of *María Candelaria*, also set in Xochimilco, another Fernández film, starring Dolores del Río. Comedian Cantinflas starred in many Mexican films and became known in the United States for his role in *Around the World in Eighty Days.*

If Mexico's golden age of cinema didn't last long, Mexico as subject matter and location has had a long life. The Durango mountains have become the film backdrop capital of Mexico. *The Night of the Iguana* was filmed in Puerto Vallarta, putting that seaside village on the map. *The Old Gringo* was filmed in Zacatecas, and *Viva Zapata!* and *Under the Volcano* were both set in Cuernavaca.

The most recent well-known film produced in Mexico is *Like Water for Chocolate*, based on Laura Esquivel's novel (Doubleday, 1992). A lusty, intimate, and wonderfully done movie, its story intertwines the secrets of traditional Mexican food preparation with a magical, surrealistic, and yet believable account of Mexican hacienda family life along the Río Grande/Río Bravo at the turn of the century.

RECORDINGS

Mexicans take their music very seriously—notice the cassettes for sale almost everywhere, the ceaseless music in the streets, and the bus drivers with collections of tapes to entertain passengers. For the collector, there are choices from contemporary rock to revolutionary ballads, ranchero, salsa, sones, and romantic trios.

Some of the best trio music is by Los Tres Diamantes, Los Tres Reyes, and Trio Los Soberanos. If you're requesting songs of a trio, good ones to ask for are "Sin Ti," "Usted," "Adiós Mi Chaparita," "Amor de la Calle," and "Cielito Lindo." Traditional ranchero music to request, which can be sung by soloists or trios, are "Tú Solo Tú," "No Volveré," and "Adiós Mi Chaparita."

Music from the Yucatán includes the recordings by the Trio Los Soberanos and Dueto Yucalpeten. Typical Yucatán songs are "Las Golondrinas Yucatecas," "Peregrina," "Ella," "El Pajaro Azul," and "Ojos Tristes." Heartthrob soloists from years past include Pedro Vargas, Pedro Enfante, Hector Cabrera, Lucho Gatica, Pepe Jara, and Alberto Vazquez.

Peña Ríos makes excellent marimba recordings. Though marimba musicians seldom ask for requests, some typical renditions would include, "Huapango de Moncayo" and "El Bolero de Ravel."

You'll arrive and leave the states of Jalisco and Colima with the sound of mariachi music playing. Among the top recording artists is Mariachi Vargas. No mariachi performance is complete without *Guadalajara, Las Mañanitas,* and *Jarabe Tapatío.* Mariachi music is played and sold all over Mexico.

One of the best recordings of recent times is the Royal Philharmonic Orchestra's rendition of classic Mexican music titled *Mexicano;* it's one purchase you must make.

Hermanos Aguascalientes, a trio of brothers who are actually from San Miguel de Allende, use stringed instruments to produce classical renditions of music from around the world. Don't rest until you find their tapes.

3

Planning a Trip to Mid-Pacific Mexico

In this chapter, the where, when, and how of your trip are discussed—the advance planning that gets your trip together and takes it on the road.

After deciding where to go, most people have two fundamental questions: What will it cost and how do I get there? This chapter not only answers those questions but also addresses such important issues as when to go, whether or not to take a tour, what pretrip health precautions should be taken, what insurance coverage to investigate, where to obtain additional information, and more.

1 Visitor Information, Entry Requirements & Money

SOURCES OF INFORMATION

The **Mexico Hotline** (☎ 800/44-MEXICO in the U.S.) is a good source for very general informational brochures on the country and for answers to the most commonly asked questions.

MEXICAN GOVERNMENT TOURIST OFFICES

Mexico has tourist offices throughout the world, including the following:

United States: 70 E. Lake St., Suite 1413, Chicago, IL 60601 (☎ 312/565-2778); 2702 N. Loop W., Suite 450, Houston, TX 77008 (☎ 713/880-5153); 10100 Santa Monica Blvd., Suite 224, Los Angeles, CA 90067 (☎ 310/203-8191); 233 Ponce de Leon Blvd., Suite 710, Coral Gables, FL 33134 (☎ 305/443-9160); 405 Park Ave., Suite 1401, New York, NY 10022 (☎ 212/755-7261); and 1911 Pennsylvania Ave. NW, Washington, DC 20006 (☎ 202/728-1750).

Canada: One Place Ville-Marie, Suite 1526, Montreal, PQ H3B 2B5 (☎ 514/871-1052); 2 Bloor St. W., Suite 1801, Toronto, ON M4W 3E2 (☎ 416/925-0704).

Europe: Weisenhüttenplatz 26, 6000 Frankfurt-am-Main 1, Germany (☎ 4969/25-3413); 60-61 Trafalgar Sq., London WC2 N5DS, United Kingdom (☎ 441/734-1058); Calle de Velázquez 126, Madrid 28006, Spain (☎ 341/261-1827); 4 rue Notre-Dame-des-Victoires, 75002 Paris, France (☎ 331/40-20-07-34); and via Barberini 3, 00187 Rome, Italy (☎ 396/482-7160).

Asia: 2.15.1 Nagato-Cho, Chiyoda-Ku, Tokyo 100, Japan (☎ 813/580-2962).

OTHER SOURCES

The following newsletters may be of interest to readers:

Mexican Meanderings, P.O. Box 33057, Austin, TX 78764, is a new six- to eight-page newsletter with photographs featuring off-the-beaten-track destinations in Mexico. It's aimed at readers who travel by car, bus, or train and is published six times annually. A subscription costs $18.

Travel Mexico, Apdo. Postal 6-1007, Mexico, DF 06600, is issued six times a year by the publishers of *Traveler's Guide to Mexico,* the book frequently found in hotel rooms in Mexico. The newsletter covers a variety of topics from news about archaeology to hotel packages, new resorts and hotels, and the economy. A subscription costs $18.

Sanborn's News Bulletin, Dept. FR, P.O. Box 310, McAllen, TX 78502, is a free newsletter produced by Sanborn's Insurance, offering tips on driving conditions, highways, hotels, economy and business, RV information, fishing, hunting, and so forth.

For other newsletters, see "For Seniors" under "Tips for Special Travelers," below.

ENTRY REQUIREMENTS

DOCUMENTS   All travelers to Mexico are required to present **proof of citizenship,** such as an original birth certificate with a raised seal, a valid passport, or naturalization papers. Those using a birth certificate should also have a current photo identification such as a driver's license. Those whose last name on the birth certificate is different from their current name (women using a married name, for example) should also bring a photo identification card *and* legal proof of the name change such as the *original* marriage license or certificate. This proof of citizenship may also be requested when you want to reenter either the United States or Mexico. Note that photocopies are *not* acceptable.

You must also carry a **Mexican tourist permit,** which is issued free of charge by Mexican border officials after proof of citizenship is accepted. The Tourist Permit is more important than a passport in Mexico, so guard it carefully. If you lose it, you may not be permitted to leave the country until you can replace it— a bureaucratic hassle that takes several days to a week at least.

A tourist permit can be issued for up to 180 days, and although your stay south of the border may be shorter than that, you should ask for the maximum time, just in case. Sometimes officials don't ask—they just stamp a time limit, so be sure to say "six months" (or at least twice as long as you intend to stay). If you should decide to extend your stay, you'll eliminate hassle by not needing to renew your papers.

This is especially important for people who take a car into Mexico. Additional documentation is required for driving a personal vehicle in Mexico (see "By Car" under "Getting There," below).

Note that children under age 18 traveling without parents or with only one parent must have a notarized letter from the absent parent or parents authorizing the travel.

Lost Documents   To replace a **lost passport,** contact your embassy or nearest consular agent, listed in "Fast Facts: Mexico," below. You must establish a record of your citizenship and also fill out a form requesting another Mexican tourist card.

Without the **tourist permit** you can't leave the country, and without an affidavit affirming your passport request and citizenship, you may have hassles at customs when you get home. So it's important to clear everything up *before* trying to leave. Mexican customs may, however, accept the police report of the loss of the tourist card and allow you to leave.

CUSTOMS   When you enter Mexico, customs officials will be tolerant as long as you have no illegal drugs or firearms. You're allowed to bring in two cartons of cigarettes, or 50 cigars, plus a kilogram (2.2 pounds) of smoking tobacco; the liquor allowance is two bottles of anything, wine or hard liquor.

When you're reentering the United States, federal law allows you to bring in duty-free up to $400 in purchases every 30 days. The first $1,000 over the $400 allowance is taxed at 10%. You may bring in a carton (200) of cigarettes or 50 cigars or 2 kilograms (4.4 pounds) of smoking tobacco, plus 1 liter of an alcoholic beverage (wine, beer, or spirits).

Canadian citizens are allowed $20 in purchases after a 24-hour absence from the country or $100 after a stay of 48 hours or more.

MONEY

CASH/CURRENCY   In 1993, the Mexican government dropped three zeroes from its currency. The new currency is called the *Nuevo Peso,* or New Peso. The purpose was to simplify accounting; all those zeroes were becoming too difficult to manage. Old Peso notes will be valid at least until 1996. Paper currency comes in denominations of 2, 5, 10, 20, 50, and 100 New Pesos. Coins come in denominations of 1, 2, 5, and 10 pesos and 20 and 50 centavos (100 centavos make one New Peso). The coins are somewhat confusing because different denominations have a similar appearance. New Peso prices appear written with *N* or *NP* beside them; and for a while the Old Peso prices will appear as well. Currently the U.S. dollar equals around NP$6; at that rate an item costing NP$5, for example, would be equivalent to U.S. 83¢.

These changes are likely to cause confusion among U.S. and Canadian travelers to Mexico in several ways. Before the New Peso was instituted, merchants and others skipped the small change; now they don't. Small change isn't always available, so cashiers often offer gum or candy to make up the difference. Also, small change appears on restaurant bills and credit cards. On restaurant bills that you pay in cash, for example, the change will be rounded up or down to the nearest five centavos. Credit-card bills, however, will show the exact amount and will have *N* written before the amount to denote that the bill is in New Pesos. Be sure to double-check any credit-card vouchers to be sure the *N* or *NP* appears on the total line.

Getting change continues to be a problem in Mexico. Small-denomination bills and coins are hard to come by, so start collecting them early in your trip and continue as you travel. Shopkeepers everywhere seem to always be out of change and small bills—that's doubly true in a market.

Note: The dollar sign ($) is used to indicate pesos in Mexico. To avoid confusion, I will use the dollar sign in this book *only* to denote U.S. currency.

Only dollar prices are listed in this book; they are a more reliable indication than peso prices. Many establishments dealing with tourists quote prices in dollars. To avoid confusion, they use the abbreviations "Dlls." for dollars and "m.n." (*moneda nacional*—national currency) for pesos.

Mexico's predicted inflation rate for 1995 is 45%. Every effort has been made to provide the most accurate and up-to-date information in this guide, but price changes are inevitable.

EXCHANGING MONEY   The 1994 devaluation of the peso has had a varied effect on tourists. First, the rate of exchange fluctuates daily, so be careful not to exchange too much of your currency at once. Don't forget, however, to allow enough to carry you over a weekend or Mexican holiday, when banks are closed. Cash can sometimes be difficult to exchange because counterfeit U.S. dollars have been circulating recently in Mexico; merchants and banks are wary, and many, especially in small towns, refuse to accept dollars in cash. In general, avoid carrying the U.S. $100 bill, the one most commonly counterfeited. Since small bills and coins in pesos are hard to come by in Mexico, the U.S. $1 bill is very useful for tipping bellboys and chambermaids.

Exchange houses in Mexico often give a rate of exchange below the official daily bank rate, and hotels usually exchange below the exchange house daily rate. Exchange houses are generally more convenient than banks since they have more locations and longer hours, but the rate of exchange will be slightly lower. Personal checks may be cashed but will delay you for weeks since a bank will wait for your check to clear before giving you your money. Canadian dollars seem to be most easily exchanged for pesos at branches of Banamex and Bancomer. *Before leaving a bank or exchange house window, always count your change in front of the teller before the next client steps up.*

Banks are open Monday through Friday from 9am to 1:30pm; a few banks in large cities offer extended afternoon hours. You'll save time at the bank or currency-exchange booths by arriving no earlier than 10am, about the time the official daily rate is received. Usually they won't exchange money until they have the official rate. Large airports have currency-exchange counters that sometimes stay open as long as flights are arriving or departing, but don't exchange money at the first one you see in an airport—there's usually more than one and you'll often find a better exchange rate farther along the concourse.

TRAVELER'S CHECKS   Traveler's checks are readily accepted nearly everywhere, but they can be difficult to cash on a weekend or holiday or in an out-of-the-way place. Their best value is in replacement in case of theft. I usually carry half of my money in cash ($1, $20, $50) and half in traveler's checks ($20 and $50). Mexican banks pay more for traveler's checks than for dollars in cash, but *casas de cambio* (exchange houses) pay more for cash than for traveler's checks. Some banks, but not all, charge a service fee as high as 5% to exchange either traveler's checks or dollars. Sometimes banks post the service charge amount so you can see it, but they might not, so it pays to ask first and shop around for a bank without a fee.

CREDIT CARDS & ATMS   You'll be able to charge some hotel and restaurant bills, almost all airline tickets, and many store purchases on your credit cards. You can get cash advances of several hundred dollars on your card, but there may be a wait of 20 minutes to 2 hours. You can't charge gasoline purchases in Mexico.

VISA ("Bancomer" in Mexico), MasterCard ("Carnet" in Mexico), and, less widely, American Express are the most accepted cards. The Bancomer bank, with branches throughout the country, has inaugurated a system of **automatic teller** machines **(ATMs)** linked to VISA International's network. If you are a VISA customer, you may be able to get peso cash from one of the Bancomer ATMs.

WIRE FUNDS   If you need cash in a hurry, **Dineros en Minutos** (Money in Minutes) is affiliated with Western Union and makes wire cash transactions at Electrika furniture/electronic stores in Mexico. Your contact on the other end presents money to Western Union, which is received by Electrika, then presented in pesos to you. The service only recently got off the ground in Mexico, but 500 outlets are planned.

BRIBES & SCAMS

BRIBES   Referred to in Mexico as *propinas* (tips), *mordidas* (bites), or worse, customary bribes and kickbacks are probably almost as old as humankind. Bribes exist in every country, but in developing countries, the amounts tend to be smaller and collected more often. You will most likely find yourself in situations where bribes are expected, so you should know how to deal with it.

Border officials have become more courteous, less bureaucratic, and less inclined to ask/hint for a bribe. I'm still wary, however; just so you're prepared, here are a few hints based on my previous experiences.

Some border officials will do what they're supposed to do (stamp your passport or birth certificate and inspect your luggage) and then wave you on through. If you don't offer a tip of a few dollars to the man who inspects your car (if you're driving), he may ask for it, as in, "Give me a tip (*propina*)." If you're charged for the stamping or inspection, ask for a receipt. If you don't get a receipt, you've paid a bribe.

Officials don't ask for bribes from everybody. Travelers dressed in a formal suit and tie, with pitch-black sunglasses and a scowl on the face are rarely asked to pay a bribe. Those who are dressed for vacation fun or seem good-natured and accommodating are targets. Ignore the request. Pretend not to understand. Don't speak Spanish. Whatever you do, avoid impoliteness, and absolutely *never* insult a Latin American official! When an official's sense of machismo is roused, he can and will throw the book at you, and you may be in trouble. Stand your ground, but do it politely.

SCAMS   As you travel in Mexico, you may encounter several types of scams. The **shoeshine scam** is an old trick, used most often in Mexico City. Here's how it works. A tourist agrees to a shine for, say, 15 pesos. When the work is complete, the vendor says, "That'll be 50 pesos" and insists that the shocked tourist misunderstood. A big brouhaha ensues involving bystanders who side with the shoeshine vendor. The object is to get the bewildered tourist to succumb to the howling crowd and embarrassing scene and fork over the money. A variation of the scam has the vendor saying the price quoted is per shoe. To avoid this scam, ask around about the price of a shine, and when the vendor quotes his price, write it down and show it to him *before* the shine.

Tourists are suckered daily into the **iguana scam,** especially in Puerto Vallarta and nearby Yelapa beach. Someone, often a child, strolls by carrying a huge iguana and says, "Wanna take my peekchur?" Photo-happy tourists seize the opportunity. Just as the camera is angled properly, the holder of the iguana says (more like mumbles), "One dollar." That means a dollar per shot. Sometimes they wait until the shutter clicks to mention money.

Because hotel desk clerks are usually so helpful, I hesitate to mention the **lost objects scam** for fear of tainting them all. But here's how it works. You "lose" your wallet after cashing money at the desk, or you leave something valuable such as a purse or camera in the lobby. You report it. The clerk has it, but instead of telling you he does, he says he will see what he can do; meanwhile, he suggests you offer a high reward. This scam has all kinds of variations. In one story a reader wrote about, a desk clerk in Los Mochis was in cahoots with a bystander in the lobby who lifted the reader's wallet in the elevator.

Another scam readers have mentioned might be called the **infraction scam.** Officials, or men presenting themselves as officials, demand money for some supposed infraction. Never get into a car with them. I avoided one begun by a bona fide policeman-on-the-take in Chetumal when my traveling companion feigned illness and began writhing, moaning, and pretending to have the dry heaves. It was more than the policeman could handle.

Legal and necessary car searches by military personnel looking for drugs are mentioned elsewhere in this book. Every now and then, however, there are police-controlled illegal roadblocks where motorists are forced to pay before continuing on their way.

Along these lines, if you are stopped by the police, I also suggest you avoid handing your driver's license to a policeman. Hold it so that it can be read but don't give it up.

Then there's the **taxi ticket scam.** This usually happens at taxi ticket booths in airports and bus stations. You're vulnerable because you may be a new arrival to the country and not yet have your peso legs, your Spanish may not be up to par, or you're preoccupied with getting where you're going. You give the ticket seller a 50-peso bill and the seller returns change for 20 pesos. I'll say this elsewhere: *Count your change before leaving the booth!* Better yet, when you hand the seller the bill, say out loud the amount of the ticket and the amount of the bill and say *cambio* (change).

Although you should be aware of such hazards and how to deal with them, I log thousands of miles and many months in Mexico each year without serious incident, and I feel safer there than at home in the United States (see also "Emergencies" and "Safety" under "Fast Facts: Mexico" later in this chapter).

2 When to Go

THE CLIMATE

From Puerto Vallarta south to Huatulco, Mexico offers one of the world's most perfect winter climates—dry, balmy, and with temperatures ranging from the 80s by day to the 60s at night. From Puerto Vallarta south, you can swim year-round. Temperatures range from 72° to 86°F year-round along the coasts of Jalisco and Colima. In the mountain village of Mazamitla, it's cold enough most of the year for gloves, heavy sweater or down jacket, wool socks, and flannel underwear.

High mountains shield Pacific beaches from *nortes* (northers—freezing blasts out of Canada via the Texas Panhandle). Jalisco and Colima, like most of Mexico, have the most rain from May through September; the rainiest months are from June through August. There is a handy temperature-conversion chart in the appendix to this book.

HOLIDAYS

On national holidays, banks, stores, and businesses are closed; hotels fill up quickly; and transportation is crowded. Mexico celebrates the following national holidays: **January 1,** New Year's Day; **February 5,** Constitution Day; **March 21,** Birthday of Benito Juárez; **March–April** (movable), Holy Week (Good Friday through Easter Sunday); **May 1,** Labor Day; **May 5,** Battle of Puebla, 1862 (Cinco de Mayo); **September 1,** President's Message to Congress; **September 16,** Independence Day; **October 12,** Day of the Race (Columbus Day in the United States); **November 1–2,** All Saints' and All Souls' days (Day of the Dead); **November 20,** Anniversary of the Mexican Revolution; **December 11–12,** Feast Day of the Virgin of Guadeloupe (Mexico's patron saint); **December 24–25,** Christmas Eve and Christmas Day.

CALENDAR OF EVENTS

The following events are celebrated nationwide; special events in cities and towns in this book are mentioned in each chapter.

January

- **Three Kings Day.** Commemorates the Three Kings' bringing of gifts to the Christ Child. On this day the Three Kings "bring" gifts to children. January 6.
- **Feast of San Antonio Abad,** Mexico City. Blessing of the Animals at the Santiago Tlatelolco Church on the Plaza of Three Cultures, at San Juan Bautista Church in Coyoacán, and at the Church of San Fernando, two blocks north of the Juárez/Reforma intersection. January 17.

February

- **Candlemas.** On January 6, Rosca de Reyes, a round cake with a hole in the middle is baked with a tiny doll inside representing the Christ Child. Whoever gets the slice with the doll must give a party on February 2. Northwest of Guadalajara in San Juan de los Lagos, Jalisco, and Buenavista near Lagos de Moreno, Jalisco, pilgrims come from all over Mexico to honor the Virgen de San Juan de los Lagos. Also in Tecomán south of Manzanillo.
- ✪ **Carnaval.** This celebration resembles New Orleans's Mardi Gras, with a festive atmosphere and parades. In Chamula, however, the event harks back to pre-Hispanic times with ritualistic running on flaming branches. On the Tuesday before Ash Wednesday in Tepoztlán and Huejotzingo, masked and brilliantly clad dancers fill the streets. In some towns there will be no special celebration, in others a few parades.

  Where: Especially celebrated in Tepoztlán, Morelos; Huejozingo, Puebla; Chamula, Chiapas; Veracruz, Veracruz; Cozumel, Quintana Roo; and Mazatlán, Sinaloa. **When:** Date variable, but always the three days preceding Ash Wednesday. **How:** Transportation and hotels will be clogged, so it's best to make reservations six months in advance and arrive a couple of days ahead of the beginning of celebrations. The latter three resemble a U.S. festival-type atmosphere. In Chamula, however, the event harks back to pre-Hispanic times with ritualistic running on flaming branches. On Tuesday before Ash Wednesday, in Tepoztlán and Huejotzingo, masked and brilliantly clad dancers fill the streets.
- **Ash Wednesday.** The start of Lent and time of abstinence. It's a day of reverence nationwide, but some towns honor it with folk dancing and fairs. Movable date.

March

- **Benito Juárez's Birthday.** Small hometown celebrations countrywide, especially in Juárez's birthplace, Gelatao, Oaxaca.
- ✪ **Holy Week.** Celebrates the last week in the life of Christ from Good Friday through Easter Sunday with somber religious processions almost nightly, spoofing of Judas, and reenactments of specific biblical events, plus food and craft fairs. Among the Tarahumara in the Copper Canyon, celebrations have pre-Hispanic overtones. Businesses close and Mexicans travel far and wide during this week.

  Where: Special in Pátzcuaro, Taxco, Malinalco, and among the Tarahumara villages in the Copper Canyon. **When:** March or April. **How:** Reserve early with a deposit. Airline seats on flights into and out of the country will be reserved months in advance. Buses to these towns or to almost anywhere in Mexico will be full, so try arriving on the Wednesday or Thursday before Good Friday. Easter Sunday is quiet.

May

- **Labor Day.** Workers' parades countrywide and everything closes. May 1.
- **Holy Cross Day,** Día de la Santa Cruz. Workers place a cross on top of unfinished buildings and celebrate with food, bands, folk dancing, and fireworks around the work site. Celebrations are particularly colorful in Valle de Bravo, in the state of Mexico, and Paracho, Michoacán. May 3.
- **Cinco de Mayo.** A national holiday that celebrates the defeat of the French at the Battle of Puebla. May 5.
- **Feast of San Isidro.** The patron saint of farmers is honored with a blessing of seeds and work animals. May 15.

June

- **Navy Day.** Celebrated by all port cities. June 1.
- ✪ **Corpus Christi.** Honors the Body of Christ—the Eucharist—with religious processions, masses, and food. Celebrated nationwide. Festivities include numerous demonstrations of the Roman *voladores* (flying pole dancers) beside the church and at the ruins of El Tajín. In Mexico City, children dressed as Indians, and their parents, gather before the National Cathedral on the Zócalo, carrying decorated baskets of fruit for the priest's blessing. *Mulitas* (mules), handmade from dried corn husks and painted, often with a corn-husk rider, and sometimes accompanied by pairs of corn-husk dolls, are traditionally sold there on that day.

  Where: Particularly special in Papantla, Veracruz. **When:** Variable date, 66 days after Easter. **How:** By bus from Tampico, Tuxpan, or Poza Rica. Make reservations well in advance.

Impressions

Involuntarily I thought of the delightful hotel at Guadalajara, with its well-prepared dinner served on an airy, roomy piazza surrounded by a fresh and fragrant garden. All these comforts were mine for the modest sum of dollars a day, Mexican money. On [the U.S.] side of the Río Grande, everything, from the small bottle of beer to the berth in the Pullman car, cost twice as much as on the other side.
—Carl Lumholtz, *Unknown Mexico,* 1902

- **Saint Peter's Day,** Día de San Pedro. Celebrated wherever St. Peter is the patron saint and honors anyone named Pedro or Peter. It's especially festive at San Pedro Tlaquepaque, near Guadalajara, with numerous mariachi bands, folk dancers, and parades with floats. June 29.

July
- **Virgin of Carmen.** A nationally celebrated religious festival centered in churches nationwide. July 16.
- **Saint James Day,** Día de Santiago. Observed countrywide wherever St. James is the patron saint and for anyone named Jaime or James or any village with Santiago in its name. Often celebrated with rodeos, fireworks, dancing, and food. July 25.

August
- **Fall of Tenochtitlán,** Mexico City. The last battle of the conquest took place at Tlatelolco, ruins that are now a part of the Plaza of Three Cultures. Wreath-laying ceremonies there and at the Cuauhtémoc monument on Reforma commemorate the event when thousands lost their lives and the last Aztec king, Cuauhtémoc, surrendered to Hernán Cortés. August 13.
- ✪ **Assumption of the Virgin Mary.** Celebrated throughout the country with special masses and in some places with processions. Streets are carpeted in flower petals and colored sawdust. At midnight on the 15th a statue of the Virgin is carried through the streets; the 16th is a running of the bulls. On August 15 in Santa Clara del Cobre, near Pátzcuaro, Our Lady of Santa Clara de Asis and the Virgen de la Sagrado Patrona are honored with a parade of floats, dancers on the main square, and an exposition of regional crafts, especially copper.
  Where: Special in Huamantla, Tlaxcala, and Santa Clara del Cobre, Michoacán. **When:** August 15 and 16. **How:** Buses to Huamantla from Puebla or Mexico City will be full, and there are few hotels in Huamantla. Plan to stay in Puebla and commute to the festivities.

September
- **Independence Day.** Celebrates Mexico's independence from Spain. A day of parades, picnics, and family reunions throughout the country. At 11pm on September 15 the president of Mexico gives the famous independence *grito* (shout) from the National Palace in Mexico City. At least half a million people are crowded into the Zócalo, and the rest of the country watches the event on television. The enormous military parade on September 16 starts at the Zócalo and ends at the Independence Monument on Reforma. Tall buildings downtown are draped in the national colors of red, green, and white, and the Zócalo is ablaze with lights; it's popular to drive downtown at night to see the spectacular lights. The day is also elaborately celebrated in Querétaro and San Miguel de Allende, where Independence conspirators lived and met. September 16 (parade day).

October
- **Cervantino Festival.** Begun in the 1970s as a cultural event bringing performing artists from all over the world to Guanajuato, a picturesque village northeast of Mexico City. Now the artists travel all over the republic after appearing in Guanajuato. Check local calendars for appearances. Early to mid-October.
- **Feast of San Francisco de Asis.** Anyone named Frances, Francis, or Francisco and towns whose patron saint is Francisco celebrate with barbecue parties, regional dancing, and religious observances. October 4.

- **Día de la Raza,** Day of the Race, or Columbus Day (the day Columbus landed in America). Commemorates the fusion of the Spanish and Mexican peoples. October 12.
- **Feast of San José.** This festival honors Saint Joseph and anyone named Joseph (José in Spanish). Ciudad Guzmán, Jalisco, between Guadalajara and Manzanillo, celebrates with a fair, processions, and regional dancing. October 21.

November

✪ **Day of the Dead.** What's commonly called the Day of the Dead is actually two days, All Saints' Day, honoring saints and deceased children, and All Souls' Day, honoring deceased adults. Relatives gather at cemeteries countrywide, carrying candles and food, often spending the night beside graves of loved ones. Weeks before, bakers begin producing bread formed in the shape of mummies or round loaves decorated with bread "bones." Decorated sugar skulls emblazoned with glittery names are sold everywhere. Many days ahead, homes and churches erect special altars laden with Day of the Dead bread, fruit, flowers, candles, and favorite foods and photographs of saints and of the deceased. On the two nights of the Day of the Dead, children dress in costumes and masks, often carrying mock coffins through the streets and pumpkin lanterns into which they expect money will be dropped.

   Where: The most famous celebration is on Janitzio, an island on Lake Pátzcuaro, Michoacán, west of Mexico City, but it has become almost too well known. Mixquic, a mountain village south of Mexico City, hosts an elaborate street fair, and around 11pm on both nights, solemn processions lead to the cemetery in the center of town where villagers are already settled in with candles, flowers, and food. **When:** November 1 and 2.

- **Revolution Day.** Commemorates the start of the Mexican Revolution in 1910 with parades, speeches, rodeos, and patriotic events. November 20.

December

✪ **Feast of the Virgin of Guadalupe.** Throughout the country the Patroness of Mexico is honored with religious processions, street fairs, dancing, fireworks, and masses. The Virgin of Guadalupe appeared to a young man, Juan Diego, in December 1531 on a hill near Mexico City. He convinced the bishop that the apparition had appeared by revealing his cloak, upon which the Virgin was emblazoned. It's customary for children to dress up as Juan Diego, wearing mustaches and red bandannas. The most famous and elaborate celebration takes place at the Basílica of Guadalupe, north of Mexico City, where the Virgin appeared. But every village celebrates this day, often with processions of children carrying banners of the Virgin and with *charreadas* (rodeos), bicycle races, dancing, and fireworks.

   Where: Basílica de Guadalupe. **When:** The week preceding December 12. **How:** Public transportation will be packed, so your best bet is a taxi, which will let you off several blocks from the basílica.

- **Christmas Posadas.** On each of the 12 nights before Christmas it's customary to reenact the Holy Family's search for an inn, with door-to-door candlelit processions in cities and villages nationwide. You may see them especially in Querétaro and Taxco.
- **Christmas.** Mexicans extend this celebration and leave their jobs often beginning two weeks before Christmas all the way through New Year's. Many

businesses close, and resorts and hotels fill up. On December 23 there are significant celebrations. Querétaro has a huge parade. In Oaxaca it's the "Night of the Radishes," with displays of huge carved radishes. On December 24 in Oaxaca processions culminate on the central plaza. On the same night Santiago Tuxtla, Veracruz celebrates with dancing the *huapango* and with *jarocho* bands in the beautiful town square. In Quiroga, Michoacán, villagers present Nativity plays (*Pastorelas*) at churches around the city on the evenings of December 24 and 25.

- **New Year's Eve.** As in the United States, New Year's Eve in Mexico is the time to gather for private parties and to explode fireworks and sound noisemakers. Places with special festivities include Santa Clara del Cobre, with its candlelit procession of Christs, and Tlacolula near Oaxaca, with commemorative mock battles for good luck in the new year.

3 Outdoor Sports, Adventure Travel & Wilderness Trips

Mexico has numerous **golf** courses, especially in the resort areas, and there are excellent ones in Puerto Vallarta, Manzanillo, El Tamarindo, and a new one in Barra de Navidad. It is sometimes easier in Mexico to rent a **horse** than a car, since horseback riding is a pastime enjoyed by many people at beach resorts as well as in the country. Sport **bicycling** has grown in popularity, so it isn't unusual to see young men (usually) making the grind of steep mountain passes during cycling club marathons.

Tennis, racquetball, squash, waterskiing, surfing, and **scuba diving** are all sports visitors can enjoy in Mexico. Both Puerto Vallarta and Manzanillo offer good scuba diving. **Mountain climbing** and **hiking volcanoes** are rugged sports in which you'll meet like-minded folks from around the world.

Mexico is behind the times with regard to ecological adventure and wilderness travel. As a result, most of the national parks and nature reserves are understaffed and/or not staffed by knowledgeable people. Most companies offering this kind of travel are U.S. operated, with trips led by specialists. The following companies offer a variety of off-the-beaten-path travel experiences:

Victor Emanuel Tours, P.O. Box 33008, Austin, TX 78764 (☎ 512/328-5221 or 800/328-8368), is an established leader in birding and natural-history tours.

Wings, Inc., P.O. Box 31930, Tucson, AZ 85751 (☎ 602/749-1967), has a wide assortment of trips, including birding in Oaxaca, Chiapas, Colima, and Jalisco.

4 Learning Vacations

SPANISH LESSONS   A dozen towns south of the border are famous for their Spanish-language programs. In the region covered by this book, the University of Guadalajara has programs for foreigners in both Guadalajara and Puerto Vallarta. Mexican Government Tourist Offices (see above) may have information about schools. Go any time of year—you needn't really wait for a "semester" or course year to start. It's best to begin on a Monday, however.

Impressions

Once an emotional bond is established . . . [the Mexican] is open and generous, willing to confide, and hospitable to extremes. All he asks is that his sincerity be reciprocated. To invite a stranger to his home becomes an act of great symbolism: He is showing the real face of how he lives by sharing the intimacy of his family.

—Alan Riding, *Distant Neighbors,* 1986

Don't expect the best and latest in terms of language texts and materials; many are well out of date. Teachers tend to be underpaid and perhaps undertrained but very friendly and extremely patient.

Try living with a Mexican family. Pay in advance for only a week or 10 days, and if things are going well, continue. If your "family stay" ends up being little more than a room rental, feel free to go elsewhere. Family stays are not particularly cheap, by the way, so you should get your money's worth in terms of interaction and language practice.

The **National Registration Center for Studies Abroad (NRCSA),** 823 N. Second St., Milwaukee, WI 53203 (☎ 414/278-0631), has a catalog ($5) of schools in Mexico. They will register you at the school of your choice, arrange for room and board with a Mexican family, and make your airline reservations. Charge for their service is reflected in a fee that's included in the price quoted to you for the course you select.

5 Health & Insurance

STAYING HEALTHY

Of course, the very best way to avoid illness or to mitigate its effects is to make sure you're in top health when you travel and you don't overdo it. Eat three wholesome meals a day, and get more rest than you normally do; also, don't push yourself if you're not feeling in top form.

COMMON AILMENTS

TURISTA   *Turista* is the name given to the persistent diarrhea, often accompanied by fever, nausea, and vomiting, that attacks so many travelers to Mexico. Doctors, who call it travelers' diarrhea, say it's not caused by just one "bug," or factor, but by a combination of consuming different food and water, upsetting your schedule, being overtired, and experiencing the stresses of travel. Being tired and careless about food and drink is a sure ticket to turista. A good high-potency (or "therapeutic") vitamin supplement, and even extra vitamin C, is a help; yogurt, which is good for healthy digestion, is becoming much more available in Mexico than in the past.

Preventing Turista: The U.S. Public Health Service recommends the following measures for prevention of travelers' diarrhea:

• *Drink only purified water.* This means tea, coffee, and other beverages made with boiled water; canned or bottled carbonated beverages and water; beer and wine; or water you yourself have brought to a rolling boil or otherwise purified. Avoid ice, which may be made with untreated water. However, most restaurants with a large tourist clientele use only purified water and ice.

• *Choose food carefully.* In general, avoid salads, uncooked vegetables, and unpasteurized milk or milk products (including cheese). Choose food that is freshly cooked and still hot. Peel fruit yourself. Don't eat undercooked meat, fish, or shellfish.

The Public Health Service does not recommend you take any medicines as preventatives. All the applicable medicines can have nasty side effects if taken for several weeks. In addition, something so simple as clean hands can go a long way toward preventing "turista." I carry packages of antiseptic towelettes for those times when wash facilities aren't available and to avoid using a communal bar of soap—a real germ carrier.

How to Get Well: If you get sick, there are lots of medicines available in Mexico that can harm more than help. Ask your doctor before you leave home what medicine he or she recommends for travelers' diarrhea.

The Public Health Service guidelines are the following: If there are three or more loose stools in an eight-hour period, especially with other symptoms (such as nausea, vomiting, abdominal cramps, and fever), see a doctor.

The first thing to do is go to bed and don't move until the condition runs its course. Traveling makes it last longer. Drink lots of liquids: Tea without milk or sugar or the Mexican *té de manzanilla* (chamomile tea) is best. Eat only *pan tostada* (dry toast). Keep to this diet for at least 24 hours, and you'll be well over the worst of it. If you fool yourself into thinking a plate of enchiladas can't hurt or beer or liquor will kill the germs, you'll have a total relapse.

The Public Health Service advises that you be especially careful to replace fluids and electrolytes (potassium, sodium, and the like) during a bout of diarrhea. Do this by drinking Pedialyte, a rehydration solution available at most Mexican pharmacies, or glasses of fruit juice (high in potassium) with honey and a pinch of salt added, or you can also try a glass of boiled pure water with a quarter teaspoon of sodium bicarbonate (baking soda) added.

ALTITUDE SICKNESS   At high altitudes it takes about 10 days to acquire the extra red blood corpuscles you need to adjust to the scarcity of oxygen. At very high altitudes, your car won't run very well, you may have trouble starting it, and you may not even sleep well at night.

Altitude sickness results from the relative lack of oxygen and the decrease in barometric pressure that characterizes high altitudes (over 5,000 feet/1,500 meters). Symptoms include shortness of breath, fatigue, headache, and even nausea.

Avoid altitude sickness by taking it easy for the first few days after you arrive at a high altitude. Drink extra fluids but avoid alcoholic beverages, which not only tend to dehydrate you but also are more potent in a low-oxygen environment. If you have heart or lung problems, talk to your doctor before going above 8,000 ft.

BUGS & BITES   Mosquitoes and gnats are prevalent along the coast and in the Yucatán lowlands. Insect repellent (*rapellante contra insectos*) is a must, and it's not always available in Mexico. If you're sensitive to bites, pick up some antihistamine cream from a drugstore at home. Rubbed on a fresh mosquito bite, the cream keeps the swelling down and reduces the itch.

Most readers won't ever see a scorpion (*alacrán*), but if you're stung, go to a doctor.

MORE SERIOUS DISEASES

You don't have to worry about tropical diseases, such as malaria, dengue fever, dysentery, cholera, and schistosomiasis if you stay on the normal tourist routes. Talk to your doctor, or a medical specialist in tropical diseases, about any precautions you should take. You can protect yourself by taking some simple precautions. In addition to being careful about what you eat and drink, don't go swimming in polluted waters. This includes any stagnant water, such as ponds, slow-moving rivers, and Yucatecan *cenotes* (wells). Mosquitoes can carry malaria, dengue fever, and other serious illnesses. Cover up, avoid going out when mosquitoes are active, use repellent, sleep under mosquito netting, and stay away from places that seem to have a lot of mosquitoes. The most dangerous areas seem to be on Mexico's west coast away from the big resorts (which are relatively safe).

To prevent malaria if you go to a malarial area, you must get a prescription for antimalarial drugs and begin taking them before you enter the area. You must also continue to take them for a certain amount of time after you leave the malarial area. Talk to your doctor about this and ask about any risks in taking the drugs; for example, people with psoriasis, or a family history of it, may not wish to take antimalarial drugs. It's a good idea to be inoculated against tetanus, typhoid, and diphtheria, but this isn't a guarantee against contracting the diseases.

EMERGENCY EVACUATION   For extreme medical emergencies there's a service from the United States that will fly people to American hospitals: **Air-Evac,** a 24-hour air ambulance (☎ 800/854-2569 in the U.S. or call collect: 713/880-9767 in Houston, 619/278-3822 in San Diego, and 305/772-0003 in Miami, 24 hours daily).

INSURANCE

HEALTH/ACCIDENT/LOSS   Even the most careful of us can experience the Murphy's Law of travel—you discover you've lost your wallet, your passport, your airline ticket, or your tourist permit. Always keep a photocopy of these documents in your luggage—it makes replacing them easier. To be reimbursed for insured items once you return, you'll need to report the loss to the Mexican police and get a written report. If you don't speak Spanish, take along someone who does. If you lose official documents, you'll need to contact both Mexican and U.S. officials in Mexico before you leave the country.

Health Care Abroad, 107 W. Federal St. (P.O. Box 480), Middleburg, VA 22117 (☎ 703/687-3166 or 800/237-6615), and **Access America,** 6600 W. Broad St., Richmond, VA 23230 (☎ 804/285-3300 or 800/628-4908), offer medical and accident insurance as well as coverage for luggage loss and trip cancellation. Always read the fine print on the policy to be sure that you're getting the coverage you want.

For British Travelers   Most big travel agents offer their own insurance and will probably try to sell you their package when you book a holiday. Think before you sign. Britain's Consumers' Association recommends that you insist on seeing the policy and reading the fine print before buying travel insurance.

You should also shop around for better deals. Try **Columbus Travel Insurance Ltd.** (☎ 071/375-0011) or, for students, **Campus Travel** (☎ 071/730-3402). If you're unsure about who can give you the best deal, contact the **Association of British Insurers,** 51 Gresham St., London EC2V 7HO, United Kingdom (☎ 071/600-333).

6 Tips on Packing

High-elevation cities such as Mazamitla, in the mountains of Jalisco, require warm wool clothing. If you're going to be in the coastal areas, however, bring light-weight cottons. The temperature is usually less than 90°F, but the humidity often reaches 100%.

Generally speaking, throughout Mexico it rains almost every afternoon or evening between May and October, so take rain gear. An easily packable rain poncho is most handy, since it fits in a purse or backpack and is ready for use in an instant.

Guadalajara and other nonresort cities and villages tend to be conservative in dress, so save shorts and halter tops for seaside resorts. For dining out in a nice restaurant in conservative Guadalajara, a jacket and tie for men and nice dress or suit for women is appropriate. In Puerto Vallarta, nice restaurants are more casual even if they are expensive. A cool dress for women and summer weight slacks and shirt for men will do fine.

GADGETS   First-class hotels generally provide washcloths, but if you're staying in moderately priced or budget hotels, bring your own washcloth or, better yet, a sponge (which dries quickly)—you'll rarely find washcloths in a budget-range hotel room. A bathtub plug (one of those big round ones for all sizes) is helpful since fitted plugs are frequently missing or don't work. Inflatable hangers and a stretch clothesline are handy. I never leave home without a luggage cart, which saves much effort and money and is especially useful in small towns where there are no porters at bus stations. Buy a sturdy one with at least four-inch wheels that can take the beating of cobblestone streets, stairs, and curbs. A heat immersion coil, plastic cup, and spoon are handy for preparing coffee, tea, and instant soup. For power failures and for visiting archaeological sites with dark interiors, a small flashlight is a help. A combination pocketknife (for peeling fruit) with a screwdriver (for fixing cameras and eyeglasses), bottle opener, and corkscrew is a must. Finally, travel-size antiseptic towelettes are handy for keeping hands clean when facilities for doing so aren't available.

7 Tips on Shopping

Known for their charm, Mexican handcrafts include pottery, textiles, ceramics, baskets, and onyx and silver jewelry, to mention only a few items.

Many of the items listed below can be found in markets and shops in both Guadalajara and Puerto Vallarta and, to a lesser extent, in Manzanillo and around Lake Chapala. Jalisco's craft villages include Tonala and Tlaquepaque near Guadalajara and Ajijic and Jocotepec near Lake Chapala. Colima makes furniture and reproductions of pre-Hispanic pottery. I have listed the cities or villages where the item is sold (and often crafted); the first place listed is the best place to buy that particular item. The larger cities, especially Guadalajara, Puerto Vallarta, and Mexico City, will have many crafts from other regions in addition to crafts from Jalisco and Colima.

It is very helpful to visit a government fixed-price shop before attempting to bargain in markets. There are two government-operated **Casas de Artesanías** in Guadalajara and one in Puerto Vallarta. These shops will give you an idea of the costs of the various crafts. The following is a list of items followed by where you can find them in Mexico:

Baskets   Woven of reed or straw: Oaxaca; Copper Canyon; Toluca; Yucatán; Puebla; Mexico City.

Blankets   Tapalpa, Jalisco; Saltillo; Toluca; Santa Ana Chiautempan, north of Puebla;, Oaxaca; and Mitla. *Note*: Make sure that the blanket you pick out is in fact the one you take since they often get switched before they are wrapped.

Cantera Stone   Guadalajara and Zacatecas.

Equipal Furniture   Tlaquepaque and Tonalá in Jalisco state; Nayarit state.

Glass   Hand-blown and molded: Tlaquepaque, Jalisco; Monterrey; and Mexico City.

Guitars   Paracho, 25 miles north of Uruapan in the state of Michoacán on Highway 37, not far from the Jalisco state line.

Hammocks and Mosquito Netting   Mérida; Campeche; Mazatlán.

Hats   In Mérida, you can find Panama hats made of sisal from the maguey cactus; also San Cristóbal de las Casas, Chiapas.

Huaraches   Leather sandals often with rubber-tire soles: Mercado Libertad in Guadalajara; San Blas.

Huipils   Hand-woven, embroidered, or brocaded overblouses indigenous to almost all Mexican states: Yucatán; Chiapas; Oaxaca; Puebla; Guerrero; and Veracruz. Most of the better huipils are in fact used garments that have been bought from the village women. Huipils can be distinguished by villages; look around before buying—you'll be amazed at the variety.

Lacquer Goods   Olinala, Guerrero, northeast of Acapulco, is known for ornate lacquered chests and other lacquered decorative items and furniture. Pátzcuaro and Uruapan, in Michoacán state, are also known for gold-leafed lacquered trays.

Leather Goods   Guadalajara; Monterrey; Saltillo; León; Mexico City; San Cristóbal de las Casas; and Oaxaca.

Masks   Wherever there is locally observed regional dancing, you'll find maskmakers. The tradition is especially strong in the states of Guerrero; Chiapas; Puebla; Oaxaca; and Michoacán.

Onyx   Puebla (where onyx is carved); Querétaro; Matehuala; Mexico City.

Pottery   Tlaquepaque and Tonalá; whimsical daily life figures in Santa Cruz de las Huertas near Tonalá; all varieties are found in the state of Jalisco. Reproductions of Colima pottery in Colima City. Also Oaxaca; Puebla; Michoacán; Coyotepec; Izúcar de Matamoras; Veracruz; Copper Canyon; Dolores Hidalgo; and Guanajuato.

Rebozos   Rectangular woven cloth, rebozos are worn by both women and men around the shoulders, in a similar manner to a shawl. Rebozos are generally made of wool or a blend of wool and cotton and sometimes silk, but synthetic fibers are creeping in, so check the material carefully before buying. Also compare the weave of different cloths since the fineness of the weave is proportional to the cost. Rebozos are sold in most markets—Oaxaca; Mitla; San Cristóbal de las Casas; Mexico City; and Pátzcuaro.

Serapes   Heavy woolen or cotton blankets with a slit for the head, serapes are worn as a poncho. Look for them in Tapalpa, Jalisco (3 hours south of Guadalajara or the same distance north of Manzanillo); Santa Ana Chiautempan (30 miles north of Puebla near Tlaxcala); San Luis Potosí; Santa María del Río (25 miles south of San Luis Potosí); Chiconcoac (1 hour's drive northeast from Mexico City, near Texcoco); Saltillo; Toluca; Mexico City.

Silver   Sterling silver is indicated by the mark "925" on the silver, which certifies that there are 925 grams of pure silver per kilogram, or that the silver is 92.5% pure. In Mexico they also use a spread-eagle hallmark to indicate sterling. Look for these marks, or you may be paying a high price for an inferior quality that is mostly nickel or even silver plate called alpaca. Look for silver especially in Taxco; Mexico City; Zacatecas; and Guadalajara.

Stones   Mexican stones include chalcedony, turquoise, lapis lazuli, and amethyst. Look for them in Querétaro; San Miguel del Allende; Durango; Saltillo; and San Luis Potosí. Opals are sold in the village of Margarita, off Highway 15 west of Tequila.

Sweaters   Beautifully made and designed sweaters using natural dyes are a cottage industry in Tapalpa, Jalisco.

Textiles   Oaxaca; Chiapas; Santa Ana near Puebla; Guerrero; and Nayarit are known for their excellent weaving, each culturally distinct and different. Ajijic and Jocotepec, both near Lake Chapala in Jalisco state, are weaving villages.

Tortoise Shell   It's illegal to buy tortoise shell in Mexico and to bring it into the United States.

8 Tips on Accommodations

Purchasing a package which includes hotel along with airfare usually saves considerable money. Never pay the public rate in expensive category hotels without first investigating package deals from your home country before arrival in Mexico.

For the best rates overall, travel during May, August, and September through November—the slowest months of the off-season (post-Easter to mid-December). Always ask about discounted rates or special packages in those months, even at budget hotels. Prices go up anywhere from 25% to 50% from mid-December through Easter week, when all the best rooms are generally booked.

It's best to have reservations in high season, but if you don't, arrive early in the day and start your search. If you are told that the rooms are full, ask if you can leave your name and return at checkout time to see if anyone has vacated.

A few things to keep in mind if you've held off on finding a hotel until you actually arrive at your destination: Hotels in the inexpensive and moderate categories will often discount the quoted price if the hotel isn't full. It never hurts to ask. If a price seems too high when compared to the price quoted in this book, ask to see their printed rates. This applies especially to budget-class hotels, where clerks have been known to jack up the price and pocket the difference.

Many budget-class hotels don't accept credit cards even if there's a sticker on the window that says they do. Any time you *can* use a credit card, it will probably pay to do so if the hotel's rates are predicated on the peso—given the currency's continuing decline against the dollar, the charge will likely amount to less by the time your monthly bill is calculated.

Some Puerto Vallarta tips: Consider travel time to and from this resort city before purchasing a two- or three-day package (you could spend half your time traveling). Most of the bargain hotels are in town, south of the Río Cuale. More expensive hotels are in the Hotel Zone, Marina Vallarta, and south to Mismaloya.

In Guadalajara, hotels in the expensive category often reduce prices on weekends, and weekdays especially in summer, meaning savings of as much as 50% off normal rates.

9 Tips for Special Travelers

FOR SENIORS Be aware that handrails are often missing. Unmarked or unguarded holes in sidewalks countrywide present problems for all visitors.

Retiring Mexico is a popular country for retirees, although their income doesn't go nearly as far as it once did. Do several things before venturing south permanently: Stay for several weeks in any place you are considering; rent before buying; and check on the availability and quality of health care, banking, transportation, and rental costs. How much it costs to live depends on your lifestyle and where you choose to live. Car upkeep and insurance, as well as clothing and health costs, are important variables to consider.

The Mexican government requires foreign residents to prove they have a specific amount of income before permanent residence is granted, but you can visit for 6 months on a tourist visa. For decades, North Americans have been living indefinitely in Mexico by returning to the border and recrossing with a new tourist card every 6 months. Recently, but not uniformly at every border crossing, Mexico has begun to crack down on this practice by refusing readmittance to someone they remember just crossed over. So if you've been there 6 months and haven't decided on permanent residency yet and want to return immediately for another stay on a tourist permit, you'll have to exercise caution about where and when you recross.

Mexican health care is surprisingly inexpensive. You can save money by living on the local economy. Buy food at the local market, not imported items from specialty stores; use local transportation and save the car for long-distance trips. Some of the most popular places for long-term stays include Guadalajara, Lake Chapala, Ajijic, and Puerto Vallarta—all in the state of Jalisco; San Miguel de Allende and Guanajuato in the state of Guanajuato; Cuernavaca, Morelos; Alamos, Sinaloa; and to a lesser extent Manzanillo, Colima, and Morelia in Michoacán. Crowds don't necessarily mean there are no other good places: Oaxaca, Querétaro,

Impressions

Often, too, ficticious names are put on the payroll sheet and the chief of the department or a higher-up pockets the salary. . . . On July 27, 1945, a cloudburst hit [Guadalajara] and damaged the principal water line. The water supply was cut and people were without water. The presidente municipal of Guadalajara announced he had put three hundred men to work repairing the damage and the system would be operating again in a few days. . . . After three weeks of the city being without water, an investigation was started. It was discovered that there were three hundred persons on the payroll, but actually working on the pipeline were twenty prisoners from the city jail!

—Herbert Cerwin, *These Are the Mexicans,* 1947

Puebla, Guanajuato, Tepoztlán, and Valle de Bravo have much to offer, even though North Americans have yet to collect there in large numbers.

The following newsletters are written for prospective retirees: *AIM,* Apdo. Postal 31–70, Guadalajara 45050, Jal., Mexico, is a well-written, candid, and very informative newsletter on retirement in Mexico. Recent issues reported on evaluated retirement in Lake Chapala, Aguascalientes, Alamos, Zacatecas, west coast beaches, Acapulco, and San Miguel de Allende. Subscriptions cost $16 to the United States and $19 to Canada. Back issues are three for $5.

The annual *Retiring in Mexico,* Apdo. Postal 50409, Guadalajara, Jal., Mexico (☎ 36/21-2348 or 36/47-9924), comes in three editions—a large January issue and smaller spring and fall supplements—all for $12. Each newsletter is packed with information about retiring in Guadalajara. It's written by Fran and Judy Furton, who also sell other packets of information as well as host an open house in their home every Tuesday for $12.

Finally, **Sanborn Tours,** 1007 Main St., Bastrop, TX 78602 (☎ 800/ 531-5440), offers a "Retire in Mexico" Guadalajara orientation tour.

FOR SINGLES   Mexico may be the land for romantic honeymoons, but it's also a great place to travel on your own without really being or feeling alone. Although combined single and double rates is a slow-growing trend in Mexico, most of the hotels mentioned in this book still offer singles at lower rates.

Mexicans are very friendly, and it's easy to meet other foreigners. Certain cities such as Acapulco, Manzanillo, and Huatulco have such a preponderance of twosomes that single travelers may feel as though an appendage is missing. On the other hand, singles can feel quite comfortable in Puerto Vallarta, San Blas, Barra de Navidad, and Guadalajara. In those places, you'll find a good combination of beachlife, nightlife, and tranquility, whichever is your pleasure.

If you don't like the idea of traveling alone, then try **Travel Companion Exchange,** P.O. Box 833, Amityville, NY 11701 (☎ 516/454-0880; fax 516/ 454-0170), which brings prospective travelers together. Members complete a profile, then place an anonymous listing of their travel interests in the newsletter. Prospective traveling companions then make contact through the Exchange. Membership costs $66 for six months or $120 for a year.

For Women   As a frequent female visitor to Mexico, mostly traveling alone, I can tell you firsthand that I feel safer traveling in Mexico than in the United States. Mexicans are very warm and welcoming people, and I'm not afraid to be friendly wherever I go. But I use the same common-sense precautions I use traveling anywhere else in the world—I'm alert to what's going on around me.

Mexicans in general, and men in particular, are nosy about single travelers, especially women. They want to know with whom you're traveling, whether you're married or have a boyfriend, and how many children you have. My advice to anyone asked these details by taxi drivers or other people with whom you don't want to become friendly is to make up a set of answers (regardless of the truth): I'm married, traveling with friends, and I have three children. Divorce may send out a wrong message about availability. Drunks are a particular nuisance to the lone female traveler. Don't try to be polite—just leave or duck into a public place.

Generally women alone will feel comfortable going to a hotel lobby bar yet are asking for trouble by going into a pulquería or cantina. In restaurants, as a general rule, single women are offered the worst table and service. You'll have to be vocal about your preference and insist on service. Don't tip if service is bad.

Finally, remember that Mexican men learn charm early. The chase is as important as the conquest (maybe more so). Despite whatever charms you may possess, think twice before taking personally or seriously all the adoring, admiring words you'll hear.

For Men I'm not sure why, but non–Spanish-speaking foreign men seem to be special targets for scams and pickpockets. So if you fit this description, whether traveling alone or in a pair, exercise special vigilance.

FOR FAMILIES Mexicans travel extensively with their families, so your child will feel very welcome. Hotels will often arrange for a baby-sitter. Several hotels in the mid- to-upper range have small playgrounds and pools for children and hire caretakers on weekends to oversee them. Few budget hotels offer these amenities.

Before leaving, you should check with your doctor to get advice on medications to take along. Bring along a supply just to be sure. Disposable diapers are made and sold in Mexico. The price is about the same as in the United States, but the quality is poorer. Gerber's baby foods are sold in many stores. Dry cereals, powdered formulas, baby bottles, and purified water are all easily available in midsize and large cities.

Cribs, however, may present a problem. Except for the largest and most luxurious hotels, few Mexican hotels provide cribs. However, rollaway beds to accommodate children staying in the room with parents are often available.

Many of the hotels I mention, even in noncoastal regions, have swimming pools, which can be a treat at the end of a day of traveling with a child who has had it with sightseeing.

FOR PEOPLE WITH DISABILITIES Travelers who are unable to walk or who are in wheelchairs or on crutches discover quickly that Mexico is one giant obstacle course. Beginning at the airport on arrival, you may encounter steep stairs before finding a well-hidden elevator or escalator—if one exists. The Guadalajara airport has an up escalator to the restaurant, but no down escalator or elevator. Airlines will often arrange wheelchair assistance for passengers to the baggage area. Porters are generally available to help with luggage at airports and large bus stations, once you've cleared baggage claim.

In addition, escalators (there aren't many in the country) are often not operating. Few handicapped-equipped restrooms exist, or when one is available, access to it may be via a narrow passage that won't accommodate a wheelchair or someone on crutches. Many deluxe hotels (the most expensive) now have rooms with baths for the handicapped and handicapped access to the hotel. Those traveling on a budget should stick with one-story hotels or those with elevators. Even so, there will probably still be obstacles somewhere. Stairs without handrails abound in Mexico. Intracity bus drivers generally don't bother with the courtesy step on boarding or disembarking. On city buses, the height between the street and the bus step can require considerable force to board. Generally speaking, no matter where you are, someone will lend a hand, although you may have to ask for it.

10 Getting There

BY PLANE

The airline situation in Mexico is changing rapidly, with many new regional carriers offering scheduled service to areas previously not served. In addition to regularly scheduled service, charter service direct from U.S. cities to resorts is making Mexico more accessible from the United States.

THE MAJOR INTERNATIONAL AIRLINES

The main airlines operating direct or nonstop flights from the United States to points in Mexico include **Aero California** (☎ 800/237-6225), **Aeroméxico** (☎ 800/237-6639); **Air France** (☎ 800/237-2747); **Alaska Airlines** (☎ 800/426-0333); **American** (☎ 800/433-7300); **Continental** (☎ 800/231-0856); **Delta** (☎ 800/221-1212); **Lacsa** (☎ 800/225-2272); **Lufthansa** (☎ 800/645-3880); **Mexicana** (☎ 800/531-7921); **Northwest** (☎ 800/225-2525); **United** (☎ 800/241-6522); and **USAir** (☎ 800/428-4322).

Southwest Airlines (☎ 800/435-9792) serves the U.S. border. The main departure points in the United States for international airlines are Chicago, Dallas/Fort Worth, Denver, Houston, Los Angeles, Miami, New Orleans, New York, Orlando, Philadelphia, Raleigh/Durham, San Antonio, San Francisco, Seattle, Toronto, Tucson, and Washington, D.C.

Bargain hunters rejoice! Excursion and package plans proliferate, especially in the off-season. A good travel agent will be able to give you all the latest schedules, details, and prices, but you may have to investigate regional airlines for yourself (see "By Plane" under "Getting Around," below).

As of press time, sample off-season, midweek, round-trip fares on Mexicana were as follows: A round-trip excursion fare from New York to Guadalajara was $561; to Puerto Vallarta, $561; and Manzanillo, $661. From Los Angeles to Guadalajara a typical fare ran from $323; to Puerto Vallarta, $279; and Manzanillo, $361. From Denver, a round-trip fare to Guadalajara was $298; to Puerto Vallarta, $298; and to Manzanillo, $477. Never pay these rates without first pricing packages that include air and hotel.

CHARTERS

Charter service is growing, especially during winter months and usually is sold as a package combination of air and hotel. Charter airlines, however, may sell air packages only, without hotel. Charter airlines include **Taesa Airlines,** which has service from several U.S. cities. **Latur** offers charters from New York to Cancún, Puerto Vallarta, and Acapulco; Chicago to Cancún; and Boston to Cancún.

Tour companies operating charters include **Club America Vacations, Apple Vacations, Friendly Holidays,** and **Gogo Tours.** You can make arrangements with these companies through your travel agent.

FROM GREAT BRITAIN   There are many airlines that fly from London to Mexico City: **British Airways, Iberia, KLM, Lufthansa, Air France, Continental,** and **American** are just a few. Your best bet is to work with a travel agent, such as Thomas Cook, to find the best deal.

BY BUS

Greyhound-Trailways (or its affiliates) offers service from around the United States to the Mexican border, where passengers disembark, cross the border, and buy a ticket for travel into the interior of Mexico. At many border crossings there are scheduled buses from the U.S. bus station to the Mexican bus station.

BY CAR

Driving is certainly not the cheapest way to get to Mexico, but it is the best way to see the country. Even so, you may think twice about taking your own car south of the border once you've pondered Mexico's many bureaucratic requirements involved in doing so.

It's wise to check and double-check all the requirements before setting out for a driving tour of Mexico. Read through the rest of this section, and then address any additional questions you have or confirm the current rules by calling your nearest Mexican consulate, Mexican Government Tourist Office, AAA, or Sanborn's (☎ 210/686-3601).

CAR DOCUMENTS

To drive a personal car into Mexico, you'll need a temporary car importation permit, granted upon completion of a long and strictly required list of documents (see below). The permit can be obtained through Banco del Ejército (Banjercito) officials, who have a desk, booth, or office at the Mexican Customs (*Aduana*) building immediately upon crossing the border into Mexico. You can obtain the permit before you travel through Sanborn's Insurance and the American Automobile Association (AAA), each of which maintains border offices in Texas, New Mexico, Arizona, and California. These companies may charge a fee for this service, but it will be worth it to avoid the uncertain prospect of traveling all the way to the border without proper documents for crossing. However, even if you go through Sanborn's or AAA, your credentials *may* be reviewed again by Mexican officials at the border—you must have them all with you since they are still subject to questions of validity.

The following requirements for border crossing were accurate at press time:

- *A valid driver's license*, issued outside of Mexico.
- *Current, original car registration and a copy of the original car title.* If the registration or title is in more than one name and not all the named people are traveling with you, then a notarized letter from the absent person(s) authorizing use of the vehicle for the trip may be required; have it ready just in case. The car registration and your credit card (see below) must be in the same name.
- *An original notarized letter from the lien holder,* if your registration shows a lien, giving you permission to take the vehicle into Mexico.
- *A valid international major credit card.* Using only your credit card, you are required to pay a $12 car-importation fee. The credit card must be in the same name as the car registration.

  Note: Those without credit cards will forego the $12 importation fee and instead will be required to post a cash bond based on the value of the car. The rules and procedures are complicated, so contact AAA or Sanborn's for details.
- *A signed declaration* promising to return to your country of origin with the vehicle. This form is provided by AAA or Sanborn's before you go or by Banjercito officials at the border. There's no charge. The form does not stipulate that you return through the same border entry you came through on your way south.

You must carry your temporary car importation permit, tourist permit, and, if you purchased it, your proof of Mexican car insurance in the car at all times.

Important reminder: Someone else may drive the car, but the person (or relative of the person) whose name appears on the car importation permit must *always* be in the car at the same time. (If stopped by police, a nonregistered family member driver, driving without the registered driver, must be prepared to prove familial relationship to the registered driver.) Violation of this rule makes the car subject to impoundment and the driver to imprisonment and/or a fine.

Only under certain circumstances will the driver of the car be allowed to leave the country without the car. If it's undrivable, you can leave it at a mechanic's shop if you get a letter to that effect from the mechanic and present it to the nearest secretaria de hacienda y credito público (a treasury department official) for further documentation, which you then present to a Banjercito official upon leaving the country. Then you must return personally to retrieve the car. If the driver of the car has to leave the country without the car due to an emergency, the car must be put under Customs seal at the airport and the driver's tourist permit must be stamped to that effect. There may be storage fees. If the car is wrecked or stolen, your Mexican insurance adjuster will provide the necessary paperwork for presentation to Hacienda officials.

If you receive your documentation at the border (rather than through Sanborn's or AAA), Mexican border officials will make two copies of everything and charge you for the copies.

The temporary car importation permit papers will be issued for six months and the tourist permit is usually issued for 180 days, but they might stamp it for half that, so check. It's a good idea also to overestimate the time you'll spend in Mexico, so that if something unforeseen happens and you have, or want, to stay longer, you'll have avoided the long hassle of getting your papers renewed.

Important note: Whatever you do, don't overstay either permit. Doing so invites heavy fines and/or confiscation of your vehicle, which will not be returned. Remember also that 6 months does not necessarily work out to be 180 days—be sure that you return before whichever expiration date comes first.

Other documentation is required for an individual's permit to enter Mexico—see "Entry Requirements," above.

MEXICAN AUTO INSURANCE

Although auto insurance is not legally required in Mexico, driving without it is foolish. U.S. insurance is invalid in Mexico; to be insured there, you must purchase Mexican insurance. Any party involved in an accident who has no insurance is automatically sent to jail and his or her car is impounded until all claims are settled. This is true even if you just drive across the border to spend the day, and it may be true even if you're injured.

All agencies selling Mexican insurance will show you a full table of current rates and recommend the coverage they think is adequate. The policies are written along lines similar to those north of the border, with the following exception: The contents of your vehicle aren't covered. It's no longer necessary to overestimate the amount of time you plan to be in Mexico because it's now possible to get your policy term lengthened by fax from the insurer. However, if you are staying longer than 48 days, it's more economical to buy a nonrefundable annual policy. For example, a car insured through Sanborn's (registered to an individual, not a business) with a value of $10,000 can be insured for $132.50 for two weeks or $71.25 for one week. An annual policy for a car valued between $10,000 and $15,000 would be a reduced rate of $519 which you get by joining Sanborn's Amigo Club for $30. (The Amigo Club membership offers hotel discounts and a newsletter.) Be sure the policy you buy will pay for repairs in either the United States or Mexico and will pay out in dollars, not pesos.

One of the best insurance companies for south of the border travel is **Sanborn's Mexico Insurance,** with offices at all of the border crossings in the United States. I never drive across the border without Sanborn's insurance. It costs the same as the competition and you get a *Travelog* that's like a mile-by-mile guide along your proposed route. With the ongoing changes in Mexico's highway system it's inevitable that the log occasionally is a bit outdated, but for the most part, it's like having a knowledgeable friend in the car telling you how to get in and out of town, where to buy gas (and which stations to avoid), what the highway conditions are, and what scams you need to watch out for. It's especially helpful in remote places. Most of Sanborn's border offices are open Monday through Friday, and a few are staffed on Saturday and Sunday. You can purchase your auto liability and collision coverage by phone in advance and have it waiting at a 24-hour location if you are crossing when the office is closed. The annual insurance includes a type of evacuation assistance in case of emergency, and emergency evacuation insurance for shorter policies is available for a small daily fee. They also offer a medical policy. For information, contact Sanborn's Mexico Insurance, P.O. Box 310, Dept. FR, 2009 S. 10th, McAllen, TX 78505-0310 (☎ 210/686-0711; fax 210/686-0732 in Texas or 800/222-0158 in the U.S.). **AAA** auto club also sells insurance.

PREPARING YOUR CAR

Check the condition of your car thoroughly before you cross the border. Parts made in Mexico may be inferior, but service generally is quite good and relatively inexpensive. Carry a spare radiator hose and belts for the engine fan and air-conditioner. Be sure your car is in tune to handle Mexican gasoline. Also, can your tires last a few thousand miles on Mexican roads?

Take simple tools along if you're handy with them; also take a flashlight or spotlight, a cloth to wipe the windshield, toilet paper, and a tire gauge—Mexican filling stations generally have air to fill tires but no gauge to check the pressure. When I am driving, I always bring along a combination gauge/air compressor sold at U.S. automotive stores; it plugs into the car cigarette lighter, making it a simple procedure to check the tires every morning and pump them up at the same time.

Not that many Mexican cars comply, but Mexican law requires that every car have **seat belts** and a **fire extinguisher.** Be prepared!

CROSSING THE BORDER WITH YOUR CAR

After you cross the border into Mexico from the United States and you've stopped to get your tourist card and car permit, somewhere between 12 and 16 miles down the road you'll come to a Mexican customs post. In the past all motorists had to stop and present travel documents and possibly have their cars inspected. Now there is a new system under which some motorists are stopped at random for inspection. All car papers are examined, however, so you must stop. If the light is green, go on through; if it's red, stop for inspection. In the Baja Peninsula the procedures may differ slightly—first you get your tourist permit then further down the road you may not be stopped for the car inspection.

RETURNING TO THE U.S. WITH YOUR CAR

The car papers you obtained when you entered Mexico *must* be returned when you cross back with your car or at some point within the time limit of 180 days. (You can cross as many times as you wish within the 180 days.) If the documents aren't returned, heavy fines are imposed ($250 for each 15 days late), and your car may be impounded and confiscated or you may be jailed if you return to Mexico. You can only return the car documents to a Banjercito official on duty at the Mexican Customs (*Aduana*) building *before* you cross back into the United States. Some border cities have Banjercito officials on duty 24 hours a day, but others do not; some also do not have Sunday hours. On the U.S. side customs agents may or may not inspect your car from stem to stern.

BY SHIP

Numerous cruise lines serve Mexico. Possible trips might cruise from California down to the Baja Peninsula (including specialized whale-watching trips) and ports of call on the Pacific coast, including Ixtapa/Zihuatanejo, Puerto Vallarta, Manzanillo, and Acapulco. Among the many cruise lines with Pacific coast itineraries is **Princess Cruises,** 10100 Santa Monica Blvd., Los Angeles, CA 90067 (☎ 800/344-2626 in the U.S.).

From a budget point of view, these are expensive if you pay the full price. However, if you don't mind taking off at the last minute, several cruise-tour specialists arrange substantial discounts on unsold cabins. One such company is **The Cruise Line, Inc.,** 4770 Biscayne Blvd., Penthouse 1–3, Miami FL 33137 (☎ 305/576-0036, 800/777-0707, or 800/327-3021).

PACKAGE TOURS

Package tours offer some of the best values to the coastal resorts, especially during high season, from December until after Easter. Off-season packages can be real bargains. However, to know for sure if the package will save you money, you must price the package yourself by calling the airline for round-trip flight costs and the hotel for rates. Add in the cost of transfers to and from the airport (which packages usually include) and see if it's a deal.

Packages are usually per person, and single travelers pay a supplement. In the high season a package may be the only way of getting to certain places in Mexico because wholesalers have all the airline seats. The cheapest package rates will be those in hotels in the lower range, always without as many amenities as higher-priced hotels. You can still use the public areas and beaches of more costly hotels without being a guest.

Travel agents have information on specific packages.

TOUR OPERATORS IN GREAT BRITAIN   BA Holidays, Airtours, and **Sunset Travel** are three of the largest companies offering package tours to Mexico. I recommend you pay a visit to the Mexican Government Tourist Office at 60–61 Trafalgar Sq., London WC2 N5DS (☎ 441/734-1058) if possible; you'll find a wealth of brochures on display.

11 Getting Around

BY PLANE

U.S. and international airlines can fly to and from Mexico letting off and picking up passengers. But to fly from point to point within the country you'll rely on Mexican airlines. Mexico has two privately owned, large national carriers, **Mexicana** and **Aeromexico,** which fly from the United States to Mexico as well as within the country, and several up-and-coming regional carriers. Several of the new regional carriers are operated by, or can be booked through, Mexicana (**Aero Caribe, Aero Cozumel,** and **Aeromonterrey**) and Aeromexico (**Aerolitoral**). The regional carriers are expensive, but they go to places that were once difficult to reach. Look for this trend to continue. In each of the sections in this book, I've mentioned the regional carriers and the major ones with all pertinent telephone numbers.

Because major airlines can book some regional carriers, read your ticket carefully to see if your connecting flight is on one of these smaller carriers—they may leave from a different airport or check in at a different counter.

AIRPORT TAXES   Mexico charges an airport tax on all departures. Passengers leaving the country on an international departure pay $12 in cash—dollars or the peso equivalent. Each domestic departure you make within Mexico costs around $6, unless you're on a connecting flight and have already paid at the start of the flight; you shouldn't be charged again if you have to change planes for a connecting flight.

RECONFIRMING FLIGHTS   Although airlines in Mexico say it's not necessary to reconfirm a flight, I always do. Also, be aware that airlines routinely overbook. To avoid getting bumped, check in for an international flight the required hour and a half in advance of travel. That will put you near the head of the line.

BY TRAIN

The Mexican government would like to privatize the railroads and recently has systematically downgraded passenger service from the high it reached a few years ago. You can't count on diner or club cars or Pullman (sleeping) cars, even on overnight journeys. No matter what is promised, *always* be prepared with food, water, and toilet paper.

However, if you find a first-class train heading your way, try it. Train travel is safer and sometimes more comfortable than bus travel, though it's slower, costs more, and schedules are likely to be less convenient. In the area covered by this book there are trains between Guadalajara, Colima, Manzanillo, and Mexico City.

BY BUS

Mexican buses are frequent and readily accessible and can get you to almost anywhere you want to go. Buses are an excellent way to get around, and they're often the only way to get from large cities to other nearby cities and small villages. There's little English spoken at bus stations, so come prepared with your destination written down, then double check the departure several times just to make sure you get to the right departing lane on time. Ticket agents can be quite brusque or indifferent, especially if there's a line; in general, however, people are willing to help, so never hesitate to ask questions if you're confused about anything.

Dozens of Mexican companies operate large, air-conditioned, Greyhound-type buses between most cities. Travel class is generally labeled first, second, and deluxe, referred to by a variety of names—*plus, de lujo, ejecutivo, primera plus,* and so on. The deluxe buses often have fewer seats than regular buses, show video movies en route, are air-conditioned, and have few stops; many run express from origin to the final destination. They are well worth the few dollars more you'll pay than you would for first-class buses. Second-class buses have many stops and cost only slightly less than first-class or deluxe buses. In rural areas, buses are often of the school-bus variety, with lots of local color.

Whenever possible, it's best to buy your reserved-seat ticket, often via a computerized system, a day in advance on many long-distance routes. Schedules are fairly dependable, so be at the terminal on time for departure.

Many Mexican cities, including Guadalajara, now have new central bus stations that are much like sophisticated airport terminals. The new terminals have replaced the bewildering array of tiny private company offices scattered all over town in such cities as Puerto Vallarta.

I've included information on bus routes in my suggested itineraries. Keep in mind that routes and times change, and as there is no central directory of schedules for the whole country, current information must be obtained from local bus stations.

For long trips, *always* carry food, water, toilet paper, and a sweater (in case the air-conditioning is too strong).

See the appendix for a list of helpful bus terms in Spanish.

BY CAR

Most Mexican roads are not up to U.S. standards of smoothness, hardness, width of curve, grade of hill, or safety marking.

Important note: Never drive at night if you can avoid it—the roads aren't good enough; the trucks, carts, pedestrians, and bicycles usually have no lights; and you can hit potholes, animals, rocks, dead ends, or bridges that are out with no warning. Enough said!

You will also have to get used to the spirited Mexican driving styles, which require other drivers to possess superior vision and reflexes. Be prepared for new procedures, as when a truck driver flips on his left-turn signal when there's not a cross street for miles. He's probably telling you the road's clear ahead for you to pass—after all, he's in a better position to see than you are. It's difficult to know, however, whether he really means that he intends to pull over on the left-hand shoulder. You may have to follow trucks without mufflers and pollution-control devices for miles. Under these conditions, drop back and be patient, take a side road, or stop for a break when you feel tense or tired. Another custom to observe is the procedure for crossing a one-lane bridge when another car is approaching from the opposite direction. Whichever car flashes its headlights first gets to cross while the other car waits.

Be prepared to pay tolls on some of Mexico's expressways and bridges. Tolls are among the highest in the world. The word for "toll" in Spanish is *cuota.*

GASOLINE   There's one government-owned brand of gas and one gasoline station name throughout the country—**Pemex** (Petroleras Mexicanas). Each station has a franchise owner who buys everything from Pemex. There are two types of gas in Mexico: **nova,** an 82-octane leaded gas, and **magna sin,** an 87-octane unleaded gas. Magna sin is sold from brilliantly colored pumps and costs around $1.25 a gallon; nova costs slightly less. In Mexico, fuel and oil are sold by the liter, which is slightly more than a quart (40 liters equals about 10^1/$_2$ gallons). Nova is readily available. Magna sin is now available in most areas of Mexico, along major highways, and in the larger cities. Even in areas where it should be available, you may have to hunt around. The usual station may be out of magna sin for a couple of days, especially on weekends, or you may be told that none is available in the area, just to get your business. Plan ahead; fill up every chance you get, and keep your tank topped off. No credit cards are accepted for gas purchases.

Here's what to do when you have to fuel up. Drive up to the pump, close enough so you'll be able to watch the pump run as your tank is being filled. Check that the pump is turned back to zero, go to your fuel filler cap and unlock it yourself, and watch the pump and the attendant as the gas goes in. Though many service-station attendants are honest, many are not. It's good to ask for a specific peso amount rather than saying "full." This is because the attendants tend to overfill, splashing gas on the car and anything within range.

As there are always lines at the gas pumps, attendants often finish fueling one vehicle, turn the pump back quickly (or don't turn it back at all), and start on another vehicle. You've got to be looking at the pump when the fueling is finished because it may show the amount you owe for only a few seconds. This "quick draw" from car to car is another good reason to ask for a certain peso amount of gas. If you've asked for a certain amount, the attendant can't charge you more for it.

Once the fueling is complete, let the attendant check the oil or radiator or put air in the tires. Do only one thing at a time, be with him as he does it, and don't let him rush you. Get into these habits, or it'll cost you.

If you get oil, make sure the can that is tipped into your engine is a full one. If in doubt, have the attendant check the dipstick again after the oil has supposedly been put in. Check your change and, again, don't let them rush you. Check that your locking gas cap is back in place.

DRIVING RULES   If you park illegally or commit some other infraction and are not around to discuss it, police are authorized to remove your license plates (*placas*). You must then trundle over to the police station and pay a fine to get them back. Mexican car-rental agencies have begun to weld the license plate to the plate frame; you may want to devise a method of your own to make the plates more difficult to remove. Theoretically, this will make the policeman move on to another set of plates that are easier to confiscate. On the other hand, he could get his hackles up and decide to have your car towed. To weld or not to weld is up to you.

Be attentive to road signs. A drawing of a row of little bumps means there are speed bumps *(topes)* across the road to warn you to reduce your speed while driving through towns or villages. Slow down when coming to a village whether you see the sign or not—sometimes they install the bumps but not the sign!

There is always a shortage of directional signs, so check frequently to be sure that you're on the right road. Don't count on plenty of notice of where to turn, even on major interchanges; more often than not, the directional sign appears without prior notice exactly at the spot where you need to make a decision—a turn, take a spaghetti bowl loop, a lane ending, and the like. Common road signs include these:

Camino en Reparación	Road repairs
Conserva Su Derecha	Keep right
Cuidado con el Ganado, el Tren	Watch out for cattle, trains
Curva Peligrosa	Dangerous curve
Derrumbes	Falling rocks
Deslave	Caved-in roadbed
Despacio	Slow
Desviación	Detour
Disminuya Su Velocidad	Slow down
Entronque	Highway junction
Escuela	School (zone)
Grava Suelta	Loose gravel
Hombres Trabajando	Men working
No Hay Paso	Road closed
Peligro	Danger

Puente Angosto	Narrow bridge
Raya Continua	Continuous (solid) white line
Tramo en Reparación	Road under construction
Un Solo Carril a 100 m.	One-lane road 100 meters ahead
Zone Escolar	School zone

TOLL ROADS   Mexico charges among the highest tolls in the world to use its network of new toll roads. As a result they are comparatively little used. Generally speaking, using the toll roads will cut your travel time between destinations. The old roads, on which no tolls are charged, are generally in good condition but overall mean longer trips since they usually pass through more mountains and are usually clotted with an abundance of slow-moving trucks. However, now that the toll roads are built, signage to the free roads is confusing and inconsistent from toll road to toll road, or is nonexistent, so it's easy to find yourself at the toll booth when you meant to take the free road.

In the region covered in this book there are new toll roads between Guadalajara and Manzanillo and a short one between Chapalilla and Compostela which bypasses Tepic (and cuts the travel time from 6 to 8 hours) on the road between Puerto Vallarta and Tepic. A new toll road between Guadalajara and Puerto Vallarta may be finished when you travel.

The toll road from Guadalajara through Colima City to Manzanillo is a dream—if an expensive one. Tolls cost around $20 for the whole distance. As you cross bridges, signboards compare heights of bridges along the route to pyramids in Mexico. The Piala Bridge, for example, is 292 ft. high, as compared to the 207 ft. for the Pyramid of the Sun. The Beltrán Bridge is 459 ft. high, compared to the Latin American Tower in Mexico City at 590 feet. It makes for an interesting bit of trivia as you travel, and some of the deep gorges from the highway are incredibly beautiful. The two-lane, free road that covers the same route is in good shape but takes longer to drive and goes through more mountainous curves.

MAPS   Guía Rojo, AAA, and International Travel Map Productions have good maps to Mexico. In Mexico, maps are sold at large drugstores like Sanborn's, at bookstores, and in hotel gift shops.

BREAKDOWNS   Your best guide to repair shops is the yellow pages. For specific makes and shops that repair them, look under "Automoviles y Camiones: Talleres de Reparación y Servicio"; auto parts stores are listed under "Refacciones y Accesorios para Automoviles." On the road, often the sign of a mechanic simply says TALLER MECÁNICO.

I've found that the Ford and Volkswagen dealerships in Mexico give prompt, courteous attention to my car problems, and prices for repairs are, in general, much lower than those in the United States or Canada. I suspect other big-name dealerships give similar satisfactory service. Often they will take your car right away and make repairs in just a few hours, sometimes minutes.

If your car breaks down on the road, help might already be on the way. Radio-equipped green repair trucks manned by uniformed English-speaking officers patrol the major highways during daylight hours to aid motorists in trouble. The **"Green Angels"** will perform minor repairs and adjustments for free, but you pay for parts and materials.

MINOR ACCIDENTS   When possible, many Mexicans drive away from minor accidents to avoid hassles with police. If the police arrive while the involved persons are still at the scene, everyone may be locked in jail until blame is assessed.

In any case you have to settle up immediately, which may take days of red tape. Foreigners who don't speak fluent Spanish are at a distinct disadvantage when trying to explain their side of the event. Three steps may help the foreigner who doesn't wish to do as the Mexicans do: If you're in your own car, notify your Mexican insurance company, whose job it is to intervene on your behalf. If you're in a rental car, notify the rental company immediately and ask how to contact the nearest adjuster. (You did buy insurance with the rental—right?) Finally, if all else fails, ask to contact the nearest Green Angels, who may be able to explain to officials that you are covered by insurance.

See also "Mexican Auto Insurance" in "By Car" under "Getting There," above.

PARKING   When you park your car on the street, lock it up and leave nothing within view inside (day or night). I use guarded parking lots, especially at night, to avoid vandalism and break-ins. This way you also avoid parking violations. When pay lots are not available, dozens of small boys will surround you as you stop, wanting to watch your car for you. Pick the leader of the group, let him know you want him to guard it, and give him a peso or two when you leave. Kids may be very curious about the car and may look in, crawl underneath, or even climb on top, but they rarely do any damage.

CAR RENTALS   With some trepidation I wander into the subject of car-rental rules, which change often in Mexico. The best prices are obtained by reserving your car a week in advance in the United States. Mexico City and most other large Mexican cities have rental offices representing the various big firms and some local ones. You'll find rental desks at airports, all major hotels, and many travel agencies. The large firms like Avis, Hertz, National, and Budget have rental offices on main streets as well. Renting a car during a major holiday may prove difficult if all the cars are booked or not returned on time. To avoid being stranded without a vehicle, if possible plan your arrival before the anticipated rush of travelers.

I don't recommend renting a car in Mexico City for 1-day excursions from the city. It can be a real hassle, and parking is also a problem.

Cars are easy to rent if you have a charge or credit card (American Express, VISA, MasterCard, and the like), are 25 or over, and have a valid driver's license and passport with you. Without a credit card you must leave a cash deposit, usually a big one. Rent-here/leave-there arrangements are usually simple to make but very costly.

Costs   Don't underestimate the cost of renting a car. When I checked recently for rental on May 15 (after Easter when rates go down) the basic cost of a 1-day rental of a Volkswagen Beetle, with unlimited mileage (but before 15% tax and $15 daily insurance) was $45 in Mexico City and $38 in Puerto Vallarta. Renting by the week gives you a lower daily rate. For renting from Avis during the week of May 15, the basic 7-day weekly rate for a VW Beetle (without tax or insurance) was $180 in Puerto Vallarta and $216 in Mexico City.

So you can see that it makes a difference where you rent, for how long, and when. Mileage-added rates can run the bill up considerably; I recommend renting with mileage included rather than with mileage added.

Rental Confirmation   Make your reservation directly with the car-rental company using its toll-free number. Write down your confirmation number and request that a copy of the confirmation be mailed to you (rent at least a week in advance so the confirmation has time to reach you). Present that confirmation slip when you appear to collect your car. If you're dealing with a U.S. company, the confirmation must be honored, even if the company has to upgrade you to another class of car—don't allow them to send you to another agency. The rental confirmation also has the agreed-on price that prevents you from being charged more, in case there is a price change before you arrive. Insist on the rate printed on the confirmation slip.

Deductibles   Be careful—deductibles vary greatly; some are as high as $2,500, which comes out of your pocket immediately in case of car damage. Don't fail to get information about deductibles.

Insurance   Many credit-card companies offer their cardholders free rental-car insurance. *Don't use it in Mexico,* for several reasons. Even though insurance policies that specifically cover rental cars are supposedly optional in Mexico, there may be major consequences if you don't have one. First, if you buy insurance, you pay only the deductible, which limits your liability. Second, if you have an accident or your car is vandalized or stolen and you don't have insurance, you'll have to pay for everything before you can leave the rental-car office. This includes the full value of the car if it is unrepairable—a determination made only by the rental-car company. While your credit card may eventually pay your costs, you will have to lay out the money in the meantime. Third, if an accident occurs, everyone may wind up in jail until guilt is determined, and if you are the guilty party, you may not be released from jail until restitution is paid in full to the rental-car owners and to injured persons—made doubly difficult if you have no rental-car insurance.

Insurance is offered in two parts. **Collision and damage** insurance covers your car and others if the accident is your fault, and **personal accident** insurance covers you and anyone in your car. I always take both.

Damage   Always inspect your car carefully, and mark all problem areas using this checklist:

- Hubcaps
- Windshield (for nicks and cracks)
- Tire tread
- Body (for dents, nicks, etc.)
- Fenders (for dents, etc.)
- Muffler (is it smashed?)
- Trim (loose or damaged?)
- Head and tail lights
- Fire extinguisher (it should be under the driver's seat, as required by law)
- Spare tire and tools (in the trunk)
- Seat belts (required by law)
- Gas cap
- Outside mirror
- Floor mats

Note every damaged or missing area, no matter how minute, on your rental agreement or you will be charged for all missing or damaged parts, including missing car plates, should the police confiscate your plates for a parking infraction (which is very costly). I can't stress enough how important it is to check your car carefully. Car companies have attempted to rent me cars with bald tires and tires with bulges; a car with a license plate that would expire before I returned the car;

and cars with missing trim, floor mats, or fire extinguishers. They've also attempted to charge me for dings that were on the auto when I rented it, which they were unable to do because the dings were marked on the agreement.

Fine Print   Read the fine print on the back of your rental agreement and note that insurance is invalid if you have an accident while driving on an unpaved road.

Trouble Number   One last recommendation: Before starting out with a rental car, be sure you know the rental company's trouble number. Get the direct number to the agency where you rented the car and write down its office hours. The large firms have toll-free numbers, but they may not be well staffed on weekends.

Problems, Perils, Deals   At present, I find the best prices are through Avis, and that's the company I use; generally I am a satisfied customer, though I sometimes have to dig in my heels and insist on proper service. I have had even more difficult problems with other agencies. I have encountered certain kinds of situations within the past 4 years that could occur with any company. These problems have included an attempt to push me off to a no-name company rather than upgrade me to a more expensive car when a VW Beetle wasn't available; poorly staffed offices with no extra cars, parts, or mechanics in case of a breakdown; and a demand I sign a credit-card voucher for 75% of the value of the car in case of an accident even though I had purchased insurance (I refused and still rented the car). Since potential problems are varied, I'd rather deal with a company based in the States so at least I have recourse if I am not satisfied.

Signing the Rental Agreement   Once you've agreed on everything, the rental clerk will tally the bill before you leave and you will sign an open credit-card voucher that will be filled in when you return the car. Read the agreement and double-check all the addition. The time to catch mistakes is before you leave, not when you return.

Picking Up/Returning the Car   When you rent the car, you agree to pick it up at a certain time and return it at a certain time. If you're late in picking it up or if you cancel the reservation, there are usually penalties—ask what they are when you make the reservation. If you return the car more than an hour late, an expensive hourly rate kicks in. Also, you must return the car with the same amount of gas in the tank it had when you drove out. If you don't, the charge added to your bill for the difference is much more than for gas bought at a public station.

CAMPING   It's easy and relatively cheap to camp south of the border if you have a recreational vehicle or trailer. It's more difficult if you only have a tent. Some agencies selling Mexican car insurance in the United States (including Sanborn's) will give you a free list of campsites if you ask. The AAA also has a list of sites.

Campgrounds here tend to be slightly below U.S. standards (with many attractive exceptions to this rule, though). Remember that campgrounds fill up just like hotels during the winter and at holiday times. Get there early. It is not wise to camp on a beach or any other remote, unofficial place.

BY RV

Touring Mexico by recreational vehicle (RV) is a popular way of seeing the country. Many hotels have hookups. RV parks, while not as plentiful as those in the United States, are available throughout the country.

BY FERRY

Ferries connect Baja California at La Paz and Santa Rosalía with the mainland at Topolobampo and Mazatlán.

BY HITCHHIKING

You see Mexicans hitching rides (for example, at crossroads after getting off a bus), but as a general rule hitchhiking isn't done. It's especially unwise for foreigners, who may be suspected of carrying large amounts of cash. I don't recommend hitching.

FAST FACTS: Mexico

Abbreviations   Dept.—apartments; Apdo.—post office box; Av.—Avenida; Calz.—Calzada (boulevard). "C" on faucets stands for *caliente* (hot), and "F" stands for *fría* (cold). PB (*planta baja*) means ground floor.

American Express   Wherever there is an office in a specific city or town, I've mentioned it.

Business Hours   In general, Mexican businesses in larger cities are open between 9am and 7pm; in smaller towns many close between 2 and 4pm. Most are closed on Sunday. Bank hours are Monday through Friday from 9 or 9:30am to 1pm. A few banks in large cities have extended hours.

Camera/Film   If your camera conks out, you can usually find a new point-and-shoot type camera for about the same price as in the U.S., although you may never have heard of the brand. Film is priced about the same as it is in the U.S. as well. Take full advantage of your 12-roll film allowance by bringing 36-exposure rolls. Also bring extra batteries: AA batteries are generally available, but AAA and small disk batteries for cameras and watches are rare. A few places in resort areas advertise color film developing, but it might be cheaper to wait until you get home.

Important note about camera use: Tourists wishing to use a video or still camera at any archaeological site in Mexico and at many museums operated by the Instituto de Historia y Antropología (INAH) may be required to pay $8.50 per video and/or still camera at each site or museum visited. (In some museums camera use is not permitted.) If you want to use either kind of camera or both, the fee must be paid for each piece of equipment. When you pay the fee, your camera will be tagged and you are permitted to use the equipment. Watchmen are often posted to see that untagged cameras are not used. Such fees are noted in the listings for specific sites and museums.

Cigarettes   Cigarettes are much cheaper in Mexico than in the United States, even U.S. brands, if you buy them at a grocery or drugstore and not a hotel tobacco shop.

Climate   See "When To Go," above, in this chapter.

Crime   See "Legal Aid" and "Safety," below, and "Bribes & Scams" under "Information & Entry Requirements," above, in this chapter.

Currency   See "Information & Entry Requirements," above, in this chapter.

Customs   Mexican customs inspection has been streamlined. At most points of entry tourists are requested to punch a button. If the resulting light is green, you go through without inspection; if it's red, your luggage or car may be inspected thoroughly or briefly.

Doctors/Dentists   Every embassy and consulate is prepared to recommend local doctors and dentists with good training and modern equipment; some of the doctors and dentists even speak English. See the list of embassies and consulates under "Embassies/Consulates," below, and remember that at the larger ones, a duty officer is on call at all times. Hotels with a large foreign clientele are often prepared to recommend English-speaking doctors. Almost all first-class hotels in Mexico have a doctor on call.

Documents Required   See "Information & Entry Requirements," above, in this chapter.

Driving Rules   See "By Car" under "Getting Around," above, in this chapter.

Drug Laws   Briefly, don't use or possess illegal drugs in Mexico. Mexicans have no tolerance for drug users, and jail is their solution, with very little hope of getting out until the sentence (usually a long one) is completed or heavy fines or bribes are paid. (*Important note:* It isn't uncommon to be befriended by a fellow user only to be turned in by that "friend," who then collects a bounty for turning you in. It's a no-win situation!) Bring prescription drugs in their original containers. If possible, pack a copy of the original prescription with the generic name of the drug.

I don't need to go into detail about the penalties for illegal drug possession upon return to the United States. Customs officials are also on the lookout for diet drugs sold in Mexico, possession of which could also land you in a U.S. jail because they are illegal here. If you buy antibiotics over the counter (which you can do in Mexico)—say, for a sinus infection—and still have some left, you probably won't be hassled by U.S. Customs.

Drugstores   Drugstores (*farmacías*) will sell you just about anything you want, with a prescription or without one. However, over-the-counter medicines such as aspirin, decongestants, or antihistamines are rarely sold. Most drugstores are open Monday through Saturday from 8am to 8pm. If you need to buy medicines after normal hours, ask for the *farmacía de turno*—pharmacies take turns staying open during off-hours. Find any drugstore, and in its window may be a card showing the schedule of which drugstore will be open at what time.

Electricity   The electrical system in Mexico is 110 volts, 60 cycles, as in the United States and Canada. However, in reality it may cycle more slowly and overheat your appliances. To compensate, select a medium or low speed for hairdryers, though they may still overheat. Older hotels still have electrical outlets for flat two-prong plugs; you'll need an adapter for using any modern electrical apparatus that has an enlarged end on one prong or that has three prongs to insert. Many first-class and deluxe hotels have the three-holed outlets (*trifácicos* in Spanish). Those that don't may loan adapters, but to be sure, it's always better to carry your own.

Embassies/Consulates   They provide valuable lists of doctors and lawyers, as well as regulations concerning marriages in Mexico. Contrary to popular belief, your embassy cannot get you out of a Mexican jail, provide postal or banking services, or fly you home when you run out of money. Consular officers can provide you with advice on most matters and problems, however. Most countries have a representative embassy in Mexico City and many have consular offices or representatives in the provinces.

The Embassy of **Australia** in Mexico City is at Jaime Balmes 11, Plaza Polanco, Torre B (☎ 5/395-9988 or 5/566-3053); it's open Monday through Friday from 8am to 1pm.

The Embassy of **Canada** in Mexico City is at Schiller 529, in Polanco (☎ 5/724-7900); it's open Monday through Friday from 9am to 1pm and 2 to 5pm (at other times the name of a duty officer is posted on the embassy door). In Acapulco, the Canadian consulate is in the Hotel Club del Sol, Costera Miguel Alemán, at the corner of Reyes Católicos (☎ 74/85-6621); it's open Monday through Friday from 8am to 3pm.

The Embassy of **New Zealand** in Mexico City is at Homero 229, 8th floor (☎ 5/250-5999 or 5/250-5777); it's open Monday through Thursday from 9am to 2pm and 3 to 5pm and Friday from 9am to 2pm.

The Embassy of the **United Kingdom** in Mexico City is at Lerma 71, at Río Sena (☎ 5/207-2569 or 5/207-2593); it's open Monday through Friday from 9am to 2pm. There are honorary consuls in the following cities: Acapulco, Hotel Las Brisas, Carretera Escénica (☎ 74/84-6605 or 74/84-1580); Ciudad Juarez, Calle Fresno 185 (☎ 16/7-5791); Guadalajara, Paulino Navarro 1165 (☎ 3/611-1678); Mérida, Calle 58 no. 450 (☎ 99/28-6152 or 99/28-3962); Monterrey, Privada de Tamazunchale 104 (☎ 83/78-2565); Oaxaca, Ev. Hidalgo 817 (☎ 951/6-5600); Tampico, 2 de Enero 102-A-Sur (☎ 12/12-9784 or 12/12-9817); Tijuana, Blvd. Salinas 1500 (☎ 66/81-7323); and Veracruz, Emparan 200 PB (☎ 29/31-0955).

The Embassy of the **United States** in Mexico City is next to the Hotel María Isabel Sheraton at Paseo de la Reforma 305, at the corner of Rió Danubio (☎ 5/211-0042). There are U.S. consulates in Ciudad Juárez, López Mateos 924-N (☎ 16/13-4048); Guadalajara, Progreso 175 (☎ 3/625-2998); Hermosillo, Calle Monterrey 141 (☎ 621/7-2375 or 621/7-2382); Matamoros, Av. Primera 2002 (☎ 88/12-4402); Mérida, Paseo Montejo 453 (☎ 99/25-6366); Monterrey, Av. Constitución 411 Poniente (☎ 83/45-2120); Nuevo Laredo, Calle Allende 3330 (☎ 871/4-0512); and Tijuana, Tapachula 96 (☎ 66/81-7400). In addition, consular agents reside in Acapulco (☎ 74/85-6600 or 74/85-7207); Cabo San Lucas (☎ 114/3-3566); Cancún (☎ 98/84-2411 or 98/84-6399); Mazatlán (☎ 69/13-4444, ext. 285); Oaxaca (☎ 951/4-3054); Puerto Vallarta (☎ 322/2-0069); San Luis Potosí (☎ 481/2-1528); San Miguel de Allende (☎ 465/2-2357 or 465/2-0068); Tampico (☎ 12/13-2217); and Veracruz (☎ 29/31-5821).

Emergencies   The 24-hour Tourist Help Line in Mexico City is 5/250-0151.

Etiquette   As a general rule, Mexicans are very polite. Foreigners who ask questions politely and say "please" and "thank you" will be rewarded. Mexicans are also very formal; an invitation to a private home, no matter how humble, is an honor. And although many strangers will immediately begin using the familiar form of the pronoun *tú* and its verb form, if you want to be correct, the formal *usted* is still preferred until a friendship is established. When in doubt use the formal form and wait for the Mexican to change to the familiar. Mexicans are normally uncomfortable with our "dutch treat" custom of dining and will usually insist on paying. It can be touchy, and you don't want to be insulting. You might, however, offer to get the drinks or insist on paying the tip. If you're invited to a home, it's polite to bring a gift, perhaps a bottle of good wine or flowers.

Guides   Most guides in Mexico are men. Many speak English (and occasionally other languages) and are formally trained in history and culture to qualify for a federally approved tourism license. Hiring a guide for a day at ruins or to squire you around Mexico City may be a worthwhile luxury if you establish boundaries in the beginning. Be specific about what you want to do and how long you want the service. The guide will quote a price. Discussion may reduce the initial quote. If your guide is using his own car, is licensed (something he can prove with a credential), and speaks English, the price will be higher and is generally worth it. If you are together at lunch, it's customary to buy the guide's meal. When bus tours from the United States diminished a few years ago, many licensed English-speaking guides became taxi drivers, so it isn't unusual to find incredibly knowledgeable taxi drivers who are experienced guides. In Mexico City these licensed guides/taxi drivers often have a permanent spot outside the better hotels and are available for private duty. If the service has been out of the ordinary, a tip is in order—perhaps 10% of the daily rate. On tours, the recommended tip is $1.50 to $2 per day per person.

Hitchhiking   Generally speaking, hitchhiking is not a good idea in Mexico. Take a bus instead—they're cheap and go everywhere.

Holidays   See "When to Go," above, in this chapter.

Information   See "Information & Entry Requirements," above, in this chapter and specific city chapters for local tourist information offices.

Language   The official language in Mexico is Spanish, but there are at least 50 Indian languages spoken and more than four times that many Indian dialects. English is most widely spoken in resort cities and in better hotels. It's best to learn some basic Spanish phrases.

Legal Aid   International Legal Defense Counsel, 111 S. 15th St., 24th Floor, Packard Building, Philadelphia, PA 19102 (☎ 215/977-9982), is a law firm specializing in legal difficulties of Americans abroad. See also "Embassies/Consulates" and "Emergencies," above.

Mail   Mail service south of the border tends to be slow (sometimes glacial in its movements) and erratic. If you're on a 2-week vacation, it's not a bad idea to buy and mail your postcards in the arrivals lounge at the airport to give them maximum time to get home before you do.

For the most reliable and convenient mail service, have your letters sent to you c/o the American Express offices in major cities, which will receive and forward mail for you if you are one of its clients (a travel-club card or an American Express traveler's check is proof). They charge a fee if you wish to have your mail forwarded.

If you don't use American Express, have your mail sent to you care of Lista de Correos (General Delivery), followed by the Mexican city, state, and country. In Mexican post offices there may actually be a "lista" posted near the Lista de Correos window bearing the names of all those for whom mail has been received. If there's no list, ask and show them your passport so they can riffle through and look for your letters. If the city has more than one office, you'll have to go to the central post office—not a branch—to get your mail. By the way, in many post offices they return mail to the sender if it has been there for more than 10 days. Make sure people don't send you letters too early.

In major Mexican cities there are also branches of such U.S. express mail companies as Federal Express and DHL, as well as private mail boxes such as Mail Boxes Etc.

Maps　AAA maps to Mexico are quite good and available free to members at any AAA office in the United States.

Newspapers/Magazines　The English-language newspaper *The News*, published in Mexico City, carries world news and commentaries, plus a calendar of the day's events including concerts, art shows, and plays. Newspaper kiosks in larger Mexican cities will carry a selection of English-language magazines.

Passports　See "Information & Entry Requirements," above, in this chapter.

Pets　Taking a pet into Mexico entails a lot of red tape. Consult the Mexican Government Tourist Office nearest you (see "Information & Entry Requirements," above, in this chapter).

Photography　All archaeological sites and many museums have restrictions on the use of personal cameras. At archaeological sites, visitors using their own video cameras are charged $8.50. A similar charge is permitted at all sites for still cameras; some sites charge it while others do not. It's courteous to ask permission before photographing anyone. In some areas, such as around San Cristóbal de las Casas, Chiapas, there are other restrictions on photographing people and villages. Such restrictions are noted in specific cities, towns, and sites.

Police　Generally, police in Mexico are to be suspected rather than trusted; however, you'll find many who are quite helpful with directions, even going so far as to lead you where you want to go.

Prices　The Mexican government now allows hotels and restaurants the right to set their own prices. Previously each entity was graded by the government and given an official price structure by which to operate. Now these businesses can charge what the traffic will bear.

When in doubt at a hotel, ask to see their rate sheet, which is required to be posted within view. If the hotel seems overpriced, leave and check with another hotel—this sends the message that the hotel is charging too much. Often desk clerks will quote a lower price if business is slack or if you suggest a slight reduction. In the past, quoted prices included the 15% IVA tax. Now a quoted price does not have to include tax, so be sure to ask before ordering a meal or taking a room. The deregulation of prices also affects taxis, tours, and car rentals.

Radio/TV　Many hotels now have antennas capable of bringing in U.S. TV channels. Large cities will have English-language stations and music.

Restrooms　The best bet in Mexico is to use restrooms in restaurants and hotel public areas. Always carry your own toilet paper and hand soap, neither of which is in great supply in Mexican restrooms. Public facilities, usually near the central market, vary in cleanliness and usually have an attendant who charges a few pesos for toilet use and a few squares of toilet paper. Pemex gas stations have improved the maintenance of their restrooms along major highways. No matter where you are, even if the toilet flushes with paper, there'll be a waste basket for paper disposal. Many people come from homes without plumbing and are not accustomed to toilets that will take paper and will throw paper on the floor rather than put it in the toilet; thus, you'll see the basket no matter what quality of place you are in. On the other hand, the water pressure in many establishments is so low that paper won't go down. There's often a sign telling you whether or not to flush paper.

Safety   Crime is more of a problem in Mexico than it used to be. Although you will feel physically safer in most Mexican cities than in comparable big cities at home, you must take some basic, sensible precautions.

First, remember that you're a tourist and an obvious target for crime. Beware of pickpockets on crowded buses, on the Metro, and in markets. Guard your possessions very carefully at all times; don't let packs or bags out of your sight even for a second. The big first-class bus lines will store your bag in the luggage compartment under the bus, and that's generally all right; however, keep your things with you on the less responsible village buses and some second-class buses on country routes.

Next, if you have a car, park it in an enclosed or guarded lot at night. Vans are a special mark. Don't depend on "major downtown streets" to protect your car—park it in a private lot with a guard or at least a fence.

Women must be careful in cities when walking alone, night or day. Busy streets are no problem, but empty streets (even if empty just for afternoon siesta) are lonely places.

Important warning: Agreeing to carry a package back to the States for an acquaintance or a stranger could land you in jail for years if it contains drugs or some other contraband. Never do it, no matter how friendly, honest, or sincere the request. Perpetrators of this illegal activity prey on innocent-looking single travelers and especially senior citizens.

Allowing anyone into your room whom you don't know could invite an instant robbery. This includes someone announcing him or herself (by phone or at your hotel room door) as room service bringing a "free" meal or drinks as compliments of the house—or anything you didn't order. When you open the door expectantly, robbers burst in. Always use caution before opening your door to anyone. When in doubt call hotel security or the reception desk.

Women travelers should see "For Women" in "Tips for Special Travelers," above, in this chapter for more specific safety information.

Seasons/Booking   Those planning to be in resorts like Puerto Vallarta, Manzanillo, San Blas, and Barra de Navidad on major holidays (Mexican as well as international) should make hotel reservations. Christmas, New Year's, and Easter week are the worst for crowding. If you discover it's a holiday when you're en route to the resort, plan to arrive early in the day.

Several readers have written to me about difficulties they encountered in making reservations by mail, and even by toll-free reservation numbers. Some report no answer or no record of their request (or deposit check) when they've arrived. Or they are quoted a higher price than the one they might have paid by just arriving without a reservation. I've experienced the same frustrations. Here's a suggestion: Only make reservations during high season if you are going to a beach area. During the off-season (unless it's a Mexican holiday), just arrive and find out what's available by calling when you arrive.

Sightseeing   As a general rule museums and archaeological sites in Mexico are free on Sunday and they are free at all times to those age 13 and below.

Taxes   There's a 15% tax on goods and services in the area covered by this book, and it's supposed to be included in the posted price.

Telephone/Fax   Telephone area codes are gradually being changed all over the country. The change may affect the area code and first digit or only the area code. Some cities are even adding exchanges and changing whole numbers. Often a personal or business telephone number will be changed without notification to the subscriber. Telephone courtesy messages announcing a phone number change are nonexistent in Mexico. You can try operator assistance for difficult-to-reach numbers, but often the phone company doesn't inform its operators of recent changes. People who have fax machines often turn them off when their offices are closed. Many fax numbers are also regular telephone numbers; you have to ask whoever answers your call for the fax tone (*Por favor darme el tono por fax*). Telephone etiquette in Mexico does not prompt the answerer to offer to take a message or to have someone return your call; you'll have to make these suggestions yourself. In addition, etiquette doesn't necessarily demand that a business answer its phone by saying its name; often you'll have to ask if you have the right place.

Public pay phones for local use are almost all Ladatel phones that use either the New Peso coins or a charge card or both. Ladatel cards are sold near pay phones, in hotel gift shops, and at newsstands, airports, and bus stations.

There are several ways to make **long-distance calls from Mexico.** The most expensive is through a hotel switchboard, which may add a service charge to your already expensive bill.

The least expensive way to make long-distance calls is to use the Ladatel phones found in bus stations, airports and downtown public areas of major cities, and touristic zones. You can use N10 peso coins or a Ladatel card purchased at many drugstores and restaurants throughout the country. To use a Ladatel phone, first have a Ladatel card or a good supply of N10 peso coins. Next, find out the approximate rate per minute for your call by picking up the handset and punching in the long-distance code (91 for Mexico, 95 for the United States and Canada, 98 for the rest of the world), plus the area or country and city codes of the number you are calling. The charge per minute in pesos will appear on the LCD display. For instance, if you press 95-212, you'll get the charge-per-minute for a call to Manhattan. Once you know the charge per minute, count your coins, make sure you have as many as you'll need, then dial your number and insert coins. The display will keep you informed of when more coins are needed. Instructions on Ladatel phones are in Spanish, English, and French.

The second costliest option, which is often faster and more convenient, is to use the *casetas de larga distancia* (long-distance telephone offices) found all over Mexico. Most bus stations and airports now have specially staffed rooms exclusively for making long-distance calls and sending faxes. Often they are efficient and inexpensive, providing the client with a computer printout of the time and charges.

To call the United States or Canada collect, dial 09 and tell the *operadora* that you want *una llamada por cobrar* (a collect call), *teléfono a teléfono* (station-to-station), or *persona a persona* (person-to-person). Collect calls are the least expensive of all, but sometimes caseta offices won't make them, so you'll have to pay on the spot.

To make a long-distance call from Mexico to another country from a *caseta* or Ladatel phone, first dial 95 for the United States and Canada, or 98 for anywhere else in the world. Then dial the area code and number you are calling. If you need the international (English-speaking) operator, dial 09.

If you have a **U.S. phone credit card** and wish to call the U.S., find a Ladatel phone. Dial 95/800/462-4242 (AT&T), 95/800/877-8000 (Sprint), or 95/800/674-7000 (MCI). Give the English-speaking operator your calling number and your phone card number.

To call **long distance** (abbreviated "lada") **within Mexico,** dial 91, the area code, then the number. Mexican area codes (*claves*) are listed in the front of the telephone directories and in the hotel listings for each area in this book. For Puerto Vallarta it's 322; for Manzanillo, 333. (As stated above, area codes are changing all over the country.)

You can save considerably by calling in off-peak periods. The cheapest times to call are daily after 11pm and before 8am and all day Saturday and Sunday. The most expensive times are Monday through Friday from 8am to 5pm.

To place a call to Mexico from your home country: dial the international service (011), then Mexico's country code (52), then the Mexican area code (for Guadalajara it's 3), then the local number.

The effects of reducing long-distance rates while hiking local rates means that hotels have begun to charge for local calls made from hotel-room phones. Until now these calls were free. So far, most of the inexpensive hotels listed in this book do not have the equipment to track calls made from individual rooms and, therefore, telephone-use charges are not added to the room bill. But hotels with more sophisticated telephone systems are charging 35¢ to 50¢ per call. To avoid checkout shock, ask at check-in if local calls are extra.

Time   Central standard time prevails throughout most of Mexico. The west-coast states of Sonora, Sinaloa, and parts of Nayarit are on mountain standard time. The state of Baja California Norte is on Pacific time, but Baja California Sur is on mountain time.

Tipping   Throw out the iron-clad 15% rule right away in budget restaurants south of the border, no matter what other travel literature may say. Do as the locals do: For meals costing under $3, leave the loose change; for meals costing from $4 to $5, leave 6% to 10%, depending on service. Above $5, you're into the 10% to 15% bracket. However, in above-average restaurants and exclusive places, the 15% rule holds. But don't tip on top of the 15% tax.

Bellhops and porters will expect about 25¢ to 50¢ per bag. You needn't tip taxi drivers unless they've rendered some special service such as carrying bags or trunks.

Tourist Offices   See "Information & Entry Requirements," above, in this chapter and also see each specific city chapter.

Villas/Condos   Renting a private villa or condominium home is a popular vacation alternative. The difference between the two, of course, is that villas are usually freestanding and condos may be part of a large or small complex. Often the villas are true private homes in exclusive neighborhoods and are rented out seasonally by their owners. Condominiums, on the other hand, may seem more like a hotel, although the secluded ones feel more exclusive. Either accommodation ordinarily comes with private kitchen and dining area, maid service, and pool. Often a full-time cook, maid, or gardener/chauffeur are on duty. I've seen prices as low as $80 a night to a high of $500 a night. Prices are seasonal, with the best deals between May and October. Of course, depending on the number of bedrooms, you can get a group together and share the cost. Two companies specializing in this type of vacation rental are: **Creative Leisure,** 951 Transport Way, Petaluma, CA 94954-1484 (☎ 707/778-1800 or 800/ 426-6367) and **Mexico Condo Reservations,** 5801 Soledad Mountain Rd., La Jolla, CA 92036 (☎ 619/275-4500, 800/262-4500 in the U.S., or 800/ 654-5543 in Canada; fax 619/456-1350). Each has brochures with photographs of properties.

Visas   See "Information & Entry Requirements," above, in this chapter.

Water   Most hotels have decanters or bottles of purified water in the rooms, and the better hotels have either purified water from regular taps or special taps marked AGUA PURIFICADA. In the resort areas, hoteliers are beginning to charge for in-room bottled water. Often, if the bottle of water in your room is an expensive imported brand such as Evian, the price for the bottle will be printed on it. Hotels with water-purifying systems frequently charge high prices for this bottled water to encourage guests to use the purified tap water instead. Virtually any hotel, restaurant, or bar will bring you purified water if you specifically request it, but you'll usually be charged for it. Bottled purified water is sold widely at drugstores and grocery stores.

4

Getting to Know
Puerto Vallarta

Despite its size—it's a city of a quarter-million people—Puerto Vallarta retains the charm of a gorgeous Mexican village. Neither its backdrop of tropical mountains hard up against the sea, nor its coves and beaches, nor its picturesque village—white buildings with red-tile roofs, streets of brick and cobblestone—have been eclipsed by all the high-rise hotels. More than any other coastal city, Puerto Vallarta balances the atmosphere of a sophisticated resort with the grace of colonial-era Mexico. This is the best place to take a vacation that combines elements of authentic inland Mexico with some of the country's best hotels, restaurants, shopping, and sports.

Once an agricultural village, Puerto Vallarta ceased to be a secret when a film version of Tennessee Williams's play *Night of the Iguana,* starring Richard Burton, Ava Gardner, and Deborah Kerr, was made here. Elizabeth Taylor came along for the filming, and the romance between Burton and Taylor became headline news, propelling Puerto Vallarta into the world's limelight. After the love affair, the tiny seaside village grew into a booming resort with a good highway and airport. Puerto Vallarta has captivated so many foreigners that a considerable colony of Americans and Canadians has taken up permanent residence here.

1 Orientation

ARRIVING & DEPARTING

BY PLANE   For a list of international carriers serving Mexico, see Chapter 3, "Planning a Trip to Mexico's Mid-Pacific Region." Local numbers of international carriers are as follows: **Alaska Airlines** ☎ 322/1-1350 or 322/1-1352; **American Airlines** ☎ 322/1-1972, 322/1-1799, or 322/1-1032; **Continental** ☎ 322/1-1025 or 322/1-1096; and **Delta** ☎ 322/1-1919 or 322/1-1032.

From other points in Mexico, **Aeroméxico** (☎ 322/4-2777 or 322/1-1055) flies from Aguascalientes, Guadalajara, La Paz, León, Mexico City, and Tijuana. **Mexicana** (☎ 322/4-8900, 322/1-1266, or 322/1-0243) has direct or nonstop flights from Guadalajara, Mazatlán, Los Cabos, and Mexico City.

The airport is close to the north end of town near the Marina Vallarta, only about 6 miles from downtown. You'll have a choice of transport from the airport. You can take the **Transportes**

❓ Did You Know?

- Puerto Vallarta is named after Ignacio Luis Vallarta (1830–93), a distinguished lawyer, diplomat, and governor of Jalisco.
- To be legally married in Mexico a civil ceremony is required; church ceremonies are optional.
- No monuments honor Hernan Cortés in Mexico.
- The poinsettia is named after Joel Poinsett, first U.S. Minister to Mexico in 1823.
- Elizabeth Taylor wasn't a member of the cast in *Night of the Iguana,* which was filmed in Puerto Vallarta and starred Ava Gardner and Richard Burton.
- Pirates once roamed the waters off the port of San Blas.

Terrestres minivan (colectivo) or taxis called **Aeromovil.** The cost of taxis or colectivo-minivans is based on the number of zones they have traversed. The closest zone to the airport is the Marina Vallarta; the next zone is anything before the Río Cuale; beyond the Río Cuale in the downtown area constitutes the next zone; and the farthest is the southern hotel zone. A shared ride in the minivan costs $3.50 to the Marina Vallarta or downtown before the Río Cuale and $6 beyond it. A private ride by Aeromovil taxi costs $8.50 to the Marina Vallarta, $10 to downtown before the river, $16.75 beyond the river, and $20 to the southern hotel zone. Be sure you know the area in which your hotel is located and double-check what you are charged—the drivers make mistakes.

Important note: Colectivos run only when they fill up after flights arrive, so avoid tarrying in the arrivals hall or you'll miss the colectivos. Between arrival times, only Aeromovil taxis operate. Another option is to walk about a block to the highway and hail a passing taxi; this option is cheaper than Aeromovil but more expensive than the colectivo. City buses also pass on the highway on their way to town and are convenient if you have only a small bag.

BY BUS   Elite, at the corner of Basillio Badillo and Constitución, has many first-class buses to Guadalajara. The deluxe-class **ETN** shares space with the first-class **Primera Plus** and the second-class **Servicios Coordinados** (☎ 322/2-6986) at Cárdenas 258, near Vallarta. ETN has several buses to Mexico City and Guadalajara. Primera Plus buses go to Guadalajara. Servicios Coordinados buses have the most frequent service to Manzanillo, Barra de Navidad, and Melaque/San Patricio.

The second-class **Autotransportes del Cihuatlan,** at the corner of Constitución and Madero (☎ 322/2-3436), has hourly buses to Manzanillo from 5am to 6pm (a 6-hour trip) and almost as frequent service to Melaque (a 4¹/₂-hour trip). **Transportes Norte de Sonora,** at Caranza 322, near Insurgentes (☎ 322/2-6666), has two daily buses via the short route to San Blas (a 3-hour trip); the route through Tepic takes at least 5 hours to reach San Blas. **Transportes del Pacífico,** Insurgentes 282 at Carranza (☎ 322/2-1015), has both first- and second-class service to Guadalajara traveling the short route (Vía Corta), which takes 6¹/₂ hours, and to Mexico City, which takes 14 hours. If you intend to head north, for instance to Mazatlán, you'll need to go to Tepic first and then catch a direct bus from there.

Puerto Vallarta Area

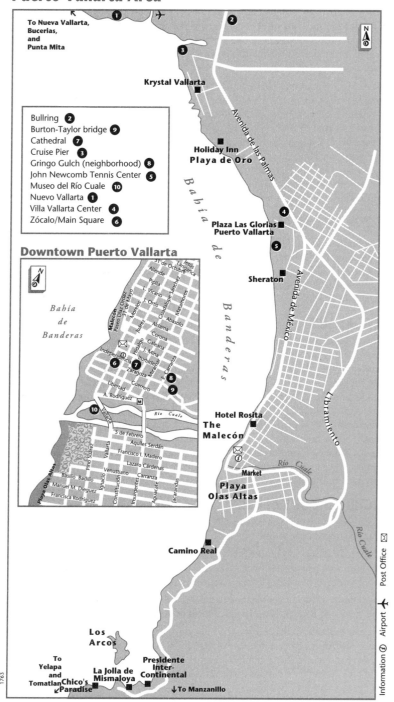

To Nueva Vallarta,
Bucerias,
and
Punta Mita

Krystal Vallarta

Avenida de las Palmas

Holiday Inn
Playa de Oro

Bahía

de

Banderas

Plaza Las Glorias
Puerto Vallarta

Sheraton

Avenida de México

Libramiento

Hotel Rosita
The
Malecón

Market

Playa
Olas Altas

Río Cuale

Camino Real

Los
Arcos

To
Yelapa
and
Tomatlan Chico's
Paradise

La Jolla de
Mismaloya

Presidente
Inter-
Continental

↓ To Manzanillo

N

Bullring ②
Burton-Taylor bridge ⑨
Cathedral ⑦
Cruise Pier ③
Gringo Gulch (neighborhood) ⑧
John Newcomb Tennis Center ⑤
Museo del Río Cuale ⑩
Nuevo Vallarta ①
Villa Vallarta Center ④
Zócalo/Main Square ⑥

Downtown Puerto Vallarta

N

Bahía
de
Banderas

31 de Octubre
Allende
Pipila
Vicario
J. Ortiz
Matamoros
Abasolo
Aldama
Corona
Galeana
I. Mina
Hidalgo
Iturbide
Zaragoza
Guerrero
Libertad
A. Rodriguez
Río Cuale
S de Febrero
Aquiles Serdán
Francisco I. Madero
Lazaro Cárdenas
Venustiano Carranza
Constitución
Insurgentes
Aguacate
Jacarandas
Basilio Badillo
Manuel M. Dieguez
Francisca Rodriguez

Malecón
Paseo Díaz Ordaz
Morelos
Juárez
Independencia

Playa Olas Altas

Pino Suárez
Vallarta
Ignacio
Matamoros
Guadalupe Sánchez
Jesús Langarica

Information ⓘ   Airport ✈   Post Office ⊠

1763

If you arrive by bus, you'll be south of the river on Madero, Insurgentes, or Constitución and close to all of the inner village hotels. Most of the bus "stations" are small offices or waiting rooms for the various lines. The city has planned a central bus station away from this downtown area for years, but so far, there has been no movement on this idea.

BY CAR The coastal Highway 200 is the only choice between Puerto Vallarta and Mazatlán to the north (a 6-hour trip) or between Puerto Vallarta and Manzanillo to the south (a 3¹/₂-hour trip). The 8-hour journey from Guadalajara through Tepic can be shortened to 6 hours by taking Highway 15A from Chapalilla to Compostela (this bypasses Tepic and saves 2 hours), then continuing south on Highway 200 to Puerto Vallarta. A new toll highway between Guadalajara and Puerto Vallarta was about to be constructed when I was last in the area and may be finished by the time you travel. With the new highway, the trip should take about 4 hours.

VISITOR INFORMATION

The **State Tourism Office,** at Juárez and Independencia (☎ 322/2-0242, 322/3-0844, or 322/3-0744; fax 322/2-0243), is in a corner of the white Presidencia Municipal building on the corner of the main square. This is also the office of the tourist police. It's open Monday through Friday from 9am to 9pm and Saturday from 9am to 1pm.

CITY LAYOUT

Puerto Vallarta has grown to the north and south of the original village along the beach. From the center of old town, nearly everything in the central village is within walking distance. The seaside promenade, or **malecón,** follows the rim of the bay from north to south, and the town stretches back into the hills a dozen blocks or more. North of the airport is **Nuevo Vallarta.** Coming into town from the airport, which is north of town, you'll pass the town pier (**Terminal Marítima**), the **Marina Vallarta** development, and the "**hotel zone,**" with many luxury hotels; downtown, the malecón is lined with shops and restaurants. **Avenida de las Palmas** (formerly called Carretera Aeropuerto or airport highway) is the beautifully landscaped, multilane thoroughfare leading from town to the northern hotel zone and airport.

NEIGHBORHOODS IN BRIEF

Listed below are the areas of Puerto Vallarta, beginning in the north and moving through town to the south:

Punta de Mita, at the northern end of the bay, has always been a beach hangout with palapa-style restaurants. A new resort is under construction, and the whole area was blocked off when I last visited; check before you go here.

Bucerías, a village of cobblestone streets, walled-in villas, and small hotels, is on the far side of Banderas Bay 19 miles north of the Puerto Vallarta airport.

Nuevo Vallarta, a planned resort, is just north of Marina Vallarta (see below), across the Ameca River in the state of Nayarit (about 8 miles north of downtown). It also has hotels, condominiums, a yacht marina, and a convention center. Nuevo Vallarta, however, is difficult to reach by public transportation, and taxis are expensive. It has several all-inclusive hotels, which are more suited for people who already know Puerto Vallarta or who are looking to simply relax in one place and aren't too interested in Puerto Vallarta's shopping and dining.

Marina Vallarta, a resort city within a city, lies at the northern edge of the hotel zone not far from the airport—you pass it on the right as you come into town from the airport. It boasts luxury hotels and condominium projects, a huge marina with 300 yacht slips, a golf course, restaurants and bars, an office park, and a shopping plaza. Between it and downtown is the area referred to as the "hotel zone."

Hotel Zone, located north of old town en route to the airport, contains many luxury hotels, including the Krystal, Sheraton and Fiesta Americana, along a fine strip of beach.

North of the Río Cuale, the original Puerto Vallarta, is the oldest part of town. The waterfront (malecón or Paseo Díaz Ordaz) is lined with shops and restaurants. The town plaza and church are here. Once you're in the center of town, you'll find nearly everything within walking distance.

Río Cuale, or Cuale river, divides north town from south town. In the middle of the river is an island that is now built up with numerous restaurants and shops.

South of the Río Cuale, once only beach, has become as built-up as the old town in the last decade. Although it's less sophisticated and more rustic than the original village, it's on its way to becoming prime tourist stomping grounds. Today, the best budget lodgings and some of the best restaurants and shops as well as the bus "stations" are located here.

Mismaloya Beach, about 6 miles from downtown, is where *Night of the Iguana* was filmed. You reach the beach by going south through the original village, winding into the hills, and passing through the southern "hotel zone," which includes the Presidente Inter-Continental and Camino Real hotels. At Mismaloya Beach, you'll find Jolla de Mismaloya Resort and Spa, and just beyond it is **Boca de Tomatlán,** which is the farthest tourist development to the south.

2 Getting Around

By Bus & Colectivo   City buses run from the airport into the Marina Vallarta, through the expensive hotel zone along Paseo Díaz Ordaz/malecón (the waterfront street), across the Río Cuale, and inland on Vallarta, looping back through the downtown hotel and restaurant districts on Insurgentes and several other downtown streets. These buses will serve just about all your transportation needs frequently and inexpensively. Buses run generally from 6am to 11pm.

The no. 02 **minivan** bus (colectivo) goes south every 10 to 15 minutes to Mismaloya Beach from Plaza Lázaro Cárdenas, a few blocks south of the river at Cárdenas and Suárez. Check with the driver to make sure this is your bus because another no. 02 goes farther to Boca de Tomatlán (a fishing village) and may not stop at Mismaloya.

To get to the northern hotel strip from old Puerto Vallarta, take the "Ixtapa" or "Aeropuerto" bus. These same buses may also post the names of hotels they pass such as Krystal, Fiesta Americana, Sheraton, and others. City buses now also pass into and through the Marina Vallarta area, where they were once prohibited.

By Boat   The town pier (**muelle**), also called **Terminal Marítima,** is where you catch pleasure boats to Yelapa, Las Animas, and Quimixto and where you depart for fishing excursions. It is located north of town near the airport and a convenient, inexpensive bus ride from town. Just take any bus marked "Ixtapa" and tell the driver to let you off at the Terminal Marítima (*ter-MEEN-ahl mah-REE-tee-mah*).

By Taxi   Most trips from downtown to the northern hotel strip and Marina Vallarta cost between $4 and $5; to or from Mismaloya Beach to the south costs $15. With such good bus service, however, there's little reason to use taxis.

FAST FACTS: Puerto Vallarta

American Express   The local office is located in the village at Morelos 660, at the corner of Abasolo (☎ 322/3-2995 or 91-800/0-0555 toll free in Mexico). It's open Monday through Friday from 9am to 6pm and Saturday from 9am to 1pm.

Area Code   The telephone area code is 322.

Business Hours   In general, businesses open around 9 or 10am. Many shops close between 2 and 4 or 5pm and reopen until 8, 9, or 10pm.

Climate   It's hot all year. Humidity rises dramatically during the summer rainy season between May and October. Rains come almost every afternoon in June and July and often continue through evening.

Currency Exchange   Bancomer has a branch on Juárez at the corner of Mina. It's open from 9am to 1:30pm; foreign currency can be exchanged only from 9:30am to noon.

Laundry   Laundries abound in old Puerto Vallarta, both north and south of the river. The Lavandería Nelly, on Guerrero near Matamoros, will wash and dry a load of clothes for about $4. It's usually open Monday through Friday from 9am to 1:30pm and 4 to 8pm, and Saturday from 9am to 1:30pm.

Pharmacy   The CMQ Farmacia, Badillo 365 (☎ 322/2-1330), is open 24 hours. It's south of the river between Insurgentes and Aguacate.

Post Office   The post office (correo) is on Mina between Juárez and Morelos. It's open Monday through Friday from 9am to 7:30pm, Saturday from 9 am to 1pm, and Sunday from 9am to noon.

U.S. Consular Agency   The office is at Miramar and Libertad, on the second floor of Parian del Puente 12A, just north of the river bridge near the market (☎ 322/2-0069, 24 hours a day for emergencies). It's open Monday through Friday from 9am to 1pm.

5

Where to Stay & Dine in Puerto Vallarta

1 Accommodations

Most of the bargain hotels are in town, south of the Río Cuale. There are more expensive hotels in the Hotel Zone, Marina Vallarta, and south to Mismaloya. For the best rates overall, travel during May, August, and September through November—the slowest months of the off-season, which runs from post-Easter to mid-December. Always ask about discounted rates or special packages in those months, even at budget hotels. Prices go up anywhere from 25% to 50% from mid-December through Easter week, when all the best rooms are generally booked.

The hotel and restaurant listings in this chapter begin in Marina Vallarta, an exclusive development immediately south of the airport and Puerto Vallarta's developed area. The list ends with hotels that are south of downtown at Mismaloya, the farthest development to the south.

MARINA VALLARTA

The Marina Vallarta, the northern extension of the "Hotel Zone," is located just before the airport. The hotels below are built around the new 400-slip marina and 18-hole golf course designed by Joe Finger. All except the Bel-Air Resort are on the beach.

Bel-Air Resort Puerto Vallarta

Pelicanos 311, Marina Vallarta, Puerto Vallarta, Jal. 48300. ☎ **322/1-0800** or 800/457-7676 in the U.S. and Canada, 91-800/3-2832 toll free in Mexico. Fax 322/1-0801. 67 suites and villas. A/C TV TEL. High season $170–$240 single or double suite; $280–$400 villa. Low season $125–$225 single or double suite; $225–$325 villa.

This stylish inn is located in the heart of the Marina Vallarta development squarely between the first and 18th holes of the golf course. Few Mexican hotels can claim such masterful use of elegant Mexican furniture; many of the gorgeous pieces are replicas of furniture found in the Museo Alfenique in Puebla—a kind of Mexican Chippendale. The suites combine those designs with sculpted faces prepared especially for the hotel by the renowned Mexican sculptor Sergio Bustamante. Some rooms have balconies and whirlpools, while others are more homelike with several bedrooms, living and dining room, and a private pool.

Dining/Entertainment: The multilevel, excellent Restaurant El Candil overlooks the golf course, wide outdoor patio, and pool; it is open from 7am to 11pm. Live harp or piano music accompanies all meals. Another restaurant/bar by the pool serves snacks during the day. The terrace bar features live nightly entertainment.

Services: Laundry, room service, car rental, concierge, transportation to the beach. Guests receive champagne and fresh juice on arrival, have separate check-in and access to the hotel's fax and secretarial services.

Facilities: Large gorgeous pool facing the golf course; golf privileges at the Marina Vallarta Golf Course at reduced rates with pick up and drop off at the hotel; 2 tennis courts; 46 private pools; a fitness center at no cost to guests. A fully staffed private beach club will open in 1995 with a restaurant and water sports.

Marriott Casamagna

Marina Vallarta, Puerto Vallarta, Jal. ☎ **322/1-0004** or 800/228-9290 in the U.S. 433 rms and suites (all with bath). A/C MINIBAR TV TEL. High season $190 single or double sunset view; $156 single or double ocean view; $330–$480 suite. Ask about low-season specials, which may include breakfast.

You'll first be impressed with the splendid openness of this grand hotel, which debuted in 1990; the enormous lobby soars, and baronial hallways lead to the rooms and beach. From the lobby en route to the beach, you cross a small artificial pond. Rooms are accented in pale sienna and pale ocher and all have ocean views and balconies, hairdryers, ironing boards and irons, and in-room safety-deposit boxes. Rooms with king-size beds have a couch; those with two double beds have an easy chair and game table.

Dining/Entertainment: Two indoor restaurants serve all three meals; one restaurant open evenings features Japanese cuisine. The poolside restaurant is open for breakfast and lunch. A lobby lounge opens at 11am, and '60s Disco Bar is open evenings.

Services: Laundry, room service, travel agency, car rental, beauty salon, barber shop, gift shop, summer children's program (ages 5 to 12) at extra cost, 14 security cameras.

Facilities: Huge oceanside pool, coed gym, five tennis courts (three lighted for night play), volleyball court.

HOTEL ZONE

The main street that comes from town and fronts the Hotel Zone has been re-named Paseo de las Palmas, but locals may still refer to it as Avenida de las Garzas or the airport road. This is handy information to keep in mind when reading or hearing addresses.

Fiesta Americana Puerto Vallarta

Av. de las Palmas s/n, Puerto Vallarta, Jal. 48300. ☎ **322/4-2010** or 800/223-2332 in the U.S. Fax 322/2-2010. 363 rms and suites. A/C MINIBAR TV TEL. High season $230–$300 single or double superior or deluxe room. Low season $115–$155 single or double superior or deluxe room. Free parking.

The Fiesta Americana's enormous thatched palapa lobby is a landmark along hotel row. With lots of plants, splashing fountains, breezes, and sitting areas, the spacious lobby has a casual, tropical feel. The nine-story building embraces a large plaza with a pool facing the beach. Marble-trimmed rooms in neutral tones with pastel accents come with pretty carved headboards and comfortable furniture. All have private balconies with sea views.

Dining/Entertainment: There are two casual and one fine-dining restaurant. During high season, there's live music nightly in the lobby bar. Friday, López is the popular disco, open from 10:30pm to 3am.

Services: Laundry, room service, travel agency, beauty shop, in-room hairdryers.

Facilities: Pool, with pool activities; children's entertainment in season; tennis privileges at the Fiesta Americana Villa Vallarta, which also has a health club with sauna and massage.

✪ Krystal Vallarta

Av. de las Palmas s/n, Puerto Vallarta, Jal. 48300. ☎ **322/4-1041** or 800/231-9860 in the U.S. and Canada. Fax 322/4-0150 or 322/4-0222. 368 rms, suites, and villas. A/C MINIBAR TV TEL. High season $180 deluxe room or villa single or double; $210–$460 single or double suite. Low season $130–$190 deluxe room or villa single or double; $170–$320 single or double suite.

Built to resemble a Mexican village with cobblestone streets, this completely self-contained resort oasis is spread out over 37 plant- and fountain-filled acres on a prime beachfront location. Interwoven in this setting are the accommodations in one- and two-story buildings. Although the resort is large, it's very quiet, and there is still a sense of seclusion, with many shaded interior walkways linking the various pool areas and restaurants.

Given the resort's seven restaurants and numerous bars, you can dine and drink without ever leaving the place, should that be your choice. The four varieties of accommodations include 38 three-bedroom villas with private pools, 22 suites with spacious living rooms, 48 junior suites, and 251 deluxe rooms. Trios of villas share a private pool. All come with tile floors, area rugs, in-room security boxes, and remote-control TV with cable channels. Some have a patio or balcony. Electric carts take guests to and from their rooms—depending on where your room is, it can be a long walk within the grounds. The hotel is not far from the main pier and airport. City buses stop right out front.

Dining/Entertainment: Among the hotel's seven restaurants is Bogart's, one of the finest places in Puerto Vallarta, open evenings, and Kamakura, an excellent Japanese restaurant also open evenings; there is also a restaurant featuring steaks. Among the six bars, the lobby bar has live music nightly. For evening entertainment, there's Cristine's disco, open from 10:30pm to 3am; Le Café in the lobby serves special coffees, tea, and pastries, and a Mexican Fiesta takes place every Tuesday and Saturday.

Services: Laundry, room service, travel agency, shops, babysitting with 12 hours' advance notice, wedding arrangements with advance notice, car rental.

Facilities: Olympic-size pool, 2 free-form pools, 38 private pools, 2 tennis courts, racquetball court.

Hacienda Buenaventura

Paseo de la Palma, Apdo. Postal 95-B, Puerto Vallarta, Jal. 48310. ☎ **322/4-6667** or 800/307-1847 in the U.S. Fax 322/4-6400. 155 rms. A/C TEL. High season $45–$57 single, $57–$69 double. Low season $29–$37 single, $36–$44 double. In low season ask about a free fourth night.

Impressions

There are a number of apartments for rent in town Puerto Vallarta. They range in price from $125 to $150 per month, including maid, utilities, etc.
—James Norman, *Terry's Guide To Mexico*, 1965

You can stay right on the hotel strip at this congenial hotel and skip the high prices of hotel row. Rooms, built around tropical gardens that include a functioning aqueduct, have soft colors, stucco walls, and alcove-type windows. The far end of the gigantic pool encircles a large palapa-roofed swim-up bar, and the other end fronts the restaurant La Cascada. Although the Hacienda has no beachfront of its own, guests are provided passes for use of the beach and facilities next door at the luxury Krystal Vallarta (see above).

NORTH OF THE RÍO CUALE

This is the real center of town, where the market, principal plazas, church, and town hall all lie. Restaurants and beaches are all close at hand.

MODERATE

Hotel Buenaventura

Av. Mexico 1301, Puerto Vallarta, Jal. 48350. ☎ **322/2-3737** or 800/223-6764 in the U.S. Fax 322/2-3546. 210 rms. A/C TEL. High season $60 single, $80 double. Low season $40 single, $50 double.

This hotel is located on the beach within walking distance of all the village shops and restaurants. The giant wood roof of the hotel lobby and restaurant sets the tone for the breezy, lush, junglelike interior filled with *equipale* leather furniture. Somewhat off the beaten tourist track, the Buenaventura holds its place in the market with appealing prices, comfort, and its beautiful beachfront. The attractive rooms have beam-and-brick ceilings and tiled floors, and some have balconies. Only fourth-floor rooms have remote-control color TV with U.S. channels; these rooms cost $5 extra. There's also a swimming pool next to the beach. The hotel is about six blocks north of the malecón between Nicaragua and San Salvador.

✪ Los Cuatro Vientos

Matamoros 520, Puerto Vallarta, Jal. 48350. ☎ **322/2-0161.** Fax 322/2-2831. 13 rms (all with bath). FAN. $40 single or double. Rates include continental breakfast. Low-season discounts.

A quiet, cozy, secluded inn set on a hillside overlooking Banderas Bay, Los Cuatro Vientos features rooms built around a small central patio and pool. A flight of stairs takes you to the second-floor patio, pool, and the cozy Chez Elena restaurant, which is open in the evenings. The cheerful and spotless rooms have small tiled baths, brick ceilings, red-tile floors, and glass-louvered windows facing outdoors. Each is decorated with simple Mexican furnishings and accented with local crafts. The whole rooftop, which offers a panoramic view of the city, is great for sunning, and it's the best place in the city for drinks at sunset. Continental breakfast is served on the terrace for guests only from 8 to 10:30am.

The friendly owner, Gloria Whiting, and the equally helpful manager, Lola Bravo, can offer many suggestions for sightseeing. The hotel is affiliated with the University of Guadalajara's language school in Puerto Vallarta and offers special packages for students attending the school. Also ask about the week-long Women's Getaway offered several times a year. The program includes cultural discussions, exercise classes, hikes, some meals and optional massages, facials, manicures, and pedicures.

To find the hotel from the central plaza, walk two blocks east on Iturbide; turn left at Matamoros and walk up Matamoros (the hill gets very steep) for three blocks. The hotel is on the right just before the corner of Corona.

INEXPENSIVE

Hotel Río

Morelos 170 (Apdo. Postal 23), Puerto Vallarta, Jal. 48300. ☎ **322/2-0366.** Fax 322/2-3235. 46 rms (all with bath). FAN. High season $16 single, $19 double. Low-season discounts.

This three-story hotel is a block north of the Río Cuale and about a block in from the beach. Its shady courtyard surrounds a tiny kidney-shaped pool. The very clean rooms come with balconies, but door locks are flimsy. Management is lax, and hotel services such as providing rooms with towels are sometimes lacking. Rooms facing Morelos will be very noisy. Try this hotel if everything else is full. It's four blocks south of the central plaza at the corner of A. Rodriguez, just before the bridge.

Hotel Rosita

Ordaz 90. (Apdo. Postal 32), Puerto Vallarta, Jal. 48300. ☎ and fax **322/2-1033.** 103 rms, 9 suites. FAN. $20–$22 single or double with A/C or poolside; $21–$23 single suite; $23–$26 double suite. Discounts Sept, Nov, May, June.

Vacationers have been flocking to the Rosita for decades, both for its ideal location on the beach and for its prices. Rooms, with dated but coordinated furnishings, are well kept. Some are carpeted, and some have tile floors. Those with air-conditioning are on the street side. A palm-shaded pool and restaurant open for all meals are by the beach. The hotel is nine blocks north of the main plaza at the corner of Diaz Ordaz and 31 de Octubre, opposite McDonald's.

SOUTH OF THE RÍO CUALE
MODERATE

Hotel Fontana del Mar

Dieguez 171, Puerto Vallarta, Jal. 48380. ☎ **322/2-0583**, 322/2-0712, or 800/221-6509 in the U.S. Fax 322/2-2418. 27 rms, 15 suites (all with bath). A/C MINIBAR TV TEL. High season $29 single, $38 double. $5–$7 more for suite. Low season $26 single, $34 double.

One of the best budget hotels in the area, this place is on a quiet street in downtown Vallarta, only two blocks from the Playa del Sol. The inviting decor includes curly white ironwork and royal-blue trim. The clean, comfortable rooms overlook the plant-filled courtyard with more frilly iron trim. Rooms have showers or bathtubs, and the suites come with balconies or kitchenettes. Guests can use the small rooftop pool or the pool and beach-club facilities at the Hotel Playa Los Arcos, a block away. The Fontana del Mar is eight blocks south of the Vallarta Bridge, near the corner of Olas Altas.

Playa Los Arcos

Olas Altas 390, Puerto Vallarta, Jal. 48380. ☎ **322/2-1583** or 800/648-2403 in the U.S. Fax 322/2-2418. 135 rms, 13 suites. A/C TEL. Dec 18–Easter $60–$75 single, $70–$85 double; $95–$110 suite. Ask about further discounts in June and Sept–Oct.

Conveniently located downtown and on the beach, this popular four-story hotel is shaped like a U facing the ocean, with a swimming pool in the courtyard. It attracts its fair share of groups and package vacationers, so there are almost always a lot of people milling about. Rooms with private balconies overlook the pool, while the 10 suites have ocean views and kitchenettes. The standard rooms are small but pleasantly decorated with pink floral spreads and carved wooden furniture painted pale pink, including two double beds, a dresser, a table, and two chairs. On the premises there are tennis courts, a restaurant, coffee shop, and beachside bar with occasional live entertainment. The hotel is seven blocks south of the river. To find it, walk five blocks south of the river on Vallarta, then right on Badillo two blocks, then left on Olas Atlas.

Hotel Molino de Agua

Vallarta 130 (Apdo. Postal 54), Puerto Vallarta, Jal. 48380. ☎ **322/2-1907,** 322/2-1957, or 800/826-9408 in the U.S., 800/423-5512 in California. Fax 322/2-6056. 12 rms, 4 suites, 25 cabins (all with bath). A/C. High season $65–$100 single or double. Low season $50–$100 single or double. Free protected parking.

This complex of cabins and small buildings reached by winding walkways is nestled into lush tropical gardens beside the river and sea; it's half a block south of the river on Vallarta at Serdán. Although the hotel is on a main street and centrally located, it's a completely tranquil oasis with big trees and open space. Some units are individual bungalows with private patios, and there's a small three-story building near the beach. Its amenities include a whirlpool beside the pool and a restaurant/bar, the Aquarena, as well as its offshoot, the Lion's Court, in the garden. The hotel is on the right immediately after you cross the Vallarta Bridge going south.

INEXPENSIVE

Hotel Azteca

Madero 473, Puerto Vallarta, Jal. 48300. ☎ **322/2-2750.** 46 rms (all with bath). FAN. $7 single, $8 double. Discounts for stays of a week or more.

This four-story (no elevator) hotel is one of the best buys in town. Many wintering northerners return to this hotel year after year. Though the rooms are very plain and basically furnished with a bed and crude table and chairs, the Villa Señor family keeps the place clean, well maintained, and safe. No visitors are allowed after 10:30pm. Rooms face the interior walkway and courtyard and are brighter than most that have this architectural arrangement. The hotel is $5^{1}/_{2}$ blocks west of the beach between Jacarandas and Naranjo.

Hotel Yasmin

Badillo 168, Puerto Vallarta, Jal. 48380. ☎ **322/2-0087.** 27 rms (all with bath). FAN. $12 single, $14 double.

The Yasmin is a great budget choice located only about a block from the beach. The hotel is a neat, hidden retreat with three stories of rooms (no elevator) built around a shady garden courtyard. The freshly painted rooms are clean and come with tile floors, firm beds with nice plaid bedspreads, small baths, and full-length mirrors. The popular Café de Olla is just off the reception/patio area. Noise created by restaurant patrons and the delightful strolling musicians catering to them lasts until about 11pm. The hotel is five blocks south of the river on Vallarta between Olas Altas and Pino Suárez.

Posada Río Cuale

Serdán 242 (Apdo. Postal 146), Puerto Vallarta, Jal. 48380. ☎ **322/2-0450** or 322/2-0914. 21 rms (all with bath). A/C. High season $23 single, $27 double. Low season $18 single, $23 double. Parking in front on the street.

This delightful two-story hotel is located at one of the town's busiest intersections. Its large rooms have arched brick windows and wooden shutters; the quietest rooms are away from Calle Vallarta. At night, the pool becomes a lighted fountain, and the courtyard around it is part of the popular Restaurant Gourmet, which has mariachi music on Friday, Saturday, and Sunday from 7 to 11pm during high season. The hotel is one block south of the Vallarta Bridge at the corner of Aquiles Serdan.

SOUTH TO MISMALOYA
EXPENSIVE

Camino Real

Hwy. 200 south to Mismaloya, km 3.2. ☎ **322/21-5000** or 800/722-6466 in the U.S. 337 rms and suites. A/C MINIBAR TV TEL. Low season $143–$170 single or double standard and superior rooms; $215–240 single or double Camino Real Club.

Not so long ago the Camino Real was the most remote hotel or establishment of any kind, 2¹/₂ miles south of town. Though it has neighbors now, further down the highway, it's still set apart with a lush mountain backdrop and has retained the exclusivity that made it popular since its beginning. The hotel is actually two buildings: the 250-room main hotel that curves gently with the shape of the Playa Las Estacas and the new 11-story, 87-room Camino Real Club, also on the beach. Rooms in the main building are large; some have sliding doors facing the bay, and others have balconies. Camino Real Club rooms from the sixth floor up have balconies with whirlpool spas. The top floor is divided among six two-bedroom Fiesta Suites with whirlpool spas on the balcony, and each has a private swimming pool. All rooms are accented with the vibrant colors of Mexico and come with hairdryers, remote-control TV (with U.S. channels), and in-room safe-deposit boxes. Camino Real Club rooms have robes besides other amenities mentioned below.

Dining/Entertainment: Three restaurants serving Mexican, French, seafood, and international food are open for all meals; there's also a beachside eatery. Live bands frequently entertain evenings in the lobby bar with dancing on weekends.

Services: Laundry; room service; travel agency; car rental; children's program December, June, July, and August.

Facilities: Two swimming pools; two lighted tennis courts; health club with weights, sauna, steam room, and weekday aerobic classes; boutiques, and convenience store. Camino Real Club guests enjoy separate check-in and concierge, daily complimentary continental breakfast, and evening cocktails and hors d'oeuvres.

Presidente Inter-Continental

Hwy. 200, km 8.5 (Apdo. Postal 448), Puerto Vallarta, Jal. 48300. ☎ **322/8-0507** or 800/ 327-0200. Fax 322/8-0116. 120 suites. A/C MINIBAR TV TEL. High season $195–$220 single or double; $235–$825 single or double suite. Low season $185–$210 single or double; $270– $925 single or double suite.

On a beautiful beach five miles south of town, this 10-story white hotel (formerly the Hyatt Coral Grand) has window boxes spilling over with vines and bougainvillea. The open-air lobby is accessed from a bridge that connects it to the street four stories above the beach. There's a serene, intimate ambiance here, with spacious suites done in white with pastel accents, tasteful art, comfortable furniture, and queen or double beds. Each suite has a living room with a couch that makes into a bed, and small balconies provide a view of the ocean. Deluxe suites have whirlpool baths, king-size beds, and robes. Master suites have two bedrooms and a whirlpool. There are two handicap-equipped rooms on the first floor and wheelchair access to the pool.

Dining/Entertainment: There are two indoor restaurants, a swim-up bar that's open for lunch, and a poolside bar open daylight hours. There's often live entertainment in the lobby bar during evening hours.

Services: Laundry, room service, travel agency, concierge, baby-sitting.

Facilities: One large pool; children's pool; one tennis court lit at night; table tennis and pool tables, plus other board games; children's game room; water sports; gym with massage service and steam baths.

2 Dining

South of the river is the best area in Puerto Vallarta for finding restaurants ranging from inexpensive to expensive. One cluster centers around the street **Olas Altas,** very close to the beach; another edges **Vallarta.** The hottest new food street is **Badillo,** which is fast becoming the south side's unofficial "restaurant row." Restaurants fronting the malecón and those on the beach are more expensive and not necessarily better in quality than others in less prominent locations.

Fine dining in Puerto Vallarta can be just as exquisite but much less expensive than the equivalent in the United States. You can expect some very fine dining in Puerto Vallarta, which is fast becoming known for the high quality and variety of its restaurants.

HOTEL ZONE
VERY EXPENSIVE

Bogart's
Krystal Vallarta Hotel, Av. de las Garzas s/n. ☎ **322/4-0202.** Full meal $35–$50. Daily 6pm–midnight. CONTINENTAL/ECLECTIC.

Just about everyone agrees that dining at Bogart's is a fantasy experience, though they admit the food is not what it once was. Even with that drawback, locals still recommend this place for a big splurge or a special occasion. Pointed Moorish arches, murmuring fountains, a silky tent ceiling, and high-backed peacock chairs create the mysterious mood of Casablanca in this softly lighted, sumptuous restaurant. A pianist plays in the background while waiters out of *Arabian Nights* serve such delicacies as Persian crêpes (sour cream, cheese, and caviar), escargots, sorbet between courses, and flambéed Shrimp Krystal. Bogart's, north of town near the main pier, is located at the front of the Krystal Hotel property, facing the main boulevard; take the "Muelle" bus.

NORTH OF THE RÍO CUALE
EXPENSIVE

Café des Artistes
Guadalupe Sánchez 740. ☎ **322/2-3228.** Reservations recommended. Main courses $12–$20. Daily 7–11pm. INTERNATIONAL.

Though it's slightly off the beaten path, you won't want to miss this charming, sophisticated indoor/outdoor eatery. It's worth a trip just to read the menu. Among the appetizers you'll find crêpes, quiche, chilled cream of prawns, and pumpkin soup. The extensive seafood menu includes sautéed shrimp with mushroom and chile guajillo salsa served with pasta. There's an interesting spring chicken flambé, stuffed with prunes and dates. The cafe is located at the corner of Vicario three blocks east of the malecón.

Chef Roger

A. Rodriguez 267, ☎ **322/2-5900.** Reservations recommended. Main courses $7–$15. Daily 6:30–11pm. NOUVELLE MEXICAN/SWISS.

This sophisticated little dinner-only restaurant has developed quite a following since it opened in 1989. Its success is partly attributable to owner Roger Dreir's prior reputation as a caterer in the city. A European-trained chef, Roger has combined elements of the cuisines of Europe, the American Southwest, and Mexico in his unique fare. Guests enjoy their meals on the patio or in one of the adjoining half open-air dining rooms. There are five or six daily specials that take advantage of what's fresh; these might include steaks and lobster and such interesting combinations as pasta with crêpes huitlacoche. The restaurant is catercorner from the craft market between Matamoros and Hidalgo.

INEXPENSIVE

✪ Café San Cristóbal

Corona 172. ☎ **322/3-2551.** Coffee $1–$2; pastries 65¢–$1.25; sandwiches $3; kilo of fresh-ground coffee $7. Daily 8am–9pm. COFFEE/PASTRIES/SANDWICHES.

This comfortable cafe is a great spot for coffee, pastries, sandwiches, and conversation. The brew, which features Mexican coffees from the states of Veracruz, Nayarit, and Chiapas, is served most any way imaginable—over ice, hot, or with milk. You can also get latte, cappuccino, or espresso, and there's Mexican chocolate as well. If you want food and drink to accompany your java, there are fresh cheese and pâté, quiche, bread, cheese and fruit plates, lemonade, and liquados. The cream cheese, cucumber, tomato, and bean sprout sandwich on fresh homemade bread is delicious. Bags of whole or ground coffee are sold by the half or full kilo. The cafe is three blocks north of the main plaza between Morelos and Juárez.

Jugos y Café Malibú

Morelos at Guerrero. ☎ **322/2-2944.** Breakfast $1.50–$2.50; juice $1.25–$1.50; burgers and sandwiches $1.35–$2. Daily 7am–11pm. JUICE DRINKS/SANDWICHES.

More than just a juice and coffee stand, this neat corner restaurant has been serving downtowners for years. The tables are ringed with stools, and the menu is listed on the wall over the kitchen and large bins of colorful fruit. Blended juice drinks come in an incredible variety of vegetable and fruit flavors, and drinks with fruit can be made with either purified water or milk. Coffee is limited to American, cappuccino, or espresso. There's a small assortment of sandwiches, hamburgers, hotcakes, and quesadillas. From the central plaza, walk two blocks south on Morelos; it's on the right at the corner of Guerrero.

✪ La Placita

Mina 452. ☎ **322/2-1194.** Breakfast $1.50; *comida corrida* $2.50. Daily 8am–noon and 1–5pm. MEXICAN HOME COOKING.

Local residents clued me in to this great peso saver in the heart of the village. Family operated, it's crisp and clean with lavender walls and cloth-covered tables. The comida corrida comes with soup, your choice of three entrées such as pork in adobo sauce, barbecue ribs, or perhaps chicken in poblano chile, fruit-flavored purified water, and dessert. It's two blocks north of the main plaza between Juárez and Hidalgo.

✪ Papaya 3

Abasolo 169. ☎ **322/2-0303.** Breakfast $2–$2.75; soups, salads, and sandwiches $2.50–$3.50; main courses $3.50–$5.35. Mon–Sat 8am–10pm. VEGETARIAN.

Opened in 1991, this fine, small restaurant serves innovative and delicious meals. Juice and fruit drinks include the "Cancún"—a blend of guayaba, coconut, melon milk, or rompope. Yogurt shakes come with fruit. Try the Shanghai salad—a large plate of steamed vegetables. Pastas are topped with imaginative sauces, and many entrées feature chicken or fish. Papaya 3 is north of the river between Morelos and Juárez.

Pietro Fonda Italiana

Zaragoza 245 at Hidalgo. ☎ **322/2-3233.** Main courses $4.75–$6.75; 12-inch pizzas $4.75–$6. Daily noon–midnight. ITALIAN.

One of the downtown mainstays, this little restaurant serves dependably good Italian food. Italian music and swags of braided garlic on the wall above a big brick oven set the mood for the fare, which includes ravioli, cannelloni, lasagne, calzone, spaghetti, and, of course, pizza. Daily specials might include seafood spaghetti and shrimp pizza. The pasta is homemade, as are the delicious soft breadsticks that arrive piping hot at your table. This place is across the street and just south of the cathedral.

Rito's Baci

Domínguez 181. ☎ **322/2-6448.** Pasta $3–$5; salads and sandwiches $1.50–$4; pizza $8–$9. Daily 1pm–midnight. ITALIAN.

Rito Calzado's grandfather emigrated from Italy, so the tradition of Italian food come naturally to this small, welcoming restaurant. Two popular pastas are the lasagne and spaghetti with oil and garlic. Pizza lovers favor the Margherite, which mingles tomato, garlic, and oregano; and the Horacio, which combines tomatoes, oregano, and basil. Sandwiches come hot or cold. If you're really hungry, order the Italian sausage sandwich, which must be consumed with two hands. Rito's offers free home or hotel delivery. It's six blocks north of the main plaza between Morelos and Juárez.

Tutifruti

Morelos 552. ☎ **322/2-1068.** Breakfast $2.75–$3.25; cinnamon coffee 65¢; fresh juices or liquados $1.35–$1.75; sandwiches $1.50–$2.50. Mon–Sat 8am–10pm. VEGETARIAN/AMERICAN.

This small, clean corner eatery is a good spot for a quick snack on stools that pull up to three narrow counters. The menu includes hot or cold sandwiches and hamburgers with all the trimmings, as well as fruit plates and yogurt. Eat at the counter or take your meal out. To get here from the main plaza, walk four blocks north on Morelos; it's on the right corner at Corona.

SOUTH OF THE RÍO CUALE

The most condensed concentration of restaurants in all price ranges lies south of the river. Basilio Badillo is known as "restaurant row" for its cluster of good restaurants. Some restaurants now close during low season. You can find inexpensive fruit, vegetables, and picnic fixings at the **municipal market** beside the Río Cuale where Libertad and Rodríguez meet. The **Supermercado Gutiérrez Ruiz,** Serdán and Constitución, has an especially large bakery and cold cut and cheese selection, as does **Gigante** on the northern hotel strip fronting Avenida de las Palmas.

EXPENSIVE

Le Bistro Jazz Café

Río Cuale. ☎ **322/2-0283.** Breakfast $3–$7.50; main courses $6–$9; wine and mixed drinks $2.50–$7. Mon–Sat 9am–11pm. INTERNATIONAL.

Of all Puerto Vallarta's restaurants, this one offers the best combination of good food, a serene and sophisticated environment, attentive service, and entertainment. The black-and-white dining area spreads out on decks overlooking the river. The cozy bar with couches and sitting areas is also outdoors. At breakfast, the appealing menu includes omelets, crêpes, and eggs Benedict. Lunch, light and casual, features sandwiches as well as chicken and steak. The evening menu has both Mexican and international offerings, mostly fish, seafood, and steaks. Many varieties of coffee are available all day. A great collection of recorded jazz plays in the background. The bistro is below the Insurgentes bridge on the left if you're arriving from the main plaza.

✪ Restaurant Argentino Los Pibes

Badillo 261. ☎ **322/2-1507.** Grilled meat $10–$15; pasta $5–$6. Daily 6pm–midnight. ARGENTINIAN GRILLED MEAT.

The food is so authentic and delicious here you may later dream of your meal, and you certainly won't forget it. Argentinean Cristina Juhas, along with her *pibes* (kids)—daughter Vanina and son Nicolás, the chef—opened this restaurant in 1994. You select your meat cut from a tray of fresh meat (portions are huge). While it's being prepared, you can try one of the wonderful empanadas filled with meat, corn, or ham and cheese or savor an order of alubias, which are marinated beans eaten with bread. The homemade sausage is delicious, and you won't find better chimchuri sauce anywhere. Besides beef, there's baby pig, lamb, and chicken fixed several Italian ways. Try the crêpes Los Pibes (cooked with apples and orange liqueur) for dessert. This slice of Argentina is 5¹/₂ blocks south of the Vallarta bridge between Vallarta and Constitución.

MODERATE

✪ Café Adobe

Badillo 283. ☎ **322/2-6720.** Main courses $7–$13. Wed–Mon 6–11pm. Closed Aug and Sept. INTERNATIONAL.

Without a doubt, this place is one of the most popular downtown restaurants for its combination of food, service, and air-conditioned southwestern decor. The Café Adobe is casually chic with jeans-clad waiters serving the imaginative food. "Adobe-style" fettuccine comes swaddled in shrimp and pesto, red snapper is topped with a smooth mango hollandaise sauce, and chicken mingles with chipotle chiles—to name just a few specialties. Owner Rudolfo Choperena is almost always on hand, which accounts for the consistently fine food and service. Café Adobe is located at the corner of Badillo and Vallarta, opposite the Restaurant Argentino Los Pibes (see above).

✪ Karpathos Taverna

Rodolfo Gomez 110 at Olas Altas. ☎ **322/3-0163.** Main courses $6–$19. Wed–Mon 4–11pm. GREEK.

The atmosphere here is very Greek—just whiff the marvelous scents from the kitchen and tune in the taped Greek music. Decorated with cloth-covered tables and posters of Greece, this is a welcoming place to take a break from Mexican food. Here, you can try sampler plates of appetizers or a combination plate for two that includes moussaka and souvlaki. The Greek salad is as good as they come. To find this place from the Vallarta bridge, cross the bridge and walk four blocks south on Vallarta; turn right on Carranza for two blocks and left on Olas Altas for four blocks. Turn right on F. Rodriguez; it's ahead on the left as you go toward the water.

Puerto Nuevo

Badillo 284. ☎ **322/2-6210.** Main courses $7–$11. Daily 12:30–11pm. MEXICAN/SEAFOOD.

Although there are tables inside, most people choose to dine on the roofed, open-air patio facing the sidewalk on Basilio Badillo. Here, they can sip a margarita, wait for the orderly succession of the meal, and watch life on PV's "restaurant row." Owner and chef Roberto Castellon presents seafood with inventive flair. Try the crab enchiladas, shrimp with lobster sauce, or smoked marlin. Salads are particularly fresh and delicious with house vinaigrette dressing. There is a wide selection of after-dinner coffees. You'll find Puerto Nuevo five blocks south of the river off Vallarta, half a block left on Badillo.

INEXPENSIVE

Café de Olla

Badillo 168. ☎ **322/3-1626.** Main courses $2.50–$5.75. High season Tues–Sun 10am–11pm. Low season Tues–Sun noon–11pm. MEXICAN.

This small and inviting place gets high marks from locals and tourists alike. It's almost always full in the evening. You'll find large portions of New York steak, fish and shrimp, American-style barbecue ribs and chicken, Oaxaca-style tamales, and a great Plato Mexicana. What they call an empanada (which should be a meat-filled pastry) is really a quesadilla—a tortilla stuffed with cheese and fried. The café is six blocks south of the Vallarta bridge near the corner of Olas Altas.

✪ El Dorado

Pulpito 102. ☎ **322/2-1511.** Breakfast $2.50–$6; main courses $3–$8; salad or sandwiches $3–$6. Daily 8am–9pm. MEXICAN.

This open-air palapa-roofed restaurant on the beach is a decades-old local favorite, especially for a hearty breakfast by the sea. Try the huevos motuleños—Yucatan-style eggs on tortillas with black beans, cheese, and tangy salsa. In the late afternoon, watch the surfers and parasailors while sipping a cool drink. Seafood is another specialty, and iced tea is always available. To get here, walk nine blocks south of the river on Vallarta, then turn right onto Pulpito to its end at the beach.

Los Arbolitos

Camino de la Rivera at Cárdenas. ☎ **322/2-4752.** Breakfast $1.50–$2; menu familiar main courses $3.25–$4.50; dinner main courses $2.75–$6.75. Daily 8am–11pm; menu familiar noon–5pm. MEXICAN/SEAFOOD.

Favored by transplanted foreigners and locals alike for its reasonably priced, well-prepared food served in ample quantities, Los Arbolitos is worth a detour from the central village. Lalo Araiza and his wife, Ramona, started the place as a taco stand with only two tables; now there are three colorful stories from which to choose, all overlooking an as yet unbeautified portion of the Río Cuale. The supremely fresh and meaty whole fish comes fixed your way with french fries, rice, and salad. Be sure to ask for the *menu familiar,* which offers the most popular main courses at a fraction of the price of the regular menu. The restaurant is located south of the river, away from the oceanfront, at the opposite end of Cárdenas where it meets the river.

✪ Memo's La Casa de Hotcakes (The Pancake House)

Badillo 289. ☎ **322/2-6272.** Breakfast $2.50–$5. Low season daily 8am–2pm. AMERICAN/ MEXICAN/BREAKFAST.

Owner Memo Barroso hosts the village's best and most popular breakfast eatery, where patrons receive true value and good food. The menu, while not limited to flapjacks, includes mouth-watering pancakes and waffles imaginatively mixed with apples, caramel, raisins, granola, chocolate, nuts, and even peanut butter. You can also enjoy great eggs Benedict, eggs Florentine, cheese blintzes, breakfast burritos, and huge omelets. Egg dishes come with delicious hash browns. A large section of the menu is called "light and fruity" and features a wide assortment of fruit, yogurt, and granola, plus whole-wheat pancakes and waffles and egg dishes using only the egg whites. The coffee keeps coming, but you only pay for it once. Memo's is six blocks south of the Vallarta bridge between I. Vallarta and Constitución.

SPECIALTY TREATS
A BAKERY

✪ Pie in the Sky Bakery

Badillo 278. ☎ **322/2-5099.** $1.75–$25. Mon–Fri 9am–9pm, Sat–Sun 10:30am–8:30pm. PASTRIES.

This is a good place to have dessert after a meal on Badillo Street or to pick up some scrumptious goodies to nibble on in your room. Owners Don and Teri Murray turn out *besos* (kisses)—an out-of-this-world cross between a brownie and a muffin—, four fabulous varieties of cheesecake, three sizes of rich carrot cake, two-layer chocolate cake and almond cake, and mint cream tarts. There are two tables where you can eat on the spot, as well as have a cup of Italian dark roast coffee. This location is six blocks south of the river, on Badillo's "restaurant row" between Constitución and Vallarta. There are two other locations—one in the Villa Vallarta shopping center, by the Continental Plaza Hotel, and one north of town at the entrance to Bucerías, with a big sign on the right side of the highway.

JUNGLE RESTAURANTS

One of the unique attractions of Puerto Vallarta is its "jungle restaurants," located to the south, toward Mismaloya. Each offers open-air dining in a magnificent tropical setting by the sea or beside a mountain river. Determine the distance from town by the kilometer in the address. For minivan transportation from Puerto Vallarta, see "Getting Around" in Chapter 4.

Chino's Paraiso

Hwy. 200, km 6.5. ☎ **322/3-0102.** Main courses $12–$30. Daily noon–5pm. GRILLED SEAFOOD/STEAK.

Tucked into some rock formations, this shady and cool jungle restaurant offers five open-air terraces overlooking a green river flanked by giant boulders under grand palapas. Guests often take a dip in the swimming holes and waterfalls before or after eating. Marimbas usually play from 1 to 3pm. To get here, take a cab or minivan as far as the entrance to La Jolla de Mismaloya Resort, then hike or hire a taxi about a mile on the dirt road on the landward side of the highway; you'll see the road and Chino's sign opposite La Jolla Resort.

El Edén

Off Hwy. 200, km 6.5. No phone. Main courses $15–$30. Daily 11am–6pm. GRILLED SEAFOOD/STEAK/CHICKEN.

With just enough jungle cleared in this lush spot beside a clear river to set up movie cameras, a crew shot scenes here for *The Predator,* starring Arnold Schwarzenegger. After the filming, the set was converted into this restaurant. Guests can dine while watching other guests dropping into the inviting green river Tarzan-style from a rope swing. El Edén is 3 miles off the highway on the mountain side farther on the same road to Chino's (see above). There's a small fee to stay without eating. It has no phone, so check first with a travel agent or at the tourist office to confirm it is open.

What to See & Do in Puerto Vallarta

6

Puerto Vallarta's beaches, fine dining and shopping, and excellent assortment of hotels are its main attractions. In addition to the suggestions on what to see and do in this chapter, look for a copy of the English-language weekly publication *Vallarta Today*, which usually has a rundown of the latest events such as art openings and new restaurants. Above all, Puerto Vallarta is a place to relax and enjoy yourself.

SUGGESTED ITINERARIES

If You Have 2 Days

On your first day, relax, amble along the beach, and have a peaceful dinner. Sleep late on your second day, then stroll around the central village. Have lunch at one of the beachside restaurants, and later select a good spot to watch the sunset at one of the restaurants mentioned in Chapter 5 and stay on for dinner.

If You Have 3 Days

Spend your first two days taking it easy on Puerto Vallarta's beaches. On your third day, take one of the boats to Yelapa or Las Animas and spend the day or afternoon on the beach; eat lunch at one of the palapa-topped restaurants there. In the evening, find an outdoor restaurant or enjoy one of the festive Mexican entertainment nights that usually include folkloric dancing, dinner, and refreshments.

If You Have 5 Days

With an extended stay in Puerto Vallarta to play with, you might want to break up your beach time with a visit to one of the jungle restaurants with a pool, a scuba-diving excursion to one of the interesting spots not far off shore, or, if you're here on a Thursday or Saturday, the house and garden tour (see "Organized Tours," below). In the evenings, set sail on one of the sunset cruises or experience Puerto Vallarta's growing nightlife, whether in throbbing dance clubs, the lobby bars of hotels, or the many lively restaurants that double as nightspots.

1 Fun On & Off the Beach

Travel agencies in Puerto Vallarta can arrange tours, fishing, and other activities.

Note: Beware of "tourist information" booths, especially along Ordaz and the malecón; they are usually time-share hawkers offering "free" or cheap Jeep rentals, cruises, breakfasts, and so forth as bait. If you're suckered in, you may or may not get what is offered, and the experience will cost at least half a day of your vacation.

SPECIAL EVENTS

Santa Cecilia, the patron saint of mariachis, is honored for a solid 24 hours on **November 22.** Beginning at midnight on the 22nd until midnight of the 23rd, different mariachi groups take turns playing in the cathedral. That evening mariachis parade and fireworks are set off in the central plaza. The week leading up to **December 12**—the "birthday" of Mexico's patron saint, the Virgin of Guadalupe—there are processions of *peregrinas* (religious pilgrims) and much merrymaking.

A STROLL THROUGH TOWN

Puerto Vallarta's tightly knit cobblestone streets are a delight to explore (provided you have good walking shoes); they are full of tiny shops, rows of windows edged with curling wrought iron, and vistas of red-tile roofs and the sea.

Start with a walk up and down the **malecón,** the seafront boulevard. Among the sights you shouldn't miss is the **municipal building,** on the main square (next to the tourism office), which has a large Manuel Lepe mural inside in its stairwell. Nearby, up Independencia, sits the **cathedral,** topped with its curious crown; on its steps women sell colorful herbs and spices to cure common ailments. Here Richard Burton and Elizabeth Taylor were married the first time—she in a Mexican wedding dress, he in a Mexican *charro* outfit.

⭐ Frommer's Favorite Puerto Vallarta Experiences

A Lazy Day on the Beach. Spend a day or more relaxing on any of Puerto Vallarta's fine wide beaches dozing, reading a book, and watching the waves.

Sunset Watching. Search out just the right place to see the sunset on Playa Olas Altas or walking along the malecón. One of the best ways to end the day is aboard a sunset dinner cruise.

Yelapa Beach. Let the boat you came on leave without you, pick one of the palapa restaurants as a base for refreshments, and spend the day on the beach. Take the last boat back to town.

Deep-Sea Fishing. A half or full day far out at sea can be a thrilling and relaxing experience. Bring back your catch and have one of the restaurants prepare it for dinner.

Jungle Restaurants. Spend an afternoon at one of the jungle restaurants swimming, relaxing, and eating.

House and Garden Tour. Join the Thursday or Saturday tour to see what's behind the walls of Puerto Vallarta's elite homes.

Three blocks south of the church, head uphill on **Libertad,** lined with small shops and pretty upper windows; it brings you to the **public market** on the river. After exploring the market, cross the bridge to the **island in the river;** sometimes a painter is at work on its banks. Walk down the center of the island toward the sea, and you'll come to the tiny **Museo del Cuale,** which exhibits pre-Columbian ceramics and works by local artists; it's open Monday through Saturday from 10am to 4pm. Admission is free.

Retrace your steps back to the market and Libertad and climb up steep Miramar to **Zaragoza.** At the top is a magnificent view over rooftops to the sea. Up Zaragoza to the right two blocks is the famous pink arched bridge that once connected Richard Burton's and Elizabeth Taylor's houses. This area, known as **Gringo Gulch,** is where many North Americans have houses.

2 Organized Tours

To get your bearings in this elongated resort town, you may find it useful to take an organized city tour or go on one of the boat trips to nearby beaches. Either of these options will give you an overview of what to do in Puerto Vallarta. However, most outings available in Puerto Vallarta, through a tour desk or travel agent, can also be done on your own.

Boat Tours   Puerto Vallarta offers a number of different boat trips, including **sunset cruises** and excursions to **Yelapa** (a tiny town on a lovely cove accessible only by boat), **Las Animas Beach,** and **Quimixto Falls,** both also only reachable by boat. Most of these make a stop at **Los Arcos** for snorkeling; some include lunch, and most provide music and an open bar on board. Most leave around 9:30am, stop for 45 minutes at Los Arcos, and arrive at the beach destination around noon for a 2^{1}/2-hour stay before returning around 3pm.

The beaches have many colorful restaurants where you can take a table under a shady umbrella on the beach while you sun, eat, and buy drinks. It's customary to make your food and drink purchases at the restaurant whose table you occupy, so on arrival, visitors are besieged by restaurant representatives. At Quimixto, where the shoreline is rocky and there's no beach, visitors can take the half-hour hike to the falls or rent a horse for a ride to the falls. Prices range from $20 for a sunset cruise or a trip to one of the beaches with open bar to $35 for an all-day outing with open bar and meals. Travel agencies have tickets and information.

If you prefer to spend a longer time at Yelapa or Las Animas without taking time for snorkeling and cruise entertainment, then try the **water taxi** south of the Río Cuale by the Hotel Marsol on Francisco Rodríguez. For around $15 round-trip, boatmen advertise direct trips to Las Animas, Yelapa, or Quimixto. Supposedly, this water taxi takes off at 10:30 and 11am and returns at 3:30pm. In reality, however, the operators of this service would rather sell the lengthy tour and don't seem too enthusiastic about the direct trips, which take 40 minutes each way; a direct trip from these folks costs only slightly less than an excursion with all the trimmings. There's also another water taxi next to the Hotel Rosita (north of the river at Diaz Ordaz and 31 de Octubre) that advertises direct trips daily at 11am for $7.

Ecological Tours   Though it may be a front for time-share sales, **Sierra Madre,** D. Ordaz 732-B, at Vicario (☎ 322/3-0661), offers a variety of ecological trips. The trendy storefront features a safari theme, as well as ecologically oriented books, tee shirts, and postcards. Supposedly, funds generated by their trips go toward several government and privately sponsored ecological reserves and studies. Among the trips they offer are treks to the mountain foothills about 1¼ hours away; "Artistic Mexico" trips to nearby villages and artisans; mountain-bike tours; whale watching; and horseback riding, all conducted by ecologically oriented leaders who point out local flora and fauna. Prices range from $15 to $45. The store is open daily from 9am to 10pm.

House and Garden Tours   A house and garden tour of four private homes in town is offered every Thursday and Saturday during high season by the **International Friendship Club** (☎ 322/2-6060), for a donation of $20 per person. The tour bus departs at 11am from the main plaza by the tourism office, at Juárez and Independencia (☎ 322/2-0242, 322/3-0844, or 322/3-0744; fax 322/2-0243), which has information about the tours. Proceeds are donated to local charities.

You can also tour the **Taylor/Burton villas** (Casa Kimberley; ☎ 322/2-1336), the two houses owned by Elizabeth Taylor and Richard Burton, located at 445 Calle Zaragoza. Tours cost $5, and proceeds go toward cleft-palate operations for area youngsters.

Tropical and Jungle Tours   Hotel travel desks and travel agencies can arrange a tropical tour ($20) or a jungle tour ($20). The "tropical tour" is really an expanded city tour that includes the workers' village of Pitallal, the posh neighborhood of Conchas Chinas, the cathedral, the market, the Taylor-Burton houses, and lunch at Chino's Paradise (see "Dining" in Chapter 5).

3 Sports & Outdoor Activities

BEACHES   Its beaches are Puerto Vallarta's main attraction. They start with **Playa de Oro** well north of town, out by the airport, and extend all around the broad Bay of Banderas. The easiest to reach is **Playa Olas Altas,** also known as **Playa Muertos** or **Playa del Sol,** just off Calle Olas Altas, south of the Río Cuale. The water is polluted here, so the beach is good for sunning but not for swimming.

Playa Mismaloya is in a beautiful sheltered cove about six miles south of town along Highway 200. The water is clear and beautiful. Entrance to the public beach is just to the left of the Mismaloya hotel. Colorful palapa restaurants dot the small beach and will rent you a beach chair for sunning, or you can stake out a table under a palapa for the day. Using a restaurant's table and palapa is a reciprocal arrangement—they let you be comfortable, and you buy your drinks, snacks, lunch there. Before choosing your spot, be sure you'll want to eat and drink there too.

The *Night of the Iguana* was filmed at Mismaloya. You can still hike up to the stone buildings that were constructed for the movie on the point framing the south side of the cove. The **Jolla de Mismaloya Resort** is to the right of the public beach, and restaurants here are available to outsiders as well. This and all beaches in Mexico are public.

Animas and **Yelapa** beaches are very good but are reached only by boat. These beaches are larger than Mismaloya but have similar layouts with restaurants fronting a wide beach. If you aren't keen on taking an expensive boat trip, see how to get to these beaches less expensively in "Boat Tours" under "Organized Tours," above.

BULLFIGHTS This Mexican traditional sport is held from December through April on Wednesday afternoons at the bullring **La Paloma,** across the highway from the Terminal Marítima. Tickets, which can be arranged through travel agencies, cost around $25.

DIVING & SNORKELING Puerto Vallarta offers good diving and snorkeling. There are three local diving areas of interest: **Las Mariettas Islands,** where there are caves; **Quimixto,** where there's good visibility and a lot of fish; and **Los Arcos,** a rock formation that's a **national underwater park.**

Underwater enthusiasts with skills ranging from beginner to expert can arrange scuba diving at **Chico's Dive Shop,** Díaz Ordaz 770–5, by Carlos Obrien's (☎ 322/2-1895). Chico's also has branches at the Marriott, Vidafel, Vila del Palmar, Camino Real, and Continental Plaza hotels. **Vallarta Divers,** in the Marina del Rey Condominium at Marina Vallarta (☎ 322/1-0492), also offers scuba outings, as well as resort courses and PADI and NAUI certification courses. Dives cost from around $35 to $60 with equipment; the price varies depending on how far you go. Snorkeling trips cost around $35.

FISHING Fishing trips can be arranged through travel agencies or through the **Cooperativo de Pescadores** (Fishing Cooperative) on the malecón, north of the Río Cuale next door to the Rosita Hotel and across from McDonald's (☎ 322/2-1202). Fishing charters cost from $200 to $300 a day for four to eight people. The price varies according to the size of the boat. Although the posted price at the fishing cooperative is the same as that given by travel agencies, you may be able to negotiate a lower price at the cooperative. It's open Monday through Saturday from 7am to 2pm, but make arrangements a day ahead of time.

Note: Most fishing trips include equipment and bait but not drinks or snacks, so arrange to bring refreshments with you.

GOLF Puerto Vallarta has two golf courses. The one nearest town is the 18-hole private course at the **Marina Vallarta** (☎ 322/1-0171), for members only. Most of the luxury hotels have memberships which their guests can use. North of town about 10 miles is the 18-hole **Los Flamingos Club de Golf** (☎ 329/8-0606), a few miles beyond the Nuevo Vallarta development. It's open from 7am to 5pm daily, with a bar (no restaurant) and full pro shop. The greens fee is $30, plus $15 for club rental and $25 for a motorized cart or $5 for a pull cart.

HORSEBACK RIDES Trips on horseback can be arranged through travel agents or directly by going to the horse owners who gather at the end of **Basilio Badillo,** south of the Río Cuale by the Restaurant Corral. Rides cost around $8 an hour. Horsemen arrive about 9am, and rides take off around 9:30am and return around 1:30pm. Ask for **Fernando Peña,** one of the horsemen, who can also take riders from his house on the outskirts of town and into the mountains. Arrange this with him a day ahead of time.

Or for a unique getaway, try **Horseback on Mexico's Hacienda Trail from Sea to Sierra Madre,** which offers several week-long journeys by horseback into the mountains. They include camping en route to stays in centuries-old haciendas. For details, contact Pam Aguirre or Ann Sherman, Rancho El Charro, Av. Francisco Villa 895, Puerto Vallarta, Jal. (☎ 322/4-1014).

MOUNTAIN-BIKE TRIPS Trips to outlying areas can be arranged through **Mountain Bike Tours,** Badillo 381 (☎ 322/2-0080). Trips cost around $30 for 4 hours and include bike, helmet, gloves, water, and an English-speaking guide. Trips start at around 8am. Make arrangements a day ahead.

WATER SPORTS   Water-skiing, parasailing, and other water sports are available at many beaches along the Bay of Banderas.

4 Shopping

Excellent quality merchandise is brought to Puerto Vallarta from all over Mexico. Prices are higher than those in the places where the goods originated, and if you're planning to visit other parts of Mexico, you might want to wait and make your purchases at the source. In Tonala and Tlaquepaque (suburbs of Guadalajara), prices are considerably lower. Puerto Vallarta, however, is becoming one of Mexico's best art centers, so works seen in galleries here may not be found anywhere else.

Puerto Vallarta's **municipal market** is just north of the Río Cuale where Libertad and A. Rodríguez meet. The *mercado* sells clothes, jewelry, serapes, shawls, leather accessories and suitcases, papier-mâché parrots, stuffed frogs and armadillos, and, of course, T-shirts. Be sure to do some comparison shopping before buying. The market is open daily from 8am to 8pm. **Calle Libertad,** next to the market, is the place to buy *huaraches*—comfortable, practical sandals made of leather strips and rubber-tire soles. Buy a pair that fits a little tightly—they stretch out quickly and can become too floppy. The **Río Cuale** under the bridge is lined with a variety of shops selling crafts, gifts, art, and clothing.

CRAFTS & FOLK ART
SOUTH OF THE RÍO CUALE

Olinala Gallery
Cárdenas 274. ☎ **322/2-4995.**

Here, you'll find two floors of fine indigenous Mexican crafts and folk art, including an impressive collection of authentic masks and Huichol beaded art. The gallery is open Monday through Saturday from 10am to 2pm and 5 to 9pm.

Pirámide Galeria
Badillo 272. ☎ **322/2-3161.**

An enormous selection of Huichol Indian art and contemporary art decorates the enormous walls here. It's open Monday through Saturday from 10am to 2pm and 6pm to 10pm.

La Rosa de Cristal Vidrio Soplado Artesanías
Insurgentes 272, between Cárdenas and Madero. ☎ **322/2-5698.**

Blown glass in all colors of the rainbow is the specialty here; the prices are the best in town, as is the selection. The items come from their factory in Tlaquepaque near Guadalajara; seconds are in the back. The shop is open Monday through Saturday from 10am to 8pm.

NORTH OF THE RÍO CUALE

Arte Mágico Huichol
Corona 178. ☎ **322/2-3077.**

As the name implies, this store specializes in Huichol Indian art, and there are rooms and rooms of it. You'll find very fine large and small yarn paintings by recognized Huichol artists, as well as intricately beaded masks, bowls, and ceremonial objects. The gallery is open Monday through Saturday from 10am to 9pm.

Casa Bombay

Morelos 527 near Corona. ☎ **322/3-0723.**

It's unusual to find European and Asian imported items in Mexico, but this shop specializes in Asian furniture, clothing, tribal jewelry, silks, and other textiles. It's open Monday through Saturday from 10am to 9pm.

El Baúl

Juárez 512, inside Las Margaritas between Corona and Galeana. ☎ **322/3-2580.**

Browse through their selection of fine decorative objects, colorful furniture, pottery, glass, and pewter. El Baúl (the trunk) is open Monday through Saturday from 10am to 2pm and 4:30 to 8pm.

El Souk

Morelos 533. ☎ **322/3-1340.**

Next door to Casa Bombay, this store features textiles, furniture, rugs, jewelry, and masks from Morocco, Tunisia, and Egypt. It's open Monday through Saturday from 10am to 9pm.

Gallery Indígena

Juárez 270, between Guerrero and Zaragoza. ☎ and fax **322/2-3007.**

This large shop features silver, Oaxaca pottery and wood carvings, lacquer chests, dance masks, pre-Hispanic pottery reproductions, and Huichol Indian art. Owner Ignacio Jacobo is usually on hand. Ask about shipping items to the United States and delivery to Puerto Vallarta hotels. It's open Monday through Saturday from 10am to 3pm and 5 to 9pm.

Instituto de la Jalisciense

Juárez 284. ☎ **322/2-1301.**

A state-operated store, this shop showcases crafts from Jalisco as well as a few other states. It's at Zaragoza catercorner from the zócalo; hours are Monday through Saturday from 10am to 2pm and 4 to 8pm.

Nacho's

Libertad 160A. ☎ **322/2-3007.**

For beautifully made silver jewelry from Taxco and lacquer ware from Olinala, come to Nacho's. The store is open Monday through Saturday from 10am to 2pm and 5 to 8pm.

Nevaj

Morelos at Libertad. ☎ **322/2-6959.**

Start here in your quest for quality folk art from Central and South America and Mexico; it's open Monday through Saturday from 10am to 2pm and 5 to 9pm.

La Reja

Juárez 501, next to Querebines. ☎ **322/2-2272.**

A great selection of Mexican ceramics and Guatemalan fabrics. It's open Monday through Saturday from 9am to 2pm and 4 to 8pm.

Querubines

Juárez 501A. ☎ **322/2-3475.**

This store is loaded with Guatemalan and Mexican wares, including embroidered and hand-woven clothing, bolts of foot-loomed fabric, wool rugs, jewelry, straw bags, and Panama hats. It's open Monday through Saturday from 9am to 9pm and Sunday 10am to 6pm. It's at the corner of Galeana.

Sergio Bustamante Gallery
Juárez 275 near Zaragoza. ☎ **322/2-1129.**

Fantastic creatures emerging from eggs and other surreal and colorful images are Bustamante's trademarks. His gold and silver jewelry is for also for sale. Two more Bustamante stores are at Ordaz 546 and at Ordaz 700. This store is open Monday through Saturday from 10am to 9pm.

Sucesos
Corner of Libertad and Hidalgo. No phone.

This is the place to buy unique, expensive hand-painted clothing. It's open Monday through Saturday from 10am to 8pm and Sunday from 11am to 3pm.

CONTEMPORARY ART
Puerto Vallarta art galleries carry works of some of Mexico's finest contemporary artists. The following galleries carry contemporary Mexican and/or foreign artists:

Arte de las Americas
Las Palmas Building, Marina Vallarta. No phone.

Opened in 1994, this gallery is displays the works of Mexico's best artists. It's open Monday through Saturday from 10am to 8pm.

Galería Uno
Morelos 561 at Corona. ☎ **322/2-0908.**

This large, bright place, operated by Janice Lavender, is the leading gallery in town. You'll find several rooms of contemporary art with special exhibits which change often. The gallery's foundation is works by a core group of artists living in Mexico. It's open Monday through Saturday from 10am to 8pm.

Galería Pacífico
Río Cuale opposite Le Bistro Jazz Café. ☎ **322/2-2748.**

Another fine gallery with carefully selected works, this place features large, often very colorful, works by contemporary artists. It's open Monday through Saturday from 10am to 9pm.

5 Puerto Vallarta After Dark

Wander down the malecón after dark, and you'll hear music pouring out from a dozen inviting restaurant/bars with their windows open to the sea or street.

RESTAURANT/BARS

Ándale
Olas Altas, 425 at A. Rodríguez. ☎ **322/2-1054.**

South of the river, Ándale is one of the wildest watering holes in town for people of all ages. The restaurant upstairs, with tables overlooking the street, is a bit quieter. Margaritas cost $1.75, and beer is $2. It's open daily from 10am to 4am or later.

Carlos O'Brian's
Paseo Díaz Ordaz 786 (the malecón), at Pipila. ☎ **322/2-1444** or 322/2-0356.

Eager patrons form a long line out front in the evening as they wait to join the party inside. Late at night, the scene resembles a rowdy college party. During the day, this place serves good food. Drinks run from $2 to $5. It's open daily from 11am to 2am. Happy hour is from 6 to 8pm.

Roxy's Music Bar & Coffee House

Vallarta 217. ☎ **322/3-2404.** No cover.

Settle in here for live rhythm and blues between 10pm and 1am and for happy hour between 6 and 9pm, when the drinks are two for the price of one. It's south of the river between Madero and Cárdenas. Hours are Monday through Saturday from 6pm to 1am.

Mariachi Loco

Cárdenas at Vallarta. ☎ **322/3-2205.** Cover $2.

Musicians start warming up in the early evening, but around 10pm, the place really comes alive with rancho music. At 11pm, the show begins with 10 vibrant mariachis. Afterward, the mariachis stroll and play as guests accompany them with impromptu singing. After midnight, the mariachis play for pay—around $8.50 per song. There are set-price meals and an à la carte menu, plus lots of drinks. It's open daily from 3pm to 2am. Food is served from 3pm to 10pm, and music is continuous from 10pm to 2am.

Mogambo

Paseo Díaz Ordaz 644 (the malecón). ☎ **322/2-3476.** No cover.

This restaurant, with big open windows facing the malecón and bay, has been here so long it's practically an institution. The theme is vaguely African, with crocodiles and other stuffed creatures on the walls, but most evenings the music is pure, live jazz. Drinks are $2.50 and up; specialty coffee is $3.50. There's food, too. It's open daily from 8am to 2am, with live jazz nightly from 9pm to 2am.

Restaurant/Bar Zapata

Paseo Díaz Ordaz 522 (the malecón). ☎ **322/2-4748.** No cover.

Climb the stairs to the second story and enjoy photographs and memorabilia from the Mexican Revolution while sitting at the bar on a horse-saddle stool. The eclectic choice of music includes tunes from the Andes, the U.S., and Mexico. National drinks (not imported) cost $2 to $3. It's open daily from noon to 1:30am; live music is played from 7pm to midnight.

SPORTS BARS & DISCOS

The discos in Puerto Vallarta are loud and expensive, but they know how to throw a party. Admission is $4 to $16; you'll generally pay $3 for a margarita, $2 for a beer, more for a whiskey and mixed drinks. Keep an eye out for the free disco passes that are frequently available in hotels, restaurants, and other tourist spots. Most discos are open from 10pm to 4am.

The malecón now has competition for the after-dark crowd. The new hip area, the south side of old Puerto Vallarta, contains parts of Vallarta, Cárdenas, Carranza, and Badillo. Some of the newer places heavily frequented by an older crowd of tourists are **La Esquina** (the Corner), Vallarta, and Cárdenas for televised sports and drinks; the younger crowd flocks to **Diva Disco,** on Vallarta, where Friday night is ladies night.

✪ Cristine

In the Krystal Vallarta Hotel, Av. de las Palmas, north of downtown off the airport road. ☎ **322/2-1459.** Cover $10.

Probably the most sophisticated disco in town, Cristine has an interior that's a cross between an octagonal jewel box and a turn-of-the-century gazebo. When the opening light show starts, the stage fogs up, lights swing down and start flashing, and suddenly you're enveloped in booming classical music like you've never heard before. After the show, video screens and disco sounds take over. Drinks go for $2.50 to $7. The disco is open nightly from 10pm to 4am; the opening light show begins at 11pm. *Note:* No shorts (for men), tennis shoes, or thongs.

Friday Lopez
In the Hotel Fiesta Americana Puerto Vallarta, north of downtown off Av. de las Palmas. ☎ **322/4-2010.** Cover $5; women free on Wed.

Live bands keep everyone hopping in this festive nightspot. Classic rock and roll is the music of choice. Drinks run $2.50 to $6. This place is open nightly from 10pm to 4am.

MEXICAN FIESTAS & HOTEL EVENTS

Mexican fiestas are held just about every night at major hotels around town and generally include a Mexican buffet, open bar, and live music and entertainment. Shows are usually held outdoors but move indoors when necessary. The state tourism office and local travel agencies can provide information on these and other hotel events; agencies can arrange tickets.

✪ La Iguana
Cárdenas 311, between Constitución and Insurgentes. ☎ **322/2-0105.** Cover $20.

Tourists seem to love this place. La Iguana offers an evening of entertainment that includes an open bar and an all-you-can-eat buffet. The eclectic show features Mexican folkloric dancing, mariachis, rope-twirling, piñatas, fireworks, and music for dancing. The show goes on Thursday and Sunday from 7 to 11pm.

Krystal Vallarta Hotel
Av. de las Garzas, north of downtown off the airport road. ☎ **322/2-1459.** Cover $35.

Krystal Vallarta hosts one of the best Mexican fiestas in town on Tuesday and Saturday at 7pm.

6 Excursions from Puerto Vallarta

If you want to take an excursion from Puerto Vallarta, try one the several boat excursions (see "Boat Tours" under "Organized Tours," above), especially to Playa Yelapa. These tours allow you to see another side of Puerto Vallarta. If you'd like to stay the night, check around with the locals and see if anyone is renting rooms; they frequently do. The horseback riding and mountain bike excursions (see "Sports & Outdoor Activities," above) also get so far off the beaten path that at the end of the journey you feel as though you've been much farther afield.

BUCERÍAS: A QUIET COASTAL VILLAGE

Only 11 miles north from the Puerto Vallarta airport, Bucerías (pronounced *boo-sah-REE-ahs*) is a small coastal fishing village of 8,000 people in Nayarit state on Banderas Bay. It's beginning to catch on as an inexpensive alternative to Puerto Vallarta.

Before you reach the town center in Bucerías, turn left when you see all the cook stands. You'll see cobblestone streets leading from the highway to the beach and glimpses of the villas and town homes behind high walls. Bucerías has already been discovered by second-home owners and by about 1,000 transplanted North Americans; casual tourists are beginning to discover its relaxed pace as well.

To get here from Puerto Vallarta, take a minivan or city bus to the stop opposite the entrance to the airport; then catch a minivan marked BUCERÍAS (they run from 6am to midnight and cost $1.15 one way). The last stop is Bucería's town square, where it departs for the return to Puerto Vallarta.

EXPLORING BUCERÍAS

Come here for a day trip from Puerto Vallarta just to enjoy the uncrowded beach and good seafood at the restaurants on the beach. If you are inclined to stay a few days, you can relax inexpensively and explore more of Bucerías while staking out an appealing place for a return trip. Sunday is street-market day, but it doesn't get going until around noon, in keeping with Bucería's casual pace.

ACCOMMODATIONS

Several small hotels and condominiums rent rooms here. The **Posada Olas Altas,** Calle Héroes de Nacozari s/n, Bucerías, Nay. 63732 (☎ 329/8-0407), is a small, basic, and inexpensive inn right on the main road in Bucerías. It's a good place to land while you poke around in search of a place that suits you. **Los Pericos Travel,** in Bucerías (☎ 329/8-0601 or 329/8-0061; fax 329/8-0601), will book accommodations, including villas, houses, condos, and the like. Call ahead or ask in Bucerías for directions to their office, which is open Monday through Friday from 9am to 2pm and 4 to 7pm, and Saturday from 9am to 2pm.

DINING

In addition to the seafood restaurants near the town square and the beach, there are inexpensive **outdoor kitchens** on the street fronting the highway that serve delicious grilled chicken marinated in orange juice. The **Pie in the Sky Bakery** is on the right, at the outskirts of Bucerías as you enter town. Stop in for straight-from-the-oven goodies for your after-dinner dessert or breakfast feast.

Adriano's
Av. Pacífico 2. ☎ **322/8-0088.** Breakfast $2.25–$3.75; seafood $6–$10; beer 85¢. Daily 8am–11pm. SEAFOOD.

Just off Bucerías's main square (on the far left) on the beach, Adriano's is an inviting place to eat while spending the day on the beach. (They have a shower and bathroom just for their beach clientele.) The extensive menu includes french toast and shrimp omelets for breakfast, seafood, and nachos. Though large, this restaurant fortunately isn't on the bus tour route, so you won't be abandoned in favor of a bus load of tourists.

✪ Mark's
Lázaro Cárdenas 56. ☎ **322/8-0303.** Pasta $6–$7; other main courses $7; nightly specials $8–$10. Wed–Mon 5:30–11pm. PASTA/STEAK/SEAFOOD.

It's worth a special trip to Bucerías just to eat at this evening-only covered patio restaurant. The most popular North American hangout, Mark's offers a great assortment of whole wheat pizzas seasoned with fresh herbs grown in the garden—in fact, everything has that wonderfully fresh taste, from the shrimp in angel hair pasta to the shrimp cakes and delicious Caesar salad. The shrimp pizza Banderas is a fresh combination of pesto, sun dried tomatoes, olives, and cheese. The restaurant is only a half a block from the beach, so you could take a dip before dining. In addition to enjoying a fine meal, you can shop in the restaurant's boutique and enjoy live music some evenings.

To find Mark's from the highway, turn left just after the bridge where there's a small sign. Then double back left at the next street (it's immediately after you turn left) and turn right at the next corner (also immediately reached). Follow that street almost to the end, where you'll see the ocean ahead and Mark's on the right.

SAN BLAS: FOR BIRDWATCHERS & SURFERS

San Blas is a rather ugly Pacific coast fishing village of 10,000 people in Nayarit State. Upon your arrival, the dirt streets and ragtag central square will make you wonder, "Is this it?" The uninviting wide beaches with hard-packed, thick-grained, grayish-colored sand sport few palm trees. At night, especially during the rainy season, the whole town is infested with "no-see-ums" that require an armor of insect repellent to ward off.

Were it not for its reputation as a birders' mecca and surfers' delight, the town would likely languish as an undesirable outpost. Still, most of the year, it attracts an assortment of tourists, some of whom are looking for an inexpensive retreat on this increasingly expensive coast and others who come just to see the birds or to surf. The few hotels are often full, especially on major Mexican holidays.

ESSENTIALS

The **Tourist Office,** next door to McDonald's restaurant (see "Dining," below) on Avenida Juárez, is open Monday through Friday from 9am to 3pm.

Transportes Norte de Sonora buses from Puerto Vallarta take the short route, but be sure to specify which route you want since the long route through Tepic takes five hours. As an alternative, you can take a **Pacífico bus** to Las Varas and change buses to San Blas; there may, however, be a wait—try to get to Las Varas before noon.

Only 150 miles from Puerto Vallarta, San Blas is an easy 3^{1}/2-hour trip now that the new nontoll highway bypasses Tepic. This new two-lane paved highway, which starts at Las Varas off Highway 200 (a sign announces Las Varas), goes through the villages of Santa Cruz and Aticama before connecting with the two-lane highway into San Blas. Signs are few, so if you're driving, keep asking directions.

As you enter the village, you'll be on **Avenida Juárez,** the principal street, which leads to the main plaza on the right. At its far end sits the old church, with a new church next to it. Across the street from the church is the bus station, and on the other side of the churches is the *mercado* (market). After you pass the square, the first one-way street to your left is **Batallón,** an important street that passes a bakery, a medical clinic, several hotels, and Los Cocos Trailer Park and ends up at **Borrego Beach,** with its many outdoor fish restaurants. Nearly everything in town is within walking distance, and there are public buses that go to the farther beaches—Matanchen and Los Cocos—on their way to Santa Cruz, the next village to the south.

As for the **climate,** October is the wettest month of the rainy season, which runs from May through October and witnesses the worst of the "no-see-um" attacks. Summer is hot and steamy.

EXPLORING SAN BLAS

After you've walked around the town and taken the river cruise, there's not a lot to do besides relax, swim, read, walk on the beach, and eat fish—unless you're a serious birdwatcher or surfer. During the winter, however, you can also look for **whales** off the coast of San Blas.

PORT OF SAN BLAS   Like Acapulco, San Blas was once a very important port for New Spain's trade with the Philippines, and the town was fortified against pirates. Ruins of the fortifications, complete with cannons, the old church, and houses all overgrown with jungle, are still visible atop the hill **La Contadura.** The fort settlement was destroyed during the struggle for independence in 1811 and has been in ruins ever since. Also, it was from San Blas that Fr. Junípero Serra set out to establish missions in California in the 18th century.

The view from La Contadura is definitely worth the trouble to get there. The entire surrounding area stretches out before you, a panorama of coconut plantations, coastline, town, and the lighthouse at Playa del Rey. To reach the ruins from San Blas, head east on Avenida Juárez about half a mile, as if you were going out of town. Just before the bridge, take the stone path that winds up the hill to your right.

BEACHES & WATER SPORTS   One of the closest beaches is **Borrego Beach,** south from the town plaza on Batallón until it ends. This is a gray sand beach edged with palapa restaurants selling fish. For a more secluded place to swim, pay a fisherman to take you across Estuary El Pozo at the southwest edge of town to the "island," actually **El Rey Beach.** Walk to the other side of the island and you might have it all to yourself, or try the beach on the other side of the lighthouse on this island. Bring your own shade, as there are no trees. The fisherman "ferry" charges about $1 one way and operates from 6am to 6pm. Canoes and small boats can also be rented at the harbor on the west side of town, following Avenida Juárez.

About three miles south of San Blas is **Matanchen Bay.** If you're driving, head out Avenida Juárez toward Tepic, cross the bridge, and turn right at the sign to Matanchen. A bus also stops there on its way south to the village of Santa Cruz; it departs from the bus station on the main square at 9 and 11am and 3 and 5pm. Check on the return stops at Matanchen Bay, which are generally an hour later. There's a little settlement here where you can have a snack or a meal or rent a boat and guide for the jungle-river cruise.

Half a mile past the settlement is a dirt road to **Las Islitas Beach,** a magnificent swath of sand stretching for miles with a few beach-shack eateries. This is a famous surfing beach with mile-long waves, and real and would-be surfing champions come from Mexico and the United States to test their mettle here, especially during September and October, when storms create the biggest waves. If you don't have a surfboard, you can usually rent one from one of the local surfers. The bodysurfing at Islitas and Matanchen is good, too. A taxi to Islitas will cost about $6 from downtown San Blas.

Farther south from Matanchen is beautiful **Playa Los Cocos,** lined with coconut palms. It's also on the bus route to Santa Cruz, but double-check on stops and schedules before boarding in San Blas.

JUNGLE CRUISE TO TOVARA SPRINGS   Almost the moment you hit San Blas, you'll be approached by a "guide" who offers "a boat ride into the jungle." This is one of Mexico's unique tropical experiences, and to make the most of it, find a guide who will leave at 6:30 or 7am. The first boat on the river encounters the most birds, and the Tovara River is like glass early in the morning, unruffled by breezes. Around 9am the boatloads of tour groups start arriving, and the serenity evaporates like the morning mist. The cost is about $40 for a boatload of one to four people for the 3- to 4-hour trip from the bridge at the edge of town on Juárez. It's less (about $30) for the shorter, 2-hour trip from the Embarcadero near Matanchen Bay, out of town. Either way, it's worth it if you take the early morning cruise through shady mangrove mazes and tunnels and past tropical birds and cane fields to the beautiful natural springs, La Tovara, where you can swim. There's a restaurant here, too, but stick to soft drinks or beer.

Note: The guide may also offer to take you to "The Plantation," which refers to pineapple and banana plantations on a hill outside of town. The additional cost of this trip is not worth it for most people.

BIRD-WATCHING   Birding is best from mid-October to April. As many as 300 species of birds have been sighted here, one of the highest counts in the western hemisphere. Birders and hikers should go to the Hotel Las Brisas Resort in San Blas (see "Accommodations," below) to buy a copy of the booklet *Where to Find Birds in San Blas, Nayarit* by Rosalind Novick and Lan Sing Wu. With maps and directions, it details all the best birding spots and walks, including hikes to some lovely waterfalls where you can swim. Ask at the Las Brisas Motel (☎ 321/5-0307 or 321/5-0558) which bilingual guide they currently recommend, and they'll put you in touch with him or her. A day's tour will cost around $100, which can be divided among the participants.

ACCOMMODATIONS
Moderate
Hotel Las Brisas Resort
Calle Paredes Sur s/n, San Blas, Nay. 63740. ☎ **321/5-0480** or 321/5-0307. Fax 321/ 5-0308 or 321/5-0112. 42 units, 5 minisuites. A/C FAN TV. $55 single, $70 double; $80 suite. Rates include breakfast. Free parking.

A block inland from the waterfront, this oasislike resort is nestled among pretty gardens of palms, hibiscus, and other tropical plants. You'll find a tranquil ambiance, two pools (one for toddlers), and one of the best restaurant/bars in town—just a few of the details that make this the nicest place to stay in San Blas. Rooms in the cottagelike fourplexes are modern, bright, airy, and immaculate, with well-screened windows and fans and air-conditioning. Several rooms have a kitchen and come with king-size beds; otherwise, most have two double beds, and a few have an extra single bed. Each room has an in-room safety deposit box. The manager, María Josefina Vazquez, is one of the most knowledgeable and helpful people I've met on the Pacific coast.

To get here, walk south from the square on Batallón about six blocks, turn right on Campeche across from the Marino Inn, then turn left on the next street, Paredes Sur.

Inexpensive
Hotel Los Bucaneros
Av. Juárez 75 Pte., San Blas, Nay. 63740. ☎ **321/5-0101.** 33 rms (all with bath). FAN. $15 single, $20 double.

A six-foot-long stuffed crocodile smiles with open jaws at visitors in the lobby of this hotel. The neat and freshly painted rooms are arranged around a courtyard, and guests enjoy the pool and patio. The hotel is on the main street one block west of the town plaza.

Motel Posada Del Rey

Calle Campeche 10, San Blas, Nay. 63740. ☎ **321/5-0123.** 12 rms (all with bath). FAN. $18 single, $22 double.

Rooms at the Posada del Rey are arranged around a tiny courtyard entirely taken up by a little pool. Six rooms have air-conditioning. An open-air bar on the third floor provides a lovely view of the ocean and palms. The motel is one block inland from the waterfront at El Pozo Estuary and five blocks south of the town plaza. Turn right at the Marino Inn, and you'll find the hotel straight ahead two blocks on the right.

DINING

For an inexpensive meal in high season on or on weekends, try fresh grilled fish from one of the little shacks on the beach. The prices are the same at all these places. From town, take Avenida Batallón south from the plaza and follow your nose when you smell the fish being grilled. There are several restaurants near the main plaza.

✪ Restaurant El Delfín

In the Hotel Las Brisas Resort, Calle Paredes Sur s/n. ☎ **321/5-0112.** Main courses $6–$13. Daily 8am–9:30pm. INTERNATIONAL.

You'll want to return often to this delightful hotel restaurant that serves the best food in San Blas. It's air-conditioned, and the new decor boasts marble floors and a pleasing pink-and-green color scheme. The chef masterfully draws from a wide repertoire of sauces. Try the exquisite shrimp or chicken with creamy chipotle pepper sauce. The spaghetti dishes include seafood marinara and spaghetti Alfredo with seafood. The homemade soups and desserts also deserve encores.

McDonald's

Juárez 36 Pte. Breakfast $2–$3; main courses $4–$7. Nov–June, daily 7am–10pm. July–Oct, Wed–Mon 7am–10pm. MEXICAN.

This family run restaurant has been a central village mainstay for more than 3 decades. Specialties of the house include mixed seafood and tenderloin brochettes and seafood platters. You'll find it one block west of the town square.

7

Getting to Know Manzanillo

Outsiders think of Manzanillo in the state of Colima as a resort community, but today this city of 90,000 is Mexico's foremost Pacific port. Sea traffic, as well as fishing and iron-ore mining, generate more income than tourism. In fact, Manzanillo has remained a relatively hidden retreat on the Pacific coast; it lacks major air links and is more than 150 miles from Puerto Vallarta and 167 miles southwest of Guadalajara. Tourists don't come in droves, as they do to those cities.

Manzanillo first began to attract foreigners seeking relief from northern winters in the 1970s, when condominiums were built on the hillsides and beaches. Today, their private enclaves on some of the most prime bay property are strung out for more than 20 miles from town center toward the airport. There are few hotels relative to private dwellings and to other Mexican resort cities, and the hotels are just as scattered as the condominiums.

Downtown Manzanillo still isn't much to look at; its town center faces the port and railroad tracks, and outlying roadways are veiled in a swirl of dust. Recently, the city has begun a long-overdue program to beautify itself, widening and resurfacing its streets and planting palms and flowers in the center medians. The appearance of the town and its main boulevards is compensated for by the beauty of the bays, the excellent climate, the few good beaches, and the town's relaxing pace. Manzanillo has a delightfully laid-back ambiance as well as some very good restaurants, and it's the ideal point from which to launch further explorations north to the coastal villages of Barra de Navidad and Melaque and inland to Colima, the state capital.

1 Orientation

ARRIVING & DEPARTING

BY PLANE **Aeroméxico** (☎ 333/3-2424 at the airport) and **Mexicana** (☎ 333/3-2323 at the airport) offer flights to and from Mexico City and Guadalajara. There are connecting flights several times a week from Monterrey, and a few flights from cold-weather cities in the United States and Canada. Ask a travel agent about the numerous charters that operate in winter from the United States.

Manzanillo Area

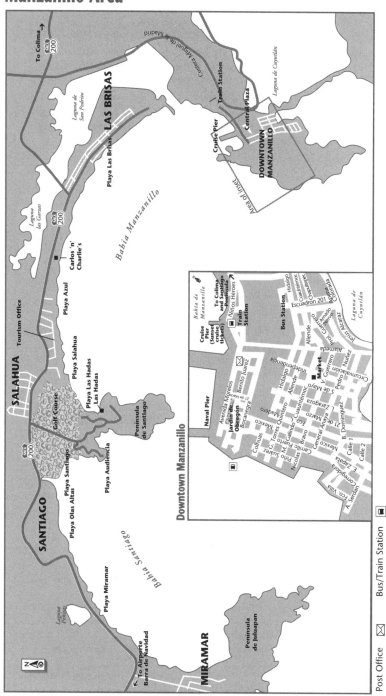

To Colima →
200

LAS BRISAS

Costera Miguel de la Madrid

Train Station

Laguna de Cuyutlán

Central Plaza

Cruise Pier

DOWNTOWN MANZANILLO

Area of Inset

Laguna de San Pedrito

Playa Las Brisas

200

Laguna las Garzas

Playa Azul

Carlos 'n' Charlie's

Bahia Manzanillo

SALAHUA

Tourism Office

Playa Salahua

Playa Las Hadas

Las Hadas

SANTIAGO

Golf Course

Playa Santiago

Peninsula de Santiago

Playa Audiência

Playa Olas Altas

200

Bahia Santiago

Playa Miramar

Laguna de Peña

MIRAMAR

Peninsula de Juluapan

← To Airport
Barra de Navidad

N

Downtown Manzanillo

Bahia de Manzanillo

To Colima and Santiago Peninsula ↗

Niños Heroes

Escuadron 201

Bus Station

Hidalgo
Cuauhtémoc
Av. Amado Nervo
Zona Carl. G
Allende
Alameda
Circunvalación

Laguna de Cuyutlán

Chapala
Obtorial
Acaraz

Cruise Pier (Sunset cruise tickets)

Train Station

Independencia

Market

Hidalgo
Allende
5 de Mayo
V. Guerrero
Pedro A. Galindo

Naval Pier

Avenida Morelos
Jardin de Obregon
21 de Marzo
Benito Juárez
Bocanegra

México
Fco. Madero
J. Zaragoza
Cuauhtémoc
Bravo
General Anaya

Colimas
Nicolas
G. Torres Quintero
Pino Suárez
Carillo Puerto
Calindo
B. Dominguez

Corregidora
A. Serdán
Fco. Villa
21 de Marzo
V. Zapata

Calle 1
Calle 2

Post Office ✉   **Bus/Train Station** ◼

❓ Did You Know?

- The name *Colima* is derived from the Náhuatl word *Coliman,* which has many interpretations, including "place of the mountain," "place of the volcano," "place of the god of fire," or "place of our ancestors."
- Manzanillo is named after a poisonous tree found growing where the port's first pier was built.
- In 1954 Manzanillo became "Mexico's Sailfish Capital" after a record catch of more than 300 sailfish in three days.
- The name *Jalisco* is a corruption of a Náhuatl word *Xaliaco,* meaning "sandy place."
- Before the conquest of Mexico, Jalisco was occupied by Purépecha- and Náhuatl-speaking tribes.
- The Revillagigedo Islands, south of Baja California, belong to Colima.
- López de Legazpi set sail for the Philippines from Barra de Navidad in 1564 and began the trade route of the Spanish galleons, which brought riches from the Orient to Mexico.
- The Volcán de Colima (Colima Volcano) first erupted in 1576; its most recent eruption was in 1991.
- In 1959, a typhoon nearly destroyed Manzanillo and Cuyutlán.
- In pre-Hispanic times a small hairless dog was bred for food in Colima; the dog traveled with nomadic traders as part of their provisions.
- Colima is the second smallest Mexican state after Tlaxcala.

The airport is 45 minutes northwest of town at Playa de Oro. The colectivo airport service, **Transportes Terrestres** (☎ 333/4-1555), picks up passengers at hotels. Call a day ahead for reservations. The one-way cost is $7 to $11; by taxi it costs $20.

BY BUS   Manzanillo's **Central Camionera** (bus station) is about 12 long blocks east of town. If you follow Hidalgo east, the Camionera will be on your right. Here, you can buy a sandwich, send a fax, make a long-distance call, or store luggage (look for the *guarda equipaje*). Taxis to town line up out front and cost around $6 to the town center.

Autotransportes Colima (also known as Los Altos; no phone) goes to Colima every 30 minutes. On a Directo the trip takes 1¹/₂ hours with two stops. An Ordinario leaves every 15 minutes and takes 2 hours, stopping frequently. Both types of bus drop off passengers within two blocks of Colima's main square rather than Colima's outlying Central Camionera.

To Barra de Navidad (1¹/₂ hours north) and to Puerto Vallarta (5 hours north), the company with the most frequent service is **Auto Camiones de Pacífico** and **Cihuatlan** (☎ 333/2-0515). It offers deluxe service (de paso), which they call "Primera Plus" (not to be confused with a line by the same name) six times a day and 10 daily second-class buses. **La Línea** (☎ 333/2-0123) has Plus (first-class) service to Colima (1¹/₂ hours) and Guadalajara (4¹/₂ hours) seven times daily. **Servicios Coordinados** (☎ 333/2-0210) has frequent first-class buses to

Guadalajara. **Primera Plus** (☎333/ 2-0210) has deluxe buses, with video movies and air-conditioning, hourly to Guadalajara and Puerto Vallarta.

BY CAR   Coastal Highway 200 leads from Acapulco and Puerto Vallarta. From Guadalajara, take Highway 54 through Colima (outside Colima you can switch to a toll road, which is faster but less scenic, into Manzanillo).

Motorists' advisory: Motorists planning to follow Highway 200 south from Manzanillo toward Lázaro Cárdenas and Ixtapa should be aware of recent reports of random car and motorist hijackings on that route, especially around Playa Azul. Before heading in that direction, ask locals and the tourism office about the current state of affairs.

VISITOR INFORMATION

The **tourism office** (☎ 333/3-2277 or 333/3-2264) in Manzanillo is on the Costera Miguel de la Madrid 4960, km 8.5. It's open Monday through Friday from 9am to 3:30pm.

NEIGHBORHOODS IN BRIEF

Downtown   The town, which is less attractive than you might expect, is at one end of a 7-mile-long curving beach facing Manzanillo Bay. The beach has four sections—**Playa Las Brisas, Playa Azul, Playa Salahua,** and **Playa Las Hadas.** The northern terminus of the beaches is the **Santiago Peninsula.** Downtown activity centers around the **plaza,** which has a brilliant poinciana tree with red blossoms, a fountain, kiosk, and a view of the bay. Train tracks run parallel to the street leading into the downtown area and then cut across the street to go inland. Large ships dock at the pier nearby. **Avenida Mexico,** the street leading out from the plaza's central gazebo, is the town's principal commercial thoroughfare and is lined with a few shops, small eateries, and juice stands. At night, swallows by the hundreds come to roost on the telephone wires around the plaza.

Las Brisas   Las Brisas peninsula fronts Manzanillo Bay and is separated from downtown by a cut large enough for ships to pass through. This peninsula lies between downtown and the Santiago Peninsula, and it's reached by the **Boulevard Costera Miguel de la Madrid** (named for a former Mexican president born in the state capital of Colima). To reach the beach, turn back left at the Las Brisas intersection of this road. A narrow paved road leads back down the peninsula past a row of small hotels fronting the beautiful Playa Las Brisas.

Salahua   Once you leave downtown, the line of commercial buildings along the highway seems almost endless; it's difficult to tell without a map when you've left one settlement and arrived at another. Salahua (whose name means "salt water") is one such settlement after Las Brisas and just before Santiago.

Lagoons   **Laguna de Cuyutlán,** almost behind the city, stretches for miles south paralleling the coast. **Laguna de San Pedrito,** north of the city, parallels the Costera Madrid; it's behind Playa Las Brisas beach. **Playa del las Garzas,** a short distance farther north, is separated from Laguna San Pedrito by a small strip of land and is behind Playa Azul. All are good places for bird watching.

Santiago Peninsula   Seven miles from downtown, beyond the San Pedrito and Las Garzas lagoons, lie Salahua (the subdivision on the right) and the Santiago Peninsula (on the left). The high, rocky peninsula juts out into the water separating Manzanillo Bay from Santiago Bay. It's the site of many beautiful homes, Las

Manzanillo, the main Pacific port for Guadalajara, Michoacán and Mexico City is a turn-of-the-century holdover, skipped over by main highways, tourists, airlines and tourist agents.
—James Norman, *Terry's Guide to Mexico*, 1965

The place [Barra de Navidad] is tropically picturesque, has magnificent stretches of golden beach and is just beginning to develop as a tourist haven.
—James Norman, *Terry's Guide to Mexico*, 1965

Hadas Resort, the La Mantarraya Golf Course owned by Las Hadas, and the best hotels in the area. The beach, **Playa Las Hadas,** is on the south side of the peninsula facing Manzanillo Bay, and **Playa Audiencia** is on the north side facing Santiago Bay. Santiago and the town are linked by the **Costera de la Madrid.** This stretch of road is also called the **Santiago Highway,** especially the extension beyond Santiago Peninsula.

Bays **Manzanillo Bay** contains the harbor, town, and beaches closest to town. It's separated by the Santiago Peninsula from the second bay, **Santiago,** which also has several beaches.

2 Getting Around

By Bus The local buses (*camionetas*) make a circuit from downtown in front of the train station. They go out along the lagoon opposite Playa Azul and then along the Bay of Manzanillo to the Santiago Peninsula and the Bay of Santiago to the north. The main buses are "Las Brisas," which goes to the Las Brisas crossroads then to the Las Brisas Peninsula and back to town; "Miramar," "Santiago," and "Salahua" buses go to outlying settlements along the bays and to most restaurants mentioned in Chapter 8. Buses marked "Las Hadas" go onto the Santiago Peninsula and make a circuit by the Las Hadas resort and the Sierra Manzanillo and Plaza las Glorias hotels. These buses are an inexpensive way to see the coast as far as Santiago and to take a tour of the Santiago Peninsula.

By Taxi Taxis in Manzanillo supposedly have fixed rates for trips within town, as well as to more distant points, but they aren't posted; ask your hotel staff what a ride should cost to get a feel for what's right, and then bargain. A taxi from the Central Camionera to the Salahua area costs around $7; a taxi to town center costs about $5.

FAST FACTS: MANZANILLO

American Express The local representative is Bahías Gemelas Travel Agency, Costera M. Madrid, km 10 (☎ 333/3-1000 or 333/3-1053; fax 333/3-0649).
Area Code The telephone area code is 333.
Bank Banamex downtown is just off the plaza on Avenida México; it's open Monday through Friday from 9:30am to 1:30pm but exchanges foreign currency only until 12:30pm.
Shopping Only a few shops in Manzanillo carry Mexican crafts and clothing, and almost all are downtown on the streets near the central plaza. You can also try exploring the new American-style malls on the road to Santiago.

8

Where to Stay & Dine in Manzanillo

1 Accommodations

The strip of coastline on which Manzanillo is located can be divided into three areas: **downtown,** with its few hotels and restaurants, shops, markets, and continual activity; **Las Brisas,** the small hotel- and condominium-lined beach area immediately to the north of the city; and **Santiago,** both the name of a town and peninsula which is virtually a suburb situated even farther north at the end of Playa Azul.

In Manzanillo, where you stay tends to define your vacation experience more so than in other Mexican resort cities that have numerous side attractions and that are not so spread out. Transportation by either bus or taxi makes all three areas fairly convenient to each other. Reservations are recommended for hotels during the Christmas and New Year's holidays.

DOWNTOWN
INEXPENSIVE

Hotel Colonial
Av. México 100 and Gonzales Bocanegra, Manzanillo, Col. 28200. ☎ and fax **333/2-1080** or 333/2-1134. 40 rms (all with bath). A/C (25 rms) FAN (15 rms). $18–$20 single or double.

An old favorite, this three-story colonial-style hotel changes little from year to year; it still offers the same beautiful blue-and-yellow tile, colonial-style carved doors and windows in the lobby and restaurant. Rooms have the same minimal furniture, red-tile floors, and basic amenities. In the central courtyard there is a restaurant/bar. The highest rates are for rooms with air-conditioning. With your back to the plaza, walk one block inland on Juárez to the corner of Galindo; the hotel is on the right corner.

Hotel Ruiseñores
Av. Teniente Azueta s/n. ☎ **333/2-2424** or 333/2-0646. 72 rms (all with bath). FAN. $13 single, $18–$20 double.

Though it's a little off the beaten path, the Ruiseñores is on the main public beach and therefore close to downtown and to public transportation. Rooms are clean, freshly painted, and comfortable, though sparsely furnished. Each comes with a small closet, a desk/ vanity, tile floors, and a worn but clean bath. In the courtyard facing the beach and ocean there are two pools—one for adults and another for children—as well as a second-story terrace. Most rooms have ceiling fans, but some have only small table fans. To find the hotel, follow the road to the edge of downtown going toward the Costera. On the right, you'll see a small half traffic circle and a sign that reads OFICINAS POTUARIOS; turn right into the half circle, then cross the highway and the railroad tracks. The hotel is on the left.

LAS BRISAS

Buses run out to the Las Brisas Peninsula from downtown. Look for "Brisas Direc" on the signboard. It's a 6-mile trundle around Manzanillo Bay, ultimately curving southward. Most hotels, bungalows, and condominiums are on the peninsula's single main road.

MODERATE

Hotel La Posada

Av. Lázaro Cárdenas 201, Las Brisas (Apdo. Postal 135), Manzanillo, Col. 28200. ☎ and fax **333/3-1899.** 24 rms. FAN. High season $75 single, $79 double. Low season $50 single, $60 double. Rates include breakfast.

Another longtime favorite of savvy travelers, this small inn has a shocking-pink stucco facade with a large arch that leads to a broad tiled patio right on the beautiful beach. The rooms have exposed brick walls and simple furnishings with Mexican decorative accents. The atmosphere here is casual and informal; you can help yourself to beer and soft drinks all day long, and at the end of your stay, owner Bart Varelmann (a native of Ohio) counts the bottle caps you deposited in a bowl with your room number. All three meals are served in the dining room or out by the pool. Breakfast, served between 8 and 11am, costs around $7; lunch and dinner (sandwiches), served between 1:30 and 8pm, cost about the same. During low season, the restaurant is open only from 8am to 3pm. You can also just come for a drink at sunset; the bar's open until 9pm all year. The hotel is at the far end of Las Brisas Peninsula—the end closest to downtown. From town center, take the "Las Brisas" bus.

INEXPENSIVE

☉ Hotel Star

Lázaro Cárdenas 1313, Manzanillo, Col. 28200. ☎ **333/3-2560** or 333/3-1980. 39 rms, 2 suites A/C FAN. $18–$25 single or double; $35 single or double suite.

In a row of modest hotels, the Hotel Star stands out for its tidy appearance and careful management. It features a two-story sunny complex facing a courtyard and a pool by the beach. The color scheme combines red tile floors with orange bedspreads and curtains. Rooms are comfortable but sparsely decorated with rattan furniture. The higher prices are for rooms with air-conditioning and television. Both suites have air-conditioning and televisions, and one has a kitchen.

SANTIAGO

Three miles north of Las Brisas is the wide Santiago Peninsula. The settlement of Salahua is on the highway at one end where you enter the peninsula to reach the hotels Las Hadas, Plaza las Glorias, and Sierra Manzanillo, as well as the Mantarraya Golf Course. Buses from town marked "Las Hadas" go every 20 minutes into the interior of the peninsula and pass by these hotels.

Past the Salahua turnoff and at the end of the settlement of Santiago, an obscure road on the left marked "Zona de Playas" leads to the hotels on the other side of the peninsula, including Hotels Marlyn and Playa de Santiago. To get to the latter hotels, take a bus to the main Santiago bus stop. Get off there and transfer to a taxi (available at all hours).

VERY EXPENSIVE

Camino Real Las Hadas

Santiago Peninsula, Manzanillo, Col. 28200. ☎ **333/3-0000** or 800/722-6466 in the U.S. and Canada. 220 rms and suites. A/C MINIBAR TV TEL. High season $260–$295 single or double; $355–$420 Camino Real Club. Low season $182–$205 single or double; $305–$370 Camino Real Club.

Anyone who has ever heard of Manzanillo has heard of Las Hadas; or say, "Las Hadas," and a lot of people think that *is* Manzanillo. You may remember it from the movie *10*, which featured Bo Derek and Las Hadas. The self-contained Eden that put Manzanillo on the map was the brainchild of the Bolivian entrepreneur Antenor Patino. The resort features Moorish-style architecture that started a trend in Mexico. Built on the beach and up a half-moon-shaped curve of the peninsula, the elegant white resort hotel is one of the most famous, popular, and exclusive in Mexico; it's among the "Leading Hotels of the World."

The rooms, which are being refurbished, are built around the hillside overlooking the bay and are connected by cobbled lanes lined with colorful flowers and palms. Covered, motorized carts are on call for transportation within the property. Though it's a large resort, it maintains an air of seclusion since rooms are large, spread out, and tucked in short rows on the landscaped grounds. The six categories of accommodations are roughly based on views, room size, and amenities. The understated, elegant, and spacious rooms have white-marble floors, sitting areas, and comfortably furnished balconies. Robes, hairdryers, in-room security boxes, and remote-control TV are standard in all rooms. Camino Real Club guests have rooms on the upper tier with great bay views, and nine rooms have private pools. Room 804 in the Camino Real Club has a whirlpool on the patio with a fabulous view of the bay.

To find the resort from the Costera, turn left at the golf course and follow the signs to Las Hadas. Entry, through a guarded gate, is only accessible to hotel guests, occupants of condominiums on an adjacent hill, patrons with restaurant reservations, or to bearers of tickets for the sunset cruise that takes off from here.

Dining/Entertainment: Of this resort's four restaurants, the most famous is elegant Legazpi Restaurant and Lounge, open in high season 6pm to midnight (see "Dining," below). Special theme nights feature patio dining and Italian, Japanese, and Mexican food, as well as mariachis, at a cost of $45 per person. There are five lounges and bars with live entertainment on the property almost every evening; the disco, Le Cartouche, is open nightly in high season from 10pm to 2am. Hours and restaurants may vary during low season.

Services: Laundry, room service, shopping arcade, travel agency, beauty and barber shops, child care, with special children's activities in high season. Camino Real Club guests have rapid check-in, continental breakfast, cocktails, concierge, preferred restaurant reservations, and late checkout.

Facilities: Club Las Hadas includes La Mantarraya, the hotel's 18-hole, 71-par golf course designed by Roy Dye; two pools; beach with shade tents; 10 tennis courts (8 hard-surface, 2 clay); marina for 70 vessels; and water sports, including scuba diving, snorkeling, sailing, and trimaran cruises. Camino Real Club guests have an exclusive pool and reserved lounge chairs at the pool and beach.

EXPENSIVE

Hotel Plaza Las Glorias

Av. de Tesoro s/n, Santiago Peninsula, Manzanillo, Jal. 28200. ☎ **333/3-0812,** 333/3-0622, 800/342-2644 in the U.S., or 91-800/3-6566 toll free in Guadalajara. Fax 333/3-1395. 86 rms, 17 Beach Club suites. A/C TV TEL. High season $125–$185 single or double. Low season $100–$165 single or double. Prices may vary more with season or holiday.

The deep burnt-orange-colored walls of this pueblo-like hotel ramble over a hillside on Santiago Peninsula. From the restaurant on top and from most rooms stretches a broad vista of other red-tiled rooftops and either the palm-filled golf course or bay. This is one of Manzanillo's hidden resorts, known more to wealthy Mexicans than to North Americans.

Originally conceived as private condominiums, the quarters were designed for living; each accommodation is spacious, stylishly furnished, and very comfortable. Each unit has a huge living room; a small kitchen/bar open to the living room; one, two, or three large bedrooms with Saltillo-tile or brick floors; large Mexican tiled bathrooms; huge closets; and large furnished private patios with views. A few of the rooms can be partitioned off and rented for the bedroom only. Water is purified in the tap, and each room has a key-locked security box. Try to get a room on the restaurant and pool level; otherwise, you'll have to climb a lot of stairs. There's a hillside rail elevator that goes from top to bottom but doesn't stop in between. The less luxurious Beach Club suites are at another location on Las Brisas Beach, several miles from the main hotel. Standard Beach Club suites have two bedrooms, two bathrooms, a fully equipped kitchen, and a separate dining area open to the sunken living room, off of which there is a terrace or balcony. Penthouse suites at the Beach Club are two stories, with the living and kitchen/dining area and a bedroom and bathroom downstairs, two bedrooms and a bathroom upstairs, and balconies on both levels. The hotel is often full weekends and holidays, so make reservations early. Package rates can cut the cost of your stay.

Dining/Entertainment: La Plazuela restaurant, a casual and informal restaurant shaped like a half-moon, is beside the pool and fronts the bay. It's open for all three meals. Live musicians often serenade diners.

Services: Laundry, room service, elevator from bottom of property to top, baby-sitters arranged with advance notice.

Facilities: One pool on the restaurant level; Beach Club on Las Brisas beach, where there's a pool and small restaurant; transportation to the Beach Club from the main hotel in the morning with return transportation in the afternoon.

Hotel Sierra Plaza Manzanillo

Av. La Audiencia 1, Los Riscos, Manzanillo, Col. 28200. ☎ **333/3-2000,** 800/333-3333, or 800/544-4686 in the U.S. Fax 333/3-2272. 333 rms and suites. A/C MINIBAR TV TEL. Low season $120–$130 single or double standard; $210–$370 single or double suite.

Opened in 1990, the 21 floors of this hotel overlook La Audiencia beach. Its architecture mimics the white Moorish style that has become so popular in Manzanillo. Inside, it's palatial in scale and covered in a sea of pale-gray marble.

The decor of the rooms picks up the pale-gray theme with washed gray armoires that conceal the TV and minibar. Most standard rooms have two double beds or a king-size bed, a small table, chairs, and desk. Several rooms at the end of most floors are small, with one double bed, small porthole-size windows, no balcony, and no view. Most rooms, however, have balconies and either ocean or hillside views. The 10 gorgeous honeymoon suites are carpeted and have sculpted shell-shaped headboards, king-size beds, and chaise lounges. Junior suites have a sitting area with couch and large bathrooms.

Dining/Entertainment: Four restaurants cover all meals and styles of dining, from casual to elegant. During high season, weekends, and holiday evenings from 8pm to 2am there's live music for dancing in Bar Sierra, which is open daily from 1pm to midnight.

Services: Laundry, room service, ice machine on each floor, hairdryers, beauty salon with massage available, travel agency, 24-hour currency exchange.

Facilities: Grand pool on the beach; children's pool; four lighted tennis courts; health spa (for an extra fee) with exercise equipment, scheduled aerobics, hot tub, and separate sauna and steam rooms for men and women. Scuba diving lessons are given in the pool, and there is excellent scuba diving within swimming distance of shore (see Chapter 9).

INEXPENSIVE

Hotel Marlyn

Peninsula de Santiago (Apdo. Postal 288), Manzanillo, Col. 28200. ☎ **333/3-0107.** 38 rms, 4 bungalows (all with bath). A/C or FAN. High season $25 single, $30 double. Low season $15–$20 single, $20 double.

White and airy, this hotel faces Audiencia Bay on the Santiago Peninsula. It has a little pool and a beachfront cafe. Some rooms have a sea view. Rates are lower for rooms with fans only.

Hotel Playa de Santiago

Santiago Peninsula (Apdo. Postal 147), Manzanillo, Col. 28860. ☎ **333/3-0055** or 333/3-0270. Fax 333/3-0344. 105 rms, 24 bungalows (all with bath). FAN TEL. $35 single or double; $38 bungalow. Free parking.

In its heyday, this 1960s-era hotel was one of the best in Manzanillo. Today, you get the essence of its former glamour at a fraction of the price. The hotel is on a small beach. Rooms in the main building are small and clean with nearly up-to-date furnishings, tile floors, tiny closets, and balconies facing the ocean. Most have two double beds. Bungalows are in a separate building next door and are rather dreary with dark-green bedspreads, old furniture, small baths, and walls that need painting. Some bungalows have kitchenettes, and all have nice size patios but no patio furniture. The restaurant/bar is positioned for its ocean views, and there are a pool and tennis court.

2 Dining

For picnic fixings, there's a big supermarket, the **Centro Comercial Conasuper,** on the road leading into town, half a block from the plaza at Morelos. The huge store sells food, produce, household goods, clothes, hardware, and more. It's open daily from 8am to 8pm.

DOWNTOWN

⑤ Cafetería/Nevería Chantilly

Juárez and Madero (across from the plaza). ☎ **333/2-0194.** Breakfast $2–$3; main courses $1.50–$4.50; *comida corrida* $3.50. Sun–Fri 7am–10pm (*comida corrida* served 1–4pm). MEXICAN.

Join locals at this informal corner cafe facing the plaza. The large menu includes club sandwiches, hamburgers, carne asada a la tampiqueña, enchiladas, fish, shrimp, and vegetable salads. The full comida corrida, a real value, might begin with fresh fruit cocktail, followed by soup, rice, the main course, dessert, and coffee.

Restaurant Roca del Mar

21 de Marzo 204. ☎ **333/2-0302** or 333/2-0424. Breakfast $1.50–$2.50; main courses $1.50–$6. Daily 7:30am–10:30pm. MEXICAN.

Cool, friendly, and open to the breeze, this popular restaurant is one of the best meeting places downtown. The large menu includes salads of chicken, fruit, seafood, and fresh vegetables, plus sandwiches, Mexican food, and seafood. It faces the main plaza, between Morelos and Juárez on the same side of the street as Helados Bing and the Bar Social.

BOTANEROS

Botaneros are a tradition almost exclusive to Manzanillo. For the price of a beer or soft drink, they serve complimentary delicious snacks—ceviche, soup, shark stew, pickled pigs' feet, tacos, and the list goes on indefinitely. The more you drink, the more the food appears. Bring a group of four or more, and the platters *really* arrive. It's customary to order at least two drinks and to tip the waitress well. She puts a box for your empties at your table and tallies the tab from its contents when you're ready to leave. Sometimes, roving musicians come in to serenade; you pay per song, so settle on the price in advance. Most botaneros have a form of a betting game, which you'll have to get a local to explain. In addition to those listed below, there's also **El Menudazo,** on the way to Santiago. Most are open daily from noon to 8pm, and all charge about the same for a beer or soft drink.

Bar Social

Facing the downtown plaza. Beer or soft drink $2. Mon–Sat noon–11pm. DRINKS/SNACKS.

More like a traditional Mexican cantina, with swinging doors and a room full of men, it's one of the original botaneros that's as popular with locals as it is with tourists. Women will feel more comfortable here in groups or with a male companion. Tables and booths are against the walls, and an enormous bar takes up the center of the room. By early evening, it gets noisy, crowded, and drunk inside, and tourists will probably want to exit before all that happens.

✪ El Último Tren

Niños Héroes. ☎ **333/2-3144.** Beer or soft drink $2. Daily noon–8pm. DRINKS/SNACKS.

Among the cheeriest of the botaneros, El Último Tren (the last train), is covered by a grand high palapa with ceiling fans. There's enough of a family feel to the place that you can feel comfortable bringing older children, although technically they aren't allowed. It's not far from downtown proper, on the right, several blocks past the train station. Just in case—women's rest rooms are named *máquinas* (cars), and the men's room is called a *garrotero* (signalman).

LAS BRISAS

In addition to Willy's, below, the hotel **La Posada** (see "Accommodations," above) offers breakfast to nonguests at it's beachside restaurant, and during other points of the day, it's a great place to mingle with North American tourists and enjoy a sunset and cocktails.

EXPENSIVE

Osteria Bugatti

Santiago and Las Brisas crossroads. ☎ **333/3-2999.** Reservations recommended after 8pm. Sonora steaks and seafood $10.75–$17; pasta $7–$8.50. Daily 1pm–1am. Closed Sept 15–27. STEAKS/SEAFOOD.

One of the best restaurants in town, this place is in a dark, vaulted cellar with a brick ceiling and soft lighting. Your English-speaking waiter arrives bearing a platter laden with quality Sonora beef, pork, and seafood. Your selection will be cooked to your specifications. There's a small selection of pastas as well. Air-conditioning and a complete international bar help to make this a popular place. It's at the Las Brisas crossroads, several miles north of town center. Take the "Las Brisas," "Salahua," "Santiago," or "Miramar" bus from town center and get off at the Las Brisas crossroads; the restaurant is across the busy boulevard. Take the "Estación" bus back to town.

✪ Willy's

Las Brisas crossroads. ☎ **333/3-1794.** Reservations required. Main courses $7–$13. Daily 7pm–midnight. SEAFOOD/INTERNATIONAL.

You're in for a treat at Willy's, one of Manzanillo's most popular restaurants. It's breezy, casual, and small, with some 13 tables inside and 10 more on the narrow balcony over the bay. Among the grilled specialties are shrimp filet imperial wrapped in bacon; red snapper tarragon; dorado basil; robalo with mango and ginger; homemade pâté; and coconut flan. The food has flair and wins over locals and tourists alike. Double back left at the Las Brisas crossroads, and you'll find Willy's on the right down a short side street that leads to the ocean. From the train station, take a "Las Brisas" bus and ask the driver to let you off at Willy's; then walk half a block toward the ocean.

MODERATE

Benedetti's Pizza

Las Brisas. ☎ **333/4-0141.** Pizza $5–$9; main courses $3.75–$11. Daily 10am–6pm. PIZZA.

Since there are several branches in town (some called Giovanni's Pizza), you'll probably find a Benedetti's not too far from where you are staying. The variety isn't extensive, but these pies taste quite good; add some chimichurri sauce for a new flavor. In addition to pizza, you can select from among pasta, sandwiches, burgers, fajitas, salad, Mexican soups, cheesecake, and apple pie. This branch is on the Costera de la Madrid, on the left just after the Las Brisas turn; it's next to Goodyear Tire. Another branch is at the Las Hadas marina (☎ 333/3-2350).

SANTIAGO ROAD

The restaurants below are on the Costera Madrid between downtown and the Santiago Peninsula which includes an area known as Salahua.

EXPENSIVE

✪ Manolo's Bistro

Costera Madrid, km 11.5. ☎ **333/3-2140.** Main courses $8–$18. Mon–Sat 6–11pm. INTERNATIONAL/STEAK/SEAFOOD.

Manolo's offers refined dining; cloth-covered tables are set with a single fresh flower and handsome wood-backed chairs with a patina reminiscent of a European dining room. Owners Manuel and Juanita Lopez and family do the serving. They cater to North American tastes—a "safe" salad is included with dinner. Among the popular entrées is filet of fish Manolo on a bed of spinach with melted cheese Florentine style and frogs' legs in brandy batter. Most guests can't leave without first being tempted by the fresh coconut or homemade pecan pie.

If you are coming from downtown, Manolo's is on the right about three blocks before the turn to Las Hadas; its yellow-colored walls are almost dwarfed next to the sprawling burnt-orange walls of El Vaquero Campestre. From town center, take a "Miramar," "Salahua," or "Santiago" bus and return on an "Estación" bus.

Bigotes III

Puesta del Sol 3. ☎ **333/3-1236.** Main courses $6–$15. Daily noon–1am. SEAFOOD.

Good food and a festive atmosphere make locals flock to this large, breezy restaurant by the water. Strolling singers serenade diners, who satisfy themselves with large portions of grilled seafood. To find Bigotes, follow the Costera de la Madrid from downtown past the Las Brisas turnoff. Look for Portofino restaurant on the right; the left turn (and a sign pointing to Bigotes) is across the street opposite Portofino's.

El Vaquero Campestre

Km 11.5, Salahua. ☎ **333/3-0475.** Main courses $5–$7; beer $1.75; wine $2.50. Daily 1–11:30pm. GRILLED MEATS.

It's hard to miss the sprawling burnt-orange stucco wall and wagon wheels along the iron work and over the door of this restaurant. Cloth-covered plastic tables and chairs are set under a couple of grand thatched palapas. The specialty here is Sonora beef cut just about any way you can think of on either side of the border—T-bone, mignon, ribeye, tampiqueña. The "arrachera" is similar to the tampiqueña (a long, thin cut), but the meat is softer. The "churrasco" is a filet for two people, charcoal-grilled then sliced and served with potatoes, beans, and tortillas. Most meats are served with grilled onions, beans, and tortillas. Most cuts are also available by the kilo for two or more people. Prices on the menu are for four people; I've listed the price per person. To get here from town, take a "Santiago," "Salahua," or "Miramar" bus.

Juanito's

Costera Madrid, km 14. ☎ **333/3-1388.** Breakfast $2–$3; hamburgers $2–$3.25; main courses $3–$6. Daily 8am–11pm. HAMBURGERS/MEXICAN/AMERICAN.

It's a long way to come for a meal, but Juanito's is worth it. This immaculate family run restaurant offers a simple recipe for success—serve the most popular culinary mainstays of the United States and Mexico. John "Juanito" Corey and his wife, Esperanza, are always on duty serving hamburgers and fries, hot dogs, club sandwiches, fried chicken, barbecued chicken and ribs, tacos, tostadas, enchiladas, milk shakes, lemonade, pie, and ice cream. They have added are a few items besides fast food, including beef or fish filet and chicken in white sauce.

The hamburgers taste just like those back home, although they're smaller, and the portions of fries are not as large as in the States.

Juanito's is 8¹/₂ miles from downtown Manzanillo on the highway going to Barra de Navidad, before the Club Maeva resort. To get here from town center, take the "Miramar" or "Fco. Villa" bus. Juanito's also offers long-distance and fax service to the public.

SANTIAGO PENINSULA
VERY EXPENSIVE

✪ Legazpi
Hotel Camino Real Las Hadas hotel, Santiago Peninsula. ☎ **333/4-0000.** Main courses $25–$45. Every other day in high season 6pm–midnight—call ahead. INTERNATIONAL.

Dine here for sheer elegance, gracious service, and outstanding food. The tranquil, candlelit room has tables covered in pale pink and white and set with silver and flowers; a pianist plays softly in the background. Enormous bell-shaped windows on two sides show off the sparkling bay below. Meals begin with a basket of warm breads, and courses are interspersed with servings of fresh fruit sorbet. The sophisticated menu includes prosciutto with melon marinated in port wine, crayfish bisque, broiled salmon, roast duck, lobster, or veal, and flaming desserts from crêes to Irish coffee. It's a dining experience you won't soon forget.

9

What to See & Do
in Manzanillo

Activities in Manzanillo depend on where you stay. Most resort hotels here are completely self-contained, with restaurants and sports all on the premises. Manzanillo is a good jumping-off point for excursions into Jalisco state; north to Barra de Navidad and Melaque; and to the individual beach resorts of Hotel Tecuan, Hotel Bel-Air El Tamarindo, Hotel Bel-Air Costa Careyes, Club Med Playa Blanca, and Las Alamandas. The curvy drive through the mountains after passing Barra de Navidad is beautiful. It's also easy to make excursions southeast of Manzanillo inland to Colima, capital of Colima state, an hour away, and on to the mountain resort town of Mazamitla, a 3-hour drive from Manzanillo in Jalisco state (see Chapter 13).

SUGGESTED ITINERARIES

If You Have 2 Days

Take it easy on your first day—go for a dip in the ocean or a pool, and have dinner at a nearby restaurant. Spend the second day by the pool or on the beach. In the evening, take a sunset cruise, then have dinner at an outdoor restaurant such as Willy's or El Vaquero Campestre (see Chapter 8).

If You Have 3 Days

Get into the slow swing of Manzanillo on your first 2 days as suggested above, then on the third day rise early and take a side trip to see the museums in Colima, the state capital located an hour to the southeast. Or spend the day on the beach at the coastal village of Barra de Navidad, 45 minutes south.

If You Have 5 Days

With an extended stay in Manzanillo, you'll have time to sample the activities described above, and then perhaps you might want to explore the beautiful coast south of Manzanillo. Select from one or two of the resorts mentioned in "Excursions from Manzanillo," below. Or for a true change of pace, spend a night or two at Mazamitla, one of Jalisco's chilly mountain resort towns, located 3 hours to the southeast (see Chapter 13).

Frommer's Favorite Manzanillo Experiences

Lazy Days. Manzanillo's lack of good shopping and sightseeing attractions makes it easy to relax without that nagging feeling that you should be touring.

Terrace Dining. Manzanillo excels in good restaurants, where you can enjoy the view and soothing breezes.

Sunset Gazing. One of my favorite places for sunset is Hotel La Posada (see Chapter 8) on the Las Brisas Peninsula, where there's always a friendly crowd of foreigners gathered on the patio for the evening ritual.

Deep-Sea Fishing. Fishing is superb here, and a day spent far out at sea is synonymous with a Manzanillo vacation.

1 Organized Tours

City Tours/Excursions   Because Manzanillo is so spread out, you might consider a city tour. I highly recommend the services **of Luís Jorge Alvarez** at **Viajes Lujo,** Av. México 143-2, Manzanillo, Col. 28200 (☎ 333/2-2919; fax 333/2-4075). Office hours are Monday through Friday from 9am to 2pm and 4 to 7pm, and Saturday from 9am to noon, but tours can take place at any time. A half-day city tour costs around $20. Other tours go to Colima ($40) and to Barra de Navidad ($40), which includes a stop at a banana and coconut plantation. Luís uses air-conditioned vehicles and speaks English.

Sunset Cruise   Buy tickets for sunset cruises from travel agents or downtown at La Perlita Dock (across from the train station) fronting the harbor. Tickets go on sale at La Perlita daily from 10am to 2pm and 4 to 7pm and cost around $15 for the La Perlita cruise. The trip is a peaceful one without music or entertainment, but both cruises include two drinks. Cruises last $1^1/_2$ to 2 hours.

2 Sports & Outdoor Activities

BEACHES   **La Audiencia Beach,** on the way to Santiago, offers the best swimming, but **San Pedrito,** shallow for a long way out, is the most popular because it's much closer to downtown. **Playa Miramar,** on the Bahía de Santiago past the Santiago Peninsula, is another of the town's popular beaches, well worth the ride out here on the local bus from town. The major part of **Playa Azul** drops off a little too steeply for safe swimming and is not recommended for waders.

BIRD WATCHING   There are many lagoons along the coast. As you go from Manzanillo up past Las Brisas to Santiago, you'll pass **Laguna de Las Garzas** (Lagoon of the Herons), also known as **Laguna de San Pedrito,** where you can see many white pelicans and huge herons fishing in the water. They nest here in December and January. Back of town, on the road leading to Colima (the capital), is the **Laguna de Cuyutlán** (follow the signs to Cuyutlán), where birds can usually be found in abundance; species vary between summer and winter.

DIVING   Manzanillo offers some unusually intriguing underwater scenery. Many locations are so close to shore there's no need for a boat, which make such dives less expensive than those using boats. Close-in dives include the jetty with coral growing on the rocks at 45 feet and a nearby sunken frigate downed in 1959 at 28 feet. Divers can see abundant sea life, including coral reefs, sea horses, giant puffer fish, and moray eels. Dives requiring a boat cost $65 each with a three-person minimum. Off-shore dives cost $50 per person. **Susan Dearing,** who pioneered diving in Manzanillo, is certified in scuba (YMCA and CMAS) and life saving and CPR by the Red Cross, and she offers divers certification in very intensive courses of various duration. For reservations contact her at the **Hotel La Posada** (☎ and fax 333/3-1899), at the spa at the **Hotel Sierra** (☎ 333/3-2000 ext. 250), or by cellular phone (☎ 90/335-80327).

FISHING   Manzanillo is famous for its fishing, particularly sailfish. Marlin and sailfish are abundant year-round. Winter is best for dolphinfish and dorado (mahimahi), and in summer, wahoo and roosterfish are in greater supply. The **international sailfish competition** is held around the November 20 holiday, and the **national sailfish competition** is in November before Thanksgiving. Fishing can be arranged through travel agencies or directly at the **fishermen's coopera-tive** (☎ 333/2-1031), downtown where the fishing boats are moored.

I can recommend **Gerardo Montes** (☎ 333/2-0817 or 333/2-5085), whose boats, the *Albatros I* and *II*, are generally docked by the Naval Station. Fishing costs $35 per hour in a 28-foot boat and $45 per hour in a 38-foot boat with a 5-hour minimum. The cost can be shared by up to seven people in the larger boat and up to four in the smaller boat.

GOLF   Lying adjacent to Las Hadas, **La Mantarraya Golf Club** (☎ 333/4-0000, ext. 782) is open from 7am to 7pm. When I checked, only guests of Las Hadas were allowed to play here. Greens fees are $35 for 18 holes or $18 for 9 holes. Carts rent for $28, clubs $18, caddies $10 to $16.

TENNIS   Several of the hotels mentioned in Chapter 8 have tennis courts with a resident pro. **La Mantarraya Golf Club**, next to Las Hadas, is open to Las Hadas guests only. The cost is $11 an hour during the day and $17 at night; the courts are open from 4:30pm to 10pm.

3 Manzanillo After Dark

Nightlife in Manzanillo consists mainly of finding a splendid sunset and dining spot followed by a good night's sleep. However, for the more active tourist, **Carlos 'n' Charlies, Costera Madrid,** km 5 (☎ 333/3-1150), on the Santiago Road (Costera Madrid), is always a good choice for food and fun. As the evening wears on, the party may resemble a fraternity bash if the crowd is of college age. Reser-vations are recommended after 6pm. In the evening during high season, there may be a required minimum order/cover if you come just to drink, but the "cover" includes three drinks. On weekends and during high season, they open the dance area.

Le Cartouche Disco, at Las Hadas resort, opens at 10pm and has a cover charge of around $16. **El Bar de Felix,** between Salahua and Las Brisas by the Avis rental car office, is open Tuesday through Sunday from 9pm to 2am; there's no cover charge. Next door and open the same days, **VOC Disco** parties from 10pm to 4am and charges a $12 cover. The 11pm light show splatters light beams over the wa-terfall, rock walls, and large central dance floor. **Jalapeños Restaurant** (by the Ford agency on the Costera) entertains patrons with live Mexican music from 9:30 to 11pm on Friday and Saturday nights.

Note: Most of these establishments have a dress code that prohibits patrons wearing *huaraches* (sandals) or shorts, but the rules generally apply to males rather than females.

4 Excursions from Manzanillo

COLIMA: A COLONIAL CITY WITH FINE MUSEUMS

Colima, the attractive capital of the state of Colima, boasts a colonial-era town center and a number of interesting museums. It is a balmy metropolis that dates from 1523; its founder was the conquistador Gonzalo de Sandoval, the youngest member of Cortés's band. Hotels and restaurants are on or near the main plaza.

From Manzanillo, you can reach Colima in an hour by taking a picturesque road that skirts the 12,870-foot **Volcano de Colima,** which last erupted in 1991. Also visible on this trip is the 14,000-foot **Nevado de Colima,** which actually lies in the state of Jalisco. Colima can also be reached by frequent bus service from the central bus station in Manzanillo. See "Arriving & Departing," in Chapter 7 for exact information on reaching Colima from Manzanillo.

Note: Policemen are abundant in this city and seem overly eager to hand out citations for speeding and other minor infractions such as driving the wrong way on a street—so beware!

EXPLORING COLIMA

Of the city's several museums, these are standouts.

Important note: Colima's museums are closed on Sunday.

✪ Museo de Occidente de Gobierno de Estado (Museum of Western Cultures)

Galvan at Ejército Nacional. No phone. Admission free. Daily 9am–7:30pm.

Also known as the Museum of Anthropology, this is one of my favorite museums in Mexico. It has many pre-Hispanic pieces, including the famous clay dancing dogs of Colima. There are fine examples of clay, shell, and bone jewelry; exquisite human and animal figures; and diagrams of tombs showing unusual funeral customs.

✪ Museo de la Cultura Popular María Teresa Pomar (Museum of Popular Culture)

University of Colima, 27 de Septiembre and Manuel Gallardo Zamora. ☎ **333/2-5140.** Admission free. Mon–Sat 9am–2pm and 4–7pm. From the Museum of Western Cultures, go left out the front door and walk five blocks to the wide Avenida Galvan, at Ejército; cross the street, and the museum will be on your right. (The front wall says INSTITUTO UNIVERSITARIO DE BELLAS ARTES.)

One of the city's most interesting museums, this attraction contains regional costumes and musical instruments from all over Mexico. There are also photographs showing the day-to-day use of costumes and masks and folk art from Oaxaca, Guerrero, and elsewhere. The section devoted to Mexican sweet bread (*pan dulce*) is set up like an authentic bakery, with each bread labeled. At the entrance is a shop selling Mexican folk art.

Museo de Historia de Colima

Portal Morelos 1. ☎ **333/2-9228.** Admission free. Tues–Sat 10am–2pm and 4–8pm.

Opened in 1988, this is the city's newest museum, dedicated to state history. Its beautiful colonial building on the plaza opposite the Hotel Ceballos is the former

Colima's Favorite Sons

Miguel de la Madrid Hurtado   President of Mexico from 1982 to 1988, de la Madrid was born in 1934 in Colima. He received a degree in law in 1957 from the Universidad Nacional Autónima de Mexico, and a master's degree in public administration in 1965 from Harvard University. He was an able administrator and a good president, who unfortunately inherited the scandalous excesses of the two presidents immediately before him, a bankrupt country with 200% inflation, and a mess from his immediate predecessor, José López Portillo, who, among other ill-advised acts, nationalized the banks overnight just before turning over the government to de la Madrid. Among de la Madrid's credits: he began returning to the private sector many government holdings; he steered Mexico toward world competition through membership in GATT (the General Agreement on Trade and Tariffs); and he managed to continue Mexico's payment on its enormous debt at great sacrifice by the Mexican people and economy. His presidency set the stage for the present one in which Mexico heads even faster into world trade, lower inflation, and greater stability.

Alfonso Michel   Born in Colima City, capital of Colima state, Michel's career took him all over the world in search of study, but it wasn't until 1942 that he began to be noticed. Using his mastery of impressionism, Michel (1897–1957) directed his themes to Mexican subjects and shared a studio with Roberto Montenegro from 1935 to 1940.

Hotel Casino, the birthplace of former Mexican president Miguel de la Madrid Hurtado. The collection includes pre-Hispanic pottery, baskets, furniture, and dance masks. After seeing the pottery here and at the Museo Occidente (see above), you'll begin to understand why the Aztec name for Colima meant "place where pottery is made." Colima is also known for its variety of pre-Hispanic tombs, and one of the best displays here shows drawings of many kinds of tombs. You may be asked to leave your purse or bag with the guard as you enter.

Sala de Exposiciones
Portal Morelos 1. No phone. Admission free. Tues–Sat 10am–2pm and 4–8pm, Sun 10am–2pm.

Next to the Museo de Historia de Colima (see above), opposite the main plaza, this museum is sponsored by the University of Colima. It's a changing showcase for fine artists from all over the world.

BARRA DE NAVIDAD & MELAQUE: A QUIET, RELAXING BEACH GETAWAY

Only 65 miles north of Manzanillo (a 1 1/2-hour trip), this pair of modest beach villages has been attracting vacationers for decades. Barra de Navidad and Melaque are only 3 miles apart from each other. Barra has the cobbled streets, good budget hotels and restaurants, and funky beach charm, while Melaque has a lineup of hotels both on and off the beach, fewer restaurants, and no funky charm, though the beach is as wide and beautiful as Barra's. Both villages appeal to those looking less for expensive, modern, and sophisticated destinations and more for quaint, quiet, and inexpensive hideaways. From Manzanillo, the highway twists through

Barra de Navidad Bay Area

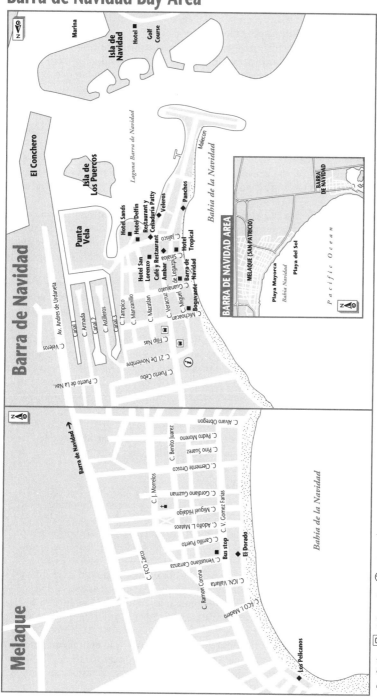

Bus Station ■   Information ⓘ   Church ⊹

some of the Pacific coast's most beautiful mountains covered in oak and coconut palm and acres of banana plantations.

Buses from Manzanillo run the route up the coast frequently on their way to Puerto Vallarta and Guadalajara. Most stop in the central villages of both Barra de Navidad and Melaque. From here, Puerto Vallarta is a 5-hour bus ride. By car, take coastal Highway 200 north; it takes 3 to 4 hours from Manzanillo.

In the 17th century, Barra de Navidad was a harbor for the Spanish fleet, and it was from here that galleons set off in 1564 to find China. Located on a gorgeous crescent-shaped bay with curious rock outcroppings, Barra de Navidad and neighboring Melaque (both are on the same wide bay) boast a perfect beach and a peaceful ambiance. So far only Barra has been "discovered," primarily by a small number of people who come from December through Easter and on Mexican holidays. Other times, it's a quiet getaway, with lots of empty hotel rooms and an easy pace.

Now that the first phase of the long-awaited **Isla Navidad Resort** project is nearing completion across the water from Barra's main pier, the area's pace may quicken. The 18-hole golf course is complete, and the first hotel was nearly completed when I last visited here. Hillside homes and condominiums are planned to follow.

The **tourism office** for both Barra de Navidad and Melaque is in Barra at the end of Legazpi (heading out of town) in the DIF building complex (☎ and fax 335/5-5100). The office is open Monday through Friday from 9am to 7pm and Saturday from 9am to 1pm.

In Barra, the main beachfront street, **Legazpi,** is lined with hotels and restaurants. From the bus station, beachfront hotels are two blocks straight ahead across the central plaza. Two blocks behind the bus station and to the right is the lagoon side, with its main street, **Morelos/Veracruz,** and more hotels and restaurants. Few streets are marked, but 10 minutes of wandering will acquaint you with the village's entire layout.

A special request: If you have any good used clothing or toys, you can deposit them with Philomena Garcia at **Los Pelicanos Restaurant** in Melaque (See "Exploring Melaque," below). She'll distribute them among needy children in the area.

EXPLORING BARRA DE NAVIDAD

Swimming and enjoying the lovely beach and bay view take up most tourists' time. Renting a small boat can be done in two ways. Go toward the malecón on Calle Veracruz until you reach the tiny **boatmen's cooperative** with fixed prices posted on the wall. You can also walk a short bit farther to the thatched gazebo at the end of the malecón itself. Prices are the same.

A round-trip by boat to the village of **Colimilla,** just across the lagoon and popular for its many pleasant restaurants, costs $7 for up to eight people, and you can stay for as long as you like. A 30-minute **tour around the lagoon** costs $12; a **tour on the sea** costs $25. **Sportfishing** is $15 per hour for up to six people. **Water-skiing** costs $15 per hour.

Unusual **area tours, house and apartment rentals,** and **sports equipment rental** can be arranged through **The Crazy Cactus,** Legazpi 138 A (☎ 335/5-5910; fax 335/5-5349), a gift shop operated by Trayce Blackstone and Mari Blanca Perez. In addition to gifts for sale, you'll find bicycles, boogie boards, snorkeling equipment, and life jackets to rent. Among the unique tours is one along the coast to lagoons and mangroves and another to nearby small towns for market days and shopping. **El Médico,** Av. Veracruz 230 (☎ 335/5-5008 and fax 335/5-5807), rents yachts and camping and fishing equipment; they also organize fishing tournaments and sell fishing lures and yacht parts.

Beer Bob's Books, Av. Mazatlán 61, between Sinaloa and Guanajuato, is a "book-lovers" institution in Barra and sort of a community service Bob does for fun. His policy of "leave a book if you take one" means vacationers can select from thousands of neatly shelved trade paperbacks. When beer was cheap, he kept a cooler stocked, and browsers could sip and read. When the price of beer went up, Bob put the cooler away, but he's still called Beer Bob.

ACCOMMODATIONS

During low season (May through November), it doesn't hurt to ask for a discount, even on rates already lowered.

Inexpensive

✪ Hotel Barra de Navidad

Legazpi 250, Barra de Navidad, Jal. 58987. ☎ **335/5-5122.** Fax 335/5-5303. 60 rms (all with bath) FAN. High season $25–$35 single, $35–$40 double. Low season $13–$15 single, $22–$25 double.

At the northern end of Legazpi, this popular, comfortable hotel on the beach has a friendly management and fine balconies overlooking the beach and bay. Rooms with a street view cost the least. A second-floor terrace restaurant overlooks the bay and swimming pool. Hotel patrons rave about the food; the restaurant is open for all meals.

Hotel Bogavante

Legazpi s/n, Barra de Navidad, Jal. 48987. ☎ **335/5-5384.** Fax 335/5-5808. 20 rms (all with bath). FAN. Low season $20 single, $25 double; $30 triple.

Although it was once shabby, this newly renovated hotel sports fresh paint and new tile throughout, making it a good value right on the beach. First-floor rooms come with a single and double bed, and second-floor rooms hold from four to eight people. Third-floor rooms all have kitchens and living areas. About half of the rooms have ocean views. The hotel is near the north end of Legazpi.

✪ Hotel Delfín

Morelos 23, Barra de Navidad, Jal. 48987. ☎ **335/5-5068.** Fax 335/5-8020 or 335/5-6020. 25 rms, 3 apts (all with bath). FAN. High season $20 single, $22 double. Low season $15 single, $17 double. Free parking in front.

One of Barra's better-maintained hotels, the three-story Delfín, on the landward side of the lagoon, is my personal favorite. It offers nice, well-cared-for rooms, each of which has a red-tile floor and either a double or two single beds (no elevator). Outside each room, there are tables and chairs on the covered walkways. The tiny courtyard with a small pool and lounge chairs is shaded by an enormous tree. A small but good breakfast buffet is served from 8:30 to 10:30am on the lovely second-level breakfast terrace (see "Dining," below).

Hotel Sands

Morelos 24, Barra de Navidad, Jal. 48987. ☎ **335/5-5018.** 43 rms (all with bath). FAN. High season $30 single or double. Low season $20 single or double.

The colonial-style Sands, catercorner from the Hotel Delfín (see above) on the lagoon side at Jalisco, offers small but homey rooms that have red-tile floors and windows with both screens and glass. Lower rooms look onto a public walkway and wide courtyard; upstairs rooms are brighter. Three rooms have air-conditioning. In back there is a beautiful pool by the lagoon. The hotel is known for its high-season happy hour from 2 to 6pm at the pool terrace bar. After 6pm, the hotel is quiet again.

Hotel San Lorenzo
Sinaloa 7, Barra de Navidad, Jal. 48987. ☎ **335/7-0139.** 24 rms (all with bath) FAN. High season $16 single, $19 double. Low season $6 per person.

During the high season, other hotels have nicer rooms at the same price and better locations than this inland one. Still, it's a family operated place that is good to know about in case other Barra hotels are full. Rooms are grouped on two levels with windows facing an inner courtyard. Each is simply furnished with tile floors and good beds. To find this hotel from the Hotel Tropical on Legazpi, walk inland two streets and turn right; it's a block ahead on the right.

DINING

Café y Restaurant Ambar
Av. Veracruz 101-A. No phone. Breakfast $2–$4; crêpes $2–$8. Daily 8am–11pm (happy hour 1pm–midnight). Closed Sept. CRÊPES/VEGETARIAN/MEXICAN.

At the corner of Veracruz and Jalisco opposite the Restaurant y Ceñaduría Patty (see below), you'll find this cozy thatched-roof upstairs restaurant open to the breezes. The crêpes are named after towns in France; the delicious crepa Paris, for example, is filled with chicken, potatoes, spinach, and green sauce. Mexican specialties include tortas and quesadillas. For something lighter, try a seafood or fruit salad. This highly recommended restaurant lies one block inland from the Hotel Tropical on Legazpi.

⊗ Hotel Delfín
Morelos 23. ☎ **335/5-5068.** Breakfast buffet $3.50–$4.50. Daily 8am–11 am. High season, beer garden, daily noon–5pm. BREAKFAST/BEER GARDEN.

The second-story terrace of this small hotel is the most pleasant place to begin the day in Barra. In high season, the self-serve buffet offers an assortment of fresh fruit, juices, granola, yogurt, milk, pastries, eggs, and the delicious banana pancakes for which the restaurant is rightfully well known. In low season, you select your order from a list, and it's delivered to your table. During both seasons, each table receives a large pot of coffee. Fresh-grilled German sausage, snacks, and beer are served afternoons during high season.

Pancho's
López de Legazpi 53. No phone. Breakfast $2–$3; main courses, $4–$10. High season, daily 9am–10pm. Low season, daily 8am–7pm. SEAFOOD.

Pancho's is on the beach, toward the far end of Legazpi. The most popular place in town, it's where locals hang out for food and conversation. Pull up a chair on the sand floor and join them. The spicy deviled shrimp was invented here, and the ground marlin ceviche, in a sauce of tomatoes and mildly hot peppers, is fabulous.

Restaurant y Ceñaduría Patty
Jalisco at Veracruz. No phone. Breakfast $2–$3; main courses $2–$7. Daily 8am–11pm. MEXICAN/REGIONAL.

This cute little corner restaurant is a pleasant place to eat, with checked tablecloths, a concrete floor, and pastel walls all open to the street. The menu includes such popular mainstays as pozole, tostadas, tacos, and sopes for dinner. The lunch menu is a bit more stout with beef, fish, and shrimp platters.

✪ Veleros

Veracruz 64. ☎ **335/5-5838.** Main courses $4–$9. High season, daily 8am–11pm. Low season, daily noon–11pm. SEAFOOD/BEEF.

Watch the small boats glide across the glassy lagoon in this clean and casual restaurant at the water's edge. Decorated with striped-cloth-covered tables, it is a tranquil spot for a lengthy meal. Depend on impeccable service and consistently good food. Seafood specialties include shrimp brochette and fish filet, but there are also steak and chicken.

BARRA DE NAVIDAD AFTER DARK

During high season, there is always happy hour from 2 to 6pm at the poolside/lagoon-side bar at the **Hotel Sands** on Calle Morelos (see "Accommodations," above). At the **Disco El Galleón,** also in the Hotel Sands, cushioned benches and cement tables encircle the round dance floor. It's all open air, but garden walls restrict airflow and there are few fans, so you can really work up a sweat dancing the night away. It serves drinks only, no snacks. Admission is $4, and it's open on Friday and Saturday from 9pm to 2am. The beachside **Capricho Disco Club,** on Legazpi (by the Pacífico Restaurant), is the most popular gathering place for sunset between 6 and 8pm, when drinks are two for the price of one.

EXPLORING MELAQUE (SAN PATRICIO)

For a change of scenery, you may want to wander over to Melaque (also known as San Patricio), 3 miles from Barra on the same bay. You can walk on the beach from Barra or take one of the frequent local buses from the bus station near the main square in Barra for 50¢. The bus is marked "Melaque." To return to Barra, take the bus marked "Cihuatlán."

Melaque's pace is even more laid-back than Barra's, and though it's a larger village, it seems smaller. It has fewer restaurants and less to do. It has more hotels, or bungalows, as they are usually called here, but none with the charm of the accommodations in Barra. If Barra hotels are full on a holiday weekend, then Melaque should be your second choice for accommodations. The paved road ends where the town begins. A few yachts bob in the harbor, and the palm-lined beach is gorgeous.

If you come by bus from Barra, you can exit the bus anywhere in town or stay on until the last stop, which is the bus station in the middle of town, a block from the beach. Restaurants and hotels line the beach, and it's impossible to get lost, but some orientation will help. Coming into town from the main road, you'll be on the town's main street, **Avenida López Mateos.** You'll pass the main square and come down to the waterfront, where there's a trailer park. The street going left (southeast) along the bay is **Avenida Gómez Farías;** the one going right (northwest) is **Avenida Miguel Ochoa López.**

Dining

In addition to the restaurants below, there are also many rustic palapa restaurants in town on the beach, and others farther along the bay at the end of the beach. You can settle in on the beach and use one of the restaurants as your base for drinking and dining.

The Turtles of Colima and Jalisco

At least four of Mexico's nine species of marine turtles nest on the beaches of Colima and Jalisco. Just before nesting time, fishermen report seeing the turtles mating offshore. Most turtles will return to the same beach to lay eggs year after year and as often as three times in a season. They only nest on dark beaches; light of any kind repels them.

It takes an hour or more for a female turtle to dig a nest in the sand with her back flippers. Of the more than 100 eggs in each nest (*nido* in Spanish), only 5% of those that hatch will live to return. Programs to save the turtles involve taking the eggs from the original nest to a fenced-off, protected area (called a *maya* in Spanish) and placing them in a nest of identical temperature, depth, and size. The hatchlings, which appear about 45 days later, wait until all their nestmates are ready before they scurry by the hundreds to the ocean.

Crabs, birds, and other ocean denizens as well as humans endanger the turtles' precarious existence. A recent Mexican law carrying serious penalties for destroying turtles or their eggs has had some effect; the belief persists, however, that turtle eggs are an aphrodisiac, and turtles are still killed for their shells and meat.

The Biological Station at Chamela, near Careyes, conducts ongoing studies of the region and produces numerous publications describing its work. The Hotel Bel-Air Careyes has a turtle program in which guests can participate.

El Dorado
Club Náutico Melaque, Gómez Farías s/n. ☎ **335/7-0770.** Breakfast $2.50–$4; main courses $6–$20. Daily 7:30am–10pm. INTERNATIONAL.

The most inviting restaurant in central Melaque, El Dorado fronts the beach behind the hotel Club Náutico Melaque. Because it's open to the breezes on three sides, it's cool on both patio levels. Try the fish amandine, in an almond butter sauce. The seafood tray serves two and comes with beer-batter-fried shrimp (it can be boiled if you prefer), octopus, plus broiled and Veracruz-style fish. To find the restaurant, walk to the right from the front of the bus station; it's on the left facing the beach.

✪ Los Pelicanos
North end of Melaque beach. No phone. Breakfast $2.25–$3; main courses $5–$12; lobster for 2 persons $30. High season, daily 9am–10pm. Low season, daily 9am–7pm. INTERNATIONAL.

Friendly ex-Pennsylvanian Phil Garcia, along with her spouse, Trine, prepares meals like you might find at home. During high season, there might be pork roast and mashed potatoes along with her usual seafood specialties. Year-round you can find burritos, nachos, and hamburgers. The tender fried squid is delectable with one of Phil's savory sauces. Order lobster 24 hours in advance. Many Barra guests come here to stake a place on the beach and use the restaurant as a day-long headquarters for sipping and napping. It's a peaceful place just to watch the pelicans bobbing in front of the restaurant. Los Pelicanos is at the far end of the bay before the Hotel Legazpi.

TECUAN: A HOTEL ON A HALF-MOON BAY

Continuing north on Highway 200 about 45 minutes from Barra de Navidad (about 18 miles beyond the turnoff sign to Tenacatita that you'll see), there is a white cone-shaped silo on the left-hand side of the road painted with a sign to El Tecuan. Turn left and drive 6¹/₂ miles on a curvy cobblestone road through a mango *ejido* (plantation). The road ends at the El Tecuan hotel.

ACCOMMODATIONS

El Tecuan

Hwy. 200, km 33.5. ☎ **335/1-5026.** Fax 335/1-5028. Reservations: Garibaldi 1676, Guadalajara, Jal. 44680 (☎ 3/616-0183; fax 3/616-6615). 40 rms, suites, and villas. A/C. $35 standard single, $40 standard double; $45 single junior suite, $50 double junior suite; $60 villa.

Built on a hill overlooking a wide half-moon bay and beach, El Tecuan is a comfortable and moderately priced standby on this coast that's becoming increasingly expensive. In addition to the wide bay spreading out in front of the hotel, there's a big, beautiful, natural lagoon to the left that's perfect for canoeing. The main building, made of stone and stucco, is built around the swimming pool and faces the bay. Suites and villas are connected via a boardwalk to the main section. Rooms have red-tiled floors and are comfortably furnished. Villas are two stories and have kitchens. Most rooms have ocean views. There's a tennis court, swimming pool, and basketball and volleyball courts. There might be bicycles, horses, and canoes for rent. One restaurant serves all three meals from 8:30am to 10:30pm. Similar to other hotels along this coast, what you see is the first part of a grand development scheme in the works.

EL TAMARINDO: AN OCEAN RESORT IN A FOREST

After Barra de Navidad, and about 25 miles north of the Manzanillo airport, you'll see a sign pointing left to El Tamarindo; turn and follow the narrow road 7 miles through the dense forest to this new and *very* exclusive resort, nestled in a dense forest beside the ocean. It's part of a larger plan that eventually will include private residences; most of the mountain lots, costing in the millions of dollars, have already been sold. When I was last here, nine holes of the projected **18-hole golf course** were complete. The course has a spectacular setting meandering on mountain tops and overlooking jagged cliffs that meet the crashing ocean; it's more like courses you may have experienced in Scotland or Ireland.

ACCOMMODATIONS

Hotel Bel-Air El Tamarindo

Km 7.5, Carretera Manzanillo-Barra de Navidad. ☎ **332/1-0071** or 800/457-7676 in the U.S. 40 villas. A/C TV. $316 one-bedroom villa; $490 two-bedroom villa; $450 junior suite; $460 ranch suite; $550 one-bedroom grand suite; $575 one-bedroom mountain villa; $590–$1030 beach villa. Rates include breakfast and dinner.

Set on 860 secluded tropical wooded acres with 9 miles of oceanfront, the 40 individual stucco villas of this resort are spread under palms and huge oaks and pines facing the beach and ocean. The resort is a member of the Small Luxury Hotels of the World.

The bright colors of Mexican and Guatemalan textiles decorate large throw pillows and furniture in the villas; the decor is reminiscent of the luxurious Las Alamandas (see below). All villas are one-story, separate, and have spacious open-air patios and living rooms with ceiling fans. The large bedrooms have fans and air-conditioning. In addition to breakfast and dinner, rates include use of the tennis courts, nonmotor water sports, and a jungle tour.

Keep in mind that if you want to explore the area, you'll need a car. If you are a nature lover or bird-watcher, the amazingly beautiful forest around the resort has been undeveloped until now and is incredibly rich in wildlife. You'll note the pains developers have taken to disturb as little as possible. Guests can tour the greenhouse and gardens where labeled native specimens are ready to be planted.

Dining/Entertainment: One restaurant serves all meals.

Services: Helicopter transfer service 10 minutes from the Manzanillo airport, laundry, room service, concierge. Airport pick up can be arranged.

Facilities: Pool, tennis courts, water sports, boat excursions, and fishing. The 18-hole golf course should be completed when you travel; nine holes were playable in 1994. Guests also have full privileges at the Hotel Bel-Air Costa Careyes (see below) 25 miles to the north, where there's an equestrian center and turtle watch, among other activities.

COSTA CAREYES: RESORTS ON THE "TURTLE COAST"

The next development is Costa Careyes (which means "turtle coast") with two resorts—the **Hotel Bel-Air Costa Careyes** (formerly the Hotel Costa Careyes), part of a 2,500-acre development, and **Club Med Playa Blanca.** Each resort has its own beaches, resort amenities, and a small, beautiful bay all to itself. The two bays adjoin but are completely separated by bluffs.

The two resorts are roughly 50 miles north of Manzanillo and 100 miles south of Puerto Vallarta. It's about a 1 1/2-hour drive north of Manzanillo on Highway 200, but only about 1 hour from the Manzanillo airport. If you haven't arranged for transportation through either hotel, taxis from the Manzanillo airport charge around $90 one way for the trip. There are car rentals at both the Manzanillo and Puerto Vallarta airports. While these resorts are completely self-contained, a car is useful for exploring the coast—Barra de Navidad and other resorts, for example—but the hotels can also make touring arrangements.

ACCOMMODATIONS

Hotel Bel-Air Costa Careyes
Hwy 200 km 53, Careyes, Jal. ☎ **335/1-0000**, 800/457-7676, or 800/525-4800 in the U.S. Fax 335/1-0100. TV TEL. High season $190–$375 single or double. Low season $140–$300 single or double.

The old Hotel Costa Careyes was gutted to create this totally luxurious hotel in a secluded setting facing the ocean. The first glimpse you see as you step into the breezy open "lobby" is the expansive lawn shaded by enormous palm trees leading to the ocean and free-form pool. It's both rustic and sophisticated, with the room facades awash in scrubbed pastels forming a U around the center lawn. It's a member of the Small Luxury Hotels of the World.

A covered arcade is lined with trendy clothing and decorative arts shops. Mexican tiles and decorative accents give each spacious room a dramatically luxurious feel—from the colony shutters to the white tile floors, handsome loomed bedspreads, and colorful pillows. Some rooms have balconies; all have ocean views, robes, hairdryers, small refrigerators, and 20 rooms have private pools.

The hotel runs a number of special-interest activities for guests. Named after the hawksbill turtle (*carey* in Spanish), the hotel, with a staff biologist, sponsors a "save the turtle" program in which guests can participate between July and December. Pacific Ridley, leatherback, black, and hawksbill turtles all nest in Playa Teopa, a nearby beach, and all are in danger of extinction. You can also arrange a birding expedition to nearby Bird Island, a natural habitat for nesting boobies between July and September. The dry months of November through May are good for birding on the mainland since many fly over during migration, but there are no official birding walks; you're on your own. Boat tours to other nearby beaches, fishing, horseback excursions, and riding lessons are available at the equestrian center. Polo clubs from around the world converge here for polo season, December through April.

Dining/Entertainment: Two restaurant/bars, both casually chic and with international menus, serve all meals in an open setting beside the beach and pool. "Just For Kids" is a program of activities for children. There are also a movie theater and library.

Services: Laundry, purified tap water, and room service. Helicopter or limo transportation from the Manzanillo can be arranged at an additional price.

Facilities: A fully equipped, state-of-the-art spa with massage, loofa scrub, wax, hot and cold plunge, steam and sauna, also has weight equipment. There's a large free-form pool by the ocean. Guests also have privileges at the super exclusive Hotel Bel-Air Tamarindo, 25 miles south, where there's a fabulous golf course.

LAS ALAMANDAS: AN EXCLUSIVE LUXURY RESORT

About 45 minutes beyond Careyes and almost equidistant between Manzanillo (1^1/$_2$ hours) and Puerto Vallarta (1^3/$_4$ hours) is a small sign pointing to Las Alamandas (toward the ocean). The dirt road winds for about a mile through a poor village to the guardhouse of Las Alamandas.

ACCOMMODATIONS

Las Alamandas

Hwy 200 Manzanillo-Puerto Vallarta. ☎ **328/5-5500.** Fax 328/5-55027. Information and reservations: 800/223-6510 in the U.S. 5 multiroom villas. $500–$1,000 one room; $1,800–$2,500 whole villa. Rates include some meals.

Part of a 1,500-acre estate and set on 70 acres against a low hill, this resort's small cluster of buildings almost spreads to the wide, clean beach. The most elite, and exclusive, resort in Mexico, it's a beautifully landscaped spot on an entirely private beach.

The architecture is a blend of Mediterranean, Mexican, and southwestern styles, and the resort has been featured in *Architectural Digest, Casa Gente, Condé Nast Traveler,* and *Vogue.* The furnishings are a stunning blend of Mexican hand-crafted furniture, pottery, and folk art, with cushy sofas beds and pillows covered in bright textiles from Mexico and Guatemala. Though exquisitely selected, the furnishings nevertheless give the rooms a relaxed, casual feel. You definitely feel like kicking back here—only 20 guests can be accommodated at any one time, and the threat of crowds is nonexistent. All of the villas are spacious and have high-pitched, tiled roofs; cool, tiled floors; and tiled verandas with ocean views. Each bedroom has its own bath. The villas have several bedrooms, which can be rented separately or as a whole house, but preference is given to guests who rent whole villas. Some are on the beach, and some are set back from the beach across a cobblestone plaza. Casa del Sol and Casa Rosa are both on the beach.

Dining/Entertainment: One restaurant serves all meals. There's an honor bar and selection of video movies. All rooms have TV with VCR, but there's no television from the outside.

Services: Room service; transportation in the hotel's van to and from Manzanillo ($250 one way) and Puerto Vallarta ($230 one way) can be arranged at the time of reservation.

Facilities: Weight room; massage; 60-foot swimming pool; lighted tennis court; horses; hiking trails for self-guided hikes; mountain bikes; boogie boards; boat tours to Río San Nicolás for birding; fishing. Private 3,000-foot paved landing strip capable of accommodating a King Air turbo prop; make advance arrangements for landing.

10

Getting to Know Guadalajara

Guadalajara (pronounced *gwa-da-la-HA-ra*), Mexico's second-largest city, is also considered by many to be the most authentically Mexican. Much of Mexican tradition developed here or nearby. The *jarabe tapatío* (the Mexican hat dance) was developed here, and Guadalajara is considered the center for *charrarería* (Mexican-style rodeo). Mariachi music, the most robust in the country, was born nearby, and tequila, the fiery liquor that's the foundation of the margarita, is produced a few miles south of the city.

In the city's charter, Emperor Charles V called Guadalajara a *muy leal y muy noble ciudad* ("most loyal and noble city"). As a result of its isolated position southwest of Mexico City, Guadalajara developed into a sophisticated city largely on its own, without a great deal of interference from Spain. Today, it is capital of the state of Jalisco, and five million people live here.

As though to emphasize the great things expected from it, Guadalajara's Spanish builders gave the city not one, but four, beautiful plazas in its center. Today the city's leaders have given it a fifth—the enormous Plaza Tapatía, an ambitious stretch of redevelopment extending for about a mile through the urban landscape. Scattered with trees and monuments and sprinkled with fountains, the superplaza links the city's major colonial buildings and joins the past with the great new buildings of the present.

By the way, *tapatío* (or *tapatía*) is a word you'll come across often in this city. In the early days of the city, people from this area were known to trade in threes (three of this for three of that) called *tapatíos*. Gradually, the people were called *tapatíos*, too, and the word has come to mean "Guadalajaran" in reference to a thing, a person, or even an idea. The way a *charro* (Mexican cowboy) gives his all or the way a mariachi sings his heart out—that's *tapatío!*

1 Orientation

ARRIVING & DEPARTING

BY PLANE   Guadalajara's international airport is a 25- to 45-minute ride from the city. Taxi and colectivo (shared ride) tickets to Guadalajara or Chapala are sold outside in front of the airport. Tickets are sold by zone. A shared taxi ride to the heart of

What's Special About Guadalajara & Environs
The Centro Histórico • With its museums, theaters, restaurants, and pedestrians-only streets, the historic center is a magnificent example of urban renewal that has preserved the city's history. Museums • The enormous Instituto Cultural Cabañas, designed by Manuel Tolsá with fabulous murals by native son José Clemente Orozco. • Tlaquepaque's Regional Ceramics Museum and Tonalá's National Ceramics Museum, exhibiting examples of Mexico's master potters. Villages • Tlaquepaque, a fascinating shopping center with pedestrians-only streets and plazas. • Tonala, famous for its street market and its artists and craftspeople. Music and Dance • The Ballet Folklórico de la Universidad de Guadalajara, acclaimed as the best folkloric company in all Mexico. • The battle of the mariachis in Tlaquepaque, under the portals of the historic El Parian.

Guadalajara costs around $12, and a private taxi costs $16. A taxi to Chapala costs around $30.

On departure from Guadalajara, you'll be required to check in at least 1 1/2 hours before takeoff for international flights and at least 1 hour before takeoff for domestic flights. Local taxis are the only transport from town to the airport.

Major Airlines   See Chapter 3, "Planning a Trip to Mexico's Mid-Pacific Region," for a list of international airlines serving the area. Local numbers for **United,** ☎ 91/800/0-0307 toll free in Mexico.

Aero California (☎ 3/826-1901 or 3/826-8850) serves Guadalajara from Tijuana, Mexico City, Los Mochis, La Paz, and Puebla; **Aeroméxico** (☎ 3/669-0202; 3/689-0028 at the airport) flies from numerous points in the United States and from Monterrey, Puerto Vallarta, Manzanillo, Mazatlán, Chihuahua, Acapulco, and Tijuana in Mexico; **Mexicana** (☎ 3/647-2222; 3/689-0119 at the airport) connects with a number of U.S. cities and with Cancún, Léon, Los Cabos, Nuevo Laredo, Zihuatancjo, Puerto Vallarta, and Tijuana in Mexico. **Saro** (☎ 3/614-7571; 3/688-5876 at the airport) flies to Mexico City, Monterrey, and Tijuana. **Taesa** (☎ 3/679-0900) flies from Mexico City, Tijuana, Morelia, some U.S. cities, and seasonally to Puerto Vallarta.

BY TRAIN   Major Trains   Guadalajara is the country's second-largest train hub, but not all trains are worth taking. The **National Railways of Mexico** (☎ 3/650-0826 or 3/650-1082) runs *El Tapatío,* which goes from Mexico City to Guadalajara, leaving Mexico City at 8:30pm and arriving in Guadalajara at 8:30am. It offers seats as well as sleeping compartments. It takes 12 1/2 hours

Guadalajara & Environs

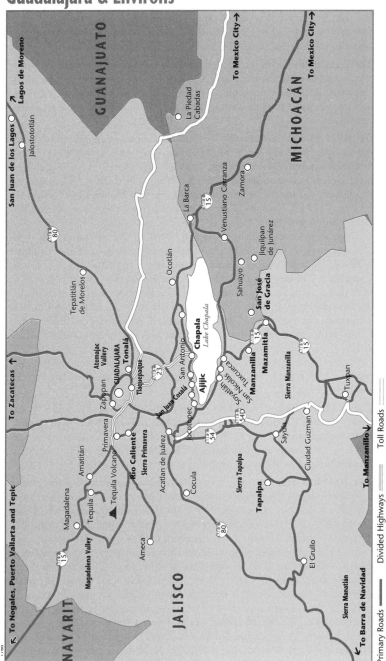

Primary Roads   Divided Highways   Toll Roads

To Nogales, Puerto Vallarta and Tepic

To Zacatecas

San Juan de los Lagos

Lagos de Moreno

To Mexico City

To Mexico City

GUANAJUATO

MICHOACÁN

NAYARIT

JALISCO

Jalostotitlán

La Piedad
Cabadas

La Barca

Venustiano Carranza

MEX 80

Zamora

Jiquilpan
de Juárez

Sahuayo

San José
de Gracia

MEX 15

Ocotlán

Tepatitlán
de Morelos

Chapala
Lake Chapala

San Antonio

Ajijic

Mazamitla
MEX 15

Mazamitla

Sierra Manzanilla

MEX 15

Tuxpan

Atemajac
Valley

Tonalá

Zapopan

GUADALAJARA

Tlaquepaque

San Juan Cosalá

Soyatlán
San Nicolás
Tuxcueca

Manzanilla

MEX 23

Jocotepec

Sayula

Rio Caliente

Sierra Primavera

Primavera

Tequila Volcano

Amatitán

Acatlán de Juárez

Cocula

54D

MEX 54

Sierra Tapalpa

Ciudad Guzmán

Magadalena

Tequila

Tequila Volcano

Ameca

Tapalpa

MEX 80

El Grullo

Magadalena Valley

MEX 15

Sierra Manatlán

To Barra de Navidad

To Manzanillo

and costs $19 to $100 one way. Considering that a bus takes 5 hours and costs $10 to $14, taking the train is the less attractive option. Other trains go to Mazatlán and Mexicali at the U.S. border, but they also take forever.

The Train Station   The station, downtown on Calzada Independencia, is too far from hotels to walk. Buses marked "Centro" go downtown, and those marked "Estación" go to the station from downtown. Otherwise, you're at the mercy of taxis that charge $5 to go the short distance anywhere between the station and the city center.

BY BUS   Two bus stations serve Guadalajara: the old one near downtown and the new one 6 miles out on the way to Tonala. A convenient place to get bus information is **Servicios Coordinados,** Calzada Independencia 254, a kind of "bus travel agency" located under Plaza Tapatía. There, travelers can make reservations, buy tickets, and receive information on the six main bus lines to all points in Mexico. The **ETN** bus line (☎ 3/614-8875 or 3/614-2479) has an office in the Hotel Carlton downtown.

To get from either station to your hotel, look for the **city buses** and white minivans marked "Centro," which pick up passengers in front of each terminal building. These are convenient only if you have a very small suitcase. **Linea Turquesa** (TUR) buses are air-conditioned and offer the most comfortable service since they accept only the number of passengers for whom there are seats. From the bus station, some go to Tonala, and others follow a route along Calzada Tlaquepaque to Tlaquepaque, Revolución, and 16 de Septiembre/Alcalde to the Centro Histórico. Some of these skip Tonala; look for the sign on the front of each bus.

You can also take a **taxi.** Taxi tickets, sold inside each terminal building, are priced by zone. A taxi from the Central Camionera to the downtown Plaza Tapatía area (a 30-minute ride) costs about $7.

The Old Bus Station   For bus trips within a 60-mile radius of Guadalajara, including to **Lake Chapala, Ajijic, Jocotepec, Mazamitla,** and **San Juan Cosalá,** go to the old bus terminal on Niños Héroes off Calzada Independencia Sur and look for **Transportes Guadalajara-Chapala** (☎ 3/619-5675), which has frequent bus and combi service beginning at 6am to Chapala (see Chapter 13).

The New Bus Station   The **Central Camionera,** about 6 miles and a 35-minute ride east of downtown toward Tonala, provides bus service to and from virtually any point in Mexico. None of the buses from here is of the school-bus variety—while the price difference between first and second class is small, the difference in speed, comfort, and convenience is often great. The new terminal resembles an international airport—seven separate buildings are connected by a covered walkway in a U shape, with one-way traffic entering on the right. Each building houses several first- and second-class bus lines. That's the only drawback—you must go to each one to find the line or service that suits you best.

Here is a breakdown of the various parts of the new station, beginning with the first building on the right: **Building 1** holds Primera Plus with deluxe service to Puerto Vallarta (5 hours), Lagos de Moreno, Colima, Manzanillo (4¹/₂ hours), and Melaque (5 hours). This building also has the ETN deluxe line to Mexico City (7 hours) and to Aguascalientes (but ETN buses leave from building 2). **Building 2** has many buses to Aguascalientes and Zacatecas. Autotransportes

Tapatío Artistry: Three Creative Native Sons

Raul Anguiano Valdez   Born in Guadalajara in 1915, at 21 Anguiano had his first exhibition at the Palacio de Bellas Artes in Mexico City. One of his most famous paintings, *The Thorn,* depicts a young Indian removing a thorn from her foot with a knife. It hangs in the National Museum of Art in Mexico City. His teaching career took him to the Escuela Nacional de Pintura y Escultura in Mexico City in 1935 when he was only 20, where he remained until 1967. Simultaneously he became a professor at the Universidad Nacional Autónima de Mexico in Mexico City in 1959, and guest professor at Trinity University in San Antonio, Texas, in 1966. One-man shows organized for him took him to Guadalajara, the Carnegie Cultural Arts Center in Oxnard, California, and the San Diego Museum of Man.

Gerardo Murillo (Dr. Atl)   Possessing enormous energy as well as political and artistic passion, Gerardo Murillo (who, for a political statement, changed his name to Dr. Atl, a Náhuatl word meaning "water") was a painter, writer, and not-too-successful politician who was driven by art and political causes and attracted by the outdoors, mountain climbing, and science. Born in Guadalajara, Murillo (1875–1964) is best known for his vast landscapes, usually including volcanoes, in which he produced an aerial feeling of the Mexican landscape. His influence on Mexican art and artists was enormous. Among his students, when he was director of the San Carlos Academy, were José Clemente Orozco and David Siquieros. One of his books, *Las Artes Populares en Mexico* (Popular Arts in Mexico), produced as a catalog for the first exhibition of Mexican folk art, upheld the common artisans of Mexico and remains a classic.

Roberto Montenegro   Another of Mexico's child prodigies, Montenegro (1887–1968), born in Guadalajara, began studying painting in 1903. The following year he went to Mexico City to study at the Escuela Nacional de Arte where he began acquaintances with some of Mexico's famous artists, Diego Rivera among them. On scholarship and working, he traveled, studied, and exhibited in Europe for almost 15 years, becoming one of Mexico's most skilled artists. When he returned to Mexico, he began an intense discovery of Mexican folk art and his paintings, besides featuring peasant folk, usually include folk art from everyday life. In 1934 he was appointed director of the Museo de Artes Populares de Bellas Artes, and for five years shared a studio in Guadalajara with fellow painter, Alfonso Michel.

Mazamitla goes to Tuxcueca, La Manzanilla, and Mazamitla hourly between 6am and 6:30pm; these buses don't go through Chapala and Ajijic; instead, they pass at the crossroads at Jocotopec. **Building 3** has Primera Plus and Autocamiones Cihuatlan with service to Manzanillo six times daily as well as to Talpa and Macota. **Building 5** has Estrella Blanca with hourly service until 6pm to Puerto Vallarta. Linea Azul Oriente has six buses to San Juan del Lago, and Turistar's deluxe buses go to Aguascalientes and Lagos de Moreno. **Building 6** has Omnibus de Mexico buses going to Mexico City and many to Zacatecas and Colima, as well as ETN buses with service to Colima, Manzanillo, Puerto Vallarta,

Mexico City, Morelia, and Aguascalientes. **Building 7** has the Expreso Futura line with many buses to Mexico City, the Rojos al Altos line with hourly service to Zacatecas, and Turistar Primera with frequent service to Lagos de Moreno, León, and Puerto Vallarta. This station is one of the nicest in Mexico, with amenities like shuttle buses, restaurants, gift shops, luggage storage *(guarda equipaje),* book and magazine shops, liquor stores, Ladatel long-distance telephones, and hotel information. There's also a large new budget hotel next door. To get to the station by bus, take any bus marked **"Central"** on Avenida 16 de Septiembre/Alcalde opposite the Rotonda de los Ilustres in downtown Guadalajara.

BY CAR   Directions   From Nogales on the California border, follow Highway 15 south. You can also take a toll road between Guadalajara and Tepic, a 6-hour drive. From Barra de Navidad or southeast on the coast, take Highway 80 northeast. A new toll road, running from Puerto Vallarta on the Pacific nearly to Tequila (30 miles west of Guadalajara), was scheduled for completion in June 1995. The trip will take 4 hours. From Mexico City, take the free Highway 90 (6 to 8 hours) or the new toll road, which takes $4^1/2$ hours. Coming from Colima, there's another toll road that takes about 4 hours.

VISITOR INFORMATION

The **State of Jalisco Tourist Information Office** is at Calle Morelos 102 (☎ 3/658-2222 or 3/658-0305; fax 3/613-0335) in the Plaza Tapatía at the crossroads of Paseo Degollado and Paraje del Rincón del Diablo. It's open Monday through Friday from 9am to 8pm and Saturday, Sunday, and festival days from 9am to 1pm. This is one of the most efficient and informative tourism offices in the country. They have a supply of maps, as well as a monthly calendar of cultural happenings in the city.

CITY LAYOUT

Guadalajara is not a difficult city to negotiate, but it certainly is big. While most of the main attractions are within walking distance of the historic downtown area, others—such as Tonala and Tlaquepaque (which are both nearby) and Lake Chapala and Ajijic (which are both farther away)—are accessible by bus. Street names downtown change at the cathedral.

NEIGHBORHOODS IN BRIEF

Centro Histórico   The heart of the city takes in the Plaza de Armas, Plaza de los Laureles, Plaza de los Hombres Ilustres, Plaza Liberación, and Plaza Tapatía. It's the tourist center and contains major museums, theaters, restaurants, hotels, and

---

Impressions

Mexico combines the modernity of today with the romance of history. Blending thirteenth-, fifteenth- and twentieth-century civilizations, it presents a stirring picture of Indian, Spanish and western civilizations living side by side. In some cities colonial palaces and cathedrals stand close to steel structures . . . . Pack burros and motor cars, ox carts and airplanes, forked-stick plows and steam tractors—all have their place in this ageless land of mañana.

—Byron Steel, *Let's Visit Mexico,* 1946

In all Latin-American cities a certain group of older men seem to spend their evenings about the plaza or in the City Club nearby. Perhaps as their wives grow older and the children grow up they lose interest at home.
    —Leonidas W. Ramsey, *Time Out for Adventure: Let's Go to Mexico,* 1934

the largest covered market in Latin America, all linked by wide boulevards and pedestrians-only streets. It's bounded east and west by Avenidas 16 de Septiembre/Alcalde and Prosperidad (across Calzada Independencia) and north and south by Avenida Hidalgo and Calle Morelos.

Parque Agua Azul   An enormous city park 20 blocks south of the Centro Histórico, it has a children's area and rubber-wheeled train. Nearby are the state crafts shop, performing-arts theaters, and the anthropology museum.

Chapultepec   A fashionable neighborhood with shops and restaurants 25 blocks west of the Centro Histórico, it is reached by Avenida Vallarta. Chapultepec is the main artery through the neighborhood.

Minerva Circle   Almost 40 blocks west of the Centro Histórico, Minerva Circle is at the confluence of Avenidas Vallarta and López Mateos and Circunvalación Washington. It's a fashionable neighborhood with several good restaurants and the Hotel Fiesta Americana, all reached by the Par Vial.

Plaza del Sol   The largest shopping center in the city, it lies south of Minerva Circle and southwest of the Centro Histórico near the intersection of Avenidas López Mateos and Mariano Otero.

Zapopan   Once a separate village founded in 1542, now it's a full-fledged suburb 20 minutes northwest of the Plaza Tapatía via Avenida Ávila Camacho. It's noted for its 18th-century basilica and the revered 16th-century image of the Virgin of Zapopan, made of corn paste and honored every October 12. The city's fashionable country club is just south of Zapopan.

Tlaquepaque   Seven miles southeast of the Centro Histórico, it's a village of former mansions turned into shops that front pedestrians-only streets and plazas.

Tonala   Four miles from Tlaquepaque, it's a village of more than 400 artists working in metal, clay, and paper. A huge street market is held on Thursdays and Sundays.

2 Getting Around

By Bus & Tren Lijero   The city has six kinds of city buses, and a rapid transit system called the **Tren Lijero**. Many of the buses run the same routes but offer different kinds of service. **Gray buses with maroon stripes** are better city buses and cost 35¢. **School bus-style buses** cost 25¢. Both of these buses carry seated passengers as well as passengers packed into the aisles. Privately operated **minivans** cost about the same as city buses. Some are numbered, and others have their destination written on the windshield. **Linea Turquesa** (turquoise line) buses, colored a pale turquoise, have the distinguishing letters "TUR" on the side and run several routes around the city. These cost $1, are air-conditioned, have padded seats, and best of all, carry only as many passengers as there are seats. Frequent TUR buses also run between the Centro Histórico, Tlaquepaque, Central Caminonera (the new bus station), Tonala, and Zapopan. Some of these go to Tonalá but not Zapopan, or to Zapopan but not Tonalá. For information on getting to Tlaquepaque and Tonalá by bus, see Chapter 13.

Two bus routes of the **"Par Vial"** (electric buses) will satisfy 90% of your intracity transportation needs. Buses bearing the sign "Par Vial" run a rectangular route going east along Independencia/Hidalgo, passing the Mercado Libertad, and going as far west as the Minerva Circle, where they turn back east on Vallarta/Juárez and pass by the Plaza de Armas on their run east.

Many buses run north-south along the Calzada Independencia (not to be confused with Calle Independencia), but the **"San Juan de Dios–Estación"** bus goes between the points you want—San Juan de Dios church, next to the Mercado Libertad, and the railroad station (*estación*) past Parque Agua Azul. This bus is best because most other buses on Calzada Independencia have longer routes (out to the suburbs, for instance) and thus tend to be heavily crowded at all times.

Section 1 of the **Tren Lijero** (rapid transit system) is finished, and section 2 should be fully operational when you travel. Section 1 serves a few tourist needs since it runs north-south along Federalismo, curving the distance of Camino de Sur/Prolongación Colón. Service 2 runs east-west along Vallarta/Juárez and Avenida Javier Mina, the eastern extension of Vallarta/Juárez. It takes passengers between the Mercado Liberación and the Parque Revolución (near the restaurants Suehiro and Copenhagen and the Museo de las Artes).

By Colectivo   Colectivos are minivans that run throughout the city day and night, picking up and discharging passengers at fixed and unfixed points. They are often a faster and more convenient way to travel than the bus. There are no printed schedules, and the routes and fixed pick-up points change frequently. However, locals know the routes by heart and can tell you where and how to use them if you tell them where you want to go.

By Car   Keep in mind several main arteries. The **Periférico** is a loop around the city that connects with most other highways entering the city. Traffic on the Periférico is slow because it's heavily potholed, filled with trucks, and only a two-lane road. Several important freeway-style thoroughfares crisscross the city. **Gonzalez Gallo** leads south from the town center and connects with the road to Tonala and Tlaquepaque or leads straight to Lake Chapala. **Highway 15** from Tepic intersects with both **Avenida Vallarta** and **Calzada Lázaro Cárdenas.** Vallarta then goes straight to the Plaza Tapatía area. **Cárdenas** crosses the whole city and intersects the road to Chapala and to Tlaquepaque and Tonala.

By Taxi   Taxis are an expensive way to get around town. A short 10- to 15-minute ride—for example, from the Plaza de Armas to the zoo and planetarium—costs an exorbitant $6 or $7, while a bus there costs only 25¢.

By Horse-Drawn Carriage   Take one of the elegant horse-drawn carriages for a spin around town. The cost is about $15, depending on route and length of ride—usually about 45 minutes. Drivers congregate in front of the Museo Regional, near the Mercado Libertad, and also behind the Plaza/Rotonda de los Hombres Ilustres and other spots around town.

Greater Guadalajara

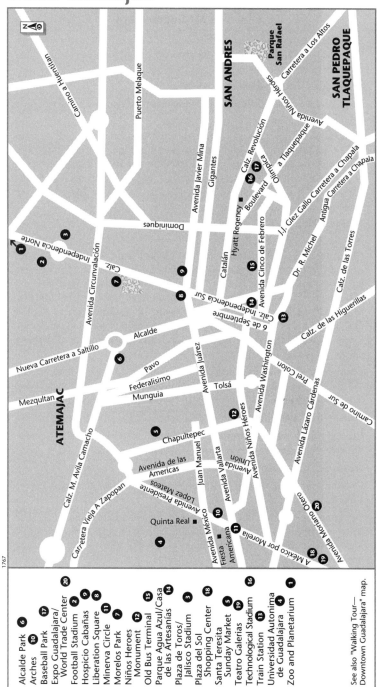

ATEMAJAC

SAN ANDRES

SAN PEDRO TLAQUEPAQUE

Parque San Rafael

Carretera a Los Altos

Camino a Huentitlán

Puerto Melaque

Avenida Javier Mina

Gigantes

Dominiques

Calz. Revolución

Olimpiaca A Tlaquepaque

Boulevard

Hyatt Regency

Catalán

Avenida Niños Héroes

J.J. Glez Gallo Carretera a Chapala

Antigua Carretera a Chapala

Independencia Norte

Avenida Circunvalación

Calz. Independencia Norte

Calz. Independencia Sur

6 de Septiembre

Avenida Cinco de Febrero

Dr. R. Michel

Calz. de las Torres

Calz. de las Higuerillas

Nueva Carretera a Saltillo

Alcalde

Pavo

Federalisimo

Munguia

Mezquitan

Avenida Juárez

Tolsá

Piel Colón

Avenida Washington

Camino de Sur

Avenida Lázaro Cárdenas

Chapultepec

Avenida de las Americas

Avenida Presidente López Mateos

Calz. M. Avila Camacho

Carretera Vieja A Zapopan

Juan Manuel

Avenida México

Avenida Vallarta

Avenida Unión

Avenida Niños Héroes

A México por Morelia

Avenida Morelia

Avenida Moreno Otero

Quinta Real

Fiesta Americana

Alcalde Park **6**
Arches **10**
Baseball Park **17**
Expo Guadalajara/ World Trade Center **20**
Football Stadium **2**
Hospicio Cabañas **9**
Liberation Square **8**
Minerva Circle **11**
Morelos Park **7**
Niños Heroes Monument **12**
Old Bus Terminal **15**
Parque Agua Azul/Casa de las Artesanias **14**
Plaza de Toros/ Jalisco Stadium **3**
Plaza del Sol **18**
Shopping Center **5**
Santa Teresita Sunday Market **19**
Teatro Galerias **16**
Technological Stadium **13**
Train Station **4**
Universidad Autonima de Guadalajara **1**
Zoo and Planetarium

See also "Walking Tour— Downtown Guadalajara" map.

1767

FAST FACTS: Guadalajara

American Express   The local office is at Av. Vallarta 2440, Plaza Los Arcos (☎ 3/615-8910); it's open Monday through Friday from 9am to 6pm and Saturday from 9am to noon.

Area Code   The telephone area code is 3.

Baby-sitters   Hotels can usually recommend baby-sitters; ask at the reception desk.

Bookstores   Gonvil, a popular chain of bookstores, has a branch across from Plaza de los Hombres Ilustres on Avenida Hidalgo and another a few blocks south at Avenida 16 de Septiembre 118 (Alcalde becomes 16 de Septiembre south of the cathedral). Sanborn's, at the corner of Juárez and 16 de Septiembre, always has a large selection of English-language magazines, newspapers, and books.

Business Hours   In Guadalajara, most stores are open Monday through Saturday from 9am to 2pm and 4 to 8pm.

Climate & Dress   Guadalajara has a mild, pleasant, and dry climate year-round. Bring a sweater for evenings during November through March. The warmest months—April and May—are hot and dry. From June through September, it's rainy and a bit cooler. Guadalajara is as sophisticated and at least as formal as Mexico City. Dress is conservative; resort wear (short shorts, halters, and the like) is out of place here, but knee-length shorts, skirts, slacks, and blouses for women, or slacks, Bermudas, and a shirt for men are fine for all but the few formal restaurants or events.

Consulates   The world's largest U.S. consular offices are here at Progreso 175 (☎ 3/625-2998 or 3/625-2700). The offices are open Monday through Friday from 8am to 4:30pm.

Crime   See "Safety," below.

Currency Exchange   Banks will change money and traveler's checks Monday through Friday from 9am to noon.

Dentists   Ask at your hotel for a referral.

Doctors   Guadalajara has many English-speaking doctors. Ask your hotel for a referral.

Drugstores   Ask at your hotel about the location of the closest pharmacy. For late-night service, try Farmacías Guadalajara, a chain throughout the city with a branch near downtown on Avenida López Cotilla (☎ 3/614-2810), open daily from 8am to 10pm.

Emergencies   Dial 02 for help in most emergencies. For the state police (☎ 3/617-5838); for the highway police (☎ 3/612-7194). During the day, call the tourist office (☎ 3/614-0606, ext. 114).

Eyeglasses   Look for the optic shop right across the plaza from the tourism office.

Holidays   February and October are the big festival months. At Christmas and Easter, many establishments are closed or have revised hours.

Hospitals   For a medical emergency, there's the Hospital México-Americano, Colomos 2110 (☎ 3/614-0089).

Information   See "Visitor Information" earlier in this chapter.

Laundry/Dry Cleaning   There are no laundries in the downtown area. Hotels generally offer this service but at a high price.

Lost Property   Call the American Consulate (see "Consulates," above), the police (see "Emergencies," above), or your bus or airline (for property lost in transit).

Luggage Storage/Lockers   Luggage storage is available in the main bus station, the Central Camionera, and at the Guadalajara airport.

Newspapers/Magazines   The Hotel Fenix, on the corner of Corona and López Cotilla, has English-language newspapers and magazines and maps. It's also a good place to buy Guadalajara's English newspaper, *The Colony Reporter*, published every Saturday, if you don't spot it on the newsstand. Sanborn's, at the corner of Juárez and 16 de Septiembre, has a wide selection of U.S. and Mexican newspapers and magazines.

Police   See "Emergencies," above.

Post Office   The main post office (Correos) is at the corner of Carranza and Calle Independencia, about four blocks northeast of the cathedral. Standing in the plaza behind the cathedral and facing the Degollada Theater, walk to the left and turn left on Carranza; walk past the Hotel Mendoza, cross Calle Independencia, and look for the post office on the left side.

Radio/TV   Many English-language U.S. cable TV stations are available in Guadalajara.

Religious Services   Check *The Colony Reporter* (see "Newspapers/Magazines," above).

Restrooms   Use the facilities in a restaurant, museum, or hotel lobby area. Always carry your own toilet paper and soap.

Safety   As in any large city, don't be careless with your belongings. There are people on the streets at all hours, but to be safe, avoid walking around alone late at night on unlighted streets. As in the rest of Mexico, pedestrians don't have the right of way, so be sure to look left, right, and behind you when crossing any street, even if you cross with the light.

Schools   Foreigners can study Spanish at the Foreign Student Study Center, University of Guadalajara, Calle Guanajuato 1047 (Apdo. Postal 12130), Guadalajara, Jal. 44100 (☎ 3/653-2150; fax 3/653-0040).

Taxis   See "Getting Around" earlier in this chapter.

Transit Information   See "Getting Around" earlier in this chapter.

11

Where to Stay & Dine in Guadalajara

Sophisticated and international, Guadalajara offers all the amenities in the way of hotels and restaurants that you'd expect of a major city. A wide range of hotels fits every budget, and restaurants serve the cuisines of the world.

1 Accommodations

In addition to these downtown hotels, check out the accommodations in nearby destinations, including the Río Caliente Spa and Ajijic on Lake Chapala (see Chapter 13).

DOWNTOWN
EXPENSIVE

Carlton Hotel
Av. Niños Héroes 125 and 16 de Septiembre, Guadalajara, Jal. 44190. ☎ **3/614-7272** or 91-800/3-6200 toll free in Mexico. Fax 3/613-5539. 222 rms and suites. A/C MINIBAR TV TEL. $150 standard single or double; $185 master suite; $195 executive suite. Ask about weekend discounts.

The Carlton is near Agua Azul Park and a short distance from the historic center. The nicely furnished rooms are unusually spacious, and all come with hairdryers and remote-control TV with U.S. channels. Master suites have large living rooms, while junior suites have a small sitting area. Each of the fifth-floor executive suites comes with continental breakfast, afternoon coffee and pastries, and open bar in the early evening. The 10th floor is reserved for nonsmokers. You'll save money by purchasing a package for this hotel through a travel agent in the United States.

Dining/Entertainment: One indoor/outdoor restaurant, facing the pool, serves all meals. There are two bars. Genesis Video Disco is open from 10pm to 1am Thursday through Saturday. Lancaster nightclub offers two evening shows of live music or singers for a cover of less than $10. Call for times.

Services: Laundry, room service, travel agency, purified tap water. For an extra charge, guests may use the hotel's fax and copy machine.

Facilities: Large pool; small, fully equipped fitness center for men from 7 to 10am and 6 to 9pm and for women all other hours.

Impressions

Not so many years ago the stage-coach between [Zapotlán] and Guadalajara used to be held up regularly, sometimes at several places in one trip. The highwaymen who came last would take from the passengers even their underwear, though with inborn chivalry they allowed the ladies to keep their crinolines. The unfortunate travelers would arrive at Zapotlán gowned in newspapers and the curtains of the coach. Whenever the curtains were seen not to be in their proper places it was at once understood in the town what had happened.

—Carl Lumholtz, *Unknown Mexico,* 1902

Fiesta Americana

Aurello Aceves 225, Glorieta Minerva, Guadalajara, Jal. 44100. ☎ **3/625-3434,** 3/625-4848, or 800/223-2332 in the U.S. Fax 3/630-3725. 396 rms. A/C MINIBAR TV TEL. $170–$175 single or double; $190 Fiesta Club.

A 22-story luxury hotel on a grand scale, the Fiesta Americana caters to the exacting demands of travelers arriving for both business and pleasure. It's a bustling hotel with a 14-story lobby and popular lobby bar with ongoing live entertainment. Like the public areas of the hotel, the individual rooms are spacious and beautifully coordinated, all with TV with U.S. channels. The 27 exclusive Fiesta Club rooms and three suites on the 12th and 14th floors come with special amenities (see "Services," below). One room is equipped for people with disabilities.

Dining/Entertainment: Three restaurants, including the popular and elegant Place de la Concorde, cater to all dining requirements. The lobby bar is open from noon to 2am. For more on the hotel's entertainment list see "Guadalajara After Dark" in Chapter 12.

Services: Laundry, dry cleaning, room service, travel agency.

Facilities: Heated rooftop swimming pool, two lighted tennis courts, and purified tap water. Fiesta Club guests have key-only access to club floors, separate check-in and checkout, concierge, remote-control TV, continental breakfast and afternoon wine and hors d'oeuvres daily, as well as business services such as secretaries, fax, copy machine, and conference room.

Hyatt Regency

Av. López Mateos Sur y, Moctezuma, Guadalajara, Jal. 45050. ☎ **3/678-1234** or 800/228-9000 in the U.S. and Canada. Fax 3/676-1222. 347 rms and suites. A/C MINIBAR TV TEL. $140–$185 single or double; $245 suite; $215–$245 Regency Club. Free parking.

The elegant 14-story Hyatt Regency Hotel anchors one end of the Plaza del Sol, the city's largest and most fashionable shopping center. Glass elevators whisk up and down the soaring lobby. Guest rooms, as stylish as the hotel's public areas, vary in size, but all are decorated in rose and green with natural wood furniture and all have a tub/shower combination. Four key-only floors are reserved for Regency Club guests who receive special amenities. Nonsmoking rooms are on the 12th floor.

Dining/Entertainment: Three restaurants, from poolside snacks to fine dining and Mexican specialties, meet guests' dining requirements. The lobby bar entertains with live music from 8 to 11:30pm. There's live music in El Pueblito Cantina Monday through Thursday from 8pm to 3am and Friday and Saturday from 6pm to 3am.

Services: Laundry, dry cleaning, room service, beauty shop, travel agency, car rental, business center with bilingual secretarial services, and 24-hour doctor. Regency Club guests receive a daily newspaper, continental breakfast, and evening cocktails in the club's separate lounge.

Facilities: Swimming pool on the 12th floor, gym, separate saunas for men and women, ice-skating rink.

✪ Quinta Real

Av. Mexico 2727, Guadalajara, Jal. 44680. ☎ **3/615-0000,** 800/445-4565 in the U.S. and Canada, or 91-800/3-6015 toll free in Mexico. Fax 3/630-1797. 78 suites. A/C MINIBAR TV TEL. $215 junior suite; $250 master suite; $275 grand-class suite.

The city's most intimate hotel is also the most difficult to book since it's almost always full. Its casual but sophisticated restaurant and bar are *the* places to be seen if you want to climb the local social or political ladder. Each of the guest rooms is different: Eight have brick cupolas, some have balconies, several have conch-shaped headboards, and four come with a whirlpool bath. All have elegant antique decorative touches, remote-control TVs with U.S. channels, tub/shower combinations, and king-size beds. The hotel is located west of the city center, two blocks from the Minerva Circle on Avenida Mexico at López Mateos.

Dining/Entertainment: The elegant off-lobby restaurant with both terrace and indoor dining is open for all meals from 7am to 1am. The adjacent bar opens from 1pm to 2am.

Services: Concierge, laundry and dry cleaning, massage by reservation, video players for rent, travel agency.

Facilities: Small heated pool.

MODERATE

✪ Calinda Roma

Juárez 170, Guadalajara, Jal. 14100. ☎ **3/614-8650,** 800/228-5151 in the U.S., or 91-800/ 9-000 toll free in Mexico. Fax 3/613-0557. 172 rms (all with bath). A/C MINIBAR TV TEL. $40–$45 single, $60–$70 double. Parking $1 daily.

Perfectly situated, the Calinda Roma is within walking distance of all downtown sights and restaurants. This quiet and comfortable hotel is one of the best in the city center. Rooms were renovated for its 100th birthday in 1993, and bathrooms will be updated next. Some rooms have exercise bicycles. Higher-priced rooms are larger. There are an excellent restaurant and bar in the lobby. The rooftop garden, with a grass putting green and a pool, is a great place to unwind. To find the hotel from the Plaza de Armas, walk two blocks south on Corona. Turn left on Juárez; the hotel is two blocks ahead at the corner of Degollado.

Hotel de Mendoza

Carranza 16, Guadalajara, Jal. 45120. ☎ **3/613-4646** or 800/221-6509 in the U.S. Fax 3/613-7310. 104 rms (all with bath). TV TEL. $75 single, $90 double.

This restored hotel is popular with foreigners for its quiet, colonial atmosphere and modern conveniences. It's at the corner of Hidalgo, only steps from Liberation Plaza and the Teatro Degollado. Almost all of the large rooms have wall-to-wall carpeting, and some have a tub and a shower. Rooms face either the street or an interior court with a swimming pool. Rates may be higher if you call or reserve them from the United States. Walk-in rates are cheaper—get them quoted in pesos. Laundry and room service are offered. The hotel has a swimming pool on the first floor and one restaurant, La Forga. El Campañario bar offers dance music. To get here from the Teatro Degollado, go to the left of the theater and look for Carranza, a block down on the left; turn left at the corner church, adjoining the hotel.

INEXPENSIVE

Hotel Nueva Galicia

Corona 610, Guadalajara, Jal. 44100. ☎ **3/614-8780.** Fax 3/613-3892. 95 rms (all with bath). A/C MINIBAR TV TEL. $20–$35 single, $26–$45 double. Free parking.

Tall and wedge-shaped, this modern hotel offers pleasant rooms with lots of windows and tub/shower combos. The interior rooms are small and dark; the larger rooms face the street and are sunny but noisy. The restaurant downstairs, Cafetería Excelsior, is open from 7am to 11pm. It's clean, bright, and spacious. Walk or take a local bus about 10 blocks south of the cathedral down 16 de Septiembre, then turn left onto Nueva Galicia and walk two blocks. The hotel is between La Paz and Independencia.

✪ Hotel San Francisco Plaza

Degollado 267, Guadalajara, Jal. 44100. ☎ **3/613-8954** or 3/613-8971. Fax 3/613-3257. 76 rms (all with bath). A/C TV TEL. $27 single, $29–$32 double. Free parking.

This highly recommended hotel facing a tiny square near Priciliano Sánchez gives you a lot for your money. Stone arches, brick-tile floors, bronze sculptures, and potted plants decorate the four spacious central courtyards. All rooms are large and attractive, and each includes either a double bed, a king-size bed, or two double beds. The English-speaking staff is friendly and helpful. A very good, inexpensive restaurant off the lobby is open daily from 8am to 10pm. To get here from the Plaza de Armas, walk five blocks south on 16 de Septiembre, turn left onto Sánchez, and walk two blocks to Degollado and to the hotel.

⑨ Posada Regis

Corona 171, Guadalajara, Jal. 44100. ☎ **3/613-3026** or 3/614/8633. 19 rms (all with bath). TV TEL. $20 single, $25 double. Discounts for stays of a week or more.

Opposite the Hotel Fenix, the Posada Regis occupies the second floor of a restored old mansion. The large, carpeted rooms are simply furnished and arranged around a tranquil, covered courtyard, a small restaurant, and potted plants. Rooms with balconies facing the street are quite noisy. Windowless interior rooms are stuffy, so ask for a fan. The mattresses have plastic covers and "nonbreathing" nylon-type sheets. Baths have open ceilings and no doors. I've stayed here and find it particularly serves my budget and my needs for safety and proximity to downtown. Video movies are shown every evening on the lobby TV.

The restaurant serves a very good and inexpensive breakfast ($1.75–$3.15) between 8am and 11am and lunch ($4–$5) from 2 to 4pm. I especially enjoy the good lunch here. Nonguests can take meals, too. It's best to call ahead and tell them you're coming, but you can also try dropping in. There's personal laundry service. To find the hotel from the Plaza de Armas, walk 2½ blocks on Corona. It's on the left almost at the corner of Madero. Enter through a small doorway and go up a flight of stairs to the second-floor hotel and lobby.

⑨ Posada Tapatía

López Cotilla 619, Guadalajara, Jal. 44100. ☎ **3/614-9146.** 10 rms (all with bath).
$12 single, $16 double.

Under the care of Alberto Guzman, the hospitable and friendly new owner, this
faded beauty of a mansion (formerly the Posada de la Plata) has been infused with
new life and is once again a good budget choice. Beautiful old tile floors and plants
enliven the once-dreary interior courtyard. Rooms are large, with high ceilings and
tall etched-glass double doors. Though basically furnished, rooms have bedside
lamps and usually a table and chairs and armoire, new mattresses, bed frames,
colorful bedspreads, shower curtains, and new bathroom fixtures. Guests can use
the washing machine and hang clothes on the rooftop to dry. To find the hotel
from the Plaza de Armas, walk south down 16 de Septiembre/Alcalde and turn
right on Cotilla; it's about $6^1/_2$ blocks farther on the left, between Barcelona and
8 de Julio.

2 Dining

Some travelers find it comforting to know that such U.S. franchise restaurants as
Kentucky Fried Chicken, McDonald's, and Dunkin' Donuts are beginning to
proliferate in Guadalajara. As long as you're in Guadalajara or anywhere in the state
of Jalisco for that matter, however, I urge you to try a local dish called *birria*—
a hearty soup of lamb, pork, or goat meat in a tasty chicken-and-tomato broth.
Restaurants around El Parian in Tlaquepaque have birria on the menu daily.
Another local specialty is the *lonche,* a sandwich made from a scooped-out *bolillo*
(a large roll) filled with a variety of meats and topped with sour cream, avocado,
onions, and chiles.

On the second floor of the **Mercado Libertad,** you can purchase economical
meals at any of the seemingly hundreds of little restaurant stands. Some people say
you should not eat here. Nonetheless, hundreds of people do eat here every day
and seem to be surviving just fine—I've even done it myself. Check it out—it's a
fascinating slice of Mexican life. The best time to go is early in the morning, while
the food is freshest. The hotel **Posada Regis** serves a very economical and filling
home-style breakfast and lunch (see "Accommodations," above.)

EXPENSIVE

Suehiro

La Paz 1701. ☎ **3/826-0094** or 3/826-3122. Reservations recommended. Main courses
$8–$25. Mon–Sat 2–5:30pm and 8–11pm. JAPANESE.

Guadalajarans love this touch of Japan in their city, and they fill every seat in the
several spacious dining rooms. The food is authentically flavored and prepared.
Teppanyaki is the specialty, but the menu offers a wide selection of tempura. You
can order a selection of sushi, too, by the plate or piece. You can also dine entirely
on sushi in the separate sushi bar, where the selection is large, fresh, delicious, and
prepared while you watch. The restaurant is about 13 blocks beyond the Parque
de la Revolución and Av. Enrique Diáz de León. To reach it, take the Par Vial
from Av. Hidalgo to Chapultepec. Get off at Chapultepec and turn left (south)
on Chapultepec for three blocks and turn left (east) on La Paz for about three
blocks; it's on the right.

MODERATE

Molino Rojo

In the Hotel Frances, Maestranza 35. ☎ **3/613-1190.** Main courses $4–$10. Daily 7:30am–10pm. INTERNATIONAL.

I can't recommend the Hotel Frances as an accommodation because of the nightly disco noise, but the off-lobby restaurant of the hotel, with its international fare, is a pleasant change from more traditional Mexican restaurants downtown. Nice but not elegant, the decor features purple, turquoise, and Mexican pottery accents. Try the spaghetti primavera (natural carrot-and-spinach pasta with fresh vegetables and parmesan cheese), the tampiqueña plate, or something more North American like the club sandwich. From the Plaza de Armas, walk one block east on Moreno to Maestranza and turn right. The hotel and restaurant are on the left.

✪ La Trattoría Pomodoro Ristorante

Niños Héroes 3051. ☎ **3/122-1977.** Pasta $4–$6; chicken, beef, and seafood dishes $6–$11. Mon–Sat 1pm–midnight, Sun 1pm–8pm. ITALIAN.

Sooner or later, visitors learn about the good food at this popular restaurant. Service is friendly and swift, and the newly decorated restaurant is refreshingly appealing with natural wood chairs, cushioned seats, and linen-clad tables. A large span of windows looks out onto Niños Héroes. There's separate seating for smokers and nonsmokers. For starters, you might want to sample the antipasto bar or the shrimp in white wine cream sauce with chiles. As a main course, the fettucine Alfredo is excellent. The superb salad bar and garlic bread are included in the price of main courses. To find this place, take the Par Vial going west on Independencia/Hidalgo. Get off when the bus turns back at the Minerva Circle. Walk one block farther to Avenida Mexico, cross the street, and get a bus going south to Niños Héroes (about 14 blocks). Cross Avenida Mexico to Niños Héroes and walk about a half a block; the restaurant is on the right behind a church.

✪ Recco

Libertad 1981. ☎ **3/625-0724.** Main courses $7–$11. Daily 1–11:30pm. ITALIAN/CONTINENTAL.

Owned by Luigi Cupurro and housed in an old mansion in one of Guadalajara's neighborhoods, this casually fashionable restaurant rates high with the locals. Dining rooms, all decked out in cloth-covered tables and cushioned chairs, are a bit too brightly lit at night to be intimate, but the service and food are good. Appetizers include small portions of pasta, seafood, and carpaccio or perhaps pâté and prosciutto and cantaloupe. Among the main courses, you'll find pepper steak, charcoal broiled trout, and veal with fettucine. To find it from the main plaza, take the Par Vial to Chapultepec and Vallarta. At Vallarta, turn left on Chapultepec for two blocks to Libertad and turn left again. You'll see the restaurant on the right less than half a block down.

INEXPENSIVE

✪ Acuarius

Prisciliano Sánchez 416. ☎ **3/613-6277.** Breakfast $3; main courses $2.50–$5; soup $2; *comida corrida* $5. Daily 9:30am–8pm (*comida corrida* served 1–4pm). VEGETARIAN.

This immaculate, airy little lunch room has soft music playing and shelves of soy sauce and vitamins. The restaurant offers breakfast, an à la carte menu, and *comida corrida*. For the *comida corrida*, there's a choice of two main dishes, which you can sample first if you can't make up your mind. When I was here, the choice was zucchini sautéed with mushrooms in tangy tomato sauce or mixed-vegetable stew. Whole grain bread and whole grain tortillas come with the meal in addition to soup, fruit, and yogurt or a salad, a tall glass of fruit juice, and dessert. If that's too much food, consider ordering from the menu that offers a daily choice of three main courses made from soy and two of vegetables. From the Plaza de Armas, walk four blocks south on 16 de Septiembre, turn right onto P. Sánchez, and walk 3¹/₂ blocks; the restaurant is on the right between D. Guerro and Ocampo.

✪ Café Madrid

Juárez 264. ☎ **3/614-9504.** Breakfast $2–$3; main courses $2–$6; Daily 7am–11pm. MEXICAN.

Conveniently located, this popular cafe serves the best coffee in Guadalajara. The aroma wafts outside the cafe in the morning—Americano, espresso, cappuccino, and café con leche are all excellent eye-openers. Signs above the counter advertise chilaquiles and "ricos hot cakes," which are indeed rich and are served with warm syrup. The extrahearty platillo tapatío includes fried chicken, a taco, an enchilada, and potatoes. From the Plaza de Armas, walk one block on Corona to Juárez and turn right; the cafe is on the right.

Denny's

Juárez 385. ☎ **3/614-0219.** Main courses $3–$7. Mon–Fri 7am–10pm; Sat–Sun 24 hours. MEXICAN/INTERNATIONAL.

This restaurant, part of a chain that bills itself as the largest in the world, always offers fast, courteous service and food at reasonable prices. The menu has pictures that appeal to foreigners who haven't mastered Spanish. Sandwiches usually come with a salad and french fries. To find Denny's from the Plaza de Armas, walk one block on 16 de Septiembre to Juárez. It's on the right corner.

⑤ La Chata Restaurant

Corona 129. ☎ **3/613-0588.** Breakfast $2.75–$4.25; main courses $2.50–$7. Daily 9am–11pm. REGIONAL.

Though it doesn't look like much from the street, La Chata comes highly recommended as the place to have authentic regional/Mexican food. The first sight of the festively clad tables and the bandanaed women stirring and frying and the first whiff of the food hook just about everyone. Locals like La Chata for *tapatío* fare from pozole and tortas ahogadas (spicy pork sandwiches) to the steaming hot atole, which some people drink over ice. To find it from the Plaza de Armas, walk 1¹/₂ blocks south on Corona; it's on the right between Juárez and López Cotilla.

✪ Los Itacates Restaurant

Chapultepec Nte. 110. ☎ **3/825-1106.** Breakfast $1.75–$4; tacos 60¢; main courses $2–$5. Mon–Sat 8am–11pm, Sun 8am–7pm. MEXICAN.

Locals can't say enough about the authenticity and quality of the Mexican food here. The atmosphere is festive, with colorfully painted chairs and table coverings. You can choose to dine on the sidewalk in front or in one of the three interior rooms. Among the specialties are pozole, sopa medula (bone marrow soup), lomo adobado (baked pork), and chiles rellenos. The chicken Itacates comes with a quarter of a chicken, two cheese enchiladas, potatoes, and rice. To find the restaurant, take the Par Vial west on Independence/Hidalgo. Get off at Chapultepec and walk to the right (north) on Chapultepec about three blocks. It's on the right.

Sanborn's

Juárez at 16 de Septiembre. ☎ **3/613-6264.** Breakfast $3–$4; main courses $3–$8. Daily 7:30am–1am. INTERNATIONAL.

As at other branches elsewhere in Mexico, foreigners always feel at home at Sanborn's, partly because the menu has food basics enjoyed by homesick foreigners—sandwiches, steaks, pancakes, milk shakes, and the like and partly because service is swift and pleasant. It's a cross between a modern department store, full-fledged pharmacy, and restaurant. The varied menu features everything from tacos and hotcakes to steaks and sandwiches. When you're finished eating, the section filled with drug items, English-language books and magazines, and gifts is *the* place to get back in touch with the world; Sanborn's is always well stocked. To find it from the Plaza de Armas, walk one block south on 16 de Septiembre to Juárez; it's on the left corner.

12

What to See & Do in Guadalajara

This modern city with its historic center and nearby excursions has enough going to keep visitors busy for several days. One of the best ways to see Guadalajara's top attractions is by taking a walking tour through the downtown area to acquaint yourself with the major historical, cultural, and architectural highlights of the city.

SUGGESTED ITINERARIES

If You Have 2 Days

On your first day in Guadalajara, familiarize yourself with the historic downtown area by taking the walking tour detailed below. Take your time browsing in the crafts section of the Libertad Market and walking the corridors of the Cabañas Cultural Institute, admiring Orozco's work. Wind up the day with dinner near the Plaza Tapatía, then stroll over to Mariachi Square to hear the battle of the singers. If your second day happens to be a Thursday, make a shopping foray to Tlaquepaque and Tonalá and have dinner in Tlaquepaque (see Chapter 13). On other weekdays, you can spend a second day further exploring the city's museums and other attractions.

If You Have 3 Days

After you've spent a couple of days getting to know Guadalajara, begin early on your third day and head for Lake Chapala; you'll probably want to go to the lakeside villages of Chapala and Ajijic (see Chapter 13). Have breakfast in Ajijic at the Posada Ajijic beside the lake, then take lunch at Manix, one of Ajijic's fine restaurants. After exploring the area and the lake, enjoy a sunset dinner at one of the lakeside restaurants.

If You Have 5 Days

After a few days taking in the pleasures of the Guadalajara area as described above, you may want to spend a couple of nights at the mountain resort town of Mazamitla, 3 hours north of Guadalajara, or you could enjoy massages, thermal waters, and vegetarian food at the Río Caliente Spa an hour west of the city.

1 The Major Attractions

Sprawling and dynamic, Guadalajara's centuries-old culture is displayed in museums and beautiful colonial-era structures, several of which are highlighted below.

Regional Museum of Guadalajara

Hidalgo at 6 de Diciembre. ☎ **3/614-9957.** Admission $4.50 for adults; children enter free. Tues–Sun 9am–3:45pm.

This building, built in 1701 in the churrigueresque style, exhibits some of the region's archaeological finds, fossils, historic objects, and art. Among the highlights are a gigantic reconstructed skeleton of a mammoth and a meteorite weighing 1,715 pounds found in 1792 in Zacatecas. On the first floor, there's a fascinating exhibit of pre-Hispanic pottery featuring unusual pieces that have been in the collection and some exquisite recent pottery and clay figures found near Tequila during the construction of the toll road. On the second floor is a small, interesting ethnography section showing the contemporary dress of the state's indigenous cultures, including the Coras, Huichols, Mexicaneros, Nahuas, and Tepehuanes.

Teatro Degollado (*deh-goh-yah-doh*)

Plaza Tapatío. ☎ **3/626-9280** or 3/614-4773, ext. 144 or 143. Mon–Fri 10am–2pm.

This beautiful neoclassic 19th-century opera house is named for Santos Degollado, a local patriot who fought with Juárez against the French and Maximilian. Notice the seven muses in the theater's triangular facade above the columns. The theater hosts various performances during the year, including the excellent Ballet Folklórico on Sunday at 10am. Plaza Libertad links the cathedral and the Degollado Theater.

Hospicio Cabañas

Plaza Tapatía. ☎ **3/617-4322.** Admission $1.50 adults, 75¢ students, and 35¢ children under age 12. Tues–Sat 10am–6pm, Sunday 10am–3pm.

Formerly called the **Cabañas Orphanage** and known today as the **Instituto Cultural Cabañas,** this impressive structure was designed by the famous Mexican architect Manuel Tolsá. It housed homeless children from 1829 until 1980. Today, it's a thriving cultural center offering art shows and classes. The main building has a fine dome, and the walls and ceiling are covered by murals painted in 1929 by José Clemente Orozco (1883–1949). Orozco's powerful painting in the dome, *Man of Fire*, is said to represent the spirit of humanity projecting itself toward the infinite. Several other rooms hold more of Orozco's work, and there are also excellent temporary exhibits. A contemporary art exhibit in the south wing features fascinating and unusual paintings by Javier Arevalo. To the left of the entrance is a bookstore.

In the far back, to the right and down a hallway beyond the first patio after you enter, is a small cafe selling pizzas, sandwiches, sweets, and hot and cold drinks. The cafe is open Monday through Friday from 10am to 8pm, Saturday from 10am to 6pm, and Sunday from 10am to 3pm. The institute's own Ballet Folklórico performs here every Wednesday at 8:30pm.

✪ Museo de las Artes de la Universidad de Guadalajara

Juárez 975. ☎ **3/625-7553**. Admission $2. Tues–Sat 10am–8pm, Sun and holidays noon–8pm.

Opened in 1994, this museum promises to be one of the most exciting in the country. The excellent opening show featured contemporary artists from all over the Americas. Several rooms house the university's collection, mostly of Mexican and Jaliscan artists, and there is always a traveling exhibition. The beautiful building housing the museum was constructed as a primary school in 1914. One wall of the auditorium and the cupola above show two of Orozco's vigorous murals entitled *Man, Creator and Rebel* and *The People and Their False Leaders*.

To reach the museum, take the Par Vial west on Independencia/Hidalgo. Get off after it makes the right turn onto Vallarta/Juárez. From the bus stop on Juárez, walk back (east) two or three blocks; it's on the right opposite the University of Guadalajara. It's also about an 11-block walk from Alcalde/16 de Septiembre, straight west on Juárez; it's four blocks beyond the Parque Revolución, which will be on your left.

✪ Museo de la Ciudad

Independencia 684 at M. Barcena. ☎ **3/658-2531**. Admission $1. Tues–Sat 10am–5pm, Sun 10am–3pm.

Opened in 1992, this fine museum, housed in a wonderful old stone convent, chronicles Guadalajara's interesting past. The eight *salas*, beginning with the first room to the right and proceeding in chronological order, cover the years just before the city's founding by 63 Spanish families up to the present. Interesting and unusual artifacts, including rare Spanish armaments and equestrian paraphernalia, give a sense of what day-to-day life was like in Guadalajara's past. As you browse, take time to read the explanations (in Spanish), which give details not otherwise noted in the displays.

WALKING TOUR
Downtown Guadalajara

Start: Plaza de Armas.
Finish: Mercado Libertad.
Time: Approximately 3 hours, not including museum and shopping stops.
Best Times: After 10am, when museums are open.
Worst Times: Mondays or holidays, when the museums are closed.

This walk through downtown Guadalajara will acquaint you with the major historical, cultural, and architectural treasures of the city. Begin the tour in the plaza beside the main cathedral on Avenida Alcalde between Avenida Hidalgo and Calle Morelos in the charming:

1. **Plaza de Armas.** This pleasant plaza has wrought-iron benches and walkways that lead like spokes to the ornate French-made iron central bandstand, directly in front of the:

2. **Palacio del Gobierno.** This eye-catching arched structure dominating the plaza was built in 1774 and combines the Spanish and Moorish influences prevalent at the time. Be sure to go inside to view the spectacular mural of Hidalgo by Clemente Orozco over the beautiful wooden-railed staircase to the right. The panel to the right is called *The Contemporary Circus* and the one on the left,

Walking Tour—Downtown Guadalajara

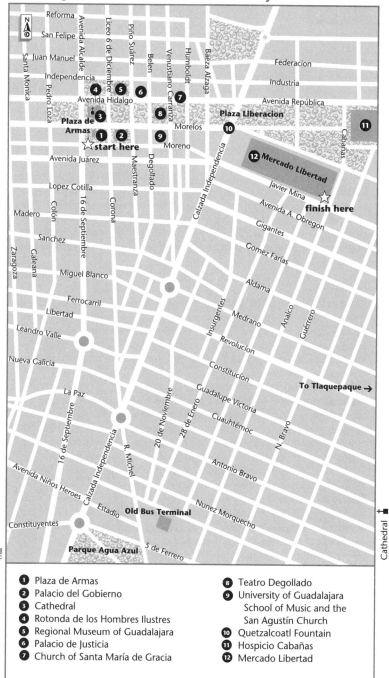

1. Plaza de Armas
2. Palacio del Gobierno
3. Cathedral
4. Rotonda de los Hombres Ilustres
5. Regional Museum of Guadalajara
6. Palacio de Justicia
7. Church of Santa María de Gracia
8. Teatro Degollado
9. University of Guadalajara School of Music and the San Agustín Church
10. Quetzalcoatl Fountain
11. Hospicio Cabañas
12. Mercado Libertad

Here I witnessed a scene which furnished a delightful contrast to the rush of prosaic modern progress which is rapidly transforming the ancient City of Guadalajara. A drowsy peon and his boy were slowly driving a large flock of turkeys along the street, keeping them in motion with the aid of long sticks with which they occasionally prodded the birds. Instead of going to a poultry shop, the housekeepers of Guadalajara buy their turkeys from these vendors as they pass through the streets.
> —W. E. Carson, *The Wonderland of the South,* 1909

The Ghost of Religion in Alliance with Militarism. The highly acclaimed Orozco was a native of Guadalajara.

Going back out the front entrance, turn right and walk to the:

3. **Cathedral.** Begun in 1561, the unusual multispired facade combines several 17th-century Renaissance styles, including a touch of Gothic. An 1818 earthquake destroyed the original large towers; the present ones were designed by architect Manuel Gómez Ibarra. Inside, look over the sacristy to see the painting believed to be the work of renowned 17th-century artist Bartolomé Murillo (1617–82).

Leave the cathedral and turn right out the front doors and walk along Avenida Alcalde to the:

4. **Rotonda de los Hombres Ilustres.** Sixteen gleaming-white columns without bases or capitals stand as monuments to Guadalajara's—and the state of Jalisco's—distinguished sons. To learn who they are, visitors need only to stroll around the flower-filled green park and read the names on the 11 nearly life-size statues of the state's heroes. There are 98 burial vaults in the park, only four of which are occupied.

East of the plaza, cross Liceo to the:

5. **Regional Museum of Guadalajara.** In a handsome 18th-century building, the history of the area from prehistoric times to the present is chronicled in fossils, archaeological discoveries, and in an ethnographic section showing contemporary clothing of area indigenous groups, the Coras, Huichols, Mexicaneros, Nahuas, and Tepehuanes. (For a full description, see "The Major Attractions," above). The museum is open from Tuesday through Sunday from 9am to 3:45pm. Outside the museum and to the right is the:

6. **Palacio de Justicia.** Built in 1588 as the first convent in Guadalajara, Santa María de Gracia later became a teachers' college and girls' school. In 1952, it was officially designated as the Palace of Justice. Inside, above the stairway, is a huge mural honoring the law profession in Guadalajara; it depicts historic events, including Benito Juárez with the 1857 constitution and laws of reform.

Outside the palacio and directly to the right, continuing east on Avenida Hidalgo is the:

7. **Church of Santa María de Gracia,** one of Guadalajara's oldest churches. It was built along with the convent next door, which eventually became the Palacio de Justicia (see above).

Opposite the church is the:

8. **Teatro Degollado** (*deh-goh-yah-doh*), a beautiful neoclassic 19th-century opera house. It's striking from the outside, and inside it's ornately decorated with red velvet and gold. It's open Monday through Friday from 10am to 2pm. (See "The Main Attractions," above, for details.)

To the right of the theater, on the opposite side of the plaza from the Santa María de Gracia church, is the:

9. University of Guadalajara School of Music and the San Agustín Church. There are continuous services in the church, and sometimes the music school is open to the public. Continuing east on the plaza, you should be sure to notice the spectacular fountain behind the Degollado Theater; it depicts Mexican history in low relief. Next, you'll pass the charming children's fountain, followed by the unusual sculpture of a tree with lions with nearby slabs of text by Charles V proclaiming Guadalajara's right to be recognized as a city.

The plaza opens up into a huge pedestrian expanse called **Plaza Tapatía,** framed by department stores and offices and dominated by the:

10. Quetzalcoatl Fountain. This towering, abstract sculpture/fountain represents the mythical plumed serpent Quetzalcoatl, which figures so prominently in Mexican legend and ancient culture and religion. The smaller pieces represent the serpent and birds; the centerpiece is the serpent's fire.

TAKE A BREAK   Take a short break at one of the small ice-cream shops or fast-food restaurants along the plaza or wait to go to the small cafeteria inside the **Hospicio** (see below), which serves hot dogs, sandwiches, cake, soft drinks, coffee, and snacks.

Looking down at the far end of the plaza, you'll spot the:

11. Hospicio Cabañas. This former 19th-century orphanage is today the city's main cultural center and one of the city's finest buildings; it was designed by the famous Mexican architect Manuel Tolsá. Simply walking through it and admiring the architecture and expansive spaces is a treat. Its seemingly endless groupings of patios, lined with arcaded porticos, houses artwork by José Clemente Orozco and others. Orozco's painting on the dome, *Man of Fire*, is best viewed by lying on the bench below it; the bench was put there for that purpose. The center is always busy with seminars and exhibits and congresses of artists. There's a small cafe on a patio off to the right of the entrance, and a bookstore is on the left. The institute's own Ballet Folklórico performs here every Wednesday at 8:30pm. To the left of the entrance is a bookstore.

For a real change of pace, turn left out the front entrance of the Cabañas and look for a stairway that leads down to the:

12. Mercado Libertad, Guadalajara's gigantic covered central market, said to be the largest in Latin America. The site has been used for a market plaza since the 1500s, and the present buildings were constructed in the early 1950s. This is a great place to buy leather goods, pottery, baskets, rugs, kitchen utensils, and just about anything else. (See "Shopping," below.)

2 More Attractions

Parque Natural Huentitán

Calz. Independencia Nte. and Flores Magón. ☎ **3/674-0318** or 3/674-0266. Zoo $3 adults, $2 children; planetarium $2.50 (movie additional $1); Pasaporte Mágico $2.50. Zoo daily 9am–6pm; planetarium Mon–Sat 9am–7pm, Sun 9am–6:30pm; Pasaporte Mágico daily 10am–5pm.

? Did You Know?

- Lake Chapala is the largest lake in Mexico.
- The U.S. Consulate in Guadalajara is the largest American consulate in the world.
- Muralist José Clemente Orozco was born in Guadalajara in 1883.
- The *jarabe tapatío* (Mexican hat dance) was developed in Guadalajara.
- The blue agave, the plant from which tequila is made, grows around Guadalajara near the town of Tequila.
- Mariachi music developed in Cocula, a small town near Guadalajara where there are now no mariachis.
- A mariachi band can be a group of as few as three musicians to a dozen or more.

This area, at the far northeastern edge of the city, holds three attractions: the city zoo, Pasaporte Mágico (a children's park), and the Centro Ciencia y Tecnología, which includes the planetarium. By local bus no. 60 north on Calzada Independencia, it's about a 30-minute ride; a taxi costs $6 to $7. Those going by bus should look for the large, yellow pillars on the right side of the street coming from downtown. From Independencia, it's another 15-minute walk up Flores Magón to the zoo's entrance through the huge parking lot on the left.

The **zoo** is set in a manicured, shaded, spread out area with meandering walkways; it's to home to polar bears, gorillas, jaguar, ocelot, tecuanes, monkeys, exotic birds, a large section of mammals, sea lions, and others. An aviary show is presented in the auditorium daily at 11:30am and 12:30 and 1:30pm. Sergio Bustamante's blue sculptures of monkeys in different positions dot the steps where you enter.

The **planetarium** (☎ 3/674-4106) is like many others you've probably seen. The hour-long movie *Mundo Desconocido* (*Unknown World*) is shown daily on a dome-shaped screen at 10 and 11:30am and 2:30, 4, and 5pm. The Centro de Ciencias y Tecnología that houses the planetarium offers dull exhibitions about space exploration, the galaxies, telephone equipment, and military aircraft.

After you enter the zoo area, you'll see the entrance to **Pasaporte Mágico** (☎ 3/674-0318), a children's park filled with all kinds of mechanical rides made just for them. Admission includes the "Mundo Marino" show at noon, 2, 4, and 6pm.

Parque Agua Azul

Located near the former bus station at the south end of Calzada Independencia, this park is a perfect refuge from the bustling city. It contains plants, trees, shrubbery, statues, and fountains. Many people come here to exercise early in the morning. The park is open daily from 7am to 6pm. Admission is adults $1; children 50¢.

Across Independencia, catercorner from a small flower market in a small one-story rock building, is the **Museo Arqueología del Occidente de Mexico.** It houses a fine collection of pre-Hispanic pottery from the states of Jalisco, Nayarit, and Colima and is well worth your time. The museum is open Tuesday through Sunday from 10am to 2pm and 4 to 7pm. There's a small admission charge.

The state-run **Casa de las Artesanías** (☎ 3/619-4664) is just past the park entrance at the crossroads of Calzada Independencia and Gallo (for details, see "Shopping," below).

Plaza de Los Mariachis

Half a block from the Mercado Libertad on Calzada Independencia and Calle Javier Mina beside the San Juan de Dios Church is the Plaza de los Mariachis, actually a short street lined with restaurants and cafes. During the day, small bands of mariachis loaf around or sip drinks, but at night the place is packed with them (see "Guadalajara After Dark," below).

Plaza and Ex-Convento del Carmen

Avenida Juarez. No phone. Tues–Sun 9am–10pm.

The **Ex-Convento del Carmen,** on Avenida Juárez four blocks west of the Centro Histórico, offers a full range of theater, films, and musical events almost nightly. Tickets are usually sold here just a short while before the performance.

Across the street, the **Plaza del Carmen,** with a bubbling fountain, roses, and shade trees, is a nice place to relax. Lovers' embraces may lead to a wedding at the small **Templo del Carmen,** an old church on the plaza. There's usually a mass, wedding, or christening in progress.

The Tequila Plant

Avenida Vallarta 3273. ☎ **3/615-6990** or 3/630-0707. Admission free. Tours 10am Mon–Fri.

Some people become fascinated with the fire liquor used in the habit-forming famous Mexican margarita and want to see how it's made. The Tequila Sauza bottling plant has regular tours. After the tour, there's a "happy hour" during which you can enjoy a variety of tequila drinks prepared by masters of the art. You can skip the tour and come just to drink from 10am to 1pm. Both the tours and the drinks are free.

By the way, this is just a bottling plant. The distillery is in the town of **Tequila,** off Highway 15 about 25 miles east of Guadalajara. You'll see the spiny blue agave plant, from which tequila is made, growing everywhere around the little town. It takes a good 2 hours to get to Tequila due to traffic. (See "Organized Tours," below).

3 Organized Tours

Several times daily, **Panoramex** (☎ 3/610-5005 or 3/610-5109) offers bilingual tours of Guadalajara, Lake Chapala, Tequila, and Zapopan; tours range from $15 to $25. Those without a car might want to consider a tour, especially to the outlying regions. Inquire at the Panoramex office (open Monday through Friday from 9am to 7pm) or at your hotel.

4 Special Events

The Jalisco State Band puts on **free concerts** in the Plaza de Armas usually every Tuesday, Thursday, and Sunday starting at about 7pm. Arrive early if you want a seat in the park.

During September, Mexicans celebrate their **independence** from Spain; Guadalajara goes all out with a month-long celebration. Look for poster-size

It is a pretty, somnolent town Guadalajara with a magnificent climate and is famous for its special style of pottery as well as for a certain type of hide chair which you will recognize instantly as the kind you have sat in wherever there was a terrace.
—Leone and Alice Leone-Moats, *Off to Mexico*, 1935

calendars listing attractions which include many performances in theaters all over the city. On **September 15,** the Governor's Palace fills with well-dressed invited guests as they and the massive crowd in the park below await his reenactment of the traditional *grito* (shout for independence) at 11pm. The *grito* commemorates Fr. Miguel Hidalgo de Costilla's pronouncement that began the Mexican War of Independence in 1810. The celebration features live music on a temporary street stage, spontaneous dancing, frequent shouting of *"Viva México!"* and fireworks. On **September 16,** there's a parade that lasts an hour or so. For the next couple of days, the park in front of the Degollado Theater resembles a country fair and Mexican market. There are games of chance with stuffed-animal prizes and a variety of food, including cotton candy and candied apples. Live entertainment goes on in the park day and night.

October is another month-long celebration called **Fiestas de Octubre,** which originally began with the procession of Our Lady of Zapopan. Nowadays, the month is a celebration of everything that is notable about Guadalajara and Jalisco. The celebration kicks off with an enormous parade, usually on the Sunday (or possibly the Saturday) nearest the first of the month. Festivities continue all month, with performing arts, rodeos (*charreadas*), bullfights, art exhibits, regional dancing, a food fair, and a Day of Nations involving all the consulates of Guadalajara. Much of the ongoing displays and events take place in the Benito Juárez Auditorium.

On **October 12** around dawn, the small, dark figure of **Our Lady of Zapopan** begins her 5-hour ride from the Cathedral of Guadalajara to the Cathedral of Zapopan in a suburb. The original figure dates from the mid-1500s, and the tradition of the procession began some 200 years later. Crowds spend the night all along the route and vie for position as the Virgin passes by in a new car provided for the occasion. During the months before October 12, the figure is carried to churches all over the city. During that time, you may see neighborhoods decorated with paper streamers and banners honoring the passing of the figure to the next church.

The last two weeks in February are marked by a series of cultural events before the beginning of **Lent.**

5 Spectator Sports

BULLFIGHTS   Many say that Guadalajara and Mexico City host the best bullfights in Mexico. Every Sunday at 4:30pm (4pm in summer), there's a bullfight at the **Plaza de Toros "Nuevo Progreso,"** across from the football stadium on Calzada Independencia Norte, north of town. Tickets range from $4 for seats in the sun (*sol*) to $80 for the best seats in the shade (*sombra*). Buy tickets downtown in the reception area of the Hotel Francés on Thursday from 10am to 2pm or at the Plaza de Toros from 4 to 7pm.

CHARREADA   To the east of Agua Azul is the **Aceves Galindo Lienzo,** or rodeo ring, at the corner of Dr. R. Michel and Calzada de las Palmas (☎ 3/19-3232). There's a Mexican rodeo (*charreada*) on Sunday at noon. Mexican rodeos are a special extravaganza with elegant costumes and grand shows of prowess in riding, roping, rope tricks, and a traditional grand promenade. Sometimes there are evening shows.

6 Shopping

The mammoth **Mercado Libertad** (see "Walking Tour—Downtown Guadalajara," above) features fresh and cooked food; crafts (including baskets, puppets, wood carvings, pottery, and dance costumes); clothing; a great selection of inexpensive watches on the second floor; household wares; and a spectacular glimpse of daily life. Although it opens at 7am, it isn't in full swing until around 10am.

In addition, Guadalajara boasts the largest modern shopping center in Latin America. The **Plaza del Sol** megacomplex sprawls over 120,000 square yards in an area at the junction of Avenidas López Mateos and Mariano Otero, outside the center of town. Here, you can buy anything from a taco to a Volkswagen; you can also cash a check, make a plane reservation, or buy a lottery ticket. Hotels and restaurants offer respite for weary shoppers. To get here, take any bus marked "Plaza del Sol" from Calzada Independencia near the Mercado Libertad or on Alcalde in front of the Rotonda de los Ilustres.

There's a convenient **pedestrian passageway** that runs under Avenida Juárez; along this passageway are many stalls selling candied fruits, leather belts, and other goods. A better place to purchase **leather goods,** however, is down on Avenida Pedro Moreno, which runs parallel to Avenida Juárez. For **shoes,** go to E. Alatorre northeast of the Centro Histórico, where there are 70 shoe stores.

One block past the entrance of Agua Azul Park in the direction of the city center (on your right at the crossroads of Calzada Independencia and Gallo) is the **Casa de las Artesanías,** Gallo 20 (☎ 3/619-4664). It's an enormous two-story state-run crafts store that sells pottery, silver jewelry, dance masks, and regional clothing from around the state and the country. There's often a great selection of colorful nativity scenes (*natividades*). However, if you're going to the villages, such as Tonalá and Tlaquepaque, you may want to postpone buying such items. On the right as you enter are museum displays showing crafts and regional costumes from the state of Jalisco. The craft store is open Monday through Friday from 10am to 6pm, Saturday from 10am to 5pm, and Sunday from 11am to 3pm.

Some of Mexico's best pottery and crafts are made in the suburbs of **Tlaquepaque** and **Tonalá.** These two villages make a wonderful excursion, especially on Thursday or Sunday, when Tonalá spreads out a huge street market. (See Chapter 13.)

7 Guadalajara After Dark

THE PERFORMING ARTS
MUSIC & DANCE

Ballet Folklórico de la Universidad de Guadalajara
Degollado Theater, Plaza Tapatía. ☎ **3/626-9280** or 3/614-4773, ext. 144 or 143. Tickets $3–$12.

Impressions

The men [of Guadalajara] are also handsome and cling to their attractive charro out-
fits and extremely large sombreros. At one time the brims of their hats were so wide that
they were declared a public nuisance. Any man caught wearing a sombrero with a brim
that extended much beyond his shoulders was arrested and fined.
>   —Burton Holmes, *Mexico,* 1939

This wonderful dance company, acclaimed as the best *folklórico* company in all of
Mexico, provides light, color, movement, and music that are pure Jalisco. For more
than a decade, it has been performing at the Degollado Theater. Performances are
on Sunday at 10am.

Ballet Folklórico Nacional del Instituto Cultural Cabañas

The Cultural Cabañas, at the far end of the Plaza Tapatía. ☎ **3/618-6003.** Tickets $6–$8.

Performances are every Wednesday at 8:30pm at the theater of the Instituto
Cultural Cabañas.

Casa de la Cultura

Between Av. 16 de Septiembre and Calzada Independencia. ☎ **3/619-3611.**

A variety of performances is offered. The Association of Composers of Jalisco
offers new works on Tuesday evenings at 8pm. The state chorus group, the Coral
del Estado, also performs here. On Thursday, there are literary readings at 8pm,
and there are experimental dance performances and Aztec music. Call for more
information.

Ex-Convento del Carmen

Av. Juárez 638. ☎ **3/614-7184.** Admission varies; call for information.

A former convent just a few blocks from the central plaza, this venue hosts many
inexpensive concerts. Performances are usually on Monday and Tuesday at 8 or
8:30pm, and tickets are usually sold shortly before the performance.

THE CLUB & MUSIC SCENE

For rousing music and local ambiance, go to the **Plaza de los Mariachis,** down
by the San Juan de Dios Church and the Mercado Libertad, at the junction of
Calzada Independencia and Avenida Juárez/Calle Javier Mina. Every evening the
colorfully dressed mariachis, in various states of inebriation, play for money (if they
can get it) or for free. Enjoy a meal, a snack, or a soft drink here or just stand
around spending nothing but time. It's fun and free; spend at least one evening
here. Pickpockets are ever-present, so be careful. It costs nothing to listen as the
mariachis belt away around other diners' tables, but if you request a song, ask the
price first.

Few places in Guadalajara are more enjoyable than **El Parian** in **Tlaquepaque,**
where mariachis serenade diners under the portals (see Chapter 13).

CABARET & JAZZ CLUBS

Hotel Fiesta Americana

Glorieta Minerva. ☎ **3/625-3434** or 3/625-4848. Cover varies.

Songs and imitations are presented in the **Caballo Negro Bar** from 11pm until
1am. There is also a continually changing show in the **lobby bar** daily from 7pm

until 1am. In another salon, **Estelaris,** there are occasional performances by nationally known artists.

Restaurant/Bar Copenhagen 77

Marcos Castellanos 140-Z. ☎ **3/625-2803.** No cover. Mon–Sat restaurant noon–12:30am; jazz 8:30pm–12:30am

This dark, cozy jazz club is by the little Parque de la Revolución, on your left as you walk down López Cotilla/Federalismo. There are linen cloths and a red rose on every table. You can come just for a drink or for the restaurant's specialty—the delicious paella Copenhagen al vino. The paella takes a while to prepare, but it's an enjoyable wait as you sip a drink and listen to the jazz.

DANCE CLUBS/DISCOS

Lobby Bar, Hotel Francés

Maestranza 35. ☎ **3/613-1190.**

Though too noisy to recommend as a place to sleep, the stately Hotel Francés is a popular downtown meeting place. Check out the lobby bar, open from 8am to 10:30pm. There's a happy hour from noon to 8pm with two national (not imported) drinks for the price of one. There's often live piano music in the late afternoon and evening.

Maxim's Disco Club

In the Hotel Francés, Maestranza 35. ☎ **3/613-1190.** No cover Mon–Thurs; $4 Fri–Sun. Daily 8pm–midnight.

Despite its name, Maxim's is not a disco but a dance hall with a singer or a live band. There are tables around the dance floor and in the lower bar section.

13 Excursions from Guadalajara

Guadalajara, while known for its cultural contributions to Mexico, its regal architecture, and sophisticated atmosphere, is in some ways almost better known for its proximity to area villages and shopping. By car, trips from Guadalajara to the villages described below take from 30 minutes to Tlaquepaque, the nearest village, to around 3 hours to Mazamitla, the farthest village. By public transportation, the trips will take longer.

Tlaquepaque and Tonalá, known for shopping, are 7 to 10 miles southeast of Guadalajara. **Río Caliente Spa** is 20 to 25 miles west. **Lake Chapala** and the village of **Chapala** are 26 miles south. **Ajijic,** a village of artists, writers, and retirees, is 4 miles west of Chapala; **San Juan Cosalá,** 9¹/₂ miles of west of Chapala, is known for its thermal waters; **Jocotepec,** where weavers reside, is 12 miles west of Chapala. **Mazamitla,** a cold mountain retreat surrounded by pine forests, is 170 miles south of Guadalajara.

1 Tlaquepaque & Tonalá

7 & 11 miles S of Guadalajara

ORIENTATION

ARRIVING & DEPARTING   By Bus   Two types of buses go from Guadalajara to Tlaquepaque and Tonalá (a 25-minute ride). Both leave from the corner of Alcalde and Independencia in front of the Cathedral. **Linea Turquesa** buses (numbered 275 A or B) pass every 10 minutes, carry only seated passengers, and cost $1. Linea Turquesa buses pass within a block of Tlaquepaque's main square (it won't be obvious, so tell the driver you want to get off in Tlaquepaque) and stop several times on the main street going to Tonalá (where you'll see the shops and street stalls). Other public buses (also numbered 275 A or B) cover the route, cost 25¢, and are often packed with both standing and seated passengers. On the public buses, you'll have to watch for the welcoming arch on the left at Tlaquepaque then get off two stops later and ask for directions to El Parian, Tlaquepaque's central building on the main square. The last stop for this bus is Tonalá (another 15 minutes), where it turns around for the return to Guadalajara.

Visitor Information   The **Tlaquepaque Tourism Office** is in the Presidencia Municipal (opposite El Parian), Calle Guillermo Prieto

80 (☎ 3/635-1503 or 3/635-0596); it's open Monday through Friday from 9am to 3pm and Saturday from 9am to 1pm.

The **Tonalá Tourism Office** (☎ 3/683-1740; fax 3/683-0590) is in the Artesanos building set back a bit from the road at Atonaltecas 140 Sur (the main street leading into Tonalá) at Matamoros. Free **walking tours** are held Monday, Tuesday, Wednesday, and Friday at 9am and 2pm and Saturday at 9am and 1pm. They include visits to artisans' workshops (exhibiting ceramic, stoneware, blown-glass, papier-mâché, and the like). Tours last between 3 and 4 hours and require a minimum of five people. Office hours are Monday through Friday from 9am to 3pm and Saturday from 9am to 1pm. Also in Tonalá, catercorner from the church, you'll see a small **tourism information kiosk** that's staffed on market days and provides maps and useful information.

Tlaquepaque and Tonalá are special treats for shoppers. **Market days** are Sunday and Thursday in Tonalá, but on Sunday many of Tlaquepaque's stores are open only from 10:30am to 2:30pm. Thursday is the best day to combine a trip to both villages, about 4 miles apart. Monday through Saturday, stores in Tlaquepaque usually close between 2:30 and 4pm. A nice day consists of wearing yourself out in Tonalá then relaxing at one of Tlaquepaque's pleasant outdoor restaurants for a sunset meal and waiting for the mariachis to warm up at El Parian.

TLAQUEPAQUE: SHOPPING & MARIACHIS

This suburban village is famous for its **fashionable stores** in handsome old stone mansions fronting pedestrians-only streets. The stores, especially on **Calle Independencia,** offer the pottery and glass for which the village is famous and the best of Mexico's crafts, including *equipal* furniture, fine wood sculptures, and papier-mâché.

The village is also known for **El Parian,** a circular building dating from the 1800s in the town center, where innumerable mariachis serenade diners in sidewalk cafes. The mariachis are especially plentiful, loud, and entertaining on weekend evenings (Sunday is best), but you'll hear them serenading there just about any time of day.

EXPLORING TLAQUEPAQUE

Tlaquepaque's **Regional Ceramics Museum,** Independencia 237 (☎ 3/35-5404), is a good place to see what traditional Jalisco pottery is all about. There are high-quality examples dating back several generations. Note the cross-hatch design known as *petatillo* on some of the pieces; it's one of the region's oldest traditional motifs. There are also a wonderful old kitchen and dining room, complete with pots, utensils, and dishes. The museum is open Tuesday through Saturday from 10am to 4pm and Sunday from 10am to 1pm. There is also the National Museum of Ceramics in Tonalá (see below.)

Across the street from the museum is **La Rosa Fábrica de Vidrio Soplado,** a glass-blowing factory. From 9:30am to 2:30pm Monday through Friday, the public is invited to go to the rear patio and watch as a dozen scurrying men and boys heat glass bottles and jars on the end of hollow steel poles. Then, blowing furiously, they chase across the room, narrowly missing spectators and fellow workers alike as they swing the red-hot glass within an inch of a man who sits placidly rolling an elaborate jug out of another chunk of cooling glass. Non-chalantly, the old man will leave his own task long enough to clip off the end of the boy's vase at the exact moment it comes within reach of his hand. Then he drops the clippers and returns once more to his own task as the youth charges back across the room to reheat the vase in the furnace.

SHOPPING

Tlaquepaque has many fine shops. Below are a few that are outstanding:

Bazar Hecht

158 Independencia. ☎ **3/657-0316.** Fax 3/635-2241.

One of the village's longtime favorites, this store sells wood objects, hand-made furniture, and antiques. Open Monday to Saturday 10am to 2:30pm and 3:30 to 6:30pm.

Sergio Bustamante

236 Independencia at Cruz Verde. ☎ **3/639-5519.**

Sergio Bustamante's imaginative and original brass, copper, ceramic, and papier-mâché sculptures are among the most sought after and the most copied in Mexico. This exquisite gallery displays his work. Open Monday to Saturday 10am to 7pm.

Caoba

156 Independencia. ☎ **3/635-9770.**

Unusual, rustic, but finely finished pottery and wood sculptures, and many table textiles and decorative objects are the specialties of this store. Open Monday to Saturday 10am to 7pm, Sunday 11am to 5pm.

Casa Canela

258 Independencia, near Calle Cruz Verde. ☎ **3/635-3717.**

Step inside this grand mansion and discover one of the most elegant stores in Tlaquepaque. Browse through the rooms of decorative arts, some of which feature imaginative use of Mexican and Guatemalan textiles on equipale furniture. Open Monday to Friday 10am to 2pm and 3 to 7pm, Saturday 10am to 6pm, Sunday 11am to 3pm.

Ken Edwards

70 Madero. ☎ **3/635-5456.**

Ken Edwards was among the first artisans to produce high-fired, lead-free stoneware in Tonalá, and his blue-on-blue pottery is sold all over Mexico. This showroom has a fine selection of his work not seen in such size or quantity elsewhere. There's a section of seconds as well. The store is next door to the Restaurant With No Name. His factory is in Tonalá. Open Monday to Saturday 10am to 6:30pm.

Tete Arte y Diseno

Juárez 173. ☎ **3/635-7347.**

Here, you'll find many large architectural decorative objects mixed in with pottery, antiques, glassware, and paintings, all in a sort of organized jumble. Open Monday to Saturday 10am to 7pm.

Tlaquepaque

DINING

Read the fine print on menus. The 15% value-added tax may not be included in Tlaquepaque; ask before ordering.

Birrería El Sope

D. Guerra 142. ☎ **3/35-6338.** Birria $3.50–$6. Mon–Sat 8am–8pm; Sun 8am–10pm. BIRRIA.

This is where locals go for that wonderful Jalisco specialty birria. Cheery and clean, the restaurant is a long, narrow room in a quiet neighborhood. The decor of cushioned French provincial chairs pulled up to covered tables topped with artificial carnations does not go along with the country menu, but the food is tasty. Choose your birria by the meat—goat, lamb, or pork—and by the cut—leg, ribs, and so on. An order comes with fresh salsa, chips, and tortillas and beans. Side orders of quesadillas or queso fundido are extra. To find this restaurant from

Impressions

Open-air cafés abound [in Tlaquepaque] and if they are far from fastidious they are at least lively, for itinerant mariachis are so numerous that their competing ballads drench the air with Latin rhythms.

—Sydney Clark, *All the Best in Mexico*, 1952

Tlaquepaque's main plaza, walk north on Madero two blocks and turn left on Guerra; it's half a block down on the right.

✪ Casa Fuerte

224-B Independencia. ☎ **3/639-6481.** Main courses $5.50–$8. Tues–Sun 10am–7pm. INTERNATIONAL.

Clothing designer Irene Pulos has turned her talents and former showroom into this popular and charming patio restaurant. The setting is pure Mexico, with pastel walls and waiters sporting colorful Pulos-designed vests. Fascinating menu offerings include shrimp in tamarindo juice, grilled brochette with banana, fresh vegetable salads, steaks, and fajitas. It's tucked in a townhouse among the row of shops on Independencia.

✪ Mariscos Progreso

Progreso 80. ☎ **3/657-4995.** Main courses $6–$11. Daily 8am–6pm. SEAFOOD/MEXICAN.

On a cozy, tree-shaped patio filled with leather-covered tables and chairs, this restaurant makes an inviting place to take a break from shopping. Charcoal-grilled seafood prepared Mexican style is the specialty here. To get here, walk two blocks south on Madero, cross Juárez (one of the streets that borders El Parian), and look for this corner restaurant on the right.

Restaurant With No Name (Sin Nombre)

Madero 80. ☎ **3/635-4520** or 3/635-9677. Breakfast $4.75–$10; main courses $8–$13. Sun–Thurs 8:30am–9pm, Fri–Sat 8:30am–midnight. HAUTE MEXICAN.

One of my all-time favorites, this place offers excellent Mexican cuisine with a flair. It's set in a spectacular garden shaded by banana, peach, palm, and other tropical trees and guarded by strutting peacocks. A trio plays music in midafternoon. The menu is spoken by the bilingual waiter, not written, so ask for prices as you order. The excellent "no name chicken" is cooked in onions, green peppers, and a buttery sauce and spread around a mound of rice. The quesadillas are outstanding. To get here from the main plaza, face the plaza (with the church to your right) and walk on Madero to the right for 1 1/2 blocks; the restaurant is on the right, between Independencia and Constitución.

TONALÁ: A TRADITION OF POTTERY MAKING

Tonalá is a pleasant, unpretentious village about 4 miles from Tlaquepaque; many find it more authentic than Tlaquepaque and easier on the wallet. The streets were paved only recently, but there aren't any pedestrians-only thoroughfares yet. The village has been a center for pottery making since pre-Hispanic times; half of the more than 400 artists who reside here produce high- and low-temperature pottery in different colors of clay with a dozen different finishes. Other local artists work with forged iron, cantera stone, brass and copper, marble, miniatures, papier-mâché, textiles, blown glass, and gesso.

EXPLORING TONALÁ

On Thursday and Sunday **market days,** vendors and temporary street stalls under flapping shade cloths fill the streets; "herb-men" sell multicolored dried medicinal herbs from wheelbarrows; magicians entertain crowds with sleight-of-hand tricks; and craftspeople spread their colorful wares on the plaza's sidewalks. Those who love the hand-blown Mexican glass and folksy ceramics will wish they had a truck to haul the gorgeous and inexpensive hand-made items back home.

Tonalá

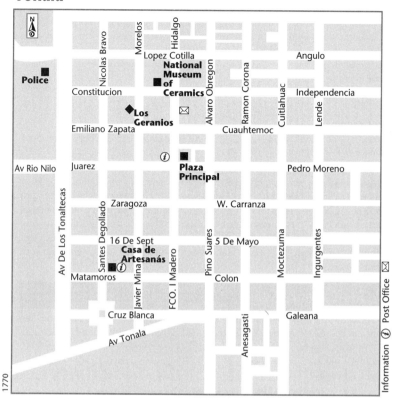

There is certainly greater variety here than in Tlaquepaque—tacky and chic are often side by side.

Tonalá is the home of the **National Museum of Ceramics,** Constitución 104, between Hidalgo and Morelos (☎ 3/683-0494). The museum occupies a huge two-story mansion and displays work from Jalisco as well as pottery from all over the country. There's a large shop in the front on the right as you enter. The museum is open Tuesday through Friday from 10am to 5pm and Saturday and Sunday from 10am to 2pm. A fee of $8.50 per camera is charged for use of any video or still cameras.

SHOPPING

José Bernabe and Sons
Hidalgo 83. ☎ **3/683-0040.** Fax 3/683-0877.

Considered among the best ceramic and stoneware artists in Tonalá, José Bernabe and his sons run this workshop and showroom half a block from the Presidencia Municipal. Prices here are high, but so is the quality, even if the items look a bit mass produced. The showroom is open Monday through Friday from 10am to 6:30pm and Saturday and Sunday from 10am to 3pm.

Santiago de Tonalá
Madero 42. ☎ **3/683-0641** or 3/639-0543.

Blown glass is made at this factory, half a block off the plaza at the corner of Zaragoza. Enter by the back door to see how the work is done. The factory is open Monday through Saturday from 7am to 3pm. There's also a sales showroom where prices are higher than elsewhere because the glassware is commercial strength, made for use in restaurants.

DINING

Los Geranios
Hidalgo 71. ☎ **3/683-0010.** Fax 3/683-0700. Main courses $3–$6. Daily 11am–5pm. MEXICAN/INTERNATIONAL.

This narrow, inviting restaurant next to El Bazar de Sermel offers a cool respite from the blazing sun. Diners relax in the clean, comfortable white canvas chairs at white-clothed tables or in the small booths. The menu includes Mexican specialties. Try the fish with almonds and mushrooms or the pork baked in orange sauce with baked potato and vegetables; there are also such quick snacks as nachos. To get here, face the church on the plaza, walk to the right turn on that street (Hidalgo) for about half a block; look on the left for a pretty stained-glass sign with red flowers.

2 Río Caliente Spa

One of Mexico's most popular spas, Río Caliente is also one of its most remote, and therein lies part of its appeal. Hidden in the Primavera Forest about 25 miles from downtown Guadalajara, it's a real getaway for those who love good vegetarian food, comfort but not luxury, thermal water bathing, and a relaxing pace—there's no rigid schedule.

Word of mouth keeps this popular and very casual spa busy.

ACCOMMODATIONS

✪ Río Caliente Spa
25 miles west, southwest of Guadalajara, Primavera Forest, La Primavera, Jal. No phone. Reservations: Marian Lewis, Spa Vacations Limited Associates, P.O. Box 897, Millbrae, CA 94030 (☎ 415/615-9543; fax 415/615 0601). 48 rms. Patio area $97 single, $161 double. Pool area $111 single, $185 double. Rates include all meals. Discounts May 1–Nov 1. Seven- and 10-night packages available.

Built along the hills of the Primavera forest and on a thermal water river, the spa's setting, at 5,550 feet, is both rugged and serene. Temperatures average 80°F year-round.

Individual rooms are clustered in two areas. Those near the activity area are smaller and more simply furnished and cost less than the newer, more stylish rooms with patios near the river and pool. All rooms have one double and one single bed, fireplace, full-length mirror, in-room safety-deposit box, desk, chest, and bed-side reading lamps. Water is purified in the pools and kitchen, and jars of fresh purified water are supplied daily in each room.

Special spa programs vary throughout the year and might include special instructors for Spanish, nutrition, and electro-acupuncture facelifts for an additional fee. A doctor comes daily. Huichol Indians sell crafts on Sunday. The help-yourself vegetarian meals are served in the cozy dining room. There's an activities room with nightly video movies or satellite TV, plus bingo and honor library. Guests have a choice of two public-area outdoor thermal water pools and two private pools and sunning areas that are separate for men and women.

Among the services are massage, with a choice of male or female massage therapist; mud wrap; antistress and antiaging therapies; live-cell therapy; and horseback riding. Sightseeing and shopping excursions are available at extra cost. Included in the cost, in addition to meals, are daily guided hikes, yoga and pool exercises, and use of scented steam room with natural steam from an underground river.

Taxi pick-up at the airport is available upon request for around $32 one way. A taxi from the airport costs around $40. If you're driving, follow Avenida Vallarta west, which becomes Highway 15, with signs to Nogales. Go straight for almost $10^{1}/_{2}$ miles and pass the village La Venta del Astillero. Take the next left after La Venta and follow the rough road through the village of La Primavera for almost five miles. Keep bearing left through the forest until you see the hotel's sign on the left. There's no phone at the spa; reservations are through the U.S. number only.

3 The Lake Chapala Region

26 miles S of Guadalajara

Mexico's largest lake and the area surrounding it have long been popular with foreign vacationers because of the near-perfect climate, gorgeous scenery, and several charming little lakeshore towns—**Chapala, Ajijic,** and **Jocotepec** among them—each with its own distinct ambiance. There's a large permanent expatriate community of around 4,000 living in settlements along the shoreline and in the villages stretching all the way from Chapala to Jocotepec.

From the mid-1970s until 1991, pollution of the Lerma River, one of the lake's water sources, caused serious concern. During that period, the lake's depth and perimeter diminished dramatically due to its heavy use as a water source by both Mexico City and Guadalajara. Recently Guadalajara developed another source of water, and the government intervened to stop pollution of the Lerma. Heavy rains in recent years have raised the lake level so much that it laps the original shore almost as it did in the past, and when you first see it, you'll think it looks like an ocean. It's a stunning sight, ringed by high, forested mountains and fishing villages.

Note: The year-round climate is so agreeable that few hotels offer air-conditioning and only a few have fans; neither is necessary.

ORIENTATION

ARRIVING & DEPARTING   By Bus   Buses to Chapala go from Guadalajara's old Central Camionera. **Transportes Guadalajara-Chapala** (☎ 3/619-5675 in Guadalajara) serves the route. Buses and minibuses run every half hour to Chapala and every hour to Jocotepec.

In Chapala, the **bus station** (☎ 376/5-2212) is about seven blocks north of the lake pier. To get to Ajijic and San Juan Cosalá from Chapala, walk toward the lake (left out of the front of the station) and look for the local buses lined up on the opposite side of the street. These buses travel between Chapala and San Juan Cosalá. At San Juan Cosalá, change buses to get to Jocotepec or take one of the buses that go directly to Jocotepec from the Chapala bus station every half hour until 8pm. The last bus back to Guadalajara from Chapala leaves at 9pm.

By Car   Those driving will be able to enjoy the lake and the surrounding towns more fully, but there is also intravillage bus service (see "By Bus," above). From

Impressions

In Jalisco, too, there are Lake Chapala and La Viuda, "the widow," who runs an open-air cantina on the shores of the lake where she sells exclusively tequila with a notorious chaser called sangre, "blood." In the past there were always mariachis to play by the hour for a few pesos. But recently La Viuda installed a juke box and most of the mariachis are out of work. Some have sought other jobs. One of them, Isodoro, now models Tarascan idols, ages them in the ground, then sells them to the tourist trade as the real thing.

—Herbert Cerwin, *These Are the Mexicans,* 1947

Guadalajara, drive to Lake Chapala via the new four-lane Highway 15/80. Leave Guadalajara via Avenida Gonzalez Gallo, which intersects with Calzada Independencia just before Playa Azul Park. Going south on Independencia, turn left onto Gallo and follow it all the way out of town past the airport, where it becomes Highway 15/80 (which may also have signs calling it Highway 44), the main road to Chapala. The first view of the lake isn't until just outside of the town of Chapala.

The highway from Guadalajara leads directly into Chapala and becomes **Madero,** which leads straight to Chapala's **pier, malécon** (waterfront walkway and street), and small **shopping and restaurant area.** The one traffic light in town (a block before the pier) is the turning point (right) to Ajijic, San Antonio, San Juan Cosalá, and Jocotopec. Chapala's **main plaza** is three blocks north of the pier, and the central food **market** flanks the park's back side.

VISITOR INFORMATION   The **Jalisco State Information Office** in Chapala is at Aquiles Serdan 26 (☎ 376/5-3141). Serdan is a narrow side street going toward the lake, one block before the Correo (post office). The office is open Monday through Friday from 9am to 6pm and Saturday and Sunday from 10am to 6pm. The staff is willing to help but doesn't have a lot of information. You may be able to get a map of the area here.

FAST FACTS   The **area code** for the whole northern lakeshore (Chapala, Ajijic, San Juan Cosalá, and Jocotopec) is 376.

A good local **bookstore** is **Libros y Revistas,** at Madero 230 (☎ 376/5-2021), near the chamber of commerce and Lloyds and opposite the plaza; it carries a wide assortment of English-language newspapers, magazines, and books—from the latest paperback novels to *Mirabella, Family Circle, Texas Monthly,* and *Scientific American.* It's open daily from 9am to 4pm.

Several outlets offer **communications services,** including fax, telephone, mail, and messages. **Centro de Mensajes Mexicano-Americano** is the local affiliate for UPS. They also have 24-hour telephone message and fax receiving service, court-approved translation ability, and secretarial service. They're at Hidalgo 236 (Apdo. Postal 872), Chapala, Jal. 45900 (☎ and fax 376/5-2102), and they're open Monday through Friday from 10am to 6pm and Saturday from 10am to 2pm. Almost next door, **Aero Flash,** Hidalgo 236 (☎ 376/5-3696; fax 376/5-3063), has a 24-hour fax service and specializes in package mailing. It's the local Federal Express office. The **post office** is on Hidalgo two blocks from the intersection of Madero. Enter down the hill and in back. It's open Monday through Friday from 9am to 1pm and 3 to 6pm, and Saturday from 9am to 1pm.

Currency exchange can be handled at the local **Banamex,** located on the right side of Madero just before the light, in Chapala. It's open Monday through

Lake Chapala

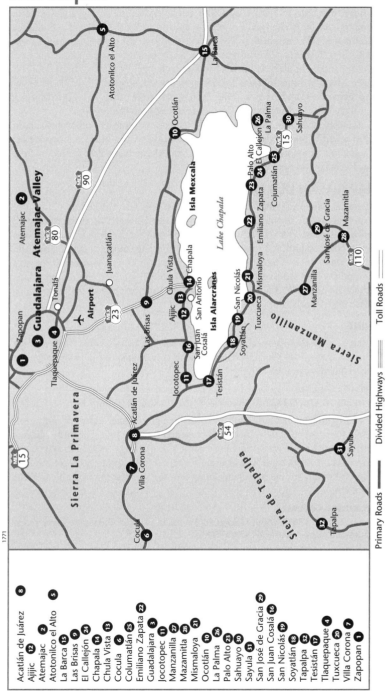

1771

Primary Roads ═══ Divided Highways ═══ Toll Roads ═══

Acatlán de Juárez **8**
Ajijic **12**
Atemajac **2**
Atotonilco el Alto **5**
La Barca **15**
Las Brisas **9**
El Callejón **24**
Chapala **14**
Chula Vista **13**
Cocula **6**
Columatlán **25**
Emiliano Zapata **22**
Guadalajara **3**
Jocotepec **11**
Manzanilla **27**
Mazamitla **28**
Mismaloya **21**
Ocotlán **10**
La Palma **26**
Palo Alto **23**
Sahuayo **30**
Sayula **31**
San José de Gracia **29**
San Juan Cosalá **16**
San Nicolás **19**
Soyatlán **18**
Tapalpa **32**
Tesistán **17**
Tlaquepaque **4**
Tuxcueca **20**
Villa Corona **7**
Zapopan **1**

Friday from 9am to 5pm; U.S. dollars can be exchanged all day, and Canadian dollars can be exchanged between 9am and 1:30pm. There's a Banamex **automated teller machine (ATM)** for Visa cards to the right of the bank's front door. Just down from Banamex (walking away from the lake), opposite the food market and main plaza, is **Lloyds Money Exchange,** by Lloyds's front door. It's open Monday through Friday from 9am to 4pm. To the left of the Hotel Nido, **Agencias de Cambios** is another money exchange office. It's open Monday through Saturday from 9am to 7pm and Sunday from 9am to 2pm.

Groceries can be purchased at any of Madero's supermarkets; probably the most convenient is **Supergrisa,** at the corner of Hidalgo and Madero, opposite the Restaurant Superior. It's open daily from 8am, closing most days at 8pm (at 3pm on Thursday and 6pm on Sunday).

CHAPALA: AN OLD LAKE RESORT

Chapala, Jalisco, founded in 1538, is the district's business and administrative center as well as the oldest resort town on Lake Chapala. Much of the town's prosperity comes from the retirees, primarily North American and Canadian, who live on the outskirts and come into Chapala to change money, buy groceries, and check their stocks. Except on weekends, when throngs of visitors fill the area around the pier and lake's edge, the town of 36,000 can be a pretty sleepy place. There are a couple of hotels in Chapala, but Ajijic (see below) is the preferable place to stay in the area.

DINING

Lake Chapala regional specialties include caviar de Chapala, *caldo michi, charales,* and *tortas ahogados.* Viuda de Sánchez Sangrita (a tequila chaser) is made locally, as is Cholula brand hot sauce.

Mariscos Guicho

Corona 20. ☎ **376/5-3232.** Main courses $4–$7.50. Wed–Mon 11am–8pm. SEAFOOD.

This brightly colored restaurant, with its lime-green walls and pink and purple table cloths, is one of the most popular restaurants on the lake. The menu includes fish prepared many ways, large juicy garlic shrimp, frogs' legs, and caviar tacos. Most main courses come with rice and bread. From Chapala's main pier, walk to the left heading for the restaurants lining the lake; this place is a long block ahead on the right.

Restaurant Cozumel

Corona 22 A. ☎ **376/5-4606.** Seafood $6–$9; steaks $7–$10; Wednesday dinner special $7. Tues–Sun 10am–9pm. SEAFOOD/STEAKS.

Boasting a loyal clientele, the Restaurant Cozumel offers a bit more atmosphere than other restaurants in town, with brick archways, hot pink walls, a ceiling full of hanging plants, and low lighting in the evening. It beats the competition by offering a free margarita and wine with the evening meal. The menu features such popular dishes as seafood brochettes, shrimp, and fish. Local favorites include breaded charales and caviar tacos. From Chapala's main pier, walk left heading for the restaurants lining the lake. You'll find this place a long block ahead on the right, two doors down from Mariscos Guicho (see above).

San Francisco Grill

Hidalgo 236-A. No phone. Brunch $4–$9; main courses $3.50–$9. Daily 8am–9:30pm (brunch served 8am–1pm). MEXICAN/AMERICAN.

Chapala Village

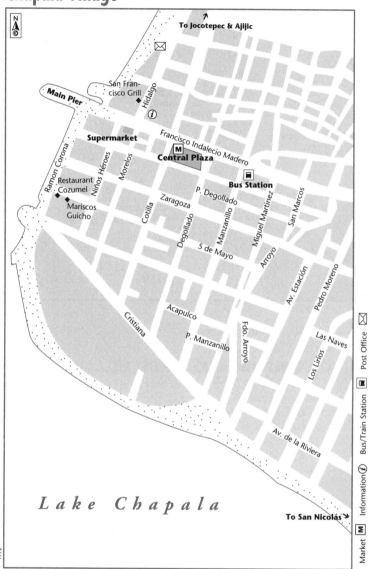

Under a giant thatched palapa with windows facing the lake, this restaurant has both inside and outside dining. It's an agreeable place to begin or end the day. Specialties include grilled meat and seafood, and there's an interesting assortment of hamburger platters with names like Broadway Burger and Nob Hill. The daily brunch begins with a choice of Bloody Mary, gin fizz, or margarita, and the price varies with the main course selected: eggs Benedict; grilled steak and eggs; shrimp Louie; and a pâté, fruit, and cheese platter. To find it from Madero, walk 1½ blocks west on Hidalgo; it's on the left down a short passage. There's also an

Ajijic

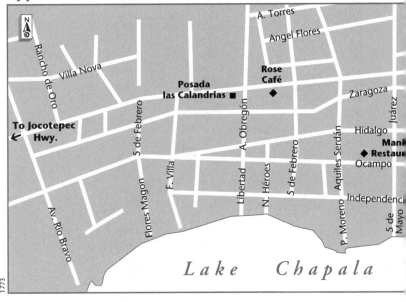

entrance from the malecón where you see the restaurant's terrace decked out with umbrella-covered tables.

AJIJIC: A QUIET FISHING AND ARTIST VILLAGE

Ajijic, another lakeside village, is a quiet place inhabited by fishermen, artists, and retirees. As you reach Ajijic, the highway becomes a wide tree-lined boulevard through **La Floresta,** a wealthy residential district. The La Floresta sign signals you've entered Ajijic, but the central village is about a mile farther on the left. To reach Ajijic's main street, **Colón** (which changes to Morelos), turn left when you see the SIX (corner grocery) sign on the left. Colón/Morelos leads straight past the main plaza and ends at the lake and the popular Restaurant La Posada Ajijic. The cobblestone streets and arts-and-crafts stores give the town a quaint atmosphere. (See "The Lake Chapala Region," above, for bus information to Ajijic.)

The **Clinica Ajijic** (☎ 376/6-0662 emergency, otherwise 376/6-0875 or 376/6-0-0500), on the main highway at the corner of Javier and Mina, has a two-bed emergency section with oxygen and electrocardiogram, ambulance, and five doctors with different specialties. The 16-bed hospital opened in 1993. The pharmacy there is open after hours for an emergency.

Linea Professional (☎ 376/6-0187; fax 376/6-0066) is a locally owned **car rental agency** in Ajijic. Make reservations as soon as possible—the cars are often all booked.

Impressions

Guadalajara is a bit too staid to go in for Acapulco-style night spots. The gaiety is left to Ajijic.

—James Norman, *Terry's Guide to Mexico,* 1965

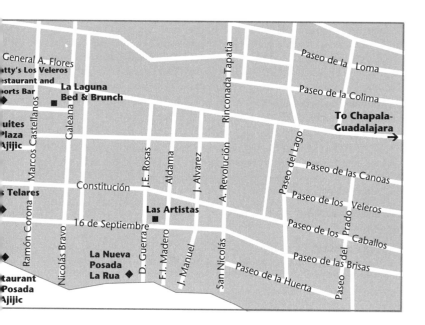

EXPLORING AJIJIC

Many visitors to placid Ajijic are also considering it for a long-term stay. Meeting the local foreign residents is easy; just go to the popular hang outs—the Restaurant Posada Ajijic, La Nueva Posada Ajijic, the Rose Café, and Los Veleros Restaurant and Sports Bar. The village, with its narrow cobblestone streets, smattering of tiny shops, and good restaurants, is best explored on foot, though there are plenty of places to park.

Thermal Pools

Five miles west of Ajijic is the lakeside settlement of **San Juan Cosalá,** known for its thermal water. The **Balneario San Juan Cosalá** allows day use of their pools. To enter, adults pay $3, and children $1.50. In addition to the large public pool, there are two huge private pools; the cost to use them is $4 per person, but you may not be allowed to use them.

Horseback Riding

At the eastern end of Ajijic, in **La Floresta**, horses for hire are tied up on the central median of 16 de Septiembre near the Hotel Real de Chapala at the intersection of Paseo del Lago. Sunset rides along the lakeshore are very popular. Adults pay $4 per hour, and children ride for $2 per hour.

SHOPPING

In La Floresta, immediately after the modernistic sculpture on the left (if arriving from Chapala), you'll see a cluster of buildings, one of which is marked ARTESANÍAS. The **state-owned shop** (☎ 376/6-0548) has a good selection of pottery from all over Mexico, as well as such locally made crafts as pottery, glassware, rugs, and wall tapestries. The shop is open Monday though Saturday from 10am to 6pm and Sunday from 10am to 2pm.

Ajijic has long been a center for weavers, but there seem to be fewer now than in the past. Still, it offers moderately good shopping; the best streets are **Colón** and those leading immediately off of it for a block or so. You'll find designer clothing and such decorative accessories as hand-loomed fabrics made into pillows and bedspreads, furniture, and pottery—but no one item in great abundance.

Boutique and Galeria Opus 1
Morelos 2 at Independencia. ☎ **376/6-0603.**

Lois Cugini is the helpful proprietor of this popular shop. She stocks a carefully chosen selection of designer clothing made from hand-loomed textiles from Mexico and Guatemala that includes the popular Opus 1 line. You can also shop for jewelry, pre-Columbian reproductions, and Mexican folk art. Open Monday to Saturday 10am–5pm and Sunday 11am–3pm.

ACCOMMODATIONS
Moderate

La Nueva Posada
Donato Guerra No. 9 (Apdo. Postal 30), Ajijic, Jal. 45900. ☎ **376/6-1444.** Fax 376/6-1344. 16 rms. $40–$45 single, $47–$50 double. Rates include full breakfast. Free parking.

As the name indicates, this is a new posada built by Michael and Elena Eager, the former owners of the popular Posada Ajijic (now a restaurant and bar under different ownership). Modeled after a gracious, traditional hacienda, La Nueva Posada looks a lot more expensive than it really is.

French doors, marble bathrooms, a wine cellar, and a small swimming pool are some of the amenities. There is an elegant dining room with a glorious lake view. Original paintings hang in all of the color-coordinated rooms and public areas. Three rooms are equipped for people with disabilities. Some rooms overlook the lake, and others have intimate patios; the former experience less disturbance from the after-hours kitchen crew. There is a paperback exchange library at the reception area, and a small pool lies in the back section of the hotel.

The hotel's restaurant, La Rusa, and casual bar (see "Dining," below) are among the most popular meeting places in the village. There's live background music most evenings and some afternoons. The Eagers' new venture is as popular as their previous hostelry, and La Nueva Posada is often booked up way in advance for holidays. To find the hotel from the plaza, walk toward the lake on Colón, then turn left on Independencia/Constitucíon; at Donato Guerro turn right, and you'll see the hotel's blue facade on the right by the lake.

✪ Las Artistas
Constitución 105, Ajijic, Jal. 45900. ☎ **376/6-1027.** Fax 376/6-0066. E-mail 74174.1257@.com. 6 rms (all with bath). $40–$60 single or double. Rates include breakfast.

A lovely walled-in home, this inn boasts a beautiful garden with a swimming pool. All rooms except one have private entry, and all are colorfully decorated but completely different in terms of size and setup. The lowest price is for the smallest room. Guests have use of the pool and run of the downstairs, which includes a beautifully furnished but comfortable living room with TV, video, and stereo; kitchen; and dining room. Breakfast is served inside or out by the pool and patio.

To find Las Artistas from the intersection of Colón/Morelos and Constitución, turn left on Constitución and walk five blocks; it's on the left, and its name is on a small tile plaque on the brick wall beside the iron gate.

Inexpensive

La Laguna Bed and Brunch

Zaragoza 29, Ajijic, Jal. 45900. ☎ **376/6-1174** or 376/6-1186. Fax 376/6-1188. 4 rms (all with bath). $25 single or double. Rates include brunch.

The rooms in this small inn are handsomely furnished with king-size beds covered in bright loomed bedspreads, thick tile floors, and fireplaces. Breakfast/brunch is served Monday through Friday from 8:30am to noon, Sunday 9am to noon. Served in the lovely glassed-in dining room facing the back patio, your meal begins with fruit and apple-bran muffins followed by a choice of eggs as you like them. Nonguests can also partake of brunch for $3 to $4.50.

To find La Laguna from the main highway, turn left on Colón and left again on the first street. The inn is 1½ blocks down on the left behind the Laguna Ajijic Real Estate Office (which faces the main highway).

Posada Las Calandrias

Main highway Poniente no. 8, Ajijic, Jal. 45900. ☎ **376/6-1052.** 29 rms (all with bath). TEL. $25 one bedroom; $35 two bedrooms.

Located outside of town, west on the main highway, this two-story brick hotel surrounds a pool with bougainvillea, mandevilla, and banana trees everywhere. The comfortable rooms have kitchens. There's a paperback book exchange at the reception desk.

◉ Suites Plaza Ajijic

Colón 33, Ajijic, Jal. 45920. ☎ and fax **376/5-4802** or 3/622-4437 in Guadalajara. 10 rms (all with bath). $20 per night single or double; $90 per week; $225 per month for three-month stay.

Located on the right side of Colón opposite Ajijic's central square, this simple but pleasant and clean hotel reopened in 1992. The lobby, which faces the street, doubles as a real-estate office. Rooms, located behind the lobby, line two sides of a fairly narrow patio. All rooms are one-bedroom apartment-like quarters; the bedrooms are separate from the kitchen areas with dining tables. A refrigerator and stove are available on request. A pleasant room in the far back of the patio serves as the common living room with a game table, a TV, a stereo, and an paperback library that operates on the honor system.

DINING

Moderate

✪ La Rusa

In the Nueva Posada Ajijic, Donato Guerra no. 9. ☎ **376/6-1444.** Reservations recommended Dec–Apr. Breakfast $3–$5; lunch $5–$7; dinner main courses $7–$12; Sun brunch $5.50–$7; garden grill $6–$9. Mon–Sat 8am–9pm, Sun 9am–8pm (Sun brunch served 9am–1pm; grill in the garden Mon–Fri 5–10pm). INTERNATIONAL.

Once you step inside the dining/drinking area of the La Nueva Posada Ajijic, you'll know the setting is right, whether you're in the *equipale*-furnished bar, the elegant dining room with garden and lake view, or the garden. La Rusa continues to be a popular dining spot with locals and *tapatíos* alike. The lunch menu is simple—crêpes, sandwiches, and salads. The dinner menu, printed on a large poster, has a dozen meat, seafood, and chicken main courses, plus soup, salad, and dessert. The Sunday brunch offers an entirely different selection. The higher-priced brunch includes wine. There's live music on Fridays and Saturdays. To reach the restaurant from the Ajijic plaza, walk toward the lake on Colón, turn left on Independencia/16 de Septiembre, and look for Donato Guerra. Turn right; La Rusa is on the right by the lake.

✪ Los Telares

Morelos 6. ☎ **376/6-0428.** Pasta $3.50–$5; main courses $5–$11. Wed–Thurs and Sun noon–9pm; Fri–Sat noon–10pm. ITALIAN/INTERNATIONAL.

Sophisticated but casual, this fashionable eatery opened in 1994. Dining tables set with hand-woven cloths and napkins are arranged around an open courtyard. The pottery was made exclusively for the restaurant by Ken Edwards of Tlaquepaque, and works of well-known international artists decorate the walls. Vegetables and herbs are organically grown in the restaurant's garden, and breads are made fresh daily. Main courses include filet of sea bass in a smooth tamarindo sauce and Pacific prawns in key lime sauce. Try the outrageously rich and unforgettably fresh fetuccine Alfredo. Los Telares is almost at the end of Colón/Morelos near the corner of Independencia/16 de Septiembre.

✪ Manix Restaurant

Ocampo 57. ☎ **376/6-0061.** *Comida corrida* $7. Mon–Sat 1–9pm. INTERNATIONAL.

This is one of my favorite restaurants in Mexico because I can always count on a delicious meal that's politely served in an extremely pleasant setting. Rainbow-colored napkins brighten the dark carved-wood furniture in this serene place. There are usually two different international *comida corridas* daily, including seafood, beef, chicken Cordon Bleu, ossu bucco, and chicken Parmesan. Servings are generous, and each *comida* comes with soup and dessert. To get here from the plaza, turn your back to the church, walk straight ahead on Colón for two blocks, and turn right on Ocampo; the restaurant is down the street on the right, but the sign is obscured by the lone tree on the street.

Restaurant La Posada Ajijic

Morelos and Independencia. ☎ **376/6-0744.** Sandwiches $3–$6; main courses $5–$10; Sunday brunch $5–$6. Mon–Thurs and Sun noon–10pm; Fri–Sat 10am–11pm; Sun brunch 9am–1pm. MEXICAN/INTERNATIONAL.

Formerly under the management of the owners of La Nueva Posada Ajijic (see "Accommodations," above), this restaurant facing the lake has reopened with graceful Mexican-inspired decor and good service. The menu covers traditional fare, including soups, salads, sandwiches, and more filling Mexican specialties, as well as imaginatively prepared beef, chicken, and seafood main courses. Sunday brunch is served on the patio facing the gardens. The bar, opposite the restaurant, is a favorite Ajijic hangout. The restaurant is at the end of Colón/Morelos; you enter through the back by the lake, where there's parking.

⑨ Rose Café

Carretera Poniente 26. ☎ **376/6-1599.** Breakfast $2–$3.50; lunch special $3.50–$4. Tues–Sun 9am–4:30pm. VEGETARIAN.

Everyone enjoys the Rose Café, both for its food and for its casual and friendly atmosphere. Tables are set outside under the pink awning and inside back a bit from the highway. Among the best breakfast selections are fresh banana and chocolate muffins, delicious hotcakes, waffles with apple-raisin sauce, fruit salad, yogurt, and a variety of omelets and frittatas. The daily lunch special might include calzones, salad, and a grapefruit drink. The cafe is beside the Second Hand Rose thrift shop on the outskirts of town on the highway going west toward Jocotepec.

AJIJIC AFTER DARK

Residents are very proud of their **Lakeside Little Theater,** reviews of which are always in the free regional tabloid found everywhere or on the bulletin board at the Nueva Posada Ajijic.

There's almost always a group or a crowd at the **Posada Ajijic Cantina,** Calle 16 de Septiembre no. 2, where a band (of sorts) plays music for dancing on Saturday and Sunday evenings. There's a happy hour Monday through Friday from noon to 1:30pm and 5 to 6pm with complimentary snacks. On Friday and Saturday evenings, between 5 and 10pm, there's a cover charge of $5. The **Nueva Posada Ajijic,** Donato Guerra 9, is a place to socialize almost anytime; happy hour, with complimentary snacks, runs from noon to 1:30pm and 5 to 6pm. For dining in a restored townhouse, catching the latest in sports on a wide-screen TV, or for just hanging out, **Patty's Los Veleros Restaurant and Sports Bar,** on Colón a block from the highway, is another popular place. It's open Sunday through Friday from 10am to 10pm and Saturday from 10am to midnight.

JOCOTOPEC: A WEAVERS' VILLAGE

West of Ajijic, this small colonial-era village is becoming a weaving center. The main street curving in front of the central plaza becomes **Hidalgo,** the main shopping street. Thursday is **market day**; the market is located at the corner where the street curves and becomes Hidalgo. Beginning on Hidalgo at the plaza, you'll find several weavers' shops with locally loomed rugs and wall hangings. The same kinds of weavings are often sold by the roadside in Ajijic.

4 Mazamitla

A 3-hour drive from Guadalajara (70 miles south of Guadalajara; 45 miles south of Chapala), this mountain resort town (population 11,000; altitude 7,500 feet) is a popular weekend getaway in the state of Jalisco. By bus, **Auto Transportes Mazamitla,** at Guadalajara's central bus station, has more than a dozen daily departures from Guadalajara to Mazamitla.

To return by bus from Mazamitla to Guadalajara, the **bus station** (☎ 353/8-0410) is opposite the market a block from the central square. From Mazamitla, six buses daily go to Guadalajara Monday through Friday, and nine buses make the route on Saturday and Sunday. All are de paso, and the last leaves Mazamitla for Guadalajara around 8:30pm—but double-check that time when you travel.

Flecha Amarilla buses (☎ 353/8-0413) in Mazamitla, half a block from the market, can take you on to Colima, Manzanillo, or to San José de Gracia. The best way to get to Mazamitla from Ajijic or Chapala (without returning to Guadalajara) is to go to the far western outskirts of Jocotepec where the highway through Jocotepec meets the highway from Guadalajara. Buses going to the Tuxcueca turnoff or to Mazamitla pass frequently. If you get one going only to Tuxcueca you can get off there and catch one of the frequent buses going to Mazamitla.

By car, the shortest way to get to Mazamitla from Guadalajara is by following Highway 44 west along the lake through Chapala, Ajijic, and Jocotepec, after which it becomes Highway 15 south as it goes along the lake's southern shoreline. Just after Tuxcueca, you'll see the right turn and crossroads with a sign to La Manzanilla, which is only 25 miles farther. (Most maps don't show the turnoff, but it's there, and the road is paved). The long way from Guadalajara is along Lake Chapala's eastern shore through La Barca and Sahuayo. Soon after the turnoff at

Tuxcueca, the road climbs and winds through the mountains, the landscape becomes covered in oak and pine trees, and the temperature drops considerably. A few miles before Mazamitla is La Manzanilla, a pretty village in which you may want to take a few minutes to walk around the plaza.

Founded soon after the conquest of Mexico, Mazamitla, only 6 miles from the state of Michoacán, architecturally resembles Michoacán more than it does Jalisco. Wide wood-beamed roof lines support dark red-tiled roofs with pine balconies and window trim—all characteristic of Michoacán. Mazamitla has retained its colonial-era charm; the village and its cobblestone streets all branch out from the shady central plaza and church, which is devoted to the Virgin of Guadalupe.

For **tourist information,** go to Colina de los Ruiseñores restaurant (see "Dining," below), where the owner, Guillermo Arias, acts as the village's unofficial tourist delegate.

Important note: Bring a heavy sweater or jacket any time of year. Long johns and heavy socks might be called for at night in unheated hotels.

EXPLORING MAZAMITLA

Although trips to this picturesque resort town are largely devoted to relaxing and strolling the streets, self-guided mountain hiking is one active option. Mazamitla is among several area villages where you can buy locally made cheese and rompope and home-canned fruits temptingly displayed in glass jars.

The town's patron, **Saint Christopher,** is honored with a large festival the last Sunday in July. Besides Saint Christopher, Mazamitla also honors the **Virgin of Guadalupe** from **December 4 to 12.** Fiestas Patrias, the Mexican **independence celebration,** takes place from **September 13 to 17.**

You can **go horseback riding** for around $5 per hour; horses for rent are on the road to Monte Verde Centro Recreacional. Look left, and you'll see them lined up under the trees. If you'd like to come just for the day and look the town over, **Viajes Copenhagen** in Guadalajara (☎ 3/621-1008) offers a day trip with picnic lunch.

ACCOMMODATIONS

Be aware that Mazamitla is a very popular getaway for Guadalajarans and hotels fill up on weekends, major Mexican holidays, and for village festival days (see "Exploring Mazamitla," above). In addition to the hotels mentioned below, the **Colina de los Ruiseñores** restaurant (see "Dining," below) has added rustically charming rooms behind the restaurant that rent doubles for $22. Should everything be full when you arrive, consider nearby San José de Gracia (see "A Side Trip to San José de Gracia," below).

Hotel Sierra del Tigre

Reforma 3 at 16 de Septiembre, Mazamitla, Jal. 49500. ☎ **353/8-0087.** 14 rms. TV. $10 per person.

Opened in 1992, this cozy two-story hotel is a welcome addition to Mazamitla's sparse hotel scene. Without windows on the outside, rooms, which are all open to the interior, are warmer than those in any other hotel in town. Each is nicely decorated with tile floors, pine furniture, and warm red-and-blue plaid bedspreads. Some come with bunk beds and a double bed, some with double beds, and some with two single beds. Most have a small refrigerator and TV with U.S. channels. There's a small sitting area on the second floor, and the restaurant is open from 8am to 10pm daily. The hotel is half a block off the main square.

Luis Barragán: An Architectural Adept

One of Mexico's most influential architects, Barragán (1902–89) was from a wealthy Guadalajara family but spent his youth in the forested mountains of Jalisco, near Mazamitla. Though a skilled landscape architect, he was known primarily as an architect/designer of homes and for his use of bold Mexican colors and incorporation of hacienda styles into modern buildings. Unschooled in either architecture or landscape gardening he nevertheless succeeded in becoming prominent in both and his techniques and designs influence Mexican architecture today. He won the coveted Pritzker Award for architecture in 1980.

Posada Alpina

Portal Reforma 8, Mazamitla, Jal. ☎ **353/8-0104** or 3/641-0681 in Guadalajara. 14 rms. $10 single, $20 double, $30 triple. Free parking in front.

Opposite the church and on the central plaza, this late 19th-century home has been converted into a rustically charming inn. Rooms in the front section, which has a large interior patio, are part of the original home, with polished plank floors and beamed ceilings. Those in the rear around a small patio have been added on and are smaller. Six of the rooms are large with three beds. Room no. 1 is one of these and opens onto the upper front porch that overlooks the plaza and church. Owner Guadalupe Toscano Hernandez will graciously help with directions or sightseeing suggestions. A small restaurant on the patio serves coffee and pastries between 5 and 10pm.

Posada Las Charrandas

Obregón 2, Mazamitla, Jal. 49500. ☎ **353/8-0254** or 3/622-7719 in Guadalajara. 10 rms. $13 small room; $23–$30 large room for two. Free parking behind the posada.

The natural pine exterior of this posada looks like it belongs in Switzerland and exudes the kind of quaint charm for which this village is known. The interior is brightly colored with orange walls, pine shutters and furniture, and fawn-colored tile floors. Rooms no. 5, 6, 7, and 8 have balconies with mountain views. Some rooms are a bit small but cheery, and all come with one or two double beds. Owner Lourdes Azpeitia keeps the place spotless. The cozy restaurant off the lobby is open daily from 8am to 9pm.

DINING

Among the regional specialties you may want to try are *bote,* which is meat cooked in pulque (the pre-Conquest alcoholic beverage made from the maguey plant); *parajito,* a mixture of fresh cow's milk, chocolate, and pure alcohol; and *atole de agua miel,* a kind of fruit wine. Everywhere, you see shelves laden with quart jars of enticing home-preserved fruits to buy and eat on the spot or to take home.

Colina de Los Ruisenores

Allende 50. ☎ **353/8-0484.** Breakfast $1–$3; main courses $2.75–$10. Daily 9am–6:30pm. REGIONAL/INTERNATIONAL.

The food at this charming little pine-decorated restaurant, in a small garden setting, is some of the best in Mazamitla—and in the country for that matter. A *ruiseñor,* by the way, is a nightingale.

Señora Arias, whose family owns and operates the place, does all the cooking using family recipes passed down through the generations. Her meat marinades are scrumptious. The pork adobada has a wonderful tangy taste, and the *bistec de res Ruiseñores,* another great marinated flavor, is in a soy sauce and vinegar base. The pork ribs are meaty and savory. The special of the day is often trout in almond sauce. There's also chicken to stay or to go, Mexican antojitos, and *lonches* (sandwiches). Arias's children and relatives do most of the serving; Senor Arias, who also sells real estate and willingly helps tourists with area information, pitches in.

A section of cozy guest rooms was being completed in back of the restaurant when I was last here. To find the restaurant from the main plaza, walk straight ahead a block (with the Posada Alpina on your right) to the market, which will be on your right; keep going to the bend in the road (about a block), and the restaurant is on the right.

Restaurant Campestre La Troje

Galeana 53. ☎ **353/8-0070.** Breakfast $1.75; main courses $6–$9. Wed–Mon 9am–7pm. REGIONAL/MEXICAN.

Campestre (country) restaurants are popular in this region, and this gleaming, spotless example is certainly deserving of the crowds it receives. Service is excellent. The place is known for charcoal-grilled meat platters that come with rice and beans. Their specialties include chicken, beef, or shrimp fajitas (or a combination of the three), shrimp prepared in four different ways, and beef brochettes. There's full bar service as well. The restaurant is at the crossroads immediately outside Mazamitla opposite the Pemex station on the road leading to the highway and Chapala.

Restaurant Posada Mazamitla

Hidalgo 2 at Reforma. ☎ **3/538-0161.** Breakfast $2–$3; main courses $3.50–$4. Daily 8:30am–6pm. REGIONAL/MEXICAN.

Opposite the church, on one corner of the square behind a small market, you'll find this colorful, popular restaurant. Fashioned out of an old home, it has a partly covered interior courtyard. Main courses usually feature pork and beef, but there are lighter choices of beans, quesadillas, and soup, all of which are very inexpensive.

A SIDE TRIP TO SAN JOSÉ DE GRACIA

Seven miles northeast of Mazamitla, just over the state line from Jalisco into the state of Michoacán, is San José de Gracia, an immaculately beautiful village. Exploring this town makes for a delightful stroll. In addition, San José's hotels come in handy when those in Mazamitla are full. It's also warmer here.

The shady **central square,** which you'll find if you keep going through town on the main highway, is the village's quiet central hub. Take time to walk around and talk to the locals, who will be quite interested in you since few visitors come here.

ACCOMMODATIONS

Hotel de Larios

Reforma y Morelos, San José de Gracia, Mich. 59500. ☎ **353/7-0580.** Fax 353/7-0236. 42 rms. TV TEL. $19 single, $37 double.

Some might count finding all of Mazamitla's hotels full a blessing since they can hop over to San José. It's generally warmer in San José, and rooms in this three-story hotel have warmth even though they aren't heated. Modern and furnished in the latest style, most rooms have tile floors, but suites are carpeted. Just off the lobby there's a restaurant which keeps irregular hours; its posted hours are Tuesday through Sunday from 1:30 to 11pm.

DINING

Restaurant Bar El Doon

Galeano 3. ☎ **353/7-0543.** Main courses $4–$10. Thurs–Tues 1–9pm. STEAK/MEXICAN.

Shiny and clean, with cloth-covered tables and good service, El Doon is *the* place to eat in San José de Gracia. An assortment of beef cuts is the specialty here, and they are grilled to your specification. You can have chicken and fish as well or try such Mexican dishes as steak Tampiqueña, charro beans, and Tarascan soup. Ask directions from the main plaza; it's between Independencia and Melchor O'Campo.

5 San Juan de Los Lagos & Lagos de Moreno

Two hours northeast of Guadalajara on Highway 80, **San Juan de los Lagos** (population 100,000; altitude 1,895 feet) receives more than five million visitors a year. The majority of tourists arrive during the months of February, May, and December and during Easter week. Most visitors are pilgrims paying homage to the Virgin of San Juan de los Lagos, whose tiny image is encased in gold leaf over the altar of the **Basílica de San Juan de los Lagos.**

The village was founded soon after the Conquest, but it wasn't until 1939 that the event that would make it a famous religious site occurred. In that year, a small girl is said to have fallen on a knife and died in the garden in front of the home of Ana Lucía. The next day, before burying the child, Ana Lucía placed the figure of the Virgin de la Concepción (which had been in her care) on the child's chest. The mourning crowd was astounded when the child returned to life.

Word of the miracle spread, and since then, penitents from around the world come to ask favors of the Virgin and to give thanks for her intervention in their lives. For years, they gathered at the chapel erected on the spot where the child came to life, which was the church of a small hospital with an adjacent guest house. Today, that place is called the Capilla del Primer Milagro (Chapel of the First Miracle); the figure has been moved to the larger Basilica de San Juan on the town's central square.

Located in an area of the state called Los Altos de Jalisco (the highlands of Jalisco), the region is rich in cattle and milk production. The abundance of milk is turned into candy, cheese, and rompope, which is sold widely, especially in San Juan de los Lagos. San Juan (as it's called locally) is a sunny city in a small, deep valley (locals refer to it as a "well") with narrow streets which eventually climb in and out of the well.

Neighboring **Lagos de Moreno** (population 140,000; altitude 1,965 feet), a city with a beautiful colonial center, was also founded in the 16th century and is only 21 miles farther. It is colder and drier than San Juan and has wide streets. Although San Juan is the focus of pilgrims and has the most shops, Lagos (as it is referred to by locals) has a greater variety of hotels, restaurants, and beautifully preserved colonial buildings.

Lagos means "lakes" in Spanish; once there were three lakes in the area, but only a small portion of one remains today. The latter part of the town's name honors

Pedro Moreno, a valiant freedom fighter who was born here and gave his life in the Mexican War for Independence. Lagos has always been a way station for travelers; it's a natural stopping-point on a journey inland to or from either coast via Guadalajara. Both Lagos and San Juan are worth a detour in your journey through this part of Mexico.

Most of the year, both cities are tranquil places, with orderly traffic and plenty of hotel space if you arrive early in the day. However, in February around 50,000 penitents arrive on foot for **Día de la Candelaria, February 2,** and they stay in and near San Juan until around February 8. Large groups carrying banners can be seen streaming toward San Juan on all the major highways of Mexico around this time, and the national news charts the progress of these pilgrims daily. Around **Easter,** at least 120,000 pilgrims come in a 15-day period.

All of May is a festival month, called the **Mez de María** (Mary's Month) and **Las Fiestas de la Primavera** (Spring Festivals). It's a combination cultural, agricultural, and religious event. There are reunions of bricklayers and other commercial groups on different days, fireworks, music, parades, and charreadas. Between **May 18** and **31,** afternoon processions feature giant papier-mâché figures. A pilgrimage for the **Assumption of the Virgin,** which culminates on **August 15th,** attracts 80,000 pilgrims, most of them traveling by bicycle. The whole month of December is given over to religious devotion, with around 150,000 visitors arriving primarily between **December 1** and **8.**

San Juan de los Lagos is easily reached from Guadalajara's Central Camionera on the first-class **La Alteña** (☎ 378/5-1223); **Transportes Frontera** (☎ 378/5-0051); **Oriente** (☎ 378/5-0625); and **Estrella Blanca** (☎ 378/5-0051) lines. **Servicios Coordinadores** (☎ 378/5-1738) has luxury service twice daily. You'll arrive in San Juan's clean bus station, which is near downtown but too far to walk with luggage. Taxis are always in front and cost around $2 to town center.

For returning to Guadalajara or going on to Lagos de Moreno, there are several choices: **La Alteña, Oriente,** and **Estrella Blanca** go to Guadalajara every hour and to Lagos every 30 minutes. **Transportes Frontera** has buses every half hour to Guadalajara and to Lagos de Moreno every hour from 9am to 11pm. **Servicios Coordinadores** has luxury buses twice daily.

The **State Tourism Office,** Callejón Fortuna 5 (☎ 378/15-0979), is in San Juan de los Lagos, only a block from the central plaza at the corner of Rita Pérez de Moreno and Fray Antonio de Segovina. Ask for José Rangel, who can answer any questions in English. The office is on the second floor and is open Monday through Friday from 9am to 8pm and Saturday from 9am to 1pm.

SAN JUAN DE LOS LAGOS: A PILGRIMS' SWEET MECCA

As you enter from Highway 80, the town spreads out below, and the towers of the Basílica de San Juan de los Lagos on the central plaza stand out prominently in the midst of it all. Parking is scarce on the narrow streets of the central city, so if you're driving, you might consider parking and taking a taxi to any sites beyond the downtown area.

EXPLORING SAN JUAN DE LOS LAGOS

The heart of the city is the **Plaza Principal,** which has the **Basílica de San Juan de los Lagos** at one end and a parklike plaza with grand fountain at the other. Strolling musicians and sellers of religious memorabilia frequent the plaza, and streets fanning out from it are chock-a-block with stores selling milk- and cream-based candy, *cajeta,* and rompope. This is the place to get the heartbeat of San Juan and to watch religion and commerce meet.

Basílica de San Juan de los Lagos
Plaza Principal. No phone.

The famed Virgin of San Juan de los Lagos is housed over the altar of the basilica, which is the focal point of the city and of the broad central square that is the city's hub. With an interior and an exterior of rose cantera stone, the basilica is especially beautiful inside; note the altar with the Virgin dressed in her blue and gold cape and crown. The basilica is plain, however, compared to the Parroquia de la Asunción in Lagos de Moreno due to remodeling early this century that removed most of its colonial adornments.

To the right of the altar is a room full of ex-votos (painted personal requests or tributes to the Virgin) made by people from all over the world. So many of these have been left over the years that the church is starting a small museum of them next to the **Posito (church) de la Virgen** at the end of Iturbide, which runs in front of the church and to the right of the basilica.

In the basilica, a private room below the altar holds religious paintings that are attributed to the school of Rubens but do not bear the master's signature. Though not open to the public, the preserved bedroom made especially for Pope John Paul II's 1990 visit is in the priest's private living area. Other rooms in that section hold photographs of the pope made during his visit.

On Sunday, the first mass is at 5:30am and thereafter almost hourly until 7:30pm. Weekdays, the first mass is at 8:30am with a daily schedule similar to Sunday and a final mass at 7:30pm. Visitors can enter any time but are requested to respect a mass in progress.

Capilla Del Primer Milagro
Luis Moreno at Primavera. No phone.

A short walk from the basilica, this small chapel and room next door commemorate the first miracle attributed to the Virgin of San Juan de los Lagos. More significant than beautiful, it is still a revered spot where thousands of visitors spend a few moments during their visit to the city. To find it from the main plaza, with your back to the front of the basilica, take the side street to the right of the

---

María Izquierdo: An Underappreciated Mexican Modernist

Born in 1906 in San Juan de los Lagos, Jalisco, Izquierdo's career was a brief but important one. A contemporary of Frida Kahlo, her work, like Kahlo's, had a skilled but primitive edge to it. Her first art lessons began at age 6 and at age 21 she spent a year in school at the Academia de San Carlos in Mexico City. The following year her first one-woman show appeared at the Galería de Arte Moderno and she began work with Rufino Tamayo, another of Mexico's renowned artists. In 1930 a one-woman show was mounted for her at the New York Art Center and in 1933 in Paris at the Galerie René Highe. Her subjects were those of everyday Mexican life. Intellectuals from around the world honored her talent and beauty with poetry and praise during her lifetime. Much of her work is in private collections, but good examples are at the Museum of Modern Art in Mexico City. She died in 1955.

basilica for four blocks. You'll see the white facade of the church on the right at the corner of Primavera.

Museo Cristero
Plaza Principal. No phone.

This small museum commemorates the Cristero Rebellion (1926–29), which was particularly brutal in this part of Mexico. When President Calles placed restrictions on the Catholic church, it set off a rebellion among the masses that is remembered to this day as one of the worst epochs in the country's history. This private museum has a small room full of photographs and newspaper clippings that chronicle the bloody event. It's open daily from 8am to 8pm. Admission is $1.

SHOPPING

In San Juan de los Lagos, it's impossible to leave without seeing the many vendors of locally made coconut and milk candy called *cajeta* (caramelized cow's milk), *rompope* (an alcoholic drink similar to eggnog), and religious objects pertaining to the Virgin de San Juan. Shop after shop sells almost the same type of goods. Scattered among them are shops selling hand-knitted and embroidered objects, including tablecloths, dresses, doilies, and sweaters; they are made by a cottage industry that's been thriving for decades. Often women set up a row of tables of these handmade items and continue knitting and embroidering while passersby browse. You can also find a small selection of pottery from Tonalá and wooden toys from Michoacán. The streets fanning out from the basilica are the most laden with goods, but your shopping could even begin with the lineup of such stalls at the bus station.

Sombreria
Plaza Principal 6. ☎ **378/5-0626.**

If you're outfitting yourself or your horse, this is the place to visit. For more than 20 years they've been decking out cowboys with straw and felt hats, boots, saddles, chaps, stirrups—the works. Just to satisfy tourists, they have a few gaudy charro hats and sun hats for women. There's no sign, but the store is on the main plaza; it's open Monday through Saturday from 9am to 2pm and 4 to 8pm.

El Corral
Hidalgo 380. ☎ **378/2-3509.**

Only a half a block from the plaza, this Western-style store, owned by cattle breeder Jesus Vega, offers a great variety of authentic charro hats, silver spurs, bone buttons, leather charro belts (with intricate designs), and knives with one-of-a-kind horn handles. Vega, a graduate of Texas A&M, is proud of the framed congratulatory graduation letter he received from Lyndon Johnson when Johnson was a senator.

ACCOMMODATIONS

Hotel Posada Arcos
Plaza Principal, San Juan de los Lagos, Jal. 47000. ☎ **378/5-1580.** Fax 378/5-1590. 140 rms. TV TEL. $25 single, $35 double; $406 suite. Free parking.

This hotel's appealing, spacious pale-gray marble lobby with black marble columns makes an inviting first impression. Halls and rooms in this four-story hotel are carpeted. Rooms, all nicely furnished, have windows facing the halls and nice-size bathrooms. This is an excellent choice on the main plaza, and there's a nice restaurant off the lobby.

DINING

The **Hotel Posada Arco** (see "Accommodations," above) has a nice restaurant, and there are several other decent lunchroom-type eateries on the main plaza. The **market,** where there are always a dozen or so small cook shops, is catercorner from the basilica.

Restaurant Señorial
Plaza Principal. ☎ **378/5-1270.** Breakfast $2–$3; main courses $3–$5; *comida corrida* $3.75. Daily 7am–10pm. MEXICAN.

You can't miss this clean lunchroom with its polite waiters; it's located opposite the basilica on the main plaza. Take a seat in the front and watch the people on the plaza. Choose from a variety of preparations of chicken, beef, pork, and enchiladas. Service is quick, friendly, and efficient, but come before 1:30pm, when the downtown lunch crowd begins to arrive.

LAGOS DE MORENO: A STROLL THROUGH COLONIAL CHARM

Located 21 miles north of San Juan de los Lagos (see above), Lagos de Moreno boasts the beautiful central **Plaza de los Constituyentes.** The plaza has an iron bandstand in the middle and is shaded by handsome magnolias, palms, flame (*flamboyan*) trees, and Indian laurel trees and is surrounded by colonial-era buildings made of the rose cantera stone so abundant in the area. On one side of the plaza is the lovely 200-year-old **Parroquía de la Asuncion,** the downtown area's most prominent church. Lagos's preserved colonial city is worth a stop to stroll the streets and nose in and out of stores and churches.

The city's main festival, **Feria de Agosto,** honors the Image of Calvario. The main day is **August 6**, but the fair goes on for a week before and after with dances, parades, charreadas, cock fights, painting expositions, and mechanical rides.

EXPLORING LAGOS DE MORENO

If you're driving, you'll be glad to know parking is not as difficult in the downtown area of Lagos as it is in San Juan. Most places of interest are in and around the central plaza called the Jardín Juárez. The **post office** is the modern building (also made with rose cantera stone) that seems a bit out of place (as it is surrounded by colonial buildings) to one side of the Jardín Juárez.

Parroquia de la Asuncion
Jardín Juárez. No phone.

The most imposing building in the central city is the parroquia, finished in 1784 with a baroque facade of rose cantera stone and a beautiful wrought-iron fence. It's used today as the parish church. The interior mesquite floors with a geometric pattern lead to the altar, over which is a mural of the Virgin Mary ascending to heaven on a cloud of cherubs. Encased to the right is what is believed to be the visible body of Saint Hermon, which was sent to San Juan in 1791. Below the main floor are crypts of priests dating from the late 1800s to the early 1900s. In the Salon Cristo Rey (a side room off the sanctuary) are paintings of the bishops of Guadalajara and the first cardinal of Mexico, José Garibi y Rivera, who gained that title in 1958.

Museo Casa de Capellanes
Off the main plaza. No phone.

Built as a temple and convent in 1756, the structure also served as a jail during the Cristero Rebellion. Now it's a museum housing the murals of Gabriel Flores, which were painted in 1964 and depict the dramatic history of the country and the area. It's open Tuesday through Sunday from 9am to 2pm and 4 to 7pm.

Templo El Calvario
On a hill above town. No phone.

With sweeping views of the town from its grand front steps, this beautiful late 19th-century stone church hovers over the town. You first notice the grand mesquite wood doors and floors, followed by the murals of saints in the cupola above the altar. In the sacristy there is a painting of the last supper with 13 apostles. When asked why there were 13 apostles, the artist replied, "One ate and ran."

SHOPPING

There aren't as many candy shops here as in San Juan, and in fact shopping is a bit scant on the whole. You'll have to wander the streets to find deals. In addition to the antique shop mentioned below, there are several other stores in the downtown area. Shops are closed between 2 and 4pm Monday through Saturday and all day Sunday.

Montecristo Antiguidades
Hidalgo 494. ☎ **474/2-0249.**

Housed in a wonderful one-story 19th-century home, Montecristo has two patios surrounded with rooms full of antiques. Hallways brim over with old doors and other architectural embellishments scavenged from the country's once-grand estates. It's open Monday through Saturday from 10am to 2pm and 4 to 7pm and Sunday from 10am to 2pm.

ACCOMMODATIONS

In addition to the hotels mentioned below, the luxury **Casa Grande,** is just outside town, on the road to Guadalajara (☎ 474/2-1392 or 474/1-1926).

Hotel Colonial
Hidalgo 279. Lagos de Moreno, Jal. ☎ **474/2-0142.** Fax 474/2-0039. 29 rms. FAN TV TEL. $30 single, $35 double. Free parking.

Wonderful blue-and-yellow tile greets you upon arrival at the Hotel Colonial, the 17th-century house of the Conde Rul. Only the lobby hints at the building's former grandeur; the two stories of rooms have long since taken on the look of a comfortable old hotel. Most rooms are carpeted and have windows opening onto the tile hallway. A nice restaurant just off the lobby serves all three meals. To find the hotel, with your back to the parroquia, walk left half a block; it's on the right.

Hotel Paris
Gonzalez León 339, Lagos de Moreno, Jal. ☎ **474/2-0200** or 474/2-0201. 36 rms. TV TEL. $12 single, $14 double.

Just opposite the parroquia, and facing the main square, this cavernous former mansion is a budget-priced alternative to the Hotel Colonial (see above). It's 50 years old and undergoing a slow renovation. Rooms, all of which have high ceilings, have one double bed or two twin beds, nice plaid bedspreads, soft mattresses, and lights over each bed. Bathrooms are aging but clean and come with either showers or tub/shower combinations but no shower curtain. The hotel is on the main plaza next to the Banco Serfin.

DINING

Adobes

Carretera Panamericana. ☎ **474/2-0625.** Main courses $10–$20. Mon–Sat 8am–11:30pm, Sun 8am–8pm. MEXICAN/INTERNATIONAL.

The newest and most sophisticated restaurant in town, Adobes caught on big when it opened in 1992 and hasn't let up. Its handsome adobe walls set a rustically beautiful background for Mexican tile, cloth-covered tables, and elegant pewter serving plates.

Beef and pork reign supreme here, but there's seafood and chicken as well. The *filete especial Adobes* is steak with bacon, mushrooms, and black-bean sauce. The pollo especial is tastefully marinated chicken breast accompanied by a fresh green salad. For dessert, the café adobe, which is coffee flavored with ice cream and rum, may catch your eye. To find this restaurant, you must ask directions; it's just out of town across the railroad tracks on Highway 80 going towards San Luis Potosí.

La Hacienda

Hidalgo 460. ☎ **474/2-0665.** Breakfast $1.25–$2.50; main courses $2–$7. Daily 8am–11pm. MEXICAN.

Another locally popular dining spot, La Hacienda is small but spiffy, with cloth-covered tables and waiters wearing black-and-white. Specialties include beef tampiqueña, lomo de cerdo adobado (pork loin baked in a spicy broth), and sopa medula (bone marrow soup). Snacks include queso fundido, tacos, and guacamole with tostados. To find La Hacienda from the main plaza, with your back to the church, walk right two blocks; it's on the corner.

La Rinconada

Constituyentes 425. ☎ **474/2-3404.** Salad and soup $2.50–$4; main courses $3–$18. Daily 1–11pm. MEXICAN/REGIONAL.

A handsome, gleaming little place with tile floors and arched doorways, La Rinconada is very popular with locals who consider it a treat to eat here. There's usually a daily special of traditional Mexican food such as chiles rellenos or almond chicken. The extensive menu features fish, shrimp, and beef, and there's a lengthy bar list. To find the restaurant from the main plaza, with your back to the front of the church, turn right one block then left; it's on the left.

Appendix

A Telephones & Mail

USING THE TELEPHONES

Area codes and city exchanges are being changed all over the country. If you have difficulty reaching a number, ask an operator for assistance. Mexico does not have helpful recordings to inform you of changes or new numbers.

Most **public pay phones** in the country have been converted to Ladatel phones, many of which are both coin and card operated. Those that accept coins accept the old 100 peso coins, but at some point may begin accepting New Peso coins. Instructions on the phones tell you how to use them. Local calls generally cost the peso equivalent of 75¢ per minute, at which time you'll hear three odd sounding beeps, and then you'll be cut off unless you deposit more coins. Ladatel cards come in denominations of 10, 20, and 30 New Pesos. If you're planning to make many calls, purchase the 30 New Peso card; it takes no time at all to use up a 10 peso card (about $3.35). They're sold at pharmacies, bookstores, and grocery stores near Ladatel phones. You insert the card, dial your number, and start talking, all the while watching a digital counter tick away your money.

Next is the *caseta de larga distancia* (long-distance telephone office), found all over Mexico. Most bus stations and airports now have specially staffed rooms exclusively for making long-distance calls and sending faxes. Often they are efficient and inexpensive, providing the client with a computer printout of the time and charges. In other places, often pharmacies, the clerk will place the call for you, then you step into a private booth to take the call. Whether it's a special long-distance office or a pharmacy, there's usually a service charge of around $3.50 to make the call, which you pay in addition to any call costs if you didn't call collect.

For **long-distance calls** you can access an English-speaking ATT operator by pushing the star button twice then 09. If that fails, try dialing 09 for an international operator. To call the United States or Canada tell the operator that you want a collect call (*una llamada por cobrar*) or station-to-station (*teléfono a teléfono*), or person-to-person (*persona a persona*). Collect calls are the least expensive of all, but sometimes caseta offices won't make them, so you'll have to pay on the spot.

To make a long-distance call from Mexico to another country, first dial 95 for the United States and Canada, or 98 for anywhere else in the world. Then, dial the area code and the number you are calling.

To call long distance (abbreviated "lada") within Mexico, dial 91, the area code, then the number. Mexico's area codes (claves) may be one, two, or three numbers and are usually listed in the front of telephone directories. In this book the area code is listed under "Fast Facts" for each town. (Area codes, however, are changing throughout the country.)

To place a phone call to Mexico from your home country, dial the international service (011), the Mexico's country code (52), then the Mexican area code (for Cancún, for example, that would be 98), then the local number. Keep in mind that calls to Mexico are quite expensive, even if dialed direct from your home phone.

Better hotels, which have more sophisticated tracking equipment, may charge for each local call made from your room. Budget or moderately priced hotels often don't charge, since they can't keep track. To avoid check-out shock, it's best to ask in advance if you'll be charged for local calls. These cost between 50¢ and $1 per call. In addition, if you make a long-distance call from your hotel room, there is usually a hefty service charge added to the cost of the call.

POSTAL GLOSSARY

Airmail   Correo Aereo
Customs   Aduana
General Delivery   Lista de Correos
Insurance (insured mail)   Seguros
Mailbox   Buzón
Money Order   Giro Postale
Parcel   Paquete
Post Office   Oficina de Correos
Post Office Box (abbreviation)   Apdo. Postal
Postal Service   Correos
Registered Mail   Registrado
Rubber Stamp   Sello
Special Delivery, Express   Entrega Inmediata
Stamp   Estampilla or Timbre

B Basic Vocabulary

Most Mexicans are very patient with foreigners who try to speak their language; it helps a lot to know a few basic phrases.

I've included a list of certain simple phrases for expressing basic needs, followed by some common menu items.

ENGLISH-SPANISH PHRASES

English	Spanish	Pronunciation
Good Day	**Buenos días**	*bway*-nohss-*dee*-ahss
How are you?	**¿Cómo esta usted?**	*koh*-moh *ess*-tah oo-*sted*
Very well	**Muy bien**	mwee byen
Thank you	**Gracias**	*grah*-see-ahss
You're welcome	**De nada**	day *nah*-dah
Goodbye	**Adios**	ah-dyohss

Please	Por favor	pohr fah-*bohr*
Yes	Sí	see
No	No	noh
Excuse me	Perdóneme	pehr-*doh*-ney-may
Give me	Déme	*day*-may
Where is . . . ?	¿Dónde esta . . . ?	*dohn*-day ess-tah
the station	la estación	la ess-tah-see-*own*
a hotel	un hotel	oon oh-*tel*
a gas station	una gasolinera	oon-nuh gah-so-lee-nay-rah
a restaurant	un restaurante	oon res-tow-*rahn*-tay
the toilet	el baño	el *bahn*-yoh
a good doctor	un buen médico	oon bwayn *may*-dee-co
the road to	el camino a . . .	el cah-*mee*-noh ah
To the right	A la derecha	ah lah day-*ray*-chuh
To the left	A la izquierda	ah lah ees-ky-*ehr*-dah
Straight ahead	Derecho	day-*ray*-cho
I would like	Quisiera	keyh-see-*air*-ah
I want	Quiero	*kyehr*-oh
to eat	comer	*ko*-mayr
a room	una habitación	oon-nuh ha-bee tah-see-*own*
Do you have?	¿Tiene usted?	tyah-nay oos-*ted*
a book	un libro	oon *lee*-bro
a dictionary	un diccionario	oon deek-see-own-ar-eo
How much is it?	¿Cuanto cuesta?	*kwahn*-to *kwess*-tah
When?	¿Cuando?	*kwahn*-doh
What?	¿Que?	kay
There is (Is there?)	¿Hay . . .	eye
Yesterday	Ayer	ah-*yer*
Today	Hoy	oy
Tomorrow	Mañana	mahn-*yawn*-ah
Good	Bueño	*bway*-no
Bad	Malo	*mah*-lo
Better (best)	(Lo) Mejor	(loh) meh-*hor*
More	Más	mahs
Less	Menos	may-noss
No Smoking	Se prohibe fumar	seh pro-*hee*-beh foo-*mahr*
Postcard	Tarjeta postal	tahr-*hay*-ta pohs-*tahl*
Insect repellent	Rapellante contra insectos	rah-pey-*yahn*-te *cohn*-trah een-sehk-tos

MORE USEFUL PHRASES

Do you speak English?   ¿Habla usted inglés?

Is there anyone here who speaks English?   ¿Hay alguien aquí qué hable inglés?

I speak a little Spanish.   **Hablo un poco de español.**

I don't understand Spanish very well.   **No lo entiendo muy bien el español.**

The meal is good.   **Me gusta la comida.**

What time is it?   ¿Qué hora es?

May I see your menu?   ¿Puedo ver su menu?

The check please.   **La cuenta por favor.**

What do I owe you?   ¿Cuanto lo debo?

What did you say?   **¿Mande? (colloquial expression for American "Eh?")**
I want (to see) a room   **Quiero (ver) un cuarto (una habitación)** . . .
   for two persons   **para dos personas**
   with (without) bath.   **con (sin) baño.**
We are staying here only   **Nos quedaremos aqui solamente** . . .
   one night   **una noche**
   one week.   **una semana.**
We are leaving tomorrow.   **Partimos mañana.**
Do you accept traveler's checks?   **¿Acepta usted cheques de viajero?**
Is there a laundromat near here?   **¿Hay una lavandería cerca de aquí?**
Please send these clothes to the laundry.   **Hágame el favor de mandar esta ropa a la lavandería.**

NUMBERS

1	**uno** (*ooh*-noh)	17	**diecisiete** (de-*ess*-ee-*syeh*-tay)
2	**dos** (dohs)	18	**dieciocho** (dee-*ess*-ee-*oh*-choh)
3	**tres** (trayss)	19	**diecinueve** (dee-*ess*-ee-*nway*-bay)
4	**cuatro** (*kwah*-troh)	20	**veinte** (*bayn*-tay)
5	**cinco** (*seen*-koh)	30	**treinta** (*trayn*-tah)
6	**seis** (sayss)	40	**cuarenta** (kwah-*ren*-tah)
7	**siete** (*syeh*-tay)	50	**cincuenta** (seen-*kwen*-tah)
8	**ocho** (*oh*-choh)	60	**sesenta** (say-*sen*-tah)
9	**nueve** (*nway*-bay)	70	**setenta** (say-*ten*-tah)
10	**diez** (dee-ess)	80	**ochenta** (oh-*chen*-tah)
11	**once** (*ohn*-say)	90	**noventa** (noh-*ben*-tah)
12	**doce** (*doh*-say)	100	**cien** (see-en)
13	**trece** (*tray*-say)	200	**doscientos** (*dos*-se-en-tos)
14	**catorce** (kah-*tor*-say)	500	**quinientos** (*keen*-ee-ehn-tos)
15	**quince** (*keen*-say)	1000	**mil** (meal)
16	**dieciseis** (de-*ess*-ee-sayss)		

BUS TERMS

Bus   **Autobus**
Bus or truck   **Camion**
Lane   **Carril**
Nonstop   **Directo**
Baggage (claim area)   **Equipajes**
Intercity   **Foraneo**
Luggage storage area   **Guarda equipaje**
Gates   **Llegadas**
Originates at this station   **Local**
Originates elsewhere; stops if seats available   **De Paso**
First class   **Primera**
Second class   **Segunda**
Nonstop   **Sin Escala**
Baggage claim area   **Recibo de Equipajes**
Waiting room   **Sala de Espera**
Toilets   **Sanitarios**
Ticket window   **Taquilla**

C Menu Terms

BREAKFAST (*DESAYUNO*)

café con crema   coffee with cream
huevos   eggs
huevos cocidos   hard-boiled eggs
huevos fritos   fried eggs
huevos pasados al agua   soft-boiled eggs
huevos poches   poached eggs
huevos revueltos   scrambled eggs

jamón   ham
jugo de naranja   orange juice
leche   milk
pan tostada   toast
mermelada   jam
té   tea
tocino   bacon

LUNCH AND DINNER

antojitos   Mexican snacks
caldo   broth
caldo de pollo   chicken broth
menudo   tripe soup
salchichas   sausages
sopa   soup
sopa clara   consomme

sopa de arroz   dry rice (not soup!)
sopa de lentejas   lentil soup
sopa de chicharos   pea soup
taco   filled tortilla
torta   sandwich
tamales russos   cabbage rolls

SEAFOOD (*MARISCOS*)

almejas   clams
anchoas   anchovies
arenques   herring
atun   tuna
calamares   squid
camarones   shrimp
caracoles   snails
corvina   bass
huachinango   red snapper
jaiba   crab
langosta   lobster
lenguado   sole

lobino   black bass
mojarra   perch
ostiones   oysters
pescado   fish
pez espada   swordfish
robalo   sea bass/snook
salmon   salmon
salmón ahumado   smoked salmon
sardinas   sardines
solo   pike
trucha arco iris   rainbow trout

MEATS (*CARNES*)

ahumado   smoked
alambre   shish kebab
albóndigas   meatballs
aves   poultry
bistec   steak
cabrito   kid (goat)
callos   tripe
carne   meat
carne fría   cold cuts
cerdo   pork
chicharrones   pigskin cracklings
chorizo   spicy sausage
chuleta   chop

conejo   rabbit
cordero   lamb
costillas   spareribs
faisán   pheasant
ganso   goose
hígado   liver
jamón   ham
lengua   tongue
lomo   loin
paloma   pigeon
pato   duck
pavo   turkey
pechuga   chicken breast

perdiz   partridge
pierna   leg
pollo   chicken
res   beef

VEGETABLES (*LEGUMBRES*)

aceitunas   olives
aguacate   avocado
arroz   rice
betabeles   beets
cebolla   onions
champinones   mushrooms
chicharos   peas
col   cabbage
coliflor   cauliflower
ejotes   string beans
elote   corn (maize)
esparragos   asparagus

FRUITS (*FRUTAS*)

chavacano   apricot
ciruela   prune
coco   coconut
durazno   peach
frambuesa   raspberry
fresas con crema   strawberries
   with cream
fruta cocida   stewed fruit
granada   pomegranate
guanabana   green pear-like fruit
guayaba   guava
higos   figs

DESSERTS (*POSTRES*)

arroz con leche   rice pudding
brunelos de fruta   fruit tart
coctel de aguacate   avocado
   cocktail
coctel de frutas   fruit cocktail
compota   stewed fruit
flan   custard

BEVERAGES (*BEBIDAS*)

agua   water
brandy   brandy
café   coffee
café con crema   coffee with cream
café de olla   coffee with cinnamon
   and sugar
café negro   black coffee

riñones   kidneys
ternera   veal
tocino   bacon
venado   venison

espinaca   spinach
frijoles   beans
hongos   mushroom
jicama   potato/turnip-like vegetable
lechug   alettuce
lentejas   lentils
papas   potatoes
pepino   cucumber
rabanos   radishes
tomate   tomato
verduras   greens, vegetables
zanahoras   carrots

lima   lime
limon   lemon
mamey   sweet orange fruit
mango   mango
manzana   apple
naranja   orange
pera   pear
piña   pineapple
platano   banana
tuna   prickly pear fruit
uva   grape
zapote   sweet brown fruit

fruta   fruit
galletas   crackers or cookies
helado   ice cream
nieve   sherbet
pastel   cake or pastry
queso   cheese
torta   cake

cerveza   beer
ginebra   gin
hielo   ice
jerez   sherry
jugo de naranja   orange juice
jugo de tomate   tomato juice
jugo de toronja   grapefruit juice

leche   milk
licores   liqueurs
licuado   fruited water or milk
manzanita   apple juice
refrescos   soft drinks
ron   rum

sidra   cider
sifon   soda
té   tea
vaso de leche   glass of milk
vino blanco   white wine
vino tinto   red wine

CONDIMENTS & CUTLERY

aceite   oil
azucar   sugar
copa   goblet
cuchara   spoon
cuchillo   knife
mantequilla   butter
mostaza   mustard

pimienta   pepper
sal   salt
taza   cup
tenedor   fork
vaso   glass
vinagre   vinegar

PREPARATIONS

a la parrilla   grilled
al horno   baked
al mojo de ajo   garlic and
butter
asado   roasted
bien cocido   well done
cocido   cooked
empanado   breaded

frito   fried
milanesa   Italian breaded
poco cocido   rare
Tampiqueño   long strip of thinly
sliced meat
Veracruzana   tomato, garlic, and
onion topped

D Menu Glossary

Achiote   Small red seed of the annatto tree.

Achiote preparada   A prepared paste found in Yucatán markets made
of ground achiote, wheat and corn flour, cumin, cinnamon, salt, onion, garlic,
and oregano. Mixed with juice of a sour orange or vinegar and put on broiled or
charcoaled fish (tikin chick) and chicken.

Agua fresca   Fruit-flavored water, usually watermelon, canteloupe, chia seed
with lemon, hibiscus flour, or ground melon seed mixture.

Antojito   A Mexican snack, usually masa-based with a variety of toppings such
as sausage, cheese, beans, onions; also refers to tostadas, sopes, and garnachas.

Atole   A thick, lightly sweet, warm drink made with finely ground rice or corn
and usually flavored with vanilla; often found mornings and evenings at markets.

Birria   Lamb or goat meat cooked in a tomato broth, spiced with garlic, chiles,
cumin, ginger, oregano, cloves, cinnamon, and thyme and garnished
with onions, cilantro, and fresh lime juice to taste; a specialty of Jalisco state.

Botana   A light snack—an antojito.

Buñelos   Round, thin, deep-fried crispy fritters dipped in sugar or dribbled
with honey.

Burrito   A large flour tortilla stuffed with beans or sometimes potatoes and
onions.

Cabrito   Grilled kid; a Northern Mexican delicacy.

Cajeta   Carmeled cow or goat milk, often used in dessert crêpes.

Carnitas Pork that's been deep-cooked (not fried) in lard, then steamed and served with corn tortillas for tacos.

Ceviche Fresh raw seafood marinated in fresh lime juice and garnished with chopped tomatoes, onions, chiles, and sometimes cilantro and served with crispy, fried whole corn tortillas.

Chiles rellenos Poblano peppers usually stuffed with cheese, rolled in a batter and baked; but other stuffings may include ground beef spiced with raisins.

Chorizo A spicy red pork sausage, flavored with different chiles and sometimes with achiote or cumin and other spices.

Choyote Vegetable pear or merleton, a type of spiny squash boiled and served as an accompaniment to meat dishes.

Churro Tube-shaped, bread-like fritter, dipped in sugar and sometimes filled with cajeta or chocolate.

Cilantro An herb grown from the coriander seed chopped and used in salsas and soups.

Cochinita pibil Pig wrapped in banana leaves, flavored with pibil sauce and pit-baked; common in Yucatán.

Corunda A triangular tamal wrapped in a corn leaf, a Michoacan specialty.

Enchilada Tortilla dipped in a sauce and usually filled with chicken or white cheese and sometimes topped with tomato sauce and sour cream (enchiladas Suizas—Swiss enchiladas), or covered in a green sauce (enchiladas verdes), or topped with onions, sour cream, and guacamole (enchiladas Potosiños).

Epazote Leaf of the wormseed plant, used in black beans and with cheese in quesadillas.

Escabeche A lightly pickled sauce used in Yucatecan chicken stew.

Frijoles charros Beans flavored with beer, a Northern Mexican specialty.

Frijoles refritos Pinto beans mashed and cooked with lard.

Garnachas A thickish small circle of fried masa with pinched sides, topped with pork or chicken, onions, and avocado or sometimes chopped potatoes, and tomatoes, typical as a botana in Veracruz and Yucatán.

Gorditas Thickish fried-corn tortillas, slit and stuffed with choice of cheese, beans, beef, chicken, with or without lettuce, tomato, and onion garnish.

Guacamole Mashed avocado, plain or mixed with onions and other spices.

Gusanos de maguey Maguey worms, considered a delicacy, and delicious when charbroiled to a crisp and served with corn tortillas for tacos.

Horchata Refreshing drink made of ground rice or melon seeds, ground almonds, and lightly sweetened.

Huevos Mexicanos Scrambled eggs with onions, hot peppers, and tomatoes.

Huevos Motulenos Eggs atop a tortilla, garnished with beans, peas, ham, sausage, and grated cheese, a Yucatecan specialty.

Huevos rancheros Fried egg on top of a fried corn tortilla covered in a tomato sauce.

Huitlacoche Sometimes spelled "cuitlacoche," mushroom-flavored black fungus that appears on corn in the rainy season; considered a delicacy.

Machaca Shredded dried beef scrambled with eggs or as salad topping; a specialty of Northern Mexico.

Manchamantel Translated means "tablecloth stainer," a stew of chicken or pork with chiles, tomatoes, pineapple, bananas, and jícama.

Masa Ground corn soaked in lime used as basis for tamales, corn tortillas, and soups.

Mixiote   Lamb baked in a chile sauce or chicken with carrots and potatoes both baked in parchment paper made from the maguey leaf.

Mole   Pronounced "*moh*-lay," a sauce made with 20 ingredients including chocolate, peppers, ground tortillas, sesame seeds, cinnamon, tomatoes, onion, garlic, peanuts, pumpkin seeds, cloves, and tomatillos; developed by colonial nuns in Puebla, usually served over chicken or turkey; especially served in Puebla, State of Mexico, and Oaxaca with sauces varying from red, to black and brown.

Molletes   A bolillo cut in half and topped with refried beans and cheese, then broiled; popular at breakfast.

Pan de Muerto   Sweet or plain bread made around the Days of the Dead (Nov.1–2), in the form of mummies, dolls, or round with bone designs.

Pan dulce   Lightly sweetened bread in many configurations usually served at breakfast or bought at any bakery.

Papadzules   Tortillas are stuffed with hard-boiled eggs and seeds (cucumber or sunflower) in a tomato sauce.

Pavo relleno negro   Stuffed turkey Yucatán-style, filled with chopped pork and beef, cooked in a rich, dark sauce.

Pibil   Pit-baked pork or chicken in a sauce of tomato, onion, mild red pepper, cilantro, and vinegar.

Pipian   Sauce made with ground pumpkin seeds, nuts, and mild peppers.

Poc-chuc   Slices of pork with onion marinated in a tangy sour orange sauce and charcoal broiled; a Yucatecan specialty.

Pollo Calpulalpan   Chicken cooked in pulque, a specialty of Tlaxcala.

Pozole   A soup made with hominy and pork or chicken, in either a tomato-based broth Jalisco-style, or a white broth Nayarit-style, or green chile sauce Guerrero-style, and topped with choice of chopped white onion, lettuce or cabbage, radishes, oregano, red pepper, and cilantro.

Pulque   Drink made of fermented sap of the maguey plant; best in state of Hidalgo and around Mexico City.

Quesadilla   Four tortillas stuffed with melted white cheese and lightly fried or warmed.

Queso relleno   "Stuffed cheese" is a mild yellow cheese stuffed with minced meat and spices, a Yucatecan specialty.

Rompope   Delicious Mexican eggnog, invented in Puebla, made with eggs, vanilla, sugar, and rum.

Salsa Mexicana   Sauce of fresh chopped tomatoes, white onions, and cilantro with a bit of oil; on tables all over Mexico.

Salsa verde   A cooked sauce using the green tomatillo and pureed with mildly hot peppers, onions, garlic, and cilantro; on tables countrywide.

Sopa de calabaza   Soup made of chopped squash or pumpkin blossoms.

Sopa de lima   A tangy soup made with chicken broth and accented with fresh lime; popular in Yucatán.

Sopa de medula   Bone marrow soup.

Sopa Tlalpeña   A hearty soup made with chunks of chicken, chopped carrots, zucchini, corn, onions, garlic, and cilantro.

Sopa Tlaxcalteca   A hearty tomato-based soup filled with cooked nopal cactus, cheese, cream, and avocado with crispy tortilla strips floating on top.

Sopa tortilla   A traditional chicken broth-based soup, seasoned with chiles, tomatoes, onion, and garlic, bobbing with crisp fried strips of corn tortillas.

Sopa Tarascan   A rib sticking pinto-bean based soup, flavored with onions, garlic, tomatoes, chiles, and chicken broth and garnished with sour cream, white cheese, avocado chunks and fried tortilla strips; a specialty of Michoacán state.

Sopa seca   Not a soup at all, but a seasoned rice which translated means "dry soup."

Sope   Pronounced "*soh*-pay," a botana similar to a garnacha, except spread with refried beans and topped with crumbled cheese and onions.

Tacos al pastor   Thin slices of flavored pork roasted on a revolving cylinder dripping with onion slices and juice of fresh pineapple slices.

Tamal   Incorrectly called tamale (tamal singular, tamales plural), meat or sweet filling rolled with fresh masa, then wrapped in a corn husk or banana leaf and steamed; many varieties and sizes throughout the country.

Tepache   Drink made of fermented pineapple peelings and brown sugar.

Tikin Xic   Also seen on menus as "tikin chick," char-broiled fish brushed with achiote sauce.

Tinga   A stew made with pork tenderloin, sausage, onions, garlic, tomatoes, chiles, and potatoes; popular on menus in Puebla and Hidalgo states.

Torta   A sandwich, usually on bolillo bread, usually with sliced avocado, onions, tomatoes, with a choice of meat and often cheese.

Torta Ahogado   A specialty of Lake Chapala is made with scooped out roll, filled with beans and beef strips and seasoned with either a tomato or chile sauce.

Tostadas   Crispy fried corn tortillas topped with meat, onions, lettuce, tomatoes, cheese, avocados, and sometimes sour cream.

Venado   Venison (deer) served perhaps as pipian de venado, steamed in banana leaves and served with a sauce of ground squash seeds.

Xtabentun   (pronounced "Shtah-ben-*toon*") A Yucatán liquor made of fermented honey and flavored with anise. It comes *seco* (dry) or *crema* (sweet).

Zacahuil   Pork leg tamal, packed in thick masa, wrapped in banana leaves, and pit baked; sometimes pot-made with tomato and masa; specialty of mid-to-upper Veracruz.

E   Metric Measures

Length

1 millimeter (mm)	=	0.04 inches (or less than $^1/_{16}$ in.)
1 centimeter (cm)	=	0.39 inches (or under $^1/_2$ in.)
1 meter (m)	=	39 inches (or about 1.1 yd.)
1 kilometer	=	0.62 miles (or about $^2/_3$ of a mile)

To convert kilometers to miles, multiply the number of kilometers by 0.62. Also use to convert kilometers per hour (kmph) to mile per hour (mph).
To convert miles to kilometers, multiply the number of miles by 1.61. Also use to convert from mph to kmph.

Capacity

1 liter	= 33.92 ounces	= 2.1 pints	= 1.06 quarts	= 0.26 U.S. gallons
1 Imperial gallon				= 1.2 U.S. gallons

To convert liters to U.S. gallons, multiply the number of liters by 0.26.
To convert U.S. gallons to liters, multiply the number of gallons by 3.79.

To convert Imperial gallons to U.S. gallons, multiply the number of Imperial gallons by 1.2.

To convert U.S. gallons to Imperial gallons, multiply the number of U.S. gallons by 0.83.

Weight

1 gram (g)	=	0.035 ounces (or about a paperclip's weight)			
1 kilogram (kg)	=	35.2 ounces	=	2.2 pounds	
1 metric ton			=	2,205 pounds	= 1.1 short ton

To convert kilograms to pounds, multiply the number of kilograms by 2.2.

To convert pounds to kilograms, multiply the number of pounds by 0.45.

Area

1 hectare (a)	=	2.47 acres		
1 square kilometer (km^2)	=	247 acres	=	0.39 square miles

To convert hectares to acres, multiply the number of hectares by 2.47.

Temperature

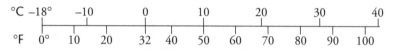

To convert degrees Fahrenheit to degrees Celsius, subtract 32 from °F, multiply by 5, then divide by 9 (example, 85°F–32 × $^5/_9$ = 29.4°C).

To convert degrees Celsius to degrees Fahrenheit, multiply °C by 9, divide by 5, and add 32 (example, 20°C × $^9/_5$ + 32 = 68°F).

Index

* For more information, see specific regional indexes.

MANZANILLO

PUERTO VALLARTA

FROMMER'S COMPLETE TRAVEL GUIDES

*(Comprehensive guides to sightseeing, dining and accommodations,
with selections in all price ranges—from deluxe to budget)*

Acapulco/Ixtapa/Taxco, 2nd Ed.	C157	Jamaica/Barbados, 2nd Ed.	C149
Alaska '94-'95	C131	Japan '94-'95	C144
Arizona '95	C166	Maui, 1st Ed.	C153
Australia '94-'95	C147	Nepal, 3rd Ed. (avail. 11/95)	C184
Austria, 6th Ed.	C162	New England '95	C165
Bahamas '96 (avail. 8/95)	C172	New Mexico, 3rd Ed.	C167
Belgium/Holland/Luxembourg,		New York State, 4th Ed.	C133
4th Ed.	C170	Northwest, 5th Ed.	C140
Bermuda '96 (avail. 8/95)	C174	Portugal '94-'95	C141
California '95	C164	Puerto Rico '95-'96	C151
Canada '94-'95	C145	Puerto Vallarta/Manzanillo/	
Caribbean '96 (avail. 9/95)	C173	Guadalajara, 2nd Ed.	C135
Carolinas/Georgia, 2nd Ed.	C128	Scandinavia, 16th Ed.	C169
Colorado '96 (avail. 11/95)	C179	Scotland '94-'95	C146
Costa Rica, 1st Ed.	C161	South Pacific '94-'95	C138
Cruises '95-'96	C150	Spain, 16th Ed.	C163
Delaware/Maryland '94-'95	C136	Switzerland, 7th Ed.	
England '96 (avail. 10/95)	C180	(avail. 9/95)	C177
Florida '96 (avail. 9/95)	C181	Thailand, 2nd Ed.	C154
France '96 (avail. 11/95)	C182	U.S.A., 4th Ed.	C156
Germany '96 (avail. 9/95)	C176	Virgin Islands, 3rd Ed.	
Honolulu/Waikiki/Oahu, 4th Ed.		(avail. 8/95)	C175
(avail. 10/95)	C178	Virginia '94-'95	C142
Ireland, 1st Ed.	C168	Yucatán '95-'96	C155
Italy '96 (avail. 11/95)	C183		

FROMMER'S $-A-DAY GUIDES

(Dream Vacations at Down-to-Earth Prices)

Australia on $45 '95-'96	D122	Ireland on $45 '94-'95	D118
Berlin from $50, 3rd Ed.		Israel on $45, 15th Ed.	D130
(avail. 10/95)	D137	London from $55 '96	
Caribbean from $60, 1st Ed.		(avail. 11/95)	D136
(avail. 9/95)	D133	Madrid on $50 '94-'95	D119
Costa Rica/Guatemala/Belize		Mexico from $35 '96	
on $35, 3rd Ed.	D126	(avail. 10/95)	D135
Eastern Europe on $30, 5th Ed.	D129	New York on $70 '94-'95	D121
England from $50 '96		New Zealand from $45, 6th Ed.	D132
(avail. 11/95)	D138	Paris on $45 '94-'95	D117
Europe from $50 '96		South America on $40, 16th Ed.	D123
(avail. 10/95)	D139	Washington, D.C. on $50	
Greece from $45, 6th Ed.	D131	'94-'95	D120
Hawaii from $60 '96 (avail. 9/95)	D134		

FROMMER'S COMPLETE CITY GUIDES

(Comprehensive guides to sightseeing, dining, and accommodations in all price ranges)

Amsterdam, 8th Ed.	S176	Minneapolis/St. Paul, 4th Ed.	S159
Athens, 10th Ed.	S174	Montréal/Québec City '95	S166
Atlanta & the Summer Olympic		Nashville/Memphis, 1st Ed.	S141
Games '96 (avail. 11/95)	S181	New Orleans '96 (avail. 10/95)	S182
Atlantic City/Cape May, 5th Ed.	S130	New York City '96 (avail. 11/95)	S183
Bangkok, 2nd Ed.	S147	Paris '96 (avail. 9/95)	S180
Barcelona '93-'94	S115	Philadelphia, 8th Ed.	S167
Berlin, 3rd Ed.	S162	Prague, 1st Ed.	S143
Boston '95	S160	Rome, 10th Ed.	S168
Budapest, 1st Ed.	S139	St. Louis/Kansas City, 2nd Ed.	S127
Chicago '95	S169	San Antonio/Austin, 1st Ed.	S177
Denver/Boulder/Colorado Springs,		San Diego '95	S158
3rd Ed.	S154	San Francisco '96 (avail. 10/95)	S184
Disney World/Orlando '96 (avail. 9/95)	S178	Santa Fe/Taos/Albuquerque '95	S172
Dublin, 2nd Ed.	S157	Seattle/Portland '94-'95	S137
Hong Kong '94-'95	S140	Sydney, 4th Ed.	S171
Las Vegas '95	S163	Tampa/St. Petersburg, 3rd Ed.	S146
London '96 (avail. 9/95)	S179	Tokyo '94-'95	S144
Los Angeles '95	S164	Toronto, 3rd Ed.	S173
Madrid/Costa del Sol, 2nd Ed.	S165	Vancouver/Victoria '94-'95	S142
Mexico City, 1st Ed.	S175	Washington, D.C. '95	S153
Miami '95-'96	S149		

FROMMER'S FAMILY GUIDES

(Guides to family-friendly hotels, restaurants, activities, and attractions)

California with Kids	F105	San Francisco with Kids	F104
Los Angeles with Kids	F103	Washington, D.C. with Kids	F102
New York City with Kids	F101		

FROMMER'S WALKING TOURS

(Memorable strolls through colorful and historic neighborhoods, accompanied by detailed directions and maps)

Berlin	W100	Paris, 2nd Ed.	W112
Chicago	W107	San Francisco, 2nd Ed.	W115
England's Favorite Cities	W108	Spain's Favorite Cities (avail. 9/95)	W116
London, 2nd Ed.	W111	Tokyo	W109
Montréal/Québec City	W106	Venice	W110
New York, 2nd Ed.	W113	Washington, D.C., 2nd Ed.	W114

FROMMER'S AMERICA ON WHEELS

(Guides for travelers who are exploring the U.S.A. by car, featuring a brand-new rating system for accommodations and full-color road maps)

Arizona/New Mexico	A100	Florida	A102
California/Nevada	A101	Mid-Atlantic	A103

FROMMER'S SPECIAL-INTEREST TITLES

Arthur Frommer's Branson!	P107	Frommer's Where to Stay U.S.A.,	
Arthur Frommer's New World		11th Ed.	P102
of Travel (avail. 11/95)	P112	National Park Guide, 29th Ed.	P106
Frommer's Caribbean Hideaways		USA Today Golf Tournament Guide	P113
(avail. 9/95)	P110	USA Today Minor League	
Frommer's America's 100 Best-Loved		Baseball Book	P111
State Parks	P109		

FROMMER'S BEST BEACH VACATIONS
(The top places to sun, stroll, shop, stay, play, party, and swim—with each beach rated for beauty, swimming, sand, and amenities)

California (avail. 10/95)	G100	Hawaii (avail. 10/95)	G102
Florida (avail. 10/95)	G101		

FROMMER'S BED & BREAKFAST GUIDES
(Selective guides with four-color photos and full descriptions of the best inns in each region)

California	B100	Hawaii	B105
Caribbean	B101	Pacific Northwest	B106
East Coast	B102	Rockies	B107
Eastern United States	B103	Southwest	B108
Great American Cities	B104		

FROMMER'S IRREVERENT GUIDES
(Wickedly honest guides for sophisticated travelers and those who want to be)

Chicago (avail. 11/95)	I100	New Orleans (avail. 11/95)	I103
London (avail. 11/95)	I101	San Francisco (avail. 11/95)	I104
Manhattan (avail. 11/95)	I102	Virgin Islands (avail. 11/95)	I105

FROMMER'S DRIVING TOURS
(Four-color photos and detailed maps outlining spectacular scenic driving routes)

Australia	Y100	Italy	Y108
Austria	Y101	Mexico	Y109
Britain	Y102	Scandinavia	Y110
Canada	Y103	Scotland	Y111
Florida	Y104	Spain	Y112
France	Y105	Switzerland	Y113
Germany	Y106	U.S.A.	Y114
Ireland	Y107		

FROMMER'S BORN TO SHOP
(The ultimate travel guides for discriminating shoppers—from cut-rate to couture)

Hong Kong (avail. 11/95)	Z100	London (avail. 11/95)	Z101